e-Book and Digital Course Materials for

Direc... ...g your
e-Book and Digital Course Materials

P9-DIA-775

Race and Racisms
A Critical Approach

BRIEF THIRD EDITION

Tanya Maria Golash-Boza

This code can be used only once and cannot be shared!

Carefully scratch off the silver coating to see your personal redemption code.

If the code has been scratched off when you receive it, the code may not be valid. Once the code has been scratched off, this access card cannot be returned to the publisher. You may buy access at **www.oup.com/he/ golash-boza-brief3e**.

The code on this card is valid for 2 years from the date of first purchase. Complete terms and conditions are available at **learninglink.oup.com.**

Access length: 6 months from redemption of the code.

VIA OXFORD learning link

Visit
www.oup.com/he/golash-boza-brief3e

Select the edition you are using and the student resources for that edition.

Click the link to upgrade your access to the student resources.

Follow the on-screen instructions.

Enter your personal redemption code when prompted.

VIA YOUR SCHOOL'S LEARNING MANAGEMENT SYSTEM

Log in to your instructor's course.

When you click a link to a protected resource, you will be prompted to register for access.

Follow the on-screen instructions.

Enter your personal redemption code when prompted.

For assistance with code redemption or registration, please contact customer support at
learninglink.support@oup.com.

OXFORD

RACE AND RACISMS

A CRITICAL APPROACH

BRIEF THIRD EDITION

TANYA MARIA GOLASH-BOZA
University of California, Merced

OXFORD
UNIVERSITY PRESS

Oxford University Press is a department of the University of Oxford.
It furthers the University's objective of excellence in research, scholarship,
and education by publishing worldwide. Oxford is a registered trade mark
of Oxford University Press in the UK and certain other countries.

Published in the United States of America by Oxford University Press
198 Madison Avenue, New York, NY 10016, United States of America.

© 2023, 2019, 2016 by Oxford University Press

For titles covered by Section 112 of the US Higher Education Opportunity
Act, please visit www.oup.com/us/he for the latest information about
pricing and alternate formats.

All rights reserved. No part of this publication may be reproduced,
stored in a retrieval system, or transmitted, in any form or by any means,
without the prior permission in writing of Oxford University Press,
or as expressly permitted by law, by license, or under terms agreed with
the appropriate reproduction rights organization. Inquiries concerning
reproduction outside the scope of the above should be sent to the Rights
Department, Oxford University Press, at the address above.

You must not circulate this work in any other form
and you must impose this same condition on any acquirer.

Cataloging-in-Publication data is on file at the Library of Congress
ISBN 978–0–19–764643–4 (paperback)
ISBN 978–0–19–764645–8 (epub)
ISBN 978–0–19–764646–5 (pdf)

9 8 7 6 5 4 3 2 1
Printed by Lakeside Book Company, United States of America

Brief Contents

Contents

Preface

This brief third edition of *Race and Racisms* engages students in significant questions related to racial dynamics in the United States. In accessible, straightforward language, the text discusses and critically analyzes cutting-edge scholarship in the field.

FEATURES

Race and Racisms includes several unique features designed to aid both teaching and learning. Each of the following features appears throughout the book:

- **Voices** sidebars highlight individual stories about race and racism, bringing personal experiences to life.
- **Thinking about Racial Justice** sidebars pose questions for students to consider in thinking about how racism could be addressed or alleviated.
- **As You Read** questions point students to the key ideas in each chapter.
- **Check Your Understanding** sections at the end of the chapter relate to the As You Read questions and help students review.
- **Critical Thinking** questions guide students in questioning their own and others' assumptions about race and racism.
- **Talking about Race** prompts at the end of each chapter suggest ways to approach discussions about race and racism.

NEW IN THIS EDITION

The goal of the third brief edition of *Race and Racisms* was not merely to keep up with our changing world but to invite students to consider their own role in it. Each chapter has been carefully updated to reflect current issues and events as well as the latest data and research. Beyond these updates, new stories and examples throughout engage readers in thinking about how racism could be addressed or alleviated. Highlights of this edition include:

- New coverage of how COVID-19 exacerbated racial inequalities
- New discussions of racial capitalism and global White supremacy
- Expanded coverage of anti-Asian racism
- Updated data and citations in each chapter
- New Voices sidebars in Chapters 4, 5, 6, 7, 8, 9, and 10

ORGANIZATION

Race and Racisms begins with a historical chapter on the origin and evolution of the idea of race. From there, it moves into an overview of racial ideologies and sociological theories of racism, and then to a historical and contemporary discussion of immigration. The next two chapters focus on racial ideologies in the media and on colorism. The final five chapters explore racial inequalities across five key areas: education, the labor market, housing, the criminal justice system, and health and the environment. Each chapter uses an intersectional framework to guide our understanding of racial dynamics.

ENHANCED EBOOK

This enhanced ebook offers interactive multimedia content integrated with the text and is ideal for self-study. Each chapter includes the following:

- Video clips to engage students in learning about race and racisms
- Flashcards to help students master new vocabulary
- Multiple-choice self-quizzes at the end of each major section and at chapter ends

OXFORD LEARNING LINK

Oxford Learning Link at www.oup.com/access/golash-boza-brief3e is your hub for a wealth of engaging digital learning tools and resources. Material hosted there includes the instructor's manual, test bank, PowerPoint presentations, videos, filmographies, activities, recommended links and readings, and all student resources. Multiple-choice self-quizzes and glossary flashcards help students review the materials and check their understanding. In addition, Oxford Learning Link Direct brings the high-quality digital teaching and learning tools for *Race and Racisms: A Critical Approach* right to your local learning management system.

ACKNOWLEDGMENTS

When I travel around the country to give talks at universities, I am always pleased and humbled when instructors tell me they use this book in their class and when students tell me how much they enjoy reading it. The positive feedback I received from the first two editions was a major motivation to revise this book. I have attempted to respond to the many helpful critiques and comments I received to make this book an even better tool for teaching about race and racism.

My interest in race and racism derives in part from my experiences growing up as a White child in a primarily Black neighborhood. I am grateful to my parents for deciding to raise our White family on the east side of Rock Creek Park in Washington, DC, and for staying in that neighborhood to this day. Had my parents made different life choices, it is likely this book would never have been written.

Writing this textbook has been much less painful than it otherwise would have been due to the extraordinary efforts of the editorial team at Oxford University Press, especially Executive Editor Sherith Pankratz, Development Editor Lauren Mine, and Editorial Assistants Maeve O'Brien and Rick Dillenberger. My deepest gratitude to this amazing and efficient team. I would also like to acknowledge the design and production teams, including Michele Laseau, Art Director at Oxford University Press and Steven Hall, Project Manager at Straive.

I did not write this book alone. In fact, many of these chapters were written in the company of fabulous colleagues in coffee shops and cabins around the world—from Belize to Hawaii to Bali. I'd like to extend a special thanks to my writing partners: Zulema Valdez, Ayu Saraswati, Christina Lux, Dalia Magaña, Whitney Pirtle, Amani Nuru-Jeter, Jemima Pierre, Winddance Twine, and Vilna Treitler.

Many thanks to our contributors for this edition: Keisha T. Jones, M.Div., Professor of Sociology and Psychology at Community College of Baltimore County and Andrew Mannheimer, Senior Lecturer in Sociology at Clemson University.

Special thanks to the reviewers who evaluated the manuscript for this brief third edition:

Michael Aquino
Pima Community College

Keisha Tamika Jones
Community College of Baltimore County

Brandi M Barnes
The University of Memphis

Armando Mejia
California State University, Long Beach

Kittye Hirsch
East Tennessee State University

Devaparna Roy
Nazareth College

Tiffany Hoard
Jackson State University

Will Tyson
University of South Florida

Tammy L Hodo
University of North Florida

Gail Wallace
University of Alabama at Birmingham

I also continue to be grateful to the many reviewers whose comments helped shape the first and second editions of this book:

David Allen
Temple University

Mark O. Melder
Northwestern State University

Amy Armenia
Rollins College

Allison T. Musvosvi
Pacific Union College

Maria Isabel Ayala
Michigan State University

Deirdre Oakley
Georgia State University

Jean Beaman
University of California, Santa Barbara

Allan Rachlin
Franklin Pierce University

David Daniel Bogumil
California State University, Northridge

Mary Roaf
Northern Arizona University

James L. Burnett Jr.,
Urbana University

Sarah Epplen Rusche
Minnesota State University, Mankato

Dianne Dentice
Stephen F. Austin State University

Matthew Schneirov
Duquesne University

Ione Y. DeOllos
Ball State University

Nadia Shapkina
Kansas State University

Johnnie M. Griffin
Jackson State University

Jack Thornburg
Benedictine University

Joachim S. Kibirige
Missouri Western State University

Santos Torres Jr.,
California State University, Sacramento

Karen McCormack
Wheaton College

Damian T. Williams
Concordia University, Chicago

Talking about Race Outside the Classroom

This book is designed primarily for classroom use. I hope teachers and students find the analyses, narratives, and data it conveys helpful in generating productive class engagements on racial justice, racial equity, and race relations. Learning, however, is a lifelong experience. And, as many of my students point out, few people you encounter in your daily life will be privy to all the knowledge and insight conveyed in this book. So, how do you—the reader—carry this knowledge from the classroom to your living room, to the coffee shop, to the dining room table, to the bar, or to your workplace? How do you talk about race outside the classroom?

Each chapter of this book concludes with a "Talking about Race" prompt that provides some suggestions on how to have conversations about the specific topics in that chapter. Here, I'd like to address the issue of discussing race more generally.

Conversations about race can be either premeditated or surprises. Premeditated conversations can be easier because you can decide ahead of time how and why you would like to broach a topic with a friend, family member, or coworker. Surprise conversations are a bit harder to deal with because you have to respond on the spot—and many times emotions can make it more difficult to have level-headed responses. Let's consider each of these two conversation types in turn, as they are quite different and require different tools.

Let's say an organization you are involved in has a policy that disadvantages people of color. You decide you would like to initiate a conversation with the leaders so that they will reconsider the policy. Here are some tips for having a productive conversation with your colleagues, drawn from a brief by the Annie E. Casey Foundation on "How to Talk about Race":

- **Emphasize shared values**. Begin the conversation by focusing on what you all may agree on.
- **Provide more than a critique**. Offer a manageable solution that can be implemented.

- **Use narratives more than numbers**. Provide concrete examples of how people are affected by the current policy and how a change could benefit them.
- **Emphasize shared goals**. Present the change you are proposing as an opportunity for the organization to move forward.

It is ideal when you have an opportunity to prepare for a discussion about race. Often, however, we encounter racial microaggressions, macroaggressions, overt acts of racism, or other forms of bigotry and have to respond on the spot. Of course, you can choose not to respond, but even silence is a response in and of itself.

How do you respond if you experience a microaggression? What if you are sitting with friends and someone makes a racial or racist joke? What if you witness someone mistreating a person based on that person's race? What is the best way to respond? Having a strategy ready ahead of time can make it easier to respond in the moment. Here are some options:

- **Respond with silence**. If you are with someone who tells a racist joke, you can be silent. By not laughing, you are sending a message that this joke is not appropriate.
- **Leave the room**. If you are with a group of people, and the conversation takes a turn toward complaining about a particular ethnic group, you can exit the room or grab your keys and leave the event. That sends a signal that their conversation is not appropriate.
- **Question the statement**. If you are with a group of people, and some of them say, for example, that all Black people are great dancers, you can ask them why they think that. You can push them and ask if they think it is genetic or cultural. You can keep asking them questions to help them see that their statement is problematic.
- **Ask the person making a racist statement if they would make the statement in different company**. For example, if someone makes a joke about Jewish people, ask the person if he or she would feel comfortable making the joke in front of Jewish people. That may help everyone in the room see that the statement is problematic.

Hearing a bigoted joke or statement—directed at you or others—can stop you in your tracks. How you respond is a personal decision that is based on your personality as well as your relationships with others. It is important to know that you have options—ranging from remaining silent to leaving to responding directly. Thinking through these options ahead of time will make you better prepared to respond.

1

The Origin
of the Idea
# of Race

AS YOU READ

1.1 What are race and ethnicity? What is racism?

1.2 How old is racism? How is race distinct from previous ways of thinking about human difference?

1.3 How did the writers of the U.S. Constitution think of slavery?

1.4 How did the Indian Removal Act affect Native Americans?

1.5 What role did science play in the propagation of racism?

Prior to the colonization of the Americas, no one would have described the population using the terms *Native American, White,* or *Black.* Instead, people identified themselves by groups such as Shawnee, Irish, and Ashanti. How, then, did our current racial categories come to be? What distinguishes the idea of race from previous ways of thinking about human difference? These are the questions we will consider in this chapter.

In the contemporary United States, one of the first things we notice about someone we meet is their race. When we aren't sure of someone's race, we may get inquisitive or begin to feel uncomfortable (Dalmage 2000). It is as if, before interacting, we have to know if the other person is White, Black, Asian, Native American, or something else. The perceived race of the other person affects how we treat one another and what we expect the other person to say and do.

It may be hard to imagine a time when the idea of race did not exist, when we did not categorize ourselves and others this way. But this time was not so long ago: although humans have long used various factors to classify one another, the idea of race as a classificatory system is a modern invention. Ancient Greeks and Romans, for example, did not think that the world's population could be divided into races (Eze 1997). Their system of social classification was much different from ours. Race is a modern **social construction**, meaning that the idea of race is not based on biological differences among people, even though race has become important in determining how we interact. It is a particular way of viewing human difference that is a product of colonial encounters.

Many people falsely believe race has a biological basis, but advances in genetic science show there is more genetic variation within races than between them. There are certainly not clear genetic boundaries between races. People who are related to one another share an ancestry and thus may share genetic similarities; however, ancestry and race are distinct concepts (Yudell et al. 2016). Your ancestry, for example, is your personal family tree—your parents, grandparents, great-grandparents, and so on. You have genetic similarities with your ancestors. In contrast, if you were to encounter someone you believe to be of the same race as you, you could not assume you have genetic similarities. You could, however, assume you may share some social experiences—as you are both racialized by others as members of the same race.

DEFINING RACE AND ETHNICITY

The word *race* refers to a group of people who share physical and cultural traits. The idea of race implies that the people of the world can be divided into biologically discrete and exclusive groups based on physical and cultural traits. This idea is further linked to notions of White or European superiority that became concretized during the colonization of the Americas. As we will see in this chapter, the history of the idea of race is critical to an understanding of its meaning. *Racism* refers to both (1) the belief that races are populations whose physical differences are linked to significant cultural and social differences within a hierarchy, and (2) the practice of subordinating races believed to be inferior.

The idea of race is slightly different from the concept of ethnicity. Races are categories of people based on a hierarchical worldview that associates ancestry, descent, and phenotype with cultural and moral attributes. **Ethnicity**, by contrast, is a group identity based on notions of similar and shared history, culture, and kinship (Cornell and Hartmann 2007). Ethnicity also has a distinct historical trajectory from race. People self-identify as belonging to an ethnic group on the basis of a perceived shared history and a concomitant set of cultural attributes. In contrast to ethnicity, race is often an externally imposed category. In the United States, people are placed into races based on socially constructed, ascribed characteristics that are often related to physical appearance, such as skin color or hair texture, regardless of self-identification. Sociologist Eduardo Bonilla-Silva (1997, 469) argues that "ethnicity has a primarily sociocultural foundation, and ethnic groups have exhibited tremendous malleability in terms of who belongs; racial ascriptions (initially) are imposed externally to justify the collective exploitation of a people and are maintained to preserve status differences."

Race is a social construction, an idea we endow with meaning through daily interactions. It has no biological basis. This might seem an odd statement, as the physical differences between a Kenyan, a Swede, and a Han Chinese, for example, are obvious. However, these physical differences do not necessarily mean that the world can be divided into discrete racial groups. If you were to walk from Kenya to Sweden to China, you would note incremental gradations in physical differences between people across space, and it would be difficult to decide where to draw the line between Africa and Europe and between

Europe and Asia. There may be genetic differences between Kenyans and Swedes, but the genetic variations within the Kenyan population are actually greater than those between Swedes and Kenyans (Smedley 2007; Yudell et al. 2016). Although race is a social, as opposed to a biological, construction, it has a wide range of consequences in our society, especially when used as a sorting and stratifying mechanism.

Race is also a historical construction, meaning that the idea of race was formulated at particular historical moments and places. Of particular note in its development are the eras of **colonialism**—the practice of acquiring political control over another country, occupying it with settlers, and exploiting it economically—and slavery in the Americas. The idea of race involves classifying humans into distinct groups. Through this classification and the assignment of cultural and moral traits to each group, Europeans and their descendants have used the idea of race to rationalize exploitation, slavery, colonialism, and **genocide**, the mass killing of a group of people, especially those of a particular ethnic or racial group.

RACE: THE EVOLUTION OF AN IDEOLOGY

An **ideology** is a set of principles and ideas that benefit the dominant group. The racial ideologies that operate today reflect our times and are rooted in the history of the Americas. The way we understand the idea of race today is distinct from previous ways of thinking about human difference. Before the conquest of the Americas, there was no worldview that separated all of humanity into distinct races (Smedley 2007; Montagu 1997; Quijano 2000). Understanding what race means today requires delving into the historical process through which the idea of race was created. Once we understand that racial categories are not natural but constructed, we can begin to think about why and how these categories were created. As we will see, European thinkers created racial categories to rationalize genocide and exploitation. This brutal history in turn raises the question of why we continue to use these categories.

Historical Precedents to the Idea of Race

Until the sixteenth century, Northern Europeans had limited knowledge of the world beyond their immediate communities. Without this knowledge, it would have been difficult to develop a worldview that classified the people of the globe into various racial groups. Southern Europeans, in contrast, had much more contact with other peoples. People from the Mediterranean region have had extensive involvement with people from Asia, Africa, and the Arab world since time immemorial. These contacts, which range from Alexander the Great's travels to India and Greek exchanges with Ethiopia to the conquest of Spain by Islamic peoples, did not lead to a racial worldview. Ancient peoples did not divide the world into distinct races based on their physical and cultural traits. Instead, Greeks had great respect for the achievements of Ethiopians (Snowden 1970), and Muslims, Christians, and Jews lived in reasonable harmony together in Spain for hundreds of years (Smedley 2007).

Although the idea of race did not develop until later, these early interactions between Europeans and other groups did provide important precedents for current ways of conceptualizing human difference. The Spanish Inquisition is one example. When the Catholic Church began to consolidate its power in Spain under the reign of monarchs Ferdinand II of Aragon and Isabella I of Castile (1479–1504), Jews were expelled from Spain, and converted Jews were subject to scrutiny. In 1480, Ferdinand and Isabella established a tribunal called the Spanish Inquisition, which was intended to ensure the orthodoxy of people who had converted from Judaism and Islam to Catholicism. The monarchs issued royal decrees in 1492 and 1501 that ordered Jews and Muslims to convert or leave the country. During the Inquisition, Jews and Muslims were obliged to convert, but conversion did not ensure their safety, as converts continued to be subject to scrutiny and suspicion. Moreover, people believed to be the descendants of Jews and Muslims also faced persecution. Discrimination against Jews and Muslims was more religious in nature than racial, yet the ideas regarding purity of blood that emerged set the stage for ideas of racial difference that were to become part of the European understanding of human differences (Smedley 2007; Quijano 2000).

Another crucial precedent to the idea of race is the English view of the Irish. England and Ireland were involved in centuries of conflict before the English first settled in North America, and English soldiers often portrayed the Irish as savage, sexually immoral, and resistant to civilizing forces. Many English colonists had been deployed to Ireland before settling in the New World. The ideas the English developed about the Irish may thus have played a role in settlers' perception of

Native Americans as savage (Allen 1994; Smedley 2007). This perception was a precursor to the racial idea that some humans were less fit for civilization than others.

Slavery before the Idea of Race

Slavery was not new to the Americas: the practice of enslaving people has existed since antiquity. In African, European, and Middle Eastern societies, conquered peoples often became slaves in the aftermath of war. As agricultural societies grew, so did the demand for labor, leading peoples such as the Greeks and Phoenicians to raid other societies for slaves. Slavery existed not only across societies but also within societies: people lacking the support of a family often had no place other than as slaves, and some people became enslaved as a means of paying off a debt or as punishment for a crime. Slavery of this latter form almost always involved persons of the same ethnic group as their masters.

The prevalence of slavery in ancient societies does not imply that racism existed then as well. Although some ancient writings refer to skin color, these references are rarely derogatory and by no means represent the general ideology of any ancient society. On the contrary, Greeks and Romans held the Egyptians as well as the Ethiopians in high esteem and admired their culture and way of life. These ancient peoples developed no known stereotypes of Black people as primitives or lacking in culture (Snowden 1983). Marriages between Egyptians and other Africans were commonplace in ancient times, and Muslim conquerors regarded anyone they succeeded in converting as brethren (Franklin 1974).

The status of slaves varied across societies. In some instances, slaves were adopted as kin after serving for a certain number of years; in other cases, slaves were permitted to marry and own property (Smedley 2007; Morgan 1975). Many slaves were granted rights not found in the system of slavery in the New World. These rights included access to education, the potential to obtain freedom for themselves and their children, the right to marry, and the right to own property. Until the eighteenth century, no society categorically denied the humanity of slaves. Denying that slaves were fully human was not seen as a necessary rationale for slavery. Although slaves were at times treated brutally, the humanity of slaves was never put into question, and slavery was never attributed to racial inferiority (Smedley 2007).

TIMELINE

The American Slave Trade

1492	Christopher Columbus lands in the Caribbean.	**1863**	Abraham Lincoln issues the Emancipation Proclamation.
1619	First African slaves arrive in Jamestown.		
1660	First slave codes enacted.	**1865**	Slavery is abolished in the United States.
1676	Bacon's Rebellion.		

European Encounters with Indigenous Peoples of the Americas

Before the arrival of the European colonizers, the Americas were home to over 100 million indigenous people. As a result of warfare, slavery, and disease, about 95 percent of this population was decimated during the first two centuries of colonization. The excerpted accounts in *Voices: The Spanish Treatment of Indigenous Peoples* below provide a small window into the extent of this massacre.

When Christopher Columbus encountered the native peoples of the Caribbean islands in 1492, he found them to be peaceable and generous. Despite the Spaniards' initial admiration for the indigenous people, the relations between the two groups soon deteriorated, as it became clear that the Spaniards' primary motive was to extract gold from the Americas. Intent upon taking as much gold as possible, the Spaniards used their weaponry to overpower and enslave the people indigenous to the Americas to compel them to find gold and silver for the Spaniards to take back to Spain (Todorov 1984). The abuse the Caribbean peoples suffered at the hands of the Spaniards was devastating: the Arawak of Santo Domingo, for example, were reduced from over 3 million people in 1496 to a mere 125 in 1570 (Jones 2003).

Reports of the Spaniards' extreme cruelty toward the indigenous people of the Americas made their way back to Spain and eventually became a subject of controversy. Fifty years after Columbus's arrival in the Caribbean islands, the enslavement of indigenous people was outlawed. The Spaniards continued to extract labor from indigenous people, however, by relying on other systems of forced labor (Wade 1997).

One of the most remarkable aspects of the conquest of the Americas is that many of the civilizations in the Americas were far more advanced than those from which the Europeans hailed. Europe in the sixteenth century was a ghastly place, with frequent famines and epidemic outbreaks of the plague and smallpox. Large cities were pestilent and dirty, with unsightly open sewers. Crime was rampant. Half of all children died before they turned ten. Thus, we can imagine the surprise and awe that the magnificent city of Tenochtitlán engendered in the Spaniards who arrived there. Tenochtitlán, an Aztec city in central Mexico, had about 350,000 inhabitants—many times the population of London or Seville at the time. When the Spanish explorer and colonizer Hernando Cortés (1485–1547) saw this city, he declared it to be the most beautiful city on earth. His companion and chronicler Bernal Díaz (1492–1585) agreed, calling it a "wonderful thing to behold." Unlike European cities of the time, Tenochtitlán boasted clean streets, amazing floating gardens, a huge aqueduct system, and a market more extensive than any the Europeans had ever seen (Stannard 1993).

When Christopher Columbus encountered the native peoples of the Caribbean, he found them to be peaceable and generous.

voices

The Spanish Treatment of Indigenous Peoples

The following excerpts are from a 1519 report of Dominicans about the Spanish treatment of indigenous peoples in the Carib Islands.

> Some Christians encounter[ed] an Indian woman, who was carrying in her arms a child at suck; and since the dog they had with them was hungry, they tore the child from the mother's arms and flung it still living to the dog, who proceeded to devour it before the mother's eyes.

> When there were among the prisoners some women who had recently given birth, if the new-born babes happened to cry, they seized them by the legs and hurled them against the rocks, or flung them into the jungle so that they would be certain to die there.

> Each of them [the foremen] had made it a practice to sleep with the Indian women who were in his workforce, if they pleased him, whether they were married women or maidens. While the foreman remained . . . with the Indian woman, he sent the husband to dig gold out of the mines; and in the evening, when the wretch returned, not only was he beaten or whipped because he had not brought enough gold, but further, most often, he was bound hand and foot and flung under the bed like a dog, before the foreman lay down, directly over him, with his wife.

Source: Todorov 1984, 139.

Despite their admiration, the Spaniards did not preserve this city. The arrival of the Spaniards led to the destruction of not only this amazing city, but also many towns and cities across the Americas. The population of central Mexico was decimated in less than a century, declining from 25 million in 1519 to barely 1.3 million in 1595. This pattern continued throughout the Americas, so that nearly 95 percent of the native populations were destroyed in less than 200 years (Stannard 1993).

Slavery and Colonization

Africans were present in the conquest of the Americas from the beginning, both as slaves and as sailors and explorers. Spain and

Portugal were slaveholding societies long before Columbus set sail in search of the Indies. Many, but not all, of the slaves in Spain in the fifteenth century were Africans. Some African residents of Spain and Portugal—enslaved as well as free—accompanied Spaniards on their initial conquest voyages to the New World. Juan Garrido (ca. 1480–ca. 1547), for example, was born in Africa and later traveled to Portugal and then to Spain, where he joined an expedition to Santo Domingo. Juan Garrido also participated in the conquest of Puerto Rica, Cuba, and then Mexico. Juan García (ca. 1495–date of death unknown), in contrast, was born in Spain as a free mulatto and traveled to Peru as a colonist (Restall 2000).

The Spanish colonists—often called conquistadores—endeavored to subdue native populations and to convert them into Catholics and subjects of the Spanish Crown. Their main goal, however, was to extract as much wealth as possible from the Americas. This extraction of wealth required labor, and the Spanish colonists enslaved the native populations to this end. The harsh conditions of this enslavement led to massive declines in the native populations, and in 1550, the Spanish Crown outlawed the practice, although it continued to allow other forms of forced labor. The ban on enslavement of indigenous people did not end the need for labor, and the Spaniards turned to Africa in their search for workers. As they realized that agricultural exploitation, particularly the harvesting of sugarcane, could bring enormous wealth, they began to bring African slaves in very large numbers to their colonies in the Americas (Smedley 2007; Franklin 1974; Morgan 1975). The Spaniards and Portuguese had long been trading with Africans and thus could imagine the possibilities for slave trading with Africa. Notably, the Spaniards were well aware of the technological advances developed in Africa and did not seek Africans as slaves because they thought they were inferior. To the contrary, the Spaniards believed enslaved Africans would be a valuable asset. Consequently, tens of millions of Africans were brought over between the early 1600s and the nineteenth century as slaves (Bowser 1974).

Exploitation in the Thirteen English Colonies

In the late fifteenth century, Europeans began to explore parts of North America where indigenous peoples had lived for thousands of years. The English, learning of the great wealth the Spanish had accrued in the New World, were anxious to fill their coffers with riches

as well. England first sent colonists to Roanoke Island in the late sixteenth century, but that attempt at settlement failed. The first permanent English settlement was at Jamestown in 1607. Much as Columbus
had recounted in 1492, these English settlers reported that the local
Native Americans were kind and generous and helped them to survive
the unfamiliar conditions. Amicable trade relations did not last long,
however, as it became clear that the Englishmen's intentions were
not benign: they planned to take over indigenous land and resources
(Zinn 2010; Morgan 1975).

European colonists engaged in constant warfare with Native Americans, often burning their lodgings and crops and enslaving entire
tribes. The English colonists justified their takeover of indigenous
lands in religious terms. They interpreted their successes as God's
will. For example, John Winthrop (1588–1649), a leader of the Massachusetts Bay Colony in the mid-seventeenth century, wrote that the
death of so many Native Americans as a result of smallpox showed that
"the Lord hathe cleared our title to what we possess" (quoted in Wood
1991, 96). It is important to note that when the English colonists interacted with Native Americans, they did not see them as belonging
to a separate race; this idea did not yet exist. Instead, the English saw
themselves as superior in religious and moral terms. These religious
justifications laid the groundwork for racial distinctions that emerged
later (Smedley 2007; Jordan 1968).

The first fifty years of the new settlement in Virginia were full of
hardship. Disease, starvation, and war caused extremely high death
rates among both Native Americans and English colonists. There were
severe food shortages, partly because the first settlers did not plant
enough corn. Morgan (1975) points out that most of the settlers in
Virginia were not farmers but nobles or gentry who thought food cul-
tivation was beneath them. Although the settlers were too proud to
grow corn to eat, they were willing to take up the enterprise of growing
tobacco to sell and expected to make their riches in this manner. As
there was no shortage of land in this vast country, the only commodity
lacking was labor power (Zinn 2010).

The English colonists were notoriously successful at decimating
the Native American population, yet less so in their attempts to use
Native Americans for labor. When the English realized they would not
become rich instantaneously through gold or silver mining, as it appeared the Spaniards had done, they turned to agricultural production

to seek wealth. For this, they needed labor—lots of it. The English were able to enslave Native Americans they captured in warfare, but most indigenous slaves either died or ran away, leaving the English in need of more labor in order to accumulate wealth (Zinn 2010).

Indentured Servitude

The lack of success at enslaving Native Americans led the colonists to turn to Britain, where they recruited poor men, women, and children from the streets of economically depressed cities such as Liverpool and Bristol. Englishmen also rounded up Irish and Scottish peasants who had been conquered in warfare, banished, or released from prison. Indentured servants from Europe who were willing to work for four to seven years to pay off their passage and debt soon became the primary source of labor for the colonies. The harsh treatment of European indentured servants needed no justification, as servitude was a way of life in Britain at the time (Smedley 2007; Zinn 2010).

Throughout the seventeenth century, indentured servants endured harsh conditions as laborers in the colonies. Hopeful laborers continued to come to the Americas, despite the difficult circumstances, because North America offered possibilities for social and economic advancement that did not exist in England. The flow of English laborers began to decline, however, with the restoration of the monarchy in England in 1660, as King Charles II implemented policies that discouraged emigration (Smedley 2007).

Enslavement of Africans

In addition to bringing English laborers, colonists brought Africans to the colonies as slaves. Most African slaves brought to North America were from West Africa and were Yoruba, Igbo, Fulani, or Mada. In 1619, English colonists brought the first group of Africans to the North American colonies. These twenty Africans occupied nearly the same social status as European indentured servants and were soon joined by African slaves brought over by Dutch and Spanish slave ships. All of these early Africans were granted rights that were later denied to all Black people in Virginia. There is no evidence that African slaves during the period before 1660 were subjected to more severe disciplinary measures than European servants. Some slaves were allowed to earn money of their own and to buy their freedom with it. There are several cases recorded in which masters set up conditions in their wills whereby Negro slaves would become free or could purchase their freedom after the master's death. The terms of these wills imply that the freed slaves would become regular members of the community (Morgan 1975; Smedley 2007; Zinn 2010).

The enslavement of Africans turned out to be especially profitable in part because Africans brought with them agricultural and craft experience. In addition, unlike people indigenous to the Americas, Africans had immunities to Old World diseases and thus could live longer in slavery. The initial justifications for bringing Africans to the colonies were not racial in nature. At the time, slavery was an accepted social system. To the extent that a justification was offered, it was that Africans were heathens and their enslavement would ensure their salvation (Smedley 2007). Over time, however, racial justifications for the enslavement of Africans emerged.

Racial differences were used to justify a new and unique form of slavery. The enslavement practices in the North American colonies differed from previous forms of enslavement in several ways. First, slaves had no human or legal rights. They were seen only as property, not as people who could marry or own property themselves. Second, slavery was permanent and the slave status was inherited. Third, slaves were forbidden to learn to read or write, thereby ensuring their inferior social status. Finally, slavery in North America was unique insofar as nearly all Africans and their descendants were enslaved, and only this group could be enslaved (Smedley 2007).

The Legal Codification of Racial Differences

Slave codes of the 1660s spelled out the legal differences between African slaves and European indentured servants. In 1667, Virginia issued a decree that slaves who had converted to Christianity could continue to be enslaved because of their so-called heathen ancestry. Whereas earlier justifications for slavery were primarily religious, the idea that ancestry could be used to determine social status set the stage for developing the idea of race. In the late seventeenth century, Virginia and Maryland each passed a series of laws that solidified the status of Black people. The strongest indicator of the solidification of the status of Africans was the prohibition of manumission: masters were not allowed to free their slaves, thereby establishing a permanent slave class. Other laws established lifelong servitude, forbade interracial marriage, and limited the rights of Black people to own property

FIGURE 1-1

REGIONS FROM WHICH CAPTURED AFRICANS WERE BROUGHT TO THE AMERICAS, 1501–1867

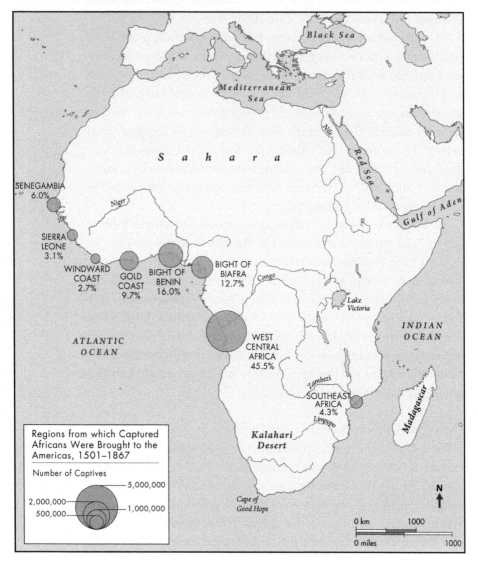

and bear arms. These laws specific to Black people both reflected the social order and solidified the status quo. For most of the seventeenth century, European indentured servants and African slaves had shared a similar social status. The slave codes gradually changed this social classification.

Laws against Intermarriage

The shared social position of African and European servants and slaves in the early years of the colonies meant that these groups intermarried and fraternized. The fact that Africans and Europeans had amicable relations is evidenced by the passage of laws that forbade these relationships. In 1661, Virginia passed a law that imposed harsh conditions on English servants who ran away with African slaves. In 1691, Virginia passed another law that prohibited free White people from intermarrying with Black and Native American people. Had these groups been naturally disinclined to intermarry or to fraternize, these laws would not have been necessary. As the 1661 law shows, plantation owners were concerned that European indentured servants and African slaves would see that they shared a common interest in fighting for more rights and better conditions. As historian Howard Zinn puts it, "only one fear was greater than the fear of black rebellion in the new American colonies. That was the fear that discontented whites would join black slaves to overthrow the existing order" (2010, 37).

When Africans and Europeans first found themselves together in the Americas, sexual relations and even marriage between these two groups were not uncommon. African men and women married European men and women (Smedley 2007). Various laws were passed, however, both to prevent and to control these relationships. The aforementioned 1662 law made it clear that when African women had children, the child's status as slave or free would be in accordance with the condition of the mother. The law also indicated that when Christians—here meaning Europeans—had sexual relations with Africans, they would pay double the normal fine for adultery. This law effectively prevented the formation of families by enslaved African women and European men.

Bacon's Rebellion

Bacon's Rebellion, which occurred in September 1676, provides one example of what could happen when Black and White people joined forces to fight for their interests. The rebellion itself was not particularly successful, but the coalition that emerged between poor White laborers and African slaves and freedmen became a cause for concern among the elite planter class, who depended on these groups for cheap labor. In Bacon's Rebellion, White indentured servants joined forces with enslaved Africans and freedmen to protest their conditions.

This massive rebellion, in which protestors demanding an end to their servitude burned Jamestown to the ground, was a clear threat to the status quo. One of the last groups to surrender was a mixed group of eighty Black and twenty White servants. This multiracial coalition indicates that Black and White people were willing to join forces to fight for their common interests as laborers. After Bacon's Rebellion, an official report arguing for the continued presence of British soldiers in Virginia stated: "Virginia is at present poor and more populous than ever. There is great apprehension of a rising among the servants, owing to their great necessities and want of clothes; they may plunder the storehouses and ships" (Zinn 2010, 37).

Howard Zinn and other historians argue that Bacon's Rebellion stirred up fear in the hearts of the elite planter class and that this fear led these elites to pass laws that divided Black and White people. For example, in the aftermath of the rebellion, the Virginia Assembly gave amnesty to the White servants who had rebelled but not to the Blacks. By extending this and other privileges to Whites that were denied to Black people, the elites succeeded in preventing future class-based alliances between Black and White people that would threaten the social order.

Wealth Imbalance and the Tenuous Social Order

Wealth in colonial North America was concentrated in the hands of very few people. In 1700, there were about 250,000 colonists, most of whom lived in horrendous conditions. In Virginia, there were only about fifty wealthy families, who depended on the labor of the other 40,000 poor colonists. This imbalance of wealth made for a tenuous social order (Zinn 2010). It soon became clear to the rich elite and the governing body that they could not continue to disregard the interests of the majority of the population. In 1705, a law was passed requiring masters to provide White servants whose indenture time was completed with ten bushels of corn, thirty shillings, a gun, and fifty acres of land (Morgan 1975, 344). This tactic of giving servants a piece of the American Dream was intended to avoid rebellion by convincing poor Whites that the rich landowners were not extortionists or enemies, but protectors of their common interests as Whites. To reinforce this impression, it was further mandated that servants had the right to possess property but that slaves did not (Morgan 1975, 333). The Virginia Assembly in 1705 also prohibited any Negro, mulatto, or Indian from raising his hand in opposition to any Christian, which meant any White man (Jordan 1968). By denying Black slaves privileges extended to White servants, the first step was taken in creating a division between Blacks and Whites (Zinn 2010).

In New York in 1708, a group of slaves was accused of murdering a farmer and his family. Shortly afterward, a law was enacted preventing the conspiracy of slaves. This meant, in effect, that slaves could not gather in private to talk about anything. In 1712, a slave rebellion involving about fifty slaves left nine Whites dead and six others wounded. Immediately thereafter, New York's repressive laws were reinforced. For example, arson committed by a slave was now considered a crime punishable by death (Szasz 1967).

One purpose of the slave codes was the prevention and deterrence of slave rebellions, which were becoming more and more of a real danger with the increasing number of slaves, especially in the southern colonies, where slaves often outnumbered Whites. In 1730, in Virginia, the governor ordered that all Whites should bring their guns with them to church on Sunday so that they would be prepared for a slave uprising in the event that slaves took advantage of their absence to conspire (Jordan 1968). The idea of a slave rebellion was even more distasteful to Whites because of the widespread idea that any slave insurrection would have as its ultimate goal not only the emancipation of slaves but also the dominance of Blacks over Whites (Jordan 1968).

Solidifying the Idea of Race

Eventually, the entire slave class was composed of Black Africans, and, as a result of manumission restrictions, most Blacks were enslaved. The creation of this sort of color line, alongside the introduction of the concept of hereditary slavery, was an important step toward solidifying the idea of race. Notably, it was not until the eighteenth century that negative beliefs about Africans became widespread among English settlers. Even then, there is ample evidence that Black and White people continued to fraternize. In 1743, a grand jury in Charleston, South Carolina, denounced "The Too Common Practice of Criminal Conversation with Negro and other Slave Wenches in this Province" (Zinn 2010).

The stories of Mary Peters and Daniel Dowdy (see *Voices: From Bullwhip Days*) elucidate the cruelty and dehumanization that were part and parcel of colonialism and enslavement in the Americas. These two phenomena—colonialism and slavery—have shaped the way people in the United States view the world. Our contemporary racial worldview is a relic of the systems of human classification that were first used in the context of the colonization of Native American territories and the enslavement of Africans in the Americas. Although such brutal practices are no longer morally or legally permissible, the ideas of racial difference that emerged from those practices persist.

voices

From *Bullwhip Days*

My mother's mistress had three boys—one twenty-one, one nineteen, and one seventeen. One day, Old Mistress had gone away to spend the day. Mother always worked in the house; she didn't work on the farm, in Missouri. While she was alone, the boys came in and threw her down on the floor and tied her down so she couldn't struggle, and one after the other used her as long as they wanted, for the whole afternoon. Mother was sick when her mistress came home. When Old Mistress wanted to know what was the matter with her, she told her what the boys had done. She whipped them, and that's the way I came to be here.

—Mary Peters describing the brutal circumstances of her own conception

I saw slaves sold. I can see that old block now. My cousin Eliza was a pretty girl, really good-looking. Her master was her father. . . . The day they sold her will always be remembered. They stripped her to be bid off and looked at. . . . The man that bought Eliza was from New York. The Negroes had made up 'nuf money to buy her off theyself, but the white folks wouldn't let that happen. There was a man bidding for her that was a Swedeland. He allus bid for the good-looking cullud gals and bought 'em for his own use. He ask the man from New York "What you gonna do with 'er when you git 'er?" The man from New York said, "None of your damn business, but you ain't got money 'nuf to buy 'er."

—Former slave Daniel Dowdy

Source: Mellon 2002, 287, 297.

SLAVERY VERSUS THE IDEAL OF FREEDOM IN THE UNITED STATES

The Declaration of Independence famously begins by stating that all men are created equal. The question is, then, why were some enslaved? Although the concept of liberty was at the core of the American Revolution, nearly half of the fifty-five men who made up the 1787 Constitutional Convention owned slaves, and most of the rest profited from slavery through their business practices. A prominent member, George Washington (1732–1799), was one of the richest men in the colonies and the owner of many slaves. These men struggled with the contradictions inherent in advocating for freedom in a slaveholding society, yet they were unwilling to outlaw slavery (Feagin 2001).

The writers of the founding documents of the United States were not willing to end slavery in part because most of them profited directly or indirectly from it. The wealth generated by slave labor in the United States had made the American Revolution possible: a significant amount of the funds that financed the American Revolution came from profits from slavery (Feagin 2001). The contradiction between the ideals of freedom and the prevalence of slavery led to justifications of slavery in terms of Black people's alleged racial inferiority. Writings by people such as Thomas Jefferson validated the belief that people of African descent were less than human. In 1787, Thomas Jefferson wrote in *Notes on Virginia*: "Blacks, whether originally a distinct race or made distinct by time and circumstance, are inferior to whites in the endowment both of body and mind" (Jefferson [1787] 2004, 98–99).

Slavery was an immensely profitable enterprise for a small number of slaveholders. In 1860, the twelve wealthiest counties in the United States could all be found in the Deep South. The profits were not evenly divided, however: about 7 percent of Southerners owned three-quarters of the 4 million slaves in the South. This concentration of wealth meant that slaveowners constituted a powerful planter class that went to great lengths to protect its property, which included humans: slaveowners saw enslaved Africans and African Americans as an investment they did not want to lose. Additionally, many Whites who did not own slaves profited indirectly from the slave system. In the southern United States, slavery was part of the economic and social fabric of society. There were fewer slaves in the northern states, but many Northerners had strong economic ties to slavery insofar as they consumed and manufactured products made on slave planta-tions. These strong economic interests in slavery meant that the prac-tice was not ended in the United States until the victory of the North in the Civil War (Wilson 1996; Feagin 2001).

On January 1, 1863, President Abraham Lincoln (1809–1865) issued the Emancipation Proclamation, which freed the slaves held in the rebel states of the Confederacy. His willingness to issue this proc-lamation was not hindered by his belief that Blacks were inferior to Whites. Five years earlier, in 1858, Lincoln had declared: "I am not nor ever have been in favor of the social and political equality of the White and Black races: that I am not nor ever have been in favor of making voters of the free negroes, or jurors, or qualifying them to hold office or having them to marry with white people. . . . I as much as any other man am in favor of the superior position being assigned to the white man" (quoted in Feagin 2001, 83–84).

In 1865, the United States finally abolished slavery. Slavery was one of the main reasons for the long and bloody Civil War that had pitted the North against the South. From the perspective of plantation owners in the South, slavery was a profitable institution that ensured the proper place of Blacks in society. From the perspective of capital-ists in the North, slavery gave southern capitalists an unfair compet-itive advantage (Feagin 2001). The end of slavery marked the end of an era of extreme exploitation. The racist ideologies that had justified the enslavement of Africans and the massacre and removal of Native Americans, however, would endure.

THE INDIAN REMOVAL ACT: THE CONTINUATION OF MANIFEST DESTINY

The **Indian Removal Act of 1830** enabled the administration of Pres-ident Andrew Jackson to use military power to displace at least 70,000 Native Americans, killing tens of thousands in the process. Indian re-moval is often associated with the Cherokee of Georgia, but there were actually many more "**Trails of Tears**," including the forced displace-ment of the Apalachicola of Florida, the Peoria of Illinois, the Shawnee of Ohio, and a host of other tribes (Littlefield and Parins 2011). These removals violated treaties the United States had made with Native Americans, even though the Indian Removal Act contained a clause guaranteeing that "nothing in this act contained shall be construed as authorizing or directing the violation of any existing treaty between the United States and any of the Indian tribes" (quoted in Cave 2003, 1335). These forced displacements, which continued until 1859, when the Seminoles were removed from Florida, wreaked havoc on indigenous communities (Littlefield and Parins 2011).

During these treacherous journeys, tens of thousands of Native Americans died from disease, cold, starvation, and exhaustion. Approximately 17,000 Cherokee were forcibly removed, and nearly half of those who embarked on this particular Trail of Tears died in the process. Large numbers of indigenous people died in other removals: about 6,000 of the 40,000 Choctaw did not survive the journey, and only about half of the Creek and the Seminole peoples survived their removals (Churchill 2002).

The justifications for Indian removal were distinct from those used for slavery, as Whites tended to see Africans as a vital source of labor. Native Americans, in contrast, were construed as hindering White expansion, and thus the racial ideologies surrounding Native Americans tended to explain and predict their gradual extinction. Notably, this extinction was imagined as occurring through both assimilation (marriage to Whites) and natural selection (death from disease). Whereas colonists' ideas about Africans served to rationalize their hyperexploitation of slaves, Whites' ideas about Native Americans aimed to rationalize the assimilation and gradual extinction of these groups, enabling Whites to appropriate Indian lands (Berger 2009).

THE RISE OF SCIENTIFIC RACISM

In the seventeenth century, people in the Americas developed and acted on folk ideas about differences between Africans, Europeans, and Native Americans that were based on daily interactions and the prevailing social order. The slow emergence of the idea of racial difference can be seen in the laws passed by legislatures and the decisions made by religious leaders. However, the rise of science in the eighteenth century would fundamentally alter this conversation. The question of human difference began to move from the realms of religion and folk ideas to that of science.

European Taxonomies

Before the rise of science, Westerners understood the world primarily in biblical terms. Theology provided explanations for nearly everything. Thus, when Europeans encountered the Americas, they attempted to place these peoples into their understanding of the history of the world, as described in their scriptures. This led to debates over which of the three sons of Noah was the ancestor of the Native Americans and even over whether Native Americans were fully human (Smedley 2007).

One of the key features of the rise of science was the emergence of taxonomy. Scholars endeavored to classify all flora and fauna known to them. Soon, scientists began to attempt to classify human beings into types. One of the first efforts to develop a classificatory system for humans appeared in a French journal in 1684. The author, François Bernier (1625–1688), divided humans into four groups: Europeans, Far Easterners, Negroes, and Lapps (people from Lapland in northern Scandinavia). His system used physical traits such as skin color and hair texture, which would later become prominent determinants of racial status, to categorize different groups. Other scholars worked on developing classificatory schemes, but it was not until 1735 that a comprehensive system of classification that resembles the modern concept of race began to be developed (Eze 1997).

In 1735, the Swedish botanist Carolus Linnaeus (1707–1778) proposed that all human beings could be divided into four groups. These four groups are consistent with the modern idea of race in two ways: all of them are still used today, and Linnaeus connected physical traits such as skin color with cultural and moral traits such as "indolence." Linnaeus described these four groups, which correspond to four of the continents, in *Systema Naturae* in 1735:

Americanus: *reddish, choleric, and erect; . . . obstinate, merry, free; . . . regulated by customs.*

Asiaticus: *sallow, melancholy, . . . black hair, dark eyes, . . . haughty, . . . ruled by opinions.*

Africanus: *black, phlegmatic, relaxed; women without shame, . . . crafty, indolent, negligent; governed by caprice.*

Europaenus: *white, sanguine, muscular; inventive; governed by laws.*

Other European men elaborated on this schema. For example, Johann Blumenbach (1752–1840), a German professor of medicine, proposed a classificatory system that divided humans into five varieties that also were associated with geographical origins: Caucasian, Mongolian, Ethiopian, American, and Malay. Both Blumenbach and Linnaeus endowed Europeans—their own group—with the most admirable qualities. It bears repeating that the idea of race was initiated by European men and that, not surprisingly, it is an idea that consistently has been used to explain and rationalize European superiority. The Scottish philosopher David Hume (1711–1776), for example, asserted in 1748 that Whites were the only "species" to have created civilized nations and to have developed arts and sciences. European explanations of White racial superiority espoused by Blumenbach, Linnaeus, and Hume soon reached the Americas, where they were used to explain and rationalize the enslavement of Africans and the continued takeover of indigenous lands (Eze 1997).

Scientific Racism in the Nineteenth Century

The nineteenth century was an age of emancipation from slavery and liberation from colonial powers. It also saw the rise of industrial capitalism and the emergence of **scientific racism**—the use of science or pseudoscience to rationalize or reproduce racial inequality. For intellectuals in the Americas and Europe, scientific racism was central to most human and social inquiries. Eighteenth-century scientists had developed elaborate systems of human classification. In the nineteenth century, scientists built on these classification systems by developing anthropometrics—tools designed to measure the qualities of humans.

With the publication between 1853 and 1855 of Comte Joseph-Arthur de Gobineau's four volumes entitled *Essays on the Inequality of the Human Races*, by the mid-nineteenth century, the idea of race was fully in place. Gobineau (1816–1882) divided humanity into three races—White, Yellow, and Black—and argued that racial differences allow us to explain fundamental differences between people. Gobineau's thinking was in line with that of Herbert Spencer (1820–1903), who contended that the superiority of the European race explained its dominant position. He pointed to the natural inferiority of Native Americans as an explanation for their decimation. Spencer's ideas of the "survival of the fittest" would hold great sway for many years to come. Both Spencer and Gobineau used ideas, arguments, and rudimentary evidence from travel accounts to make their claims. Other scientists, however, were developing anthropometric techniques that enabled them to measure differences between people (Gould 1996).

Samuel George Morton (1799–1851), a scientist and physician who worked in Philadelphia, amassed an impressive collection of human skulls. He began his collection in the 1820s, and by the time of his death in 1851, he had over 1,000 skulls. Morton used these skulls to test his hypothesis that brain size could be used to rank the various human races. In his initial efforts to measure brain size, Morton filled the cranial cavity with mustard seeds. Later, when he realized that mustard seeds did not provide consistent measurements, he switched to lead shots with a one-eighth-inch diameter that produced less variable results. Through use of both mustard seeds and lead shots, Morton's measurements consistently showed that Europeans had larger brains than Africans or American Indians. In 1977, however, evolutionary biologist and scientific historian Stephen Jay Gould reanalyzed Morton's raw data and found several examples of unconscious bias in his work (Gould 1996).

Morton found that American Indians had the smallest skull sizes. Gould explains that Morton arrived at this conclusion because he had included 155 skulls of Peruvian Incas, who had an average brain size of seventy-five cubic inches, yet he only included three skulls of Iroquois people, who had, on average, a much larger skull size. In contrast, in the Caucasian group, Morton eliminated the Hindus, who had the smallest skulls, from his sample. Had Morton ensured equal representation from each of the American Indian and Caucasian groups, he would have found no significant differences in skull size.

Stephen Gould explains that skull size is related to body size, and yet he contends that Morton never took body size into account when he measured skulls. As women tend to be smaller than men, women often have smaller skulls. When Morton compared the brain sizes of Africans and Europeans, his African sample was entirely female and his English sample entirely male. Of course, he found that Europeans had larger brains. What is remarkable about Morton's research is not just that it is full of unconscious bias, but also that his biases are consistently in favor of his expectations. Morton set out to prove, through science, that Europeans were superior. All of his miscalculations favored his hypothesis. In this sense, Morton was similar to nearly all of his contemporaries: European and American male scientists of the nineteenth century developed a plethora of methods to measure human abilities and consistently found that White men were superior to all other groups.

Paul Broca (1824–1880), a French anthropologist, built on Samuel Morton's work to develop more elaborate techniques for measuring humans. Broca believed strongly that there was a direct correlation between brain size and intelligence, and he spent much of his career measuring the brains of dead people. Broca eventually ran into trouble with his arguments when he measured the brains of eminent scholars who had passed on and discovered that many people considered to be highly intelligent turned out to have small brains. Undeterred, Broca accounted for those anomalies by asserting that they had died at a very advanced age or that their brains had not been properly preserved. When a study of criminal brains revealed that criminals had abnormally large brains, Broca argued that their sudden death by execution meant that their brains did not atrophy, as did those of people who died of natural causes. Broca eventually went on to measure other characteristics of brains and bodies; not surprisingly, his scientific measurements always showed what he set out to prove: that Europeans were superior to other groups (Gould 1996).

Intelligence Testing

When nineteenth-century scientists compared the skulls of Blacks to those of Whites, they used science to demonstrate what they thought they already knew: that the White race was superior to all others. Nineteenth-century **craniometry**—the measurement of cranial capacity—provided the first opportunity for scientists to bring massive amounts of data to bear on their ideas of human hierarchy. These data on brain size supposedly provided "scientific" proof of White superiority. Eventually, however, craniometry lost its appeal, and scientists looked for new ways to measure human difference and argue for European supremacy. These new methods revolved around measuring intelligence directly (Gould 1996).

In the United States, **intelligence testing**—the quantification of intellectual ability using scientific measures—became popular in the early twentieth century. Such tests were used in attempts to demonstrate the alleged superiority of not only Europeans as a whole but also particular groups of Europeans. When the United States began to receive large numbers of immigrants from southern and eastern Europe, American scientists used intelligence testing to draw distinctions among them (Gould 1996; Brodkin 1998).

Intelligence tests were not originally designed to find out which races were the most intellectually fit. Instead, the goal was to identify children who needed extra help in school. Alfred Binet (1857–1911), director of the psychology laboratory at the Sorbonne in Paris, dedicated much of his scholarly career to developing ways to measure children's intellectual ability. It was only when Binet's test was taken to the United States that it began to be used to determine which groups were innately superior or inferior.

One of the first psychologists to use Binet's test was H. H. Goddard (1866–1957), who adapted it for use in the Vineland Training School for Feeble-Minded Boys and Girls. Goddard firmly believed that feeble-mindedness was inherited, attributing intelligence to a single gene. To provide evidence for his beliefs, Goddard took Binet's test to Ellis Island, where he administered the exam to arriving immigrants who spoke little English. Many received a low score, but instead of questioning the conditions under which he performed the exam, Goddard concluded that immigrants were of low intelligence. He further argued that, given these results, immigration had to be curtailed. Later in his career, Goddard conceded that perhaps what he defined as feeble-mindedness could be cured through education (Gould 1996).

The next prominent psychologist to use intelligence testing was Lewis Terman (1877–1956), a professor of psychology at Stanford University. Terman modified the Binet test, endeavoring to standardize it such that the average person would score 100. This number should sound familiar, as it is still used today as the mean for IQ—the intelligence quotient—in what's known as the Stanford-Binet test. Terman's colleague R. M. Yerkes (1876–1956) carried on Terman's work and developed the Army Mental Tests, which aimed to measure innate intelligence. Yerkes succeeded in convincing the U.S. Army to allow him to administer the tests to all of its recruits. This massive sample of over a million respondents gave significant quantitative weight to the emerging field of intelligence testing (Gould 1996).

Stephen Gould argued that the primary error in intelligence testing is that of reification—making intelligence into a scientific concept by measuring it. Some people know more facts and trivia, are more quick-witted, can calculate sums in their heads faster, and are more eloquent in speech and writing than others. But as Gould contends, intelligence tests are flawed because they cannot truly measure this wide range of abilities. Moreover, instead of promoting the idea that each of these skills can be learned and nurtured, intelligence testing implies that they are innate (Gould 1996).

Eugenics

The **eugenics** movement, which had its heyday from about 1900 to 1930, promoted the idea that not only intelligence but also alcoholism, laziness, criminality, poverty, and other moral and cultural traits could be inherited. Based on this notion, eugenicists advocated the selective breeding of Americans and the sterilization of the biologically unfit as a way of creating a superior breed of people. During this period, many Americans believed that the American population was in decline as a result of immigration and the high birth rate among poor people (Lindsay 1998).

One of the main proponents of eugenics was Madison Grant (1865–1937), a lawyer, historian, and physical anthropologist. In much of his work, including the 1916 book *The Passing of the Great Race*, Grant proposed that Europe could be divided into three races: "Nordics," "Alpines," and "Mediterraneans." He forcefully argued that Nordics were the most fit of the three and that measures should be taken to ensure their racial purity and survival. His ideas made it into the mainstream both through his book and through his position as chairman of the U.S. Committee on Selective Immigration. In that capacity, he advocated for a reduction in the number of Alpines and Mediterraneans admitted into the United States. The views of Madison Grant and other eugenicists played an important role in the development of immigration policy in the 1920s, placing limits on the immigration of "undesirable" groups (Jacobson 1998).

Madison Grant's ideas—particularly that Nordics were the "master race" and that it was incumbent upon the state to ban interracial marriages and sterilize inferior races—found a large audience in Germany. Adolf Hitler referred to Grant's book *The Passing of the Great Race* as his "bible," and the German translation became widely read in the 1930s (Spiro 2008). Hitler put Grant's ideas into practice when he passed the Eugenic Sterilization Law in 1933, which led to the sterilization of 225,000 people in Germany in just three years. Similar to sterilization laws in the United States, this law was intended to improve the population. The Nazis then took these ideas several steps further, first to euthanasia and then to gas chambers (Smedley 2007).

CONCLUSION AND DISCUSSION

The brutal, troubled history of the idea of race clearly demonstrates the power of ideologies about human difference. The idea that the world's population can be divided into discrete racial groups is a product of a specific series of events: colonialism, slavery, and the rise of scientific racism. Europeans developed ideologies of racial inferiority to rationalize their desire to take land from indigenous peoples in the Americas and to extract labor from Africans.

Alongside this large-scale theft of land and exploitation of labor, science began to emerge as a field of study concerned largely with the classification of all objects and species into specific groups. Scientists rushed to develop taxonomies of flora and fauna, including classifications of humans. Europeans who proposed these classifications put their own group at the top of the hierarchy.

This subjective (and overt) bias of Europeans continued with the development of anthropometric and other measurement techniques in the nineteenth century. European scientists measured human skulls, brains, and every other imaginable part of the human body and arrived at the same conclusion: Europeans are superior. This recounting of history offers a revealing look at not only the past but also the present. We cannot simply look at the past and point fingers at those "racists" of yesteryear. Instead, we should also be compelled to explore the assumptions and ideologies that govern our behavior today.

THINKING
ABOUT
RACIAL
JUSTICE

IN THIS CHAPTER, we have seen that the idea of race was created to rationalize mass genocide and brutal exploitation. We have also seen that there is as much diversity and genetic difference within any racial group as there is across racial groups, if not more. But race is an important part of our identities nevertheless. How does what you learned in this chapter affect the way you think of yourself? Write a 500-word essay that (1) shows what your racial identity is and how you usually think of yourself, (2) provides evidence that race is a social construction and not a biological reality, (3) demonstrates how this evidence affects how you think of your own racial identity, and (4) reflects on how this knowledge might be used in the pursuit of racial justice.

Key Terms

social construction 2	slave codes 13
race 3	Indian Removal Act of 1830 20
racism 3	Trails of Tears 20
ethnicity 3	scientific racism 23
colonialism 4	craniometry 25
genocide 4	intelligence testing 25
ideology 4	eugenics 27

CHECK YOUR UNDERSTANDING

1.1   What are race and ethnicity? What is racism?

- *Race* refers to a group of people who share physical and cultural traits. Race is a social construction and has no biological basis. *Ethnicity* is a group identity based on notions of similar and shared history, culture, and kinship.
- *Racism* refers to the belief that some races are superior to others, as well as the practice of subordinating races believed to be inferior.

Q   Why do sociologists argue that race is a social construction?

1.2   How old is racism? How is race distinct from previous ways of thinking about human difference?

- There are historical precedents to the idea of race, including the Spanish Inquisition and the subjugation of the Irish by the English.
- Slavery existed long before the invention of the idea of race.
- When the Spanish colonists arrived in the Americas, they displayed extreme cruelty to the native people of the Americas.
- Africans were enslaved in the Americas to meet labor needs.
- The idea of race emerged to rationalize slavery and colonization.

Q   When was the idea of race invented? Why do sociologists argue that race is a historical construction?

1.3   How did the writers of the U.S. Constitution think of slavery?

- Although the Declaration of Independence declares that "all men are created equal," nearly half of the authors were slaveowners.
- Slavery was not abolished in the United States until 1865.

Q   Why were slavery and freedom in tension during the writing of the Declaration of Independence?

1.4 How did the Indian Removal Act affect Native Americans?

- The Indian Removal Act of 1830 resulted in the death of tens of thousands of Native Americans as a result of forced displacements.

Q   How and why were the rationalizations for Indian removal distinct from those used for slavery?

1.5 What role did science play in the propagation of racism?

- The idea of race was originally based on simple taxonomies. However, as science developed, scientists created more complex explanations of the differences among racial groups.
- In the nineteenth century, scientists measured skulls in an attempt to assess differences among racial groups.
- In the early twentieth century, scientific racism continued. In an attempt to scientifically demonstrate the superiority of the White race, scientists used intelligence testing, and many promoted eugenics.

Q   How did bias influence early scientific measurements of various racial groups?

Critical Thinking

1. Why is it important to clarify that the idea of race is a modern invention?
2. Can you imagine a world in which racial classifications had no importance? Why or why not?
3. What are today's prevailing racial ideologies in the United States? In what ways do those ideologies work to rationalize the current racial hierarchy?
4. How and why do racial ideologies related to Native Americans and African Americans differ?
5. What biases toward race might be present in today's sciences and social sciences?

Talking about Race

Imagine someone said to you that African Americans are naturally gifted at basketball. How could you respond to such a statement in a constructive way? The first step is to ask for further explanation. Listen to any evidence provided to support the claim. The person who made the statement may provide anecdotal evidence or possibly cite national trends. You should be able to draw from the knowledge you gained in this chapter to respond to the contention that there are natural or genetic differences between racial groups. Use your sociological imagination to encourage your conversational partner to think of explanations other than genetics for racial differences in basketball skills.

Learn more with this chapter's digital tools, including video clips from the author, web links, filmography, and chapter self-assessment quizzes at www.oup.com/he/golash-boza-brief3e.

2

Racial Ideologies and Sociological Theories of Racism

AS YOU READ

2.1 How is individual racism linked to institutional inequality?

2.2 How do systemic racism and structural racism create racial disparities?

2.3 What are racial ideologies, and how have they functioned and changed over time?

2.4 What is racial formation, and how does this concept inform our understanding of racial inequality?

2.5 What does the perspective of Indigenous studies reveal about racism in the contemporary United States?

2.6 In what ways do race, class, and gender oppression work together?

2.7 What is White privilege, and how does it function?

Racial inequality is pervasive in the contemporary United States. We see it in the criminal legal system, where Black and Latinx people are several times more likely to go to prison than White people. We can find racial inequality in employment as well: audit studies have shown that Black people are less likely than White people to be interviewed and, once interviewed, to get a job. Once Black people have jobs, they are less likely to get promoted. Black business owners have more trouble getting contracts. In education, the picture is equally bleak. Many schools in the United States are racially segregated, and the quality of education is lower at primarily Black and Latinx schools. Within schools, White students are given preferential treatment. When White parents visit schools, they get more attention from staff members, and teachers are more likely to recommend White students for gifted programs. Sociologists and other researchers have carried out study upon study demonstrating such inequality. Yet how do we explain it?

This is where **sociological theories of racism** come into play; they are lenses that help make sense of patterns such as the overrepresentation of African Americans in the criminal legal system. Sociologists use evidence from their studies to develop explanations, known as theories, for how racial inequality is created and reproduced.

Before we begin an examination of these theories, what do you think? How would you explain the racial disparities in the criminal legal system, for example? Do you think Black people commit more crimes? Do you think police officers spend more time policing Black communities? Do you think police officers are biased against African Americans? All of these questions can be translated into hypotheses that can be tested through scientific studies. First, let's look at how racism can be the basis of an explanation for racial inequality.

PREJUDICE, DISCRIMINATION, AND INSTITUTIONAL RACISM

Racism encompasses both racial **prejudice**—the belief that people belong to distinct races and that these racial groups have innate hierarchical differences that can be measured and judged—and racial **discrimination**—the practice of treating people differently on the basis of their race. For example, an employer can think African Americans are less competent than Whites; this belief constitutes racial prejudice. When that employer decides to hire a White person instead of an equally qualified Black person, that decision constitutes racial discrimination. Both prejudice and discrimination are widespread in U.S. society.

In one survey, Joe Feagin (2001) found that three-quarters of Whites agreed with prejudicial statements about Blacks, such as "Blacks have less native intelligence" than Whites (109). Eduardo Bonilla-Silva (2013) found that most Whites use color-blind discourses that reproduce and rationalize racial inequality. In 1995, researchers conducted a study in which they asked participants to close their eyes for a second and imagine a drug user. Fully 95 percent of respondents reported imagining a Black drug user (Alexander 2010). The reality is that African Americans account for only 15 percent of drug users in the United States and are just as likely as Whites to use drugs. However, Americans have an unconscious bias against Black people and imagine them to be more likely than other groups to use drugs (Alexander 2010). These and other studies show the widespread nature of racial prejudice.

Many Americans, even those who do not believe they are racially prejudiced, have implicit biases that operate at the level of the subconscious. It is hard to avoid these biases because of the barrage of racialized messages we receive in the media and through our personal networks. Racial prejudice and implicit biases inevitably lead to racial discrimination. (Curious about your own implicit bias? Take the Implicit Association Test at https://implicit.harvard.edu/implicit.)

Individual Racism

Discrimination can occur at the individual level when one person discriminates against another. Audit studies have consistently shown that Black candidates are less likely to be interviewed for jobs than White candidates and that Black and Latinx people face housing discrimination on a regular basis (Feagin 2001; Pager, Western, and Bonikowski 2009; Auspurg, Schneck, and Hinz 2019). Racially discriminatory actions by individuals such as not calling back an interviewee for a job because of their race or telling a person on the phone that the apartment is taken because he or she has a Spanish accent or lives on a reservation constitute **individual racism**. Individual acts of racial discrimination and bigotry are commonplace in our society and help to reproduce racial inequalities.

How widespread is individual racism? Researchers have consistently found that racial discrimination is pervasive. One study of Department of Defense employees revealed that nearly half of the Black employees had heard racist jokes in the previous year (Feagin 2001). Another survey conducted by Feagin and McKinney (2003) revealed that 80 percent of Black respondents had encountered racial hostility in public places. One African American secretary detailed the consequences of constant discrimination as follows: "I had to see several doctors because of the discrimination, and I went through a lot of stress. And, then, my blood pressure . . . went on the rise" (82). This woman, like many other African Americans interviewed in this study, displayed high levels of stress as a result of her mistreatment in the workplace and consequently developed health issues. In another study, Dwanna Robertson (2015) found that Native Americans constantly face the consequences of negative stereotypes about them. One of her participants told her, "I hear things like: 'Show me an Indian, I'll show you a drunk Indian.' 'Indians are lazy'" (130). A study by Raúl Pérez and Geoff Ward (2019) pointed to the prevalence of racist joking among police officers. One of the examples they discuss comes from Ferguson, MO, just prior to the 2014 police killing of a young Black man, Michael Brown. That joke refers to an abortion by a Black woman as an event that leads to a reduction in crime.

It is remarkable that individual racism is widespread in a society that usually condemns overt acts of racism. If a television announcer were to make a racially charged or overtly racist statement such as "African Americans are inherently more violent than Whites," we can be sure that the following day, critics would forcefully condemn the racist statement. If racial discrimination is frowned upon, how can it be so widespread?

One way that individual racism persists, even in a society that decries racism, is through **racial microaggressions**—daily, commonplace insults and racial slights that cumulatively affect the psychological well-being of people of color. The consequences of these microaggressions can be severe, and studies of African Americans, Latinx Americans, and Asian Americans have uncovered the continued prevalence of microaggressions. One study of African Americans on college campuses, for example, found that White students and professors consistently doubted the academic potential of African Americans. One Black student was presumed to have cheated after getting an "A" on a difficult math quiz. Another Black student found that people assumed his scholarship was for sports, when, in fact, it was for his academic achievements. These students reported that the cumulative effect of these slights was to make them tired, discouraged, and frustrated—especially since they had expected more from their professors and peers (Solorzano, Ceja, and Yosso 2000). These microaggressions can have severe consequences: a recent study among African American college students found that certain types of racial microaggressions were associated with elevated levels of suicide ideation (Hollingsworth et al. 2017).

In a study of Asian Americans' experiences of discrimination, Derald Wing Sue and his colleagues found that Asian Americans experienced a wide variety of microaggressions, ranging from the assumption of foreignness to exoticization of Asian women to invisibility. For example, Asian Americans reported that White Americans consistently asked them questions such as "Where are you from?" or made comments such as "You speak good English," when the only indication that they might not be from the United States was their Asian appearance. Other Asian Americans pointed out that people presumed they were good at math and that men presumed Asian women would be submissive lovers. The Asian Americans in this study recounted that the constant barrage of microaggressions angered them but that they also felt disempowered to respond, as any single event could seem inconsequential by itself (Sue, Bucceri, Lin, Nadal, and Torino. 2007). These experiences are commonplace: a study of 152 Asian Americans found that 78 percent of them experienced microaggressions during a two-week period (Ong, Burrow, Fuller-Rowell, Ja, and Sue 2013).

Kevin Nadal and his colleagues conducted a study of multiracial people's experiences of microaggressions and found them to be pervasive (Nadal et al. 2011). Their studies of both Asian Americans and multiracial individuals reveal that well-intentioned Whites often deliver microaggressions because of their insensitivity toward and ignorance about non-Whites. This can be seen, for example, when a White person speaks Japanese to a Chinese American or tells a biracial woman with a Black mother and a White father that being half-White makes it easier to get along with her. In the first instance, the White person may be trying to show a cultural interest in Asian people, although her act simultaneously tries to erase the differences between Japanese and Chinese people and reasserts the presumed foreignness of Asian Americans. In the second instance, this assertion reinforces White supremacy by implying that the biracial woman is better than other Black people because she has a White parent.

Microaggressions and other forms of individual racism continue to pose a problem on college campuses. Studies have consistently found that individual acts of bigotry are commonplace (Harper and Hurtado 2007). In a study of 2500 college students published in 2018, C. C. Levchak found that 90 percent of Black students and 80 percent of Asian students reported experiencing a microaggression (Levchak 2018). Notably, the study took place at both a primarily White institution and a racially diverse one, and students reported high levels of microaggressions at both places. A qualitative study of 30 Mexican college students found that they experienced multiple microaggressions (Ballinas 2017). Educational professionals consistently made them feel as if college was not for them. Over half of the students reported having their academic capabilities, accomplishments, or goals questioned. One student reported, "every exam it was the same thing: he [his eleventh-grade history teacher] thought I was cheating because I would score 97, 98, good grades . . . So he would always be monitoring me. And in my work he would mark it really specific, he would take off all these little points and I would talk to my [White] friends in class and ask if he took [points] off for them. . . He wouldn't take off half the stuff he took off me" (Ballinas 2017: 398). Other students reported being steered toward community colleges and away from "good four-year universities" by White high school guidance counselors—often with some variation of "Oh, those [four-year universities] are for rich white people. Why don't we look into a community college?" (Ballinas 2017: 398).

voices

Microaggressions

Individuals who have had the following experiences and consider them to be racial microaggressions posted these reports on the website microaggressions.com. How do you feel as you read these reports? What would you say if you overheard such comments? What would you say if someone directed one of these comments at you?

- Often when I have dinner at people's houses, they ask me if I would prefer chopsticks, regardless of the meal!
- I am a registered nurse and always get told that I speak English so well. I was born in Australia and I am of Filipino background. I don't think about my appearance until a patient or their family member points it out, and they are quite amazed/baffled that someone who appears Asian "speaks so well" and could be considered a "real Australian."

(continued)

continued.

Microaggressions

The presumption that Asian Americans use chopsticks at every meal is based on an idea of inherent cultural differences. We don't see these same presumptions applied to third-generation Italian Americans or Irish Americans.

- I always get asked to be an interpreter for patients who are not native English speakers, specifically for those of Asian background. Because I am of Asian background as well, there is this assumption that I speak every language in Asia or that there is only one language/country in Asia. Unbelievable.
- "Sorry, that must be my Black coming out." [Said by] my biracial friend (African American and Mexican). Whenever she does or says something negative, she blames it on the "Black" side of her. Makes me feel angry, belittled, resentful.
- I express that my brother attends a private university. Immediately a girl in the car responds in a very sure voice, "Oh, he plays football?" This is the second time this has happened. As if a young Black male can only attend a prestigious private college on a football scholarship.
- "You're really unintimidating for a Black guy." Said by White male. I am a freshman in college. Made me feel as though I should be intimidating because I'm Black.
- Ohmygawd. You're totally not what people think of when they think of Muslim women. You're so cool.
- Wow. Don't get the Muslim mad, guys. We don't want a blown-up school tomorrow.
- Substitute teacher: Quiet down! You're acting like a bunch of wild Indians!
- Oh, but you're Latin, so you must love the heat! While discussing the summer weather. I'm from Bogotá—the average temperature is 60°F. I feel like nobody in the States bothers to understand that Latinos are not just one monolithic entity.

Source: The Microaggressions Project.

Institutional Racism

In the late 1960s and 1970s, sociological thinking on racism moved away from a focus solely on prejudice and individual acts of racism toward an institutional approach. Carmichael and Hamilton (1967) introduced the idea of **institutional racism**—the policies, laws, and institutions that reproduce racial inequalities—in their book *Black Power*. They explained that the high rates of Black infant mortality in Birmingham, Alabama, and the prevalence of Black families in slums are best understood through an analysis of institutional racism.

In an essay published in 1979, Carol Camp Yeakey posited that research on institutional racism in the late 1960s and throughout the 1970s represented a marked departure from previous research, which had not focused on "the attributes of the majority group and the institutional mechanisms by which majority and minority relations are created, sustained, and changed" (Yeakey 1979, 200). Yeakey then argued that racism operates on both a covert and an overt level and takes two related forms: "The first is on an individual level. The second is on an institutional level where racism as a normative, societal ideology operates within and among the organizations, institutions, and processes of the larger society. And the overt acts of individual racism and the more covert acts of institutional racism have a mutually reinforcing effect" (200).

Understanding the framework of institutional racism is essential for understanding racism in the United States, as racism amounts to more than individual acts of discrimination. An individual police officer may have prejudicial beliefs that Blacks are more likely to be violent than Whites. Based on this prejudice, the officer may be more likely to racially discriminate against Blacks and more likely to use more physical force against Blacks than Whites. What do we call it, though, when this kind of discrimination happens repeatedly? An analysis of the 1,217 U.S. police shootings between 2010 and 2012 found that young Black males are 21 times more likely to be killed by police than are their White counterparts (Gabrielson, Grochowski Jones, and Sagara 2014). Although African Americans only make up 12 percent of the U.S. population, they accounted for 47.3 percent of wrongful convictions between 1989 and 2012 (Free 2017). How do we explain these disparities?

In overwhelmingly Black neighborhoods in Washington, D.C., and Chicago, nearly three-quarters of Black men have been incarcerated. In some states, Black men go to jail on drug charges at fifty times the rate of White men. In seven states, Black people constitute over 80 percent of drug offenders sent to prison (Alexander 2010). These extraordinary disparities cannot be explained by individual acts of discrimination alone.

Instead, it makes sense to argue that racial discrimination has become institutionalized in the criminal legal system. This is because racial discrimination happens at every level of this system. The laws are written in ways that discriminate against Black people—the disparities in sentences for possession of crack and possession of cocaine are one example (Alexander 2010). Police officers are consistently more likely to pull over and arrest Black men than they are White men. Blacks are more likely to get harsher sentences or even the death penalty (Gottschalk 2015). When we look at the system as a whole and see that the criminal legal apparatus more harshly affects Blacks than Whites, and when we can see that racial discrimination is consistent and systematic, we can say that the criminal legal system is a prime example of institutional racism. Institutional racism also exists in other institutions, including the educational system, housing, and the labor market.

SYSTEMIC RACISM AND STRUCTURAL RACISM

Stokely Carmichael and Charles Hamilton (1967) developed the idea of institutional racism in the 1970s. Since that time, many thinkers have enhanced their conceptual models and developed more complex and integrative ways of thinking about institutional racism. In 1969, Samuel Robert Friedman (1969, 20) defined *structural racism* as a "pattern of action in which one or more of the institutions of society has the power to throw on more burdens and give less benefits to the members of one race than another on an on-going basis." In 1979, Carol Camp Yeakey wrote about "the interrelated and cumulative nature of systemic or institutional discrimination and racism," the way racism works in "social systems" (203), and explained:

> *The resource allocation of city schools; residential segregation and housing quality; the location, structure, and placement of transport systems; hiring and promotion practices; academic underachievement of racial and ethnic minority youth; availability of decent health care; behavior of policemen and judges; a legal order that incarcerates more minorities than majorities; stereotypical images prevalent in the media and school curricula; price gouging in ghetto stores; morbidity, mortality, and longevity rates; lack of political clout and effective legislative representation—these and a myriad of*

other forms of social, political, and economic discrimination concurrently interlock to determine the status, welfare, and income of the racial and ethnic minorities of color.

Unfortunately, nearly forty years later, we can make the same assessment with regard to institutional racism. Fortunately, scholars of race and racism continue to refine these theories and approaches. In this section, we explore some of these current approaches.

Systemic Racism

Sociologist Joe Feagin defines **systemic racism** as "a diverse assortment of racist practices; the unjustly gained economic and political power of Whites, the continuing resource inequalities; and the White-racist ideologies, attitudes, and institutions created to preserve white advantage and power" (2001, 16). He explains that systemic racism encompasses daily microaggressions, deep-seated inequalities, and anti-Black ideologies. Taken together, systemic racism includes:

- Patterns of unjust impoverishment of non-Whites
- Vested group interests of Whites to maintain racism
- Omnipresent and routinized discrimination against non-Whites
- The rationalization of racial oppression
- An imbalance of power whereby Whites are able to reproduce inequality through control of major political and economic resources

Systemic racism theory gives primacy to history and to anti-Blackness: Feagin explains that systemic racism exists because of the history of the United States as a slaveholding nation. Racial oppression was foundational to and is deeply ingrained in our nation's history. The legal system of the United States—based on the Constitution and Supreme Court cases—is rife with examples of entrenched racism. Systemic racism in history and the present day has created a "White racial frame" that shapes individuals and institutions in the United States. Feagin emphasizes that racism and racial inequality were created by Whites and continue to be perpetuated by White individuals and White-owned institutions (Feagin, 2001).

The unjust enrichment of Whites through slavery and privileged access to resources since the beginning of the United States is at the core of an understanding of systemic racism. This unjust enrichment has led to unjust impoverishment of African Americans. Past and continuing discrimination has created a situation in which African Americans have been denied resources many Whites have come to take for granted, including good jobs, great schools, and nice neighborhoods (Feagin and McKinney 2003; Feagin 2001). The pervasiveness of everyday acts of discrimination, combined with a legacy of unequal distribution of resources throughout every aspect of U.S. society, constitutes systemic racism.

Structural Racism

Proponents of the idea of **structural racism** take a slightly different approach in their analysis of racial inequality. As we have seen, institutional racism focuses on practices within institutions, and systemic racism focuses on accumulated acts of racism across history and throughout one's lifetime. Structural racism differs by pointing to interinstitutional interactions across time and space. For example, racial inequality in housing leads to racial inequality in schooling, which in turns leads to racial inequality in the labor market. Across generations, this chain of events becomes a cycle because parents who are less well positioned in the labor market cannot afford housing in the better neighborhoods, which means that their children will be less likely to attend better schools. A structural understanding of racism underscores the "structural relationships that produce racialized outcomes" (powell 2008, 798). This emphasis on the relationships among structures of institutional inequality provides new insights into how racial inequality is reproduced across generations.

Eduardo Bonilla-Silva proposes the concept of **racialized social systems**. By this term, he means "societies in which economic, political, social, and ideological levels are partially structured by the placement of actors in racial categories" (1997, 469). Bonilla-Silva places particular emphasis on racial hierarchies and points to how these hierarchies influence all social relations. Societies that have racialized social systems differentially allocate "economic, political, social, and even psychological rewards to groups along racial lines" (442). Bonilla-Silva's framework reflects a structural racism perspective because he focuses on structures of inequality, hierarchies, and social relations and practices that reproduce and rationalize racial disparities.

Melvin Oliver and Thomas Shapiro (2006) offer a keen analysis of the role of structural racism in reproducing wealth inequalities. They explain that wealth inequality "has been structured over many generations through the same systemic barriers that have hampered Blacks throughout their history in American society: slavery, Jim Crow, so-called de jure discrimination, and institutionalized racism" (12–13). Oliver and Shapiro (2006) point to three instances of structural inequalities that work together: (1) Blacks' transition from slavery to freedom without a material base, (2) the suburbanization of Whites and the ghettoization of Blacks, and (3) contemporary institutional racism in the lending and real estate markets. These three inequalities work together to create a situation in which the median net worth of one White household is ten times that of a Hispanic or Latinx household and thirteen times that of a Black household (Kochhar and Fry 2014) (Figure 2-1).

Oliver and Shapiro (2006) explain how laws and policies, even those that do not mention race, can still work to enhance racial inequality. Our tax policies provide one example. In the United States, capital gains are taxed at a lower rate than income, and tax deductions are offered for home mortgages. These policies are ostensibly designed to help the middle class and encourage economic growth. However, they provide many more advantages to Whites than to Blacks because Blacks rarely have capital gains income, are less likely to own a home, and, when they do own a home, have houses that are worth less than Whites' houses (Shapiro 2004). These state policies work to widen the wealth gap between Blacks and Whites by providing advantages to those who are already wealthier and who are more likely to be White.

FIGURE 2-1

MEDIAN NET WORTH OF WHITE, HISPANIC/LATINX, AND BLACK HOUSEHOLDS, 2014

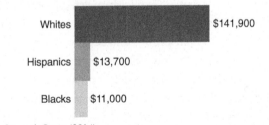

Source: Pew Research Center (2014)

RACIAL IDEOLOGIES

Patricia Hill Collins (2004) explains: "When ideologies that defend racism become taken-for-granted and appear to be natural and inevitable, they become hegemonic. Few question them and the social hierarchies they defend" (96). When Collins explains that racial ideologies are **hegemonic**, she means they become so widely accepted that they become common sense. An ideology is more than an individual prejudice: it is a set of principles and ideas that embodies the interests of a societal group. A **racial ideology**, then, is a set of principles and ideas that (1) divides people into different racial groups and (2) serves the interests of one group. Ideologies are usually created by the dominant group and reflect the interests of that group. Both historically and today, the dominant racial group in the United States includes Whites (Feagin 2001). Our individual prejudices and acts of discrimination are directly related to our acceptance (conscious or unconscious) of racial ideologies.

Many scholars make a distinction between old racism—which permitted the internment of the Japanese and the enslavement of Africans, for example—and a new but related ideology that perpetuates racism without such practices. In **new racism**, it is no longer acceptable to make overtly racist statements or to have overtly racist laws (P. H. Collins 2004; Bonilla-Silva 2013; Logan 2011; Wingfield and Feagin 2010). Racism did not disappear with the dismantling of slavery and **Jim Crow laws**, nor did the civil rights era mark the end of racism. Race scholars generally agree that the post–1965 era is distinct. Theorists Michael Omi and Howard Winant (1994) explain that whereas the government could once be overtly violent toward non-Whites, "in the post–civil rights era, the racial state cannot merely dominate; it must seek *hegemony*" (147) (emphasis in original). By this statement Omi and Winant meant that policymakers must seek to make the current racial order seem natural and normal, as it is no longer viable to have laws and practices that are explicitly racist.

Racial inequality persists today both because of our history— colonialism, slavery, and Jim Crow—and because of ongoing practices of discrimination and exclusion. The new racism is an outgrowth of past racial inequality; mass media and popular beliefs "help manufacture the consent that makes the new racism appear to be natural, normal, and inevitable" (P. H. Collins 2004, 34). Racial inequality in the United States has become naturalized. We have come to think of it as normal that African American men are overrepresented among prisoners and that White men are overrepresented among the elite, even though we would never accept laws that overtly discriminated against African Americans.

In the United States, most people do not consider themselves to be racist, and laws are in place that prevent overt acts of discrimination. Despite this massive change in attitudes and laws over the past century, however, racial inequality persists. African Americans have, on average, a mere 10 percent of the wealth that Whites have (Oliver and Shapiro 2006). African American men are seven times more likely than White men to go to prison (Feagin 2001). On almost any measure, Black and Latinx people are doing worse socially and economically than White people in the United States (Logan 2011). How do we explain the persistence of racial inequality despite the social stigma associated with being a racist? One way is by looking at how different forms of racism operate. This allows us to see how some forms of racism are more acceptable than others, even though all racial ideologies serve the same purpose: to explain, rationalize, and normalize racial inequality and injustice.

Another reason to examine racial ideologies closely is that despite trends that demonstrate widespread racial inequality, a few prominent exceptions make it seem as if racism is a problem of the past. Most notably, the United States had an African American president, has a woman of African American and Indian descent serving as vice-president, and a Latina and an African American serving on the Supreme Court. How do we explain these developments? Clearly, we need new ways to think and talk about race and racism. In this section, we will discuss different forms of racism and consider the extent to which these racial ideologies persist.

Biological Racism

Biological racism is the idea that Whites are genetically superior to non-Whites. This idea has its origins in the scientific racism of the nineteenth century, which set out to prove Whites' superior innate intelligence. In the 1920s, the American lawyer Madison Grant argued that Nordics were the "master race" and that the United States should pass laws banning interracial marriages and ensuring the sterilization of inferior races. In the twenty-first century, it would be difficult to find people who openly advocate for the sterilization of Blacks because of their biological inferiority. Nevertheless, these ideas have not completely disappeared.

One of the most prominent examples of biological racism in recent decades is a 1994 book called *The Bell Curve*. In this book, Richard Herrnstein and Charles Murray argue that intelligence is quantifiable. For Herrnstein and Murray, as for a century of intelligence testers before them, the fact that Blacks scored lower on intelligence tests than Whites provided support for the idea that Blacks are innately inferior to Whites (Herrnstein and Murray 1994). More recently, Frank Miele and Vincent Sarich argued in *Race: The Reality of Human Differences* (Miele and Sarich 2004) that races are a biological reality and that there are measurable intellectual differences among racial groups. The publication of *The Bell Curve, Race: The Reality of Human Differences*, and other books and articles in this vein provide evidence of the persistence of the belief that Whites are genetically or biologically superior to non-Whites. However, most academics reject these views, and few Americans openly express such opinions in public spaces today. Biological racism still exists, but it is waning and is subject to virulent criticism whenever expressed.

Cultural Racism

Cultural racism is a way of thinking that attributes disadvantaged racial groups' lack of prosperity to their behavior and culture rather than to structural factors. Unlike biological racism, which claims that some races are inferior because of lower intelligence, cultural racism is the standpoint that a particular culture—African American or Latinx culture, for example—inhibits success.

The 1965 publication of a report by the U.S. politician Daniel Patrick Moynihan (1927–2003) planted the seeds for many of the ideas inherent in cultural racism (Moynihan 1965). The document, which has come to be known as the Moynihan Report, acknowledged the pervasiveness of poverty in the Black community and pointed to the breakdown of the Black family as one of the principal causes of this poverty. Moynihan argued that the history of slavery and racism had had detrimental consequences for the Black family. He made the gendered argument that the central problem of Black America was that there were too many single Black mothers who were incapable of raising children on their own. His proposed solution to Black poverty was restoration of Black men to their rightful place as breadwinners and heads of families.

For Moynihan, the solution to Black poverty was to "fix" Black families. This stance—which ignores structural factors such as discriminatory employment policies and practices—is typical of cultural racism. Essentially, the cultural racism argument points to the behavioral patterns and culture of African Americans as the primary cause of their poverty. Cultural racism persists today. For example, pundits often blame Blacks' educational failures on dysfunctional families or parenting styles rather than on failing schools and pervasive poverty.

Cultural racism also takes another form: teachers perceive children who invoke African American language and style as less intelligent than those who conform to the dominant culture. Ann Arnett Ferguson (2001) found in her research in an elementary school that Black students were more likely to get into trouble at school because of the way teachers and school administrators responded to their body language, oral expressiveness, manners, and styles. She found that children who conformed to White, middle-class cultural norms were less likely to get into trouble and were more likely to do well in school, and that the use of African American forms of expressiveness in school was grounds for punishment. Ferguson also argues that when children are White or behave in a White middle-class way, they are perceived to be self-disciplined and good, while children who "behave Black" are perceived as troublemakers. Ferguson's findings point to the persistence of cultural racism: whereas White, middle-class children are rewarded for behaving in school as they and their parents do at home, working-class and poor Black children are punished for speaking and acting as their parents do.

Cultural racism also affects other racialized groups in the United States. Latinas are often portrayed as "pregnant breeders" who plan to have "anchor babies" in the United States (Hondagneu-Sotelo 1995). Asians feel the brunt of the "model minority" stereotype—the myth that Asians are smarter, harder-working, and more successful than other minorities. And Native Americans are perceived alternatively as "savages" or "wise men." The racialized stereotypes of Native Americans, Asian Americans, and Latinx Americans are discussed further in Chapter 4.

Color-Blind Racism

Sociologist Eduardo Bonilla-Silva offers a framework for understanding how pervasive racial inequality exists even though no one wants to be called a racist. In his work, Bonilla-Silva (2013) presents the notion of **color-blind racism**, a racial ideology that explains contemporary racial inequality as the outcome of nonracial dynamics, such as market dynamics, naturally occurring phenomena, and non-Whites' supposed cultural limitations. This racial ideology ignores or marginalizes people of color's distinctive needs, experiences, and identities. Bonilla-Silva argues that although race is a social construction, the idea of race is real in a social sense and has produced a racial structure that systematically privileges Whites.

How is it possible that racial inequality is widespread when most Whites claim there is no racism and that they are not racist? Bonilla-Silva offers an explanation in his book *Racism Without Racists* (2013). His research team interviewed Whites and asked them questions about their views on race in the United States. He found that Whites use several "frames" of color-blind racism to rationalize and reproduce racial inequality.

One frame Bonilla-Silva mentions is **abstract liberalism**. This frame involves using liberal ideas such as equality of opportunity or freedom of choice to explain or rationalize racial inequality. For example, when presented with the fact that African Americans still live in underserved, poorer neighborhoods than Whites do, a person using this frame would explain this inequality by saying that people live in such neighborhoods because they choose to do so. Nothing prevents them from leaving, so their situation arises not because of racism but because of individual choices. This response, however, ignores the structural factors that have created segregation and continue to perpetuate it. Similarly, the **naturalization** frame permits people to explain racial phenomena as if they were natural. The explanation for segregation would be that people like to be around others who are like them. Again, segregation develops not because of structural factors, but because it's normal or natural.

The aforementioned frames represent explanations that Whites consistently offered in interviews about their racial attitudes. In addition, Bonilla-Silva found that Whites used specific **rhetorical strategies**, or ways of expressing ideas, to rationalize their own racial prejudices and discriminatory actions. These rhetorical strategies permit Whites to reproduce racism without being labeled as racists. Bonilla-Silva argues that because post–civil rights racial norms do not permit the open expression of racial views, Whites have developed hidden ways of voicing them.

As Bonilla-Silva found, one common rhetorical strategy is to preface discriminatory claims with "I am not a racist, but. . . ." Alternatively, a White person would say, "Some of my best friends are Black, but. . . ." For example, when asked if he would mind if his daughter married a Black man, a White person would respond, "I am not a racist, but I don't think interracial marriages work." Or the White person might use another rhetorical strategy called projection, according to which she would respond: "I don't mind if my daughter marries a Black man, but you have to think about the children." These rhetorical strategies allow Whites to express discriminatory or prejudiced ideas without seeming racist.

In his research, Bonilla-Silva found that color-blind racial ideology is used in everyday speech patterns to *rationalize* racial inequality. It influences rhetorical strategies, stories, and etiquette that allow Whites to explain why racial inequality exists even though most people are not racist. In addition to rationalizing racial inequality, color-blind racism *reproduces* racial inequality by permitting people to engage in discriminatory actions without being labeled as racists.

Islamophobia and Anti-Arab Racism

Islam is a religion. Does it make sense, then, to define **Islamophobia**—the systematic marginalization of Muslims—as racism? Because race and religion are distinct phenomena, religious discrimination and racial discrimination are not identical. Nevertheless, it is clear that the United States is a Christian-centric society and that people who are not Christians face various forms of marginalization. To what extent should these forms of exclusion be considered racism?

Ramón Grosfoguel and Eric Mielants (2006) state that Islamophobia began as religious discrimination and has evolved into racial/ethnic discrimination. They point out that, at the same time that the Spaniards set out to colonize the Americas, they expelled Jews and Arabs from the Spanish peninsula. During this time, religious beliefs were the primary motivation for the marginalization of Jews and Arabs. Grosfoguel and Mielants argue that in more recent times, however, Islamophobia and anti-Arab sentiment have primarily taken the form of cultural racism—a concept discussed in more detail in Chapter 3. They explain that the tropes used to describe Muslims and Arabs such as "uncivilized," "barbarian," "savage," "primitive," "underdeveloped," "authoritarian," and "terrorist" (4) are markers of cultural racism.

For Grosfoguel and Mielants (2006), Islamophobia is a form of racism. Steven Salaita (2006) argues, however, that it is important to draw a distinction between Islamophobia and anti-Arab racism. Despite the American conflation of Arabs and Muslims, only one-fifth of the world's total Muslim population is Arab, and not all Arabs are Muslim (Grosfoguel and Mielants 2006). Salaita (2006) maintains that anti-Arab racism goes beyond dislike or distaste for Islam: it is used to rationalize U.S. military interventions in the Middle East.

RACIAL FORMATION

Whereas analyses of structural and systemic racism focus on racism itself, Michael Omi and Howard Winant consider racial meanings (Omi and Winant 1994). They introduce the concept of **racial formation** to help us understand how racial dynamics work in the United States. Omi and Winant define racial formation as "the sociohistorical process by which racial categories are created, inhabited, transformed, and destroyed," and as a "process or historically situated project" (56). They argue that the state (i.e., the national government) is the primary site where race is constructed and contested. According to this theory, the state can reproduce or alleviate racial inequality through its institutions and policies. Omi and Winant explore "how concepts of race are created and changed" and argue that "concepts of race structure both state and civil society" (vii).

When Omi and Winant's book was first published in 1986, it was a welcome change from earlier works that studied race as a variation of ethnicity, class, or nation. Instead, Omi and Winant presented race as a topic worthy of study in itself. Their groundbreaking work has greatly enhanced our understanding of how race works in the United States.

Omi and Winant (1994) draw from the Italian theorist Antonio Gramsci to argue that racial dynamics in the United States have changed from domination to hegemony. Domination refers to direct rule by coercion, whereas hegemony involves rule by both coercion and consent. For example, Omi and Winant contend that the United States prior to the civil rights era could be characterized as a racial dictatorship in which racial inequality was enforced through domination. During slavery and the Jim Crow era, White domination was legal, state-enforced, and difficult to contest openly. In the current era of racial hegemony, racial stratification and White dominance are achieved more subtly through coercion and consent. Omi and Winant argue that the United States is undergoing a slow, gradual, and contentious transition from a racial dictatorship to a racial democracy.

The concept of racial formation blends an understanding of social structures with an understanding of cultural representations. Omi and Winant use the concept of a **racial project**, which they define as being "simultaneously an interpretation, representation, or explanation of racial dynamics, and an effort to reorganize and redistribute resources along particular racial lines" (1994, 56). Racial projects give meaning to racial categories through both cultural representations and social structures. For example, Doris Marie Provine and Roxanne Lynn Doty (2011) argue that the criminalization of immigrants through intensified immigration policy enforcement is a racial project. In this example, the state targets immigrants and draws attention to their vulnerable status. The increased law enforcement and resulting media attention reinforce the marginalization of immigrants as a racialized group.

For Omi and Winant, a racial project is defined as racist if it "creates or reproduces structures of domination based on essentialist categories of race" (1994, 71). They are careful to distinguish between race and racism and to point out that not all racial projects are racist. Projects are racist only when they reproduce structures of domination and hegemony. For example, one could argue that the criminalization of Latinx immigrants is a racist project because it reinforces the marginalized status of this racialized group. Omi and Winant argue that every state institution is a racial institution. They don't go so far as to say that every state institution is *racist*. This is because they believe the state can also use racial schemas to promote racial equality.

WHITE SUPREMACY AND SETTLER COLONIALISM

What if we consider present-day racism in the United States from the perspective of Indigenous studies? From this perspective, we are forced to contend with questions related to the meaning of White control of lands that once belonged to Native Americans. What would the end of racism look like for Indigenous peoples? Native Americans' claims are different from those of African Americans.

Andrea Smith (2012) argues that there are three pillars of White supremacy: (1) anti-Black racism, (2) genocide, and (3) orientalism (Table 2-1). Anti-Black racism defines people as property, thereby

TABLE 2-1
Pillars of White Supremacy

	Anti-Black Racism	Genocide	Orientalism
BASIS	Capitalism	Colonialism	Security
POSITION	People can be property.	Native people are disappearing and must disappear.	Certain nations or peoples pose a permanent threat to Western civilization.
CONCLU-SION	Slavery and current forms of exploitation are justified.	Non-Native people have a right to all that once belonged to Native people.	War against such nations or peoples is justified.

Source: Based on A. Smith 2012.

rationalizing slavery and current forms of exploitation, and is rooted in a logic of capitalism—that is, designed to extract profit. Genocide is rooted in colonialism. This is the idea that Native people are disappearing and must disappear, and that therefore non-Native people have a right to everything that once belonged to Native people. Orientalism is rooted in the idea that certain nations or peoples pose a permanent threat to Western civilization and is thereby used to rationalize war.

Although the United States is no longer engaged in the mass murder and expulsion of Native Americans, many Indigenous scholars contend that the logics of genocide and settler colonialism endure (A. Smith 2012). Native Americans continue to have a unique legal position in the United States: they are citizens both of the United States and of the tribes to which they belong. Scholars such as Andrea Smith (2012) contend that capitalist ideas of property ownership and White supremacist ideas of Indigenous inferiority work together to justify the expropriation (seizure) of Indigenous lands. From this perspective, simply returning lands to Native Americans would not solve the problem of Indigenous expropriation. The more fundamental problem is the nation-state itself and the idea that people can control territory and keep other human beings out of it.

Once we recognize that the United States is a nation rooted in White supremacy, it becomes clear that the state will never grant Native peoples self-determination. For some Indigenous scholars, this recognition means that the struggle against racism requires a challenge to the very existence of the United States as a legitimate state (A. Smith 2012).

Joe Feagin (2001), in his systemic racism framework, contends that anti-Black oppression is at the center of U.S. society, even though the United States was formed through genocide. Andrea Smith (2012) contests this framework, arguing that the United States exists precisely because of the disappearance of Indigenous people and that this genocide continues today. One's framework for understanding the experience of Native peoples is critical because it shapes how we view racial progress or regression. Smith points to the example of high rates of intermarriage between Native Americans and Whites. Is this progress? Or is it a continuation of a pattern of genocide?

Using these perspectives, we can see how frameworks shape research questions and answers. From the perspective of settler colonialism, one might argue that the United States is an illegitimate state founded on genocide and must be dismantled. From a systemic racism perspective, one can argue that the United States is founded on a history of racism and that the Constitution must be rewritten. From a racial formation perspective, the United States is headed in the right direction and through more struggles for justice and civil rights will complete the transition from racial dictatorship to racial democracy.

INTERSECTIONAL THEORIES OF RACE AND RACISM

In what ways do race, class, and gender oppression work together? Some race scholars argue that we need to develop a concrete understanding of how race and racism work before we can understand other forms of oppression. Feminist scholars, however, often contend that we must look at class, race, and gender oppression simultaneously—a concept known as **intersectionality**.

Intersectionality is not a question of counting our identities to see how many marginalized identities we have. Intersectionality is not something that applies only to people of color or to women. It applies to us all, because intersectionality involves an analysis of how multiple systems of oppression shape all of our lives.

For example, White supremacy, patriarchy, and capitalism are three interlocking systems of oppression (see Table 2-2). White supremacy is a system of racial stratification that places Whites at the top of the hierarchy. Patriarchy is a system of gender oppression where men hold the power and are the central figures in the family, community, government, and

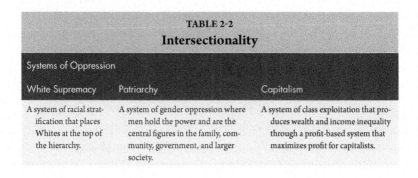

TABLE 2-2
Intersectionality

Systems of Oppression		
White Supremacy	Patriarchy	Capitalism
A system of racial stratification that places Whites at the top of the hierarchy.	A system of gender oppression where men hold the power and are the central figures in the family, community, government, and larger society.	A system of class exploitation that produces wealth and income inequality through a profit-based system that maximizes profit for capitalists.

larger society. Capitalism is a system of class exploitation that produces wealth and income inequality through a profit-based system that maximizes profit for capitalists (Valdez 2011).

Sociologist Patricia Hill Collins argues that these three systems are interdependent, and that we cannot understand one system without looking at the others. Feminist theorist bell hooks describes these systems of oppression as the White-supremacist capitalist patriarchy. hooks explains that "interlocking systems of classism, racism, and sexism work to keep women exploited and oppressed" (2000). Jordanna Matlon (2016) defines **racial capitalism** as "an economic system that organizes and justifies exploitation by racial classification." With its history of colonialism and slavery, it is clear that capitalism in the US context is deeply racialized. Similarly, notions of gender and sexuality in the US context cannot be separated from race. Patriarchy is also racialized.

Kimberlé Crenshaw (1991) uses the concept of intersectionality in her work, making her point with the example of a group of Black and Latina women in a battered women's shelter. Taken together, the factors of race, class, and gender elucidate how these women ended up in the shelter. The women faced abuse in part because of gender oppression, but their economically vulnerable situation and race also help us understand their situation. If they had the economic resources, they likely would have gone elsewhere—not to a shelter. If they were White, they wouldn't have faced racial discrimination in employment, meaning that they may have had more resources. If they were men, their chances of being battered would have been much lower. Any proposed method of helping these women must pay attention to their gender-based, class-based, and racially based oppression. A narrow lens that focuses on just race, gender, or class would miss crucial aspects of these women's situations.

Patriarchy, White supremacy, and capitalism shape how the state and society respond to women. To understand why women of color are overrepresented in domestic violence shelters, and on the welfare rolls we need an understanding of how the White-supremacist capitalist patriarchy works. This understanding allows for a deeper analysis both of how people experience oppression and of how these systems of oppression operate.

Intersectionality is part of a **critical race theory** tradition. Critical race theory differs from other theories of race insofar as these theories center the voices of people of color, focus on the eradication (and not just the analysis) of racist oppression, and require reflexive thinking.

From a critical race perspective, the only good reason to study race is to work towards the elimination of racial oppression. Taking this task on requires reflexivity about one's own positionality as well as an intentional effort to center the voices and experiences of people of color. As you develop your own ideas about what racism is and how it works, think about the extent to which a critical race theory framework is useful for you.

WHITE PRIVILEGE

Whereas most studies of racism focus on oppression, those scholars who use a White privilege framework focus on privilege—the opposite side of oppression. **White privilege** refers to the advantages inherent in being categorized as White. The concept derives from earlier work by African American sociologist W. E. B. DuBois (1868–1963), who observed that White workers in the United States over time came to see themselves as White like their bosses, as opposed to developing working-class solidarity with recently freed Black slaves. DuBois argued in 1936 that White workers received a psychological "**wage of Whiteness**" by aligning with the dominant group; they were poor, but at least they were White. Additionally, by reserving certain segments of the labor market for Whites only, White laborers were able to reap material rewards from their Whiteness. Other scholars, mostly historians, have built on DuBois's insights to explain how waves of European immigrants learned to be White and to reap the privileges of Whiteness (Allen 1994; Jacobson 1998; Roediger 1999).

Prior to coming to the United States, European immigrants of the early twentieth century did not think of themselves as White. And, in some cases, people in the United States did not see them as White. Irish immigrants learned to capitalize on their Whiteness by forming unions and excluding Blacks from them. And although Jews faced discrimination during and after World War II, as Whites, they were able to reap the benefits of the GI bills and Federal Housing Administration and Department of Veterans Affairs mortgages that were denied to Blacks, which propelled many Whites into the middle class (Brodkin 2005). Whereas these European immigrants had to learn to be White, most Whites today never have to think about Whiteness.

In the contemporary United States, Whiteness is an unmarked identity. Whereas African, Latinx, Asian, and Native Americans are constantly reminded of their race, European Americans easily can forget that they too have a race (Dalton 2005). When we talk about race (or, more recently, diversity), the focus is usually on non-Whites, as if White were not also a race (Lewis 2004). When we think of race in the United States, Whiteness usually is not the first thing that comes to mind. The reason is that Whiteness has become normalized—"whiteness makes itself invisible precisely by asserting its normalcy" (Frankenberg 1997, 6).

Privilege is often hard to notice. If you are White, it can be difficult to notice that you are not being followed around the store; that people are smiling at you on the street instead of clutching their purses; that no one asks you if you speak English; that you are not asked for identification when paying with a credit card. Instead, you are likely to think that these things are normal—that this is simply how things are. To notice these privileges as a White person, you likely would have to walk down the street with an African American friend or accompany a Latinx friend to get a driver's license. Then, you may notice a difference in terms of how White people respond to you and your non-White friend. Few Whites notice they are treated better than non-Whites, and most are unlikely to attribute that better treatment to privilege. Privilege is largely invisible to those who have it.

White privilege only becomes visible when people point it out. For example, in 2015, a White Stanford student by the name of Brock Allen Turner was found sexually assaulting an unconscious, semi-naked woman behind a dumpster. She was taken to the hospital, where a nurse noted that significant trauma had been inflicted on the victim's genitalia. When the case went to trial, the jury found Turner guilty on three felony counts, and the prosecution argued he should get a six-year sentence. However, Judge Aaron Persky was hesitant to punish Turner this severely and gave him six months in county jail instead. The judge explained: "A prison sentence would have a severe impact on him." *Huffington Post* writer Alanna Vagianos wrote in response: "Turner's lenient punishment is the perfect example of what happens when rape culture and white privilege collide." By *rape culture*, Vagianos is referring to the normalization of sexual abuse of women in our society. Because of Turner's Whiteness and class privilege, the judge had sympathy for him. Turner was held in protective custody and ultimately spent only three months behind bars (Vagianos 2016).

The case of Brock Turner, as well as many other cases of White privilege, makes it clear that White privilege doesn't simply exist—it is enacted. The judge gave Turner a light sentence because he did not believe Turner to be a dangerous man, despite the evidence that Turner had committed rape. When shopkeepers are not suspicious of White shoppers, the White shopper is the beneficiary of the privilege, but only because the shopkeeper has accepted the racist idea that Whites are less likely to shoplift. White privilege, then, is related to White supremacy: White privilege exists because of past and current practices that reproduce racism.

We can also ask, however, whether racism can be harmful to Whites even though White privilege exists. In *Whiteness: The Power of Privilege*, the antiracism activist and writer Tim Wise contends that "the price we pay to stay one step ahead of others is enormous" (Wise 2005, 120). The vast majority of working people could earn higher wages and have better benefits if Whites and non-Whites worked together to demand them as a common goal. Whites are less likely to go to prison than Black or Latinx people, yet the enormous amount of resources the United States invests in the prison-industrial complex are resources that don't go into better schools, parks, libraries, and universities. For these reasons, W. E. B. DuBois and others have referred to the "psychological wage of whiteness": racism makes all Whites *think* they are getting a better deal, but the reality is that racism affects all of us, albeit in different ways. DuBois argued that the psychological wage of Whiteness drives a wedge between White and Black laborers, who otherwise share an interest in working together to fight for better material conditions.

It is important to think about White privilege for several reasons. First of all, if we want to understand racial oppression, it is crucial to understand how it looks from the other side. Second, White privilege often remains invisible, and by bringing it to light we can develop a better understanding of how racism works in our society.

WHITENESS, CLASS, GENDER, AND SEXUALITY

An important point to keep in mind when thinking about White privilege is that although it certainly benefits some Whites, not all Whites experience White privilege in the same way. When an employer gives a White applicant the benefit of the doubt because he is White, the applicant experiences White privilege, whether or not he is aware of it. However, a poor lesbian White woman in rural South Carolina, for example, will experience her Whiteness—and her White privilege—in different ways than a wealthy White heterosexual male stockbroker in New York. The White stockbroker will have doors opened to him that will remain shut to a poor woman of any race.

White privilege can be hard to see. Similarly, class privilege also often remains invisible. In a study that compared middle-class White students with poor White students, Kirby Moss found that middle-class White students "overwhelmingly perceived class position as nearly nonexistent within White culture" (Moss 2003, 32). It was very difficult for these middle-class Whites to see that they had advantages that working-class and poor Whites did not. In contrast, the working-class and poor Whites criticized the middle-class Whites for being lazy and entitled and for not having to work for anything in life.

The privileges associated with being White were not the same for these two groups. The poor Whites experienced a contradiction in their identities—Whites were not supposed to be poor, yet they were. These poor Whites found it difficult to envision taking advantage of their Whiteness, as their poverty presented obstacles to enjoying the privileges of Whiteness. Although they were White, they did not have the "set of cultural practices" (Frankenberg 1993, 43) associated with Whiteness because of their class background. Moreover, many of these poor Whites lived in poor, primarily non-White neighborhoods, where their Whiteness presented obstacles to acceptance in their own neighborhoods.

Past and present-day practices of individual and institutional racism have created segregated neighborhoods in the United States. Whites' privileged access to primarily White neighborhoods is part of White privilege. The other side of this coin is that working-class and poor Whites cannot always afford to live in middle-class White neighborhoods and thus are unable to reap this particular benefit of Whiteness. As Kirby Moss (2003) contends, poor Whites sometimes live in primarily non-White neighborhoods because that is where they can afford to live. Living in those neighborhoods, poor Whites encounter many of the same challenges that their non-White neighbors encounter, such as crime, violence, and lack of access to resources.

This is one example that makes it evident that White privilege does not always work in the same way for working-class and poor Whites as it does for wealthier Whites. It is important to note here, however, that most poor Whites live in primarily White neighborhoods, just as most poor Blacks live in primarily Black neighborhoods (Bischoff and Reardon 2014). A White man who enters a primarily Black neighborhood may be made aware of his Whiteness once he finds himself surrounded by Blacks and receiving stares (or even glares) from residents who want to know why a White person is in their neighborhood. In the narrow space of a primarily Black neighborhood, a White person may not feel she is experiencing White privilege. However, a middle-class White man often can live his whole life without ever having to enter a space where his Whiteness will present a challenge. He can avoid primarily Black neighborhoods because there is no reason for him to ever go there. In contrast, a Black man may need to go to a White neighborhood because that is where his job is located, or he may want to move into such a neighborhood because that is where the good schools are. A Black man may encounter problems with law enforcement or neighborhood watch associations if he walks around a middle-class White neighborhood.

Just as Whiteness is linked to class, it is also defined by gender and sexuality. White womanhood has historically been linked to sexual virtuosity, and for women, White privilege can hinge on maintaining an appearance of sexual respectability. Amy Wilkins (2004) uses the case of Puerto Rican wannabes—White girls and young women who draw on Puerto Rican cultural styles to attract men of color—to explain how race, class, gender, and sexuality are co-constructed. Puerto Rican wannabes manipulate their gender and sexual identities to cross racial boundaries: by defying conceptions of White womanhood by dressing provocatively, they can claim to identify with Puerto Rican-ness. Notably, they reject Whiteness through the rejection of mainstream notions of sexuality.

Catrin Lundström (2014) explored Whiteness at the other end of the spectrum of White womanhood—Swedish Whiteness. Through interviews with married female Swedish immigrants in the United States, Lundstrom found that their American husbands placed tremendous value on their wives' Swedish heritage. These American men viewed Swedish women as representing an ideal form of Whiteness that encompasses White purity, beauty, and sensuality. Lundstrom's work adds nuance to sociological understandings of Whiteness, as it allows us to see that there are degrees of Whiteness in the United States and that these ideas of Whiteness are intertwined with ideas of gender, sexuality, and White womanhood.

CONCLUSION AND DISCUSSION

Theories of systemic, structural, and institutional racism provide us with different frameworks to understand the deep-seated nature of racial inequality in the United States. These analyses place the emphasis on racism; Feagin and Elias (2013) argue that only through an understanding of racial oppression can we grasp the true nature of racial meanings. In contrast, racial formation theory focuses on how race is constructed, and we can use these analyses to deepen our understanding of racism (Omi and Winant 1994). Analyses of White privilege focus on privilege to show how racial oppression works. Still other scholars invoke settler colonialism as the primary framework for understanding racial oppression. Which perspective is the most valuable?

There is no right answer to this question. Instead, the usefulness of a perspective depends on the kind of question you are asking. For example, imagine you were examining why African Americans and Latinx Americans fared worse economically than Whites in the aftermath of the Great Recession. An analysis based on systemic or structural racism would be especially useful in this case (Kochhar, Fry, and Taylor 2011). If you were considering why Indonesian women use whitening creams, even though they express no desire to be Caucasian, a racial formation perspective would offer valuable nuances (Saraswati 2010). Both of these studies are grounded in the field of racial and ethnic studies, but they have different research questions and goals and thus draw from different frameworks.

The frameworks set forth by Indigenous and feminist scholars can also be more or less useful, depending on the kinds of questions you decide to ask. A consideration of Mayan migration to Houston would likely benefit from Andrea Smith's (2012) pillars of White supremacy framework, and an analysis of violence in youth gangs in Oakland would likely be enriched by an intersectional perspective that focuses on race, class, gender, and sexuality. A study of Whiteness and class in an economically diverse White neighborhood would do well to interrogate the White privilege perspective. No theory can be expected to shed light on every aspect of our society. Moreover, sociologists and other thinkers continue to develop ways for us to understand inequality. Readers of these texts can decide for themselves which frameworks are most useful for understanding the questions that are important to them. What about you? What frameworks do you find most compelling, and why?

THE UNITED STATES has one of the highest incarceration rates in the world. African American men are seven times more likely than White men to go to prison. Explain this statistic using two different perspectives from this chapter (e.g., cultural racism, institutional racism, structural racism, White privilege). Can either of these perspectives help us to understand this disparity? Is either of these perspectives useful in terms of racial justice?

THINKING ABOUT RACIAL JUSTICE

Key Terms

sociological theory of racism   33
prejudice   33
discrimination   33
individual racism   34
racial microaggressions   35
institutional racism   38
systemic racism   41
structural racism   42
racialized social systems   42
hegemonic   44
racial ideology   44
new racism   44
Jim Crow laws   44

biological racism   45
cultural racism   46
color-blind racism   48
abstract liberalism   48
naturalization   48
rhetorical strategies   48
Islamophobia   49
racial formation   50
racial project   51
intersectionality   53
racial capitalism   54
critical race theory   55
White privilege   55
wage of Whiteness   55

CHECK YOUR UNDERSTANDING

2.1 How is individual racism linked to institutional inequality?

Prejudice, discrimination, and institutional racism are interconnected and thus should not be studied in isolation. Prejudice refers to beliefs about racial difference; discrimination refers to actions; and institutional racism describes the larger context in which prejudice and discrimination occur.

Q How widespread is individual racism, and how does it persist?

Q What are some examples of racial microaggressions?

Q What is the relationship between individual and institutional racism?

2.2 How do systemic racism and structural racism create racial disparities?

Systemic racism and structural racism are two theoretical frameworks that aim to explain how racism is deeply rooted in society. While systemic racism focuses on accumulated acts of racism across history and throughout one's lifetime, structural racism points to interinstitutional interactions across time and space.

Q What is one key difference between systemic racism and structural racism?

Q How does structural racism explain wealth inequalities?

2.3 What are racial ideologies, and how have they functioned and changed over time?

A racial ideology is a set of principles and ideas that (1) divides people into different racial groups and (2) serves the interests of one group. Racism has changed over the years yet continues to benefit Whites.

Q What is an example of racism pre-1965?

Q What is an example of racism post-1965?

Q What are the differences among biological, cultural, and color-blind racisms?

Q How is Islamophobia related to racism?

2.4 What is racial formation, and how does this concept inform our understanding of racial inequality?

Racial formation is one of the most influential theories of race and racism in the United States. It focuses on racial meanings—how racial categories are "created, inhabited, transformed, and destroyed," as Omi and Winant (1994) describe.

Q What do Omi and Winant mean when they say the United States is transitioning from a racial dictatorship to a racial democracy?

Q What is an example of a racial project?

2.5 What does the perspective of Indigenous studies reveal about racism in the contemporary United States?

One way to consider how racism works is to examine it from the perspective of Indigenous studies. This leads us to consider settler colonialism theory, which offers a broad critique of racism and capitalism.

Q What are the three pillars of White supremacy?

Q Why is it important to understand genocide in relation to contemporary race relations?

2.6 In what ways do race, class, and gender oppression work together?

Ideas of race, gender, class, and sexuality all shape how racism works, and intersectional scholars take these factors seriously as they build their frameworks.

Q What is an example of a scenario that intersectional theory helps us understand?

2.7 What is White privilege, and how does it function?

White privilege refers to the advantages associated with being categorized as White and can be a useful analytic for understanding racial oppression. Whiteness and White privilege vary by class, gender, and sexuality.

Q Who benefits from White privilege, and why?

Critical Thinking

1. Think of an issue related to racial inequality and use one of the frameworks discussed in this chapter to explain it. Justify your selection of this framework over the others.

2. What are some of the key differences between systemic racism and structural racism, and how might they shape your research agenda?

3. Most of the scholars cited in the section on intersectionality are women of color. Why do you think these scholars have been at the head of these debates and discussions?

Talking about Race

Structural ideas of racism help us understand how racial inequality can be reproduced even in the absence of overtly racist acts. What racial disparities in your community could be explained by a structural theory? How can you use what you have learned in this chapter to explain such disparities? Some examples might include a lack of green spaces in non-White neighborhoods, a preponderance of minorities in lower-quality schools, or a concentration of non-Whites in poorer areas of the city.

Learn more with this chapter's digital tools, including video clips from the author, web links, filmography, and chapter self-assessment quizzes at www.oup.com/he/golash-boza-brief3e.

3

Racism and Nativism in Immigration Policy

AS YOU READ

3.1 Examine the racialized history of U.S. immigration policy.
3.2 Describe U.S. policy responses to undocumented immigration.
3.3 Analyze the relationship between nativism and racism in the twenty-first century.

I n 2021, over 20,000 men, women, and children were behind bars in the United States who were not waiting for a trial and were not serving time for a crime. These people were not citizens of the United States and were held in preventive detention, mostly waiting to find out if they would be deported to their countries of birth. Some had already been ordered deported and were waiting for the day of their deportation. Many were asylum seekers, fleeing persecution in their home countries.

The detention of immigrants in the United States is just one aspect of our immigration law enforcement system. Today, as in the past, our harsh immigration policies primarily affect people considered non-White. This chapter describes the history of immigration policy in the United States and the extent to which racist and nativist sentiments have played a role in U.S. immigration legislation. Although the country's immigration policy has shifted dramatically over the years, two trends have remained constant: (1) nativism has always been an integral part of debates over immigration policy, and (2) the consequences of immigration policy have been more disadvantageous to people considered non-White than to those considered White. What has changed over time is the removal of explicitly discriminatory language from U.S. immigration laws. This chapter explores how immigration laws can have racially disparate consequences, even when the laws do not mention race. Whereas racism presumes the superiority of a racial group, **nativism** presumes the superiority of native-born citizens, favoring the allocation of resources to them over immigrants and promoting a fear of foreign cultures.

As Robert Bautista's story makes clear (see *Voices: Robert Bautista—Denied Due Process*), U.S. immigration policy can be draconian—even long-term legal residents can have their rights stripped away for minor transgressions of the law. In this chapter, we explore the history of U.S. immigration policy, as well as present-day laws and policies. The historical overview shows how lawmakers have used immigration policy to influence the racial and ethnic makeup of the nation. In this process, racism and nativism often have become indistinguishable.

Immigration policy continues to be at the forefront of the political agenda in the United States today. It is hard to imagine a time when the country had no immigration policy, yet just one hundred years ago, there was no Border Patrol, and passports and visas were not required to enter the United States. When the United States began to pass immigration laws governing the entry and residency conditions of the foreign-born at the end of the nineteenth century, the laws were overtly racialized and expressed a clear preference for people from northern and western Europe.

voices

Robert Bautista—Denied Due Process

In 2009, immigration agents arrested Robert Bautista as he was returning from vacation in the Dominican Republic, his country of birth. Once arrested, Mr. Bautista was placed in detention without the possibility of a bond hearing. He had been a legal permanent resident of the United States for twenty-five years, had been married for over a decade, had three school-age children, and was the owner of a successful business in Pennsylvania. His mandatory detention caused his business to be destroyed and his family to lose their home. His children, all of whom are U.S. citizens, had to bear witness to their father being treated as if he were a criminal, but without the procedural protections normally accorded to people charged with crimes.

Mr. Bautista's immigration detention was not pursuant to any criminal convictions. In 2002, Mr. Bautista had been found guilty of third-degree attempted arson for carrying a container of gasoline near his own vehicle, but by 2009 he had completed his parole. When immigration agents arrested him, it was not because he was being charged with a new crime. Instead, he was detained because the Department of Homeland Security (DHS) ruled that his 2002 conviction was a crime involving moral turpitude (CIMT). Because of this prior conviction, Mr. Bautista was considered to be seeking admission to the United States, as if he were not present in the country and as if he had not been living and working in the country for over two decades. As a person not technically inside the United States, Mr. Bautista was not protected by the Constitution.

Just one hour before his immigration hearing, DHS made an additional argument: that third-degree attempted arson is also an aggravated felony, meaning that Mr. Bautista would be subject to mandatory detention and deportation without judicial review. In such a case, it does not matter if you have lived in the United States for three decades, if you have three children, if you have no relatives in your country of origin, or if your family depends on you for their survival. Noncitizens convicted of aggravated felonies are not given a fair and reasonable hearing of the sort that would meet international human rights standards.

In October 2011, the Board of Immigration Appeals (BIA) heard Mr. Bautista's case and decided that third-degree attempted arson is an aggravated felony, as DHS had charged. This determination means that Mr. Bautista could not challenge his deportation on the

(continued)

Robert Bautista—Denied Due Process

basis of his ties to the United States. Instead, he faced mandatory deportation to the Dominican Republic, where he would be labeled a criminal deportee and face a bleak future. The Dominican government treats arriving criminal deportees as if they are criminals. They are booked at the city jail, and their deportation is recorded on their criminal record, making it nearly impossible to secure employment.

If Mr. Bautista had been afforded the due process protections we give to criminals, he would have had a bond hearing and likely would not have been detained for over two years. Instead, he would have had the opportunity for a trial in which a judge could weigh the equities in his case, and he may have been eligible for a public defender. Mr. Bautista was fortunate that a lawyer decided to take his case pro bono. With the help of this lawyer, in February 2014, in an appeals case, the U.S. Third Circuit Court of Appeals found that third-degree attempted arson is not an aggravated felony, thereby overturning the BIA decision and permitting Bautista to apply for cancellation of removal.

Source: Golash-Boza 2012a; *Bautista v. Attorney General of the United States*, No. A038-509-855 (3rd Cir. LAR 34.1(a) September 20, 2012).

THE RACIALIZED HISTORY OF U.S. IMMIGRATION POLICY

The history of U.S. immigration policy is a reflection of societal racism and nativism. As various scholars have noted (e.g., Lippard 2011; Sanchez 1997; Johnson 2004), racist nativism is a prominent feature of contemporary American society: the fear of foreigners is clearly racialized, and nativist sentiments are directed at particular racial groups, such as Mexicans and people from the Middle East. Through an examination of the history of immigration policy and nativist responses to immigration, we will see how nativism and racism have been intertwined in U.S. history and how the nativism of today is distinct from that of the past.

Race and the Making of U.S. Immigration Policies: 1790 to 1924

The United States was a sovereign nation for a full century before immigration restrictions became a subject of political debate, let alone law. Although the country did not begin to pass immigration laws until the late 1800s, Congress passed an important piece of legislation in 1790 related to people born abroad. The **Naturalization Act of 1790** was not an immigration policy in that it did not regulate entry; instead, it stated that only free White persons who had lived in the United States for at least two years were eligible for citizenship. This first piece of legislation related to the foreign-born is particularly notable because it contained a racialized provision, defining citizenship as accessible solely to White persons. The purpose of this clause was to deny citizenship to African-descended slaves, and it was later used to deny Asians **naturalization**, or the granting of citizenship after birth.

When large numbers of immigrants began to arrive on the shores of the United States fifty years after passage of the Naturalization Act of 1790, the question of who was White gained importance. Between 1846 and 1855, over 3 million immigrants came to the United States, including 1,288,307 from Ireland and 975,311 from Germany. There is no reason to believe that the millions of Irish who came to the United States in the mid-nineteenth century thought of themselves as "White" when they lived in Ireland. In a context in which everyone is Irish, Whiteness has little meaning. As each of these groups integrated into the United States, they experienced both a process of *assimilation*, through which Irish, Italians, and Germans became Americans, and a process of *racialization*, through which Celts, Hebrews, and Mediterraneans became White. This process was not smooth, as Irish faced discrimination, and Italians and Jews were lynched in the South alongside African Americans (Jacobson 1998). Racialized fears of European and Asian immigrants eventually translated into laws that ended these immigration flows.

TIMELINE

U.S. Immigration and Deportation Policy

1790	Naturalization Act	1965	Immigration and Nationality Act
1882	Chinese Exclusion Act	1986	Immigration Reform and Control Act
1924	Immigration Act (Johnson–Reed Act)	1996	Anti-Terrorism and Effective Death Penalty Act (AEDPA)
1924	Creation of Border Patrol		
1942–1964	Bracero program	1996	Illegal Immigration Reform and Immigrant Responsibility Act (IIRIRA)
1943	Repeal of Chinese Exclusion Act		
1950–1954	Operation Wetback	1996	Personal Responsibility and Work Opportunity Reconciliation Act (PRWORA)

The first major piece of immigration legislation was the **Chinese Exclusion Act**, signed into law in 1882. This act denied entry to one specific group: Chinese laborers. In specifically excluding a group because of race and class, the Chinese Exclusion Act set the stage for twentieth-century immigration policy, which had both overt and covert racial and class biases (E. Lee 2002). Although the Chinese Exclusion Act was repealed in 1943, the court cases that stemmed from it continue to shape how we treat immigrants today.

The Chinese Exclusion Act compelled the federal government to put into place the bureaucratic machinery needed to patrol the borders of the country. As the act excluded specific groups of people from entering the United States, it required that the government establish immigration controls and checks. The act required the creation of an immigration inspection force, one that eventually would evolve into the Border Patrol. It further required the creation of certificates of residence—the precursors to today's "green cards"—for Chinese individuals who were permitted to remain in the United States. It was not until 1928 that other immigrants had to carry proof of legal presence. In 1940, these cards were replaced by "alien registration cards," which continue to be used today (Lee 2002).

A landmark 1893 Supreme Court case, *Fong Yue Ting v. United States*, involved three Chinese nationals who claimed they deserved constitutional protections in their deportation cases. The court held that the power to deport noncitizens was inherent in the nature of sovereignty and that constitutional protections, including the right to a trial by jury, did not apply. This case defined deportation as simply an administrative procedure and not a punishment. The idea of deportation as a nonpunitive action was based on a distinction between deportation and banishment. Banishment removes a person from a country where he or she belongs, whereas deportation returns a person to where he or she belongs and thus is not considered a punishment. According to the *Fong Yue Ting* decision, which still holds in court today, deportation is a procedure to ensure that people abide by the terms of their visas. When they do not, they face the possibility of being returned to where they belong. It is remarkable that this court decision, which was made in the context of strong anti-Chinese sentiment, continues to hold the status of legal precedent today.

The Chinese Exclusion Act was passed in the midst of a great wave of immigration from both Europe and China. In the 1840s, the United

States began to experience large-scale immigration for the first time since its founding. This influx dramatically changed both the country's cultural landscape and its official stance toward immigrants. Between 1841 and 1850, 1.7 million immigrants arrived in the United States (see Figure 3-1), and in the following decade, 2.6 million arrived. In 1870, immigrants constituted nearly 14 percent of the total population. In each subsequent decade until 1924, millions continued to arrive. Toward the end of this wave of immigrants in the early twentieth century, the United States began to implement policies governing the entry of the foreign-born.

The **Immigration Act of 1917** expanded the Chinese Exclusion Act to deny entry to anyone coming from the "Asiatic Barred Zone," which included India, Burma, the Malay States, Arabia, and Afghanistan (Calavita 2000; Lee 2002). Between 1917 and 1952, the United States placed strict immigration limits on people from Asia while welcoming those from preferred European countries. The intent behind these laws was to improve the racial composition of the United States.

In 1924, the U.S. Congress implemented the overtly racialized **Immigration Act of 1924**, or the **Johnson–Reed Act**, which greatly

FIGURE 3-1

IMMIGRANTS AS TOTAL NUMBER AND AS A PERCENTAGE OF THE U.S. POPULATION, 1850–2015

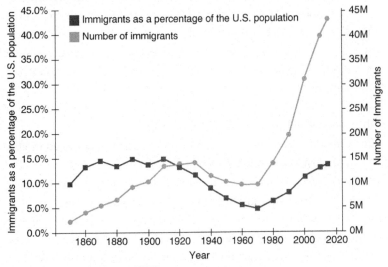

Source: Migration Policy Institute (2015)

reduced immigration from southern and eastern Europe by introducing quotas, or limits on the number of people from these countries who
were allowed to enter the United States. The Johnson–Reed Act was
overtly racist in that it was designed to increase the Nordic population
in the United States and halt the growth of other groups. The act made
passports and visas a requirement for entry to the United States and
established national-origin quotas for European immigrants. These
quotas dictated the number of immigrants who could enter the United
States in any given year. Calculated on the basis of the U.S. population's composition in 1890, the quotas were applicable only to the European population. Specifically, the law stipulated that the quotas not
take into account the following four groups: (1) immigrants from the
Western Hemisphere, (2) aliens ineligible for citizenship (e.g., Asians),
(3) the descendants of slaves, and (4) Native Americans. By basing
national-origin quotas exclusively on the European population at the
time, the law made it clear that Africans, Asians, and Native Americans were not considered to be part of the nation (Ngai 2004).

The Johnson–Reed Act was implemented through the lobbying efforts of the *eugenics* movement (see Chapter 1). Eugenicists advocated
the selective breeding of Americans, the sterilization of the biologically unfit, and selective immigration policies as a way of creating a
superior breed of people. Members of Congress took the ideas of eugenicists into account when they voted to restrict the immigration of
people they deemed undesirable and to promote the immigration of
those whom they expected might improve the American stock. The
quotas that took effect in 1929 reflect these preferences: Great Britain and Northern Ireland were granted a quota of 65,271 immigrants;
Italy, 5,802; Yugoslavia, 845; and most African and Asian countries,
100 (Ngai 2004).

Nativism Between 1924 and 1964

The period between 1924 and 1964 was an exceptional period in U.S.
history in that the country welcomed relatively few immigrants. The
1924 measures significantly curbed the flow of immigrants until the
1965 overhaul of U.S. immigration laws. These trends are evident in
Figure 3-1 and in Figure 3-2, which display the number of people who
attained legal permanent resident status by decade. A **legal permanent
resident** is a foreign national who is granted the right to remain in the
United States and who will be eligible for naturalization after a period of

FIGURE 3-2

NUMBER OF PEOPLE TO ATTAIN LEGAL PERMANENT RESIDENT STATUS IN THE UNITED STATES BY DECADE, 1820–2018

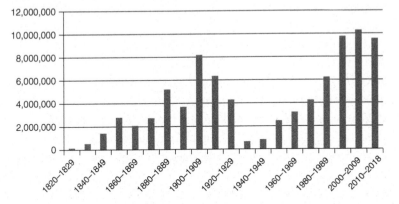

Source: U.S. Department of Homeland Security, Office of Immigration Statistics (2018).

three to five years. To become a U.S. citizen today, a legal permanent resident must have been a permanent resident for at least five years if he or she is not married to a U.S. citizen or for at least three years if he or she is the spouse of a U.S. citizen. The applicant must also be a person of good moral character; have basic knowledge of U.S. history and government; and, in most cases, be able to read, write, and speak basic English. In addition, the applicant must pay the filing fees, which were $725 in 2021.

Mass Deportation of Mexicans

Mexicans have a long history of immigration to the United States. The first group of Mexicans to enter the United States were not immigrants, however, but became Americans following the U.S. takeover of large swaths of Mexican land under the 1848 Treaty of Guadalupe Hidalgo. The first substantial wave of Mexican immigrants came between 1910 and 1930, when the Mexican immigrant population tripled from 200,000 to 600,000. This wave was due largely to instability caused by the Mexican Revolution and to the growth of agribusiness in the United States (Massey, Durand, and Malone 2002; Ngai 2004; Hernandez 2010).

The second wave of Mexican immigration came during the **bracero program** (1942–1964). Under this program, created by the U.S government to meet labor shortages caused by World War II,

4.6 million Mexicans, called *braceros* (a Spanish term that can be roughly translated as "farmhands"), came to work in agriculture in the United States. Mexicans also continued to immigrate to the United States illegally because not all workers qualified for the bracero program and the costs associated with immigrating as a bracero were prohibitive to some.

The United States carried out mass deportations of Mexicans twice during this period, first in the 1930s and again in the 1950s, when the bracero program was in full swing. The United States deported 1,751 Mexicans in 1925, but this number increased dramatically to 15,000 in 1929, when the U.S. stock market crash triggered the onset of the Great Depression. Subsequently, the Immigration and Naturalization Service, in cooperation with local officials, mounted a repatriation campaign, under which over 400,000 people of Mexican origin were returned to Mexico (Ngai 2004). In the 1950s, the U.S. Border Patrol deported over a million Mexican immigrants under Operation Wetback.

World War II created a Mexican American middle class, and during this time Mexicans were also accorded an improved social standing in the borderlands. By the late 1940s, "No Mexicans Allowed" signs had disappeared, and high schools were increasingly integrated. At the same time, the Border Patrol became more firmly entrenched as part of the federal government, meaning that its policies often reflected Washington's interests more than local interests along the border. This shift created tensions, as ranchers and farmers in Texas wanted to employ undocumented Mexicans, whereas it was the duty of Border Patrol agents to stop immigrants from crossing over (Hernandez 2010).

In 1950, the Border Patrol began massive roundups of Mexicans in a series of operations that would come to be known as **Operation Wetback**. One example of an Operation Wetback raid happened on July 30, 1952. At dawn, about one hundred Border Patrol agents began to arrest Mexicans by the hundreds in an area near Brownsville, Texas. By the end of the day, they had made 5,000 arrests and had transported all of those people to the bridge that led back to Mexico. These sorts of roundups continued through 1954. In October 1954, the Border Patrol announced it had deported more than one million Mexican immigrants. These mass arrests created fear and tension in immigrant communities, as Mexicans were forced to leave their loved ones, their belongings, and their lives in the United States and return to Mexico (Hernandez 2010).

Mexican workers in a flax field, 1946. The U.S. government's Bracero Program (1942–1964) sparked a wave of immigration from Mexico, but in the 1950s, an initiative known as Operation Wetback led to deportations.

The 1965 Immigration and Nationality Act and the Changing Face of Immigration

One of the most significant changes to U.S. immigration law in the twentieth century was the **1965 Immigration and Nationality Act**, also called the 1965 **Hart–Cellar Act**. This act put an end to the racially biased quotas set forth in the Immigration Act of 1924. In the spirit of the civil rights movement, the 1965 act set a universal quota of 20,000 immigrants for every country in the world. Each country could send up to 20,000 qualified immigrants a year, with no racial restrictions. Potential immigrants could now qualify for entry based on either family ties to the United States (relatives could petition for their entry) or their skills (employers could request immigrants based on their skills and education). The 1965 act had two main consequences: (1) it increased immigration from Asia, Latin America, and the Caribbean; and (2) it increased undocumented immigration from Mexico.

Asian Immigration

Historically, immigrants from India, China, Japan, the Philippines, and Korea had come to the United States to work as laborers. However, the longstanding prohibitions on Asian immigration between 1882 and 1965 greatly decreased Asian immigration. The 1965 act opened up the possibility of immigration from Asia by removing racial quotas, and large numbers of Asians began to migrate to the United States once again.

Between 1820 and 1849, only 210 people came to the United States from Asia as legal permanent residents. In the 1850s, 36,080 people from Asia became legal permanent residents. Asian immigration peaked in the first decade of the twentieth century, with nearly 300,000 people from Asia becoming legal permanent residents. After the passage of the 1924 Immigration Act, this number dropped off, and only 19,231 Asians gained legal permanent residency in the 1930s. Asian immigration again increased in the 1950s to 135,000 and then increased exponentially to nearly 1.5 million in the 1970s, 2.4 million in the 1980s, and 2.9 million in the 1990s (see Figure 3-3). In the first decade of the twentieth century, almost 3.5 million Asians became legal permanent residents. The most prominent countries of origin of Asian immigrants today are China, the Philippines, India, Korea, and Vietnam—each with its own history of immigration to the United States. By 2015, Asia was the largest sending

FIGURE 3-3

NUMBER OF ASIANS TO ATTAIN LEGAL U.S. PERMANENT RESIDENT STATUS, BY DECADE

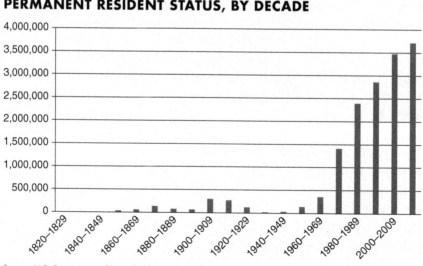

Source: U.S. Department of Homeland Security, Office of Immigration Staticstics (2018).

region for legal permanent residents. In that year, 419,297 Asians (40 percent of the total) became legal permanent residents of the United States (Baugh and Wistman 2017). More recently, immigration from Asia has declined slightly while Latin American migration has increased: in 2018, 10 percent more (100,673) more people from the Americas (497,860) attained legal permanent residency than from Asia (397,187) (Baugh 2019).

Immigration from Asia increased dramatically with the passage of the 1965 Immigration and Nationality Act. Asians did not come from every country in the region, but specifically from countries with which the United States had longstanding ties. In fact, with the exception of Vietnam, those Asian countries that send large numbers of immigrant to the United States today are the same countries that sent substantial numbers of immigrants in the late nineteenth and early twentieth centuries. These immigration patterns can be directly linked to both family ties and high skills provisions in the 1965 Immigration and Nationality Act.

Chinese immigrants to the United States predate many other immigrant groups; the large-scale migration of Chinese to the United States began when U.S. contractors recruited laborers to build railroads in the mid-nineteenth century. Around the same time, recruiters in Hawaii (which would not become a U.S. state until 1959) brought tens of thousands of Chinese migrants to work in agriculture and other industries. Chinese immigration peaked in the 1870s, with 133,000 Chinese becoming legal permanent residents of the United States. Following the Chinese Exclusion Act of 1882, however, immigration dropped off dramatically and did not begin to rise again until decades after the act was repealed in 1943.

Following the 1943 repeal of the Chinese Exclusion Act, Chinese immigration to the United States slowly began to pick up again. The presence of Chinese immigrants and their descendants in the United States facilitated future waves of immigration. In the 1980s, 171,000 Chinese immigrated to the United States. Chinese immigration increased in the next decade to 342,000 and to 592,000 in the first decade of the twenty-first century.

The United States has a longstanding relationship with the Philippines, as well as a protracted migration history. This helps explain why this relatively small (with a population of 88 million, compared to China and India's billion-plus people) and quite distant country sends large numbers of its nationals to the United States. The Philippines was a U.S. colony from 1898 until 1946. From 1898 to 1934, Filipinos were American nationals and could freely come to the United States. Many were recruited as laborers by Hawaiian sugar plantations, and by 1931, around 113,000 had migrated to Hawaii alone. Manufacturers and vineyard owners in California also recruited Filipinos as workers, attracting over 5,000 to the mainland by 1920. With the passage of the 1924 Immigration Act, which ended the flow of Japanese laborers, agribusiness turned to Mexican and Filipino labor, such that by 1930, there were 56,000 Filipinos on the West Coast. As the numbers of Filipinos began to increase in the 1920s, Whites increasingly began to see Filipinos as a problem and a threat. In 1929, the California legislature asked Congress to restrict Filipino immigration. Congress eventually responded by passing the Tydings–McDuffe Act in 1934, which limited Filipino immigration to an annual quota of fifty—the smallest of any country. The onset of World War II and racial violence on the West Coast also contributed to slowing Filipino immigration. Between 1946 and 1965, 33,000 Filipinos immigrated to the United States, nearly half of whom were wives of U.S. servicemen (Liu, Ong, and Rosenstein 1991; White, Biddlecom, and Guo 1993; Ngai 2004).

As with other countries, the 1965 Immigration and Nationality Act changed immigration patterns from the Philippines to the United States. Between 1965 and 1985, about 667,000 Filipinos obtained visas to come to the United States. These Filipino migrants consisted of two groups of people. The first group, which constituted about two-thirds of Filipino immigrants, came on family reunification visas from the networks of the pre-1965 migrants. The second group included migrants who obtained employment visas, mostly as professionals and other highly trained individuals (Liu et al. 1991). In 2015, 5 percent of all new legal permanent residents were from the Philippines, making it the fourth-largest sending country (Baugh and Wistman 2017).

India is another country that sent large numbers of immigrants to the United States prior to passage of the Johnson–Reed Act. As with other Asian countries, immigration from India resumed after 1965. Between 1966 and 1981, a total of 215,640 Asian Indians came to the United States. This rate of 14,376 immigrants per year is twenty times higher than the rate at the previous peak in the period just before World War I. The majority of these new immigrants were professionals, with less than 1 percent working in farm labor occupations (Gonzales 1986).

In 2015, India was the third-largest sending country for legal permanent residents, as 64,116 Indians became legal permanent residents
that year (Baugh and Wistman 2017).

The pattern is similar for Korea. Over 7,000 Koreans migrated to
Hawaii to work on sugar plantations between 1903 and 1905. Korean
migration was cut off, first as a result of restrictions placed on emigration by the Japanese imperial power and later by the 1924 restrictions. These restrictions were lifted in the aftermath of the Korean
War (1950–1953), and more than 3,000 Koreans were admitted between 1950 and 1965, the vast majority of whom were wives of U.S.
servicemen stationed in Korea. With passage of the 1965 Immigration
and Nationality Act, Koreans quickly became one of the largest immigrant groups in the United States. In 1965, a total of 2,165 Koreans
entered the United States. In 1970, the figure was 9,314. And in 1977,
the number increased to 30,917 (Reimers 1981; Min 1990). Between
1975 and 1990, Korea sent more immigrants to the United States than
any other country, with the exception of Mexico and the Philippines.
Korean immigrants were relatively highly educated, and 30 percent in
the 1970s came on skills-based visas. The remaining 70 percent came
on family reunification visas (Min 1990).

Vietnam is distinct from the other Asian countries in that there
were almost no Vietnamese in the United States in the early twentieth century, or even prior to the Vietnam War. Today, there are over
one million Vietnamese in the United States. The first wave came as
refugees; between 1971 and 1980, 150,000 Vietnamese were admitted
to the United States (White, Biddlecom, and Guo 1993). The reunification provisions of the 1965 act led to the growth of the Vietnamese population in the United States well after the Vietnam War ended
(Kelly 1986). Those Vietnamese who were in the United States already
had the right to bring their family members to the country under the
family reunification provisions of the Immigration and Nationality
Act. Legal immigration through family reunification policies, combined with illegal immigration, led to the continued growth of the
Vietnamese population. The 2000 census reported the presence of
over one million Vietnamese, nearly a quarter of whom had been born
in the United States (Hoefer, Rytina, and Campbell 2007). In 2010,
Vietnam came in at number nine in the list of the top twenty countries
sending legal permanent residents to the United States, with 310,000
Vietnamese legal permanent residents in the country (Rytina 2011).

FIGURE 3-4

REGION OF BIRTH OF UNDOCUMENTED IMMI-GRANTS RESIDING IN THE UNITED STATES, 2013

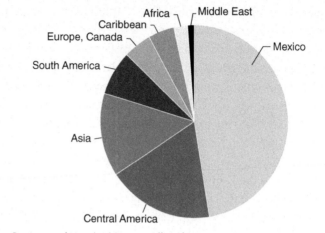

Source: Department of Homeland Security, Office of Immigration Statistics (2017).

Three other countries in Asia had larger populations of legal perma-nent residents in the United States: the Philippines (560,000), China (550,000), and India (500,000).

Figure 3-4 shows the distribution of the population of undocu-mented immigrants in the United States in 2013: 56 percent of undoc-umented migrants in the United States come from Mexico, 15 percent from Central America, and 14 percent from Asia.

Latin American and Caribbean Immigration

As noted earlier, the 1965 Immigration and Nationality Act instituted quotas of 20,000 immigrants per country. At first glance, this blan-ket quota may seem fair. However, most of the 180-plus countries in the world do not send 20,000 immigrants per year to the United States, and a handful of countries send many more. Mexico is a case in point. Prior to 1965, there were no limits on the number of immi-grants that could be admitted from Mexico, and tens of thousands of Mexicans came to the United States each year. The 1965 act initially established a ceiling of 120,000 immigrant visas for the entire Western Hemisphere. In 1976, the law came fully into effect, and a quota of 20,000 immigrants per year was extended to all countries in the West-ern Hemisphere, including Mexico (Joppke 1998). The imposition of a quota of 20,000 immigrants from Mexico was unrealistic in the 1970s because of the need for Mexican labor and the desire of many Mexicans to work in the United States.

The restrictions on the number of immigrants from countries in the Western Hemisphere did not end large-scale migration from Mexico. Because many employers depended on Mexican labor, workers came illegally to the United States. At this time, there were hardly any Border Patrol agents, and it was easy for Mexicans to enter the United States illegally. Thus, Mexicans continued to arrive. The imbalance between the quota and the need for Mexican labor to sustain economic growth in the United States led to increased undocumented immigration (Massey et al. 2002).

Up until the 1970s, over 80 percent of Mexicans who came to the United States were temporary farm workers. By the end of the twentieth century, only 40 percent of Mexicans could be described as such (Massey et al. 2002). With the passage of the 1965 Immigration and Nationality Act and the subsequent 1986 mass legalization laws, increasing numbers of Mexicans have chosen to reside permanently in the United States. Figure 3-5 shows the number of people who obtained legal permanent resident status who were from Latin America and the Caribbean (all of the Americas except for Canada).

FIGURE 3-5

PERSONS FROM THE AMERICAS ATTAINING LEGAL PERMANENT RESIDENT STATUS, 1820–2015

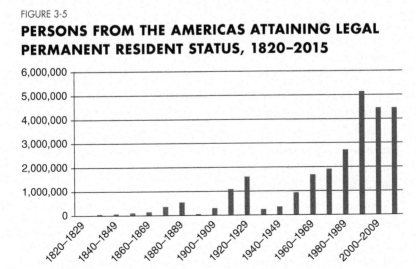

Source: U.S. Department of Homeland Security, Office of Immigration Statistics (2015).

Latin American migrants account for a substantial proportion of immigrants to the United States. In 2018, 38 percent of the one million people who became legal permanent residents came from the Americas. In that same year, 36 percent came from Asia and 10 percent from Africa. 15 percent of all people who became legal permanent residents in 2018 were from Mexico (Baugh 2019).

Central Americans have been coming to the United States since the late nineteenth century, but they did not begin to arrive in large numbers until the 1960s, with the passage of the 1965 Immigration and Nationality Act. Around 8,000 Central Americans entered the United States legally between 1900 and 1910; this number increased to 17,000 in the next decade, around 6,000 in the 1930s, 21,000 in the 1940s, and about 45,000 in the 1950s. In the 1960s, the presence of U.S. companies in Central America increased, with a concomitant increase in the presence of Central Americans in the United States. Between 1971 and 1980, more than 130,000 Central Americans legally entered the United States (Hamilton and Chinchilla 1991).

In the 1980s, immigration to the United States from El Salvador and other Central American countries increased rapidly as a result of both political violence in Central America and the economic setbacks that this violence entailed (Hamilton and Chinchilla 1991). In neighboring Nicaragua, the U.S. Central Intelligence Agency financed and organized a counterrevolution against the Sandinista government. In El Salvador, the U.S. government supplied military equipment to the government in the 1980s, which was used to kill thousands of civilians (Hamilton and Chinchilla 1991). As part of its Cold War strategy, the U.S. government also supplied the Salvadoran government with more than $6 billion in military and economic aid between 1980 and 1992 (Quan 2005). The civil war in El Salvador caused massive population displacements, and many of those displaced came to the United States. While the conditions in El Salvador were the motivation for leaving, the nation's longstanding ties to the United States turned the latter country into a preferred destination when Salvadorans began to seek refuge (Menjívar 2000).

Immigrants have been coming to the United States from the Caribbean for as long as the nation has been keeping records. Between 1820 and 1900, nearly 90,000 people from the Caribbean came to the United States. Immigration from this region reached a peak in the first three decades of the twentieth century, when 300,000 people from the Caribbean became legal permanent residents. In the last three decades of the twentieth century, 2.5 million people from the Caribbean became legal permanent residents of the United States. Another million migrated legally in the first decade of the twenty-first century (Golash-Boza 2012b). Since the passage of the 1965 Immigration and Nationality Act, large numbers of immigrants from the Dominican Republic, Cuba, and Jamaica have entered the country.

The United States has been heavily involved in the affairs of the Dominican Republic and has been the destination of many immigrants as a consequence of this close relationship. Between 1961 and 1968, for example, the United States was closely entangled in the Dominican Republic's presidential elections, to the point of ensuring that the democratically elected left-wing president Juan Bosch was ousted in 1965. This time of intense involvement in the Dominican Republic coincided with the passage of the 1965 Immigration and Nationality Act, which paved the way for Dominicans to enter the United States. During this time, more people from the Dominican Republic entered the United States than from any other country in the Western Hemisphere except Mexico. Emigration from the Dominican Republic has continued to rise. By 1980, there were 169,000 Dominican immigrants in the United States. By 1990, there were 348,000, and by 2012, there were nearly a million (Garrison and Weiss 1979; Hernández 2004; Nwosu and Batalova 2014).

Cuba is another Caribbean country that has had a longstanding relationship with the United States. In the early twentieth century, more than 20,000 Cubans lived in the United States, and by the end of the 1950s, that number was about 50,000. This population continued to increase following Fidel Castro's victory in the Cuban Revolution in 1959. By the end of the 1980s, there were nearly one million Cubans in the United States (Perez 2003). The exiles who came in the early 1960s came because of a long history of U.S. military interventions into Cuba, with the expectation that the U.S. government would assist in ousting Castro's government. Those migrants who come today come more often because of economic than political motives and because of ties they have in the United States, in the context of an immigration policy that has been generally favorable toward Cubans. President Lyndon B. Johnson established an "open door" policy that encouraged Cuban emigration. In the mid-1990s, President Bill Clinton changed that policy to a "wet foot, dry foot" policy that repatriated

Cubans found at sea but allowed those who reached land to stay. In his last days in office in January 2017, President Obama ended this policy, thereby ending Cuban migrants' special treatment (Eckstein and Barberia 2002; Perez 2003; Pew Hispanic Center 2006).

Relatively few Jamaicans came to the United States prior to 1965, in part because Jamaicans were primarily emigrating elsewhere: to Central America, other islands, and Great Britain. However, just as Great Britain passed a series of restrictive immigration laws in the 1960s, the United States passed the 1965 Immigration and Nationality Act, which facilitated the increased immigration of Jamaicans on skills- and family-based visas. By 2009, there were about 637,000 Jamaican migrants in the United States (Glennie and Chappell 2010). Nearly half of Jamaicans in the United States live in New York City, and another 28 percent live in southern Florida. There are also significant populations in Connecticut, New Jersey, Washington, DC, and Atlanta (Vickerman 1999). Notably, over half of Jamaican migrants to the United States are women (Foner 2008; Glennie and Chappell 2010).

Migrants to the United States from Puerto Rico are not technically immigrants, as Puerto Ricans are U.S. citizens. Nevertheless, Puerto Ricans share a similar migration history with other Caribbean countries, in terms of its relationship to the U.S. mainland. Spain ceded Puerto Rico to the United States in 1898, and the island became a U.S. territory. In 1917, Puerto Ricans became citizens of the United States. Shortly thereafter, employers in the United States began to recruit Puerto Ricans to work in the mainland United States due to labor shortages caused by World War I. The recruitment of Puerto Ricans—and thus the migration—intensified in the aftermath of World War II when labor shortages in the mainland United States were even more severe. Just as Mexicans filled key labor needs in the western and southwestern United States during this time, Puerto Ricans were the primary source of migrant labor in the northeastern United States in the aftermath of World War II. The post–World War II period of massive migration of Puerto Ricans to the northeastern United States is often referred to as the "Great Migration" owing to the large numbers of Puerto Ricans who left the island. This migration tapered off in the late 1960s and 1970s, as migrants from other Caribbean countries were able to more easily migrate to the United States following the passage of the 1965 Immigration Act (Portes and Grosfoguel 1994). There has been a resurgence of migration from Puerto Rico to the mainland United States in recent years, related to a protracted economic crisis on the island. Between 2010 and 2013, an average of 48,000 Puerto Ricans left the island each year, which is over three times the average number that left each year in the 1980s and 1990s. By 2012, about 1.4 million Puerto Ricans were living on the mainland (Cohn, Patten, and Lopez 2014). The number of Puerto Ricans in Florida increased yet again following the devastating Hurricane Maria in 2017.

ILLEGAL IMMIGRATION AND POLICY RESPONSE

In the 1970s, undocumented immigration reached unprecedented levels and became a matter of public debate for the first time. During the 1980s, public opposition to undocumented immigration grew, and politicians began to get tough on immigration. Eventually, another major legislative change took place in 1986.

The Immigration Reform and Control Act of 1986 (IRCA) and Nativism

The debates leading up to passage of the **Immigration Reform and Control Act of 1986 (IRCA)** invoked racialized sentiments about Mexicans taking jobs from Americans, overusing welfare, and refusing to assimilate, despite evidence to the contrary. As Pierrette Hondagneu-Sotelo (1994) argues, the debates surrounding IRCA were not so much about the presence of Mexicans as about the reality that increasing numbers of Mexicans were settling in the United States. Hondagneu-Sotelo (1994) contends that the nativism pervading the debates over IRCA focused on three claims: (1) allegations that immigrants were stealing jobs from Americans, (2) concerns that immigrants were overusing the welfare system, and (3) worries that the newcomers were too different and "unassimilable." By the end of the twentieth century, immigration restrictionists were no longer concerned about the inability of southern and eastern Europeans to assimilate. Now, the target was Mexicans.

The passage of IRCA involved a series of compromises and constituted the last mass legalization of the twentieth century. As the name implies, IRCA included immigration reform and control provisions. The twin prongs of IRCA were (1) to offer a legalization option for people who lived in the United States but did not have the proper authorization to work in the country, and (2) to impose sanctions on employers who hired people not authorized to work in the United States. The imposition of sanctions was meant to deter employers from hiring undocumented workers. Instead, these sanctions ultimately created an industry that produced fraudulent documentation, making it easy for anyone to obtain the (false) documents they needed to work (Fragomen and Bell 2007).

One of the major consequences of IRCA was to encourage the permanent settlement of Mexican immigrants, who had formerly come primarily as temporary workers (Avila, Fuentes, and Tuirán 2000). The legalization of temporary workers encouraged more migrants to settle permanently in the United States and to bring their families with them (Massey et al. 2002). Once migrants obtained legal residence or citizenship, they were able to bring over family members under family reunification provisions. As increasing numbers of Mexicans settled permanently in the United States, racialized fears of immigrants intensified.

Proposition 187 and the Lead-Up to the Illegal Immigration Reform and Immigrant Responsibility Act of 1996 (IIRIRA)

Fear of immigrants often has racial undertones. The vast majority of immigrants to the United States are people of color (Figure 3-6). In 2015, one million people became legal permanent residents. Just

FIGURE 3-6

U.S. IMMIGRANT POPULATION BY ORIGIN, 1960–2015

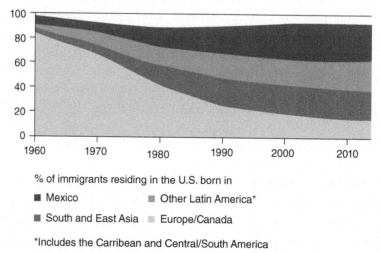

% of immigrants residing in the U.S. born in

■ Mexico   ▨ Other Latin America*

■ South and East Asia   ▨ Europe/Canada

*Includes the Carribean and Central/South America

Source: Adapted from LA Times Graphics

over 10 percent were from primarily White countries: 90,789 of them were from Europe, 3,795 from Australia, 978 from New Zealand, and 19,309 from Canada. Thus, any discourse about immigration today has the subtext of minority incorporation into society (Johnson 2004). The racialization of immigrants, and especially of undocumented immigrants, became clear in the campaign to push forward Proposition 187 in California, a ballot initiative that would deny social services and educational opportunities to the undocumented.

When Proposition 187 was being debated in the early 1990s, California was on the verge of becoming a majority–minority state, and demographic changes were at the center of the fears expressed by Proposition 187 supporters. For example, in Robin Dale Jacobson's interviews with supporters, one of her respondents told her that the proposition was a response to the "Mexican impact on the state of California." Another interviewee was more forthright: "So, I just wanted something to be done about too many Mexican people all of a sudden" (Jacobson 2008, 39). In addition to criminalizing undocumented immigrants, much of the discourse surrounding Proposition 187 racialized undocumented immigrants as Mexican. Thus, many of its supporters interpreted the "invasion" of undocumented workers as a racial takeover of California (Jacobson 2008, 117).

The political campaigns that promoted the passage of Proposition 187 drew on racial imagery. Television ads supported by Governor Wilson "showed shadowy Mexicans crossing the border in large numbers" (Johnson 2004, 43). While it would have been politically unsavory to launch an overtly racist attack on people of color, targeting undocumented immigrants without mentioning race directly was permissible.

In the context of an economic downturn, job losses, and state cutbacks in social services, many Californians found undocumented immigrants to be appropriate scapegoats for their economic troubles, and in 1994, Proposition 187 was passed (Alvarez and Butterfield 2000). Although there was no clear connection between the presence of a large undocumented population and hard economic times, gubernatorial and state legislature candidates in California were able to use the presence of undocumented people to their advantage by advocating for harsh policies that were not guaranteed to improve the fiscal health of the state. Politicians used undocumented immigrants as scapegoats by blaming them for the poor economic conditions, and their promises to get tough on illegal immigration helped them win elections. In California, 60 percent of voters voted in favor of Proposition 187. The bill was not implemented, however, as it was found to be unconstitutional in 1997 (Diamond 1996).

Although Proposition 187 was found to be unconstitutional, the debates surrounding it set the stage for the passage of three laws in 1996 that negatively affected immigrants: the **Anti-Terrorism and Effective Death Penalty Act (AEDPA)**, the **Illegal Immigration Reform and Immigrant Responsibility Act (IIRIRA)**, and the **Personal Responsibility and Work Opportunity Reconciliation Act (PRWORA)**.

The PRWORA was designed to "end welfare as we know it." It also had nativist provisions that denied services to noncitizens. Contrary to popular belief, undocumented migrants are not eligible for welfare services such as cash benefits, Medicaid, food stamps, or public housing. The root of the myth that undocumented migrants benefit from need-based programs such as food stamps is that their U.S.-citizen children are eligible for the same set of benefits as any other U.S. citizen. When PRWORA was passed, it extended the limitations on welfare benefits to legally present immigrants. Touted as a money-saving measure, PRWORA denied most benefits to legally present migrants, at least for the first five years of their stay in the United States (Tumlin and Zimmerman 2003).

Before we turn to the other two laws passed in 1996, let's briefly consider the composition of the immigrant population. An immigrant is any person living in the United States born in another country. In 2017, of the 45.6 million people living in the United States who were born abroad, 45 percent were citizens, 27 percent were legal permanent residents, and 23 percent were undocumented migrants (see Figure 3-7; Passel and Cohn 2019). Immigrants are often juxtaposed against citizens in popular discourse, yet nearly half of all immigrants are indeed citizens. The legal permanent resident category is often ignored in conversations about immigrants, yet these 12.3 million people were deeply affected by the laws passed in 1996.

FIGURE 3-7

FOREIGN-BORN POPULATION ESTIMATES, 2017

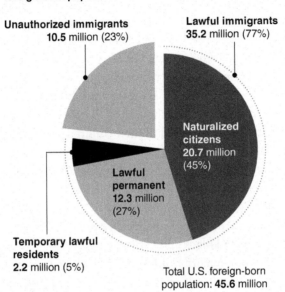

Unauthorized immigrants are a quarter of the U.S. foreign-born population

Unauthorized immigrants
10.5 million (23%)

Lawful immigrants
35.2 million (77%)

Naturalized citizens
20.7 million (45%)

Lawful permanent
12.3 million (27%)

Temporary lawful residents
2.2 million (5%)

Total U.S. foreign-born population: **45.6 million**

The 1996 Laws and the Detention and Deportation of Black and Latinx Immigrants

AEDPA and IIRIRA were striking in that they eliminated judicial review of some deportation orders, required mandatory detention for many noncitizens, and introduced the potential for the use of secret evidence in certain cases. Some of the most pernicious consequences of these laws are related to the deportation of legal permanent residents, commonly referred to as "green card holders."

Under IIRIRA, legal permanent residents like Robert Bautista (whose story is featured in *Voices: Robert Bautista—Denied Due Process* earlier) face mandatory deportation if they are convicted of "aggravated felonies." These include crimes for which a person is sentenced to at least one year in prison, regardless of whether the sentence is served or suspended. These crimes can also be relatively minor, such as the theft of baby clothes from a department store or two counts of minor drug possession. These cases do not require judicial review—that is, people do not have the right to have a judge hear the specifics of the case or consider the ties that a person has to the United States. Furthermore, the law can be applied retroactively. This means that any legal permanent resident charged with a crime at any time during his or her stay in the United States could be subject to deportation. For example, a person could have come to the United States legally at age two, been convicted of resisting arrest at age eighteen, and—twenty years later, after the passage of IIRIRA—be subject to deportation at age thirty-eight. Even adopted children of U.S. citizens have faced deportation under these laws, specifically in those cases in which parents failed to naturalize their children prior to age eighteen (Morawetz 2000; Master 2003). In light of the heavy policing of Black and Latinx neighborhoods, and of Black and Latinx youth in particular, immigrants from Latin America and the Caribbean are more likely to face deportation because of these laws.

The 1996 laws are punitive and harsh. Moreover, they have disproportionately affected Black and Latinx people. Johnson (2004) argues that since the vast majority of immigrants who come to the United States each year are people of color, the differential treatment of noncitizens in U.S. legal practices amounts to racial discrimination. As noted in Chapter 2, Joe Feagin (2001, 16) defines systemic racism as "a diverse assortment of racist practices; the unjustly gained economic and political power of Whites; the continuing resource inequalities; and the White-racist ideologies and attitudes created to preserve white advantage and power." He further contends that "one can accurately describe the United States as a 'total racist society' in which every major aspect of life is shaped to some degree by the core racist realities." The system of deportation and detention of immigrants is no exception: it is clearly shaped by the "core racist realities" of the United States.

The criminal legal system systematically disadvantages Black and Latino men. Even though Black and White men have similar levels of criminal activity, Black men are seven times more likely than White men to be imprisoned, and Latinos are four times as likely (P. Collins 2004; Feagin 2001; Western 2006). In the case of drug offenses, the data are particularly striking. In the United States, Black men are sent to prison on drug charges at thirteen times the rate of White men, yet five times as many Whites use illegal drugs as Blacks (Alexander 2010). Although Whites use drugs more frequently than Blacks, Blacks are much more likely to end up incarcerated. These data are important for understanding deportations, as about a third of all deportees are deported for drug charges, and most criminal deportees are men (Golash-Boza 2015).

Racism in the criminal legal system has severe implications for Black and Latinx immigrants. Many Jamaicans, Dominicans, and Haitians experience the same set of resource deprivations and racist ideologies and practices that have led to the mass incarceration of Black men. Immigrants from Latin America often live in Latinx neighborhoods that are heavily policed. Thus, immigrants of African and Latin American descent are more likely to be jailed and eventually deported than immigrants of European or Asian descent, who are not subject to the same set of prejudices and discriminatory actions. Whereas the immigrant population includes many Whites and Asians, Black and Latinx immigrants almost exclusively make up the group of detainees and deportees. Black and brown people from Latin America and the Caribbean are substantially more likely to be deported than are Whites or Asians; 98 percent of deportees are sent to the Americas (see Table 3-1).

voices

Hector, a Guatemalan Deportee

Hector moved to the United States with his mother in 1984, when he was three years old. They joined his father, who had been there since he was a newborn. In 1990, his parents applied for political asylum, as Hector's mother had worked for the Guatemalan government and could be subject to persecution if they returned. They were issued work permits and waited for their cases to be heard. In 1999, Hector and his family were able to legalize under the Nicaraguan Adjustment and Central American Relief Act (NACARA). Hector became a legal permanent resident of the United States.

Hector spent most of his childhood in the San Fernando Valley, where he completed elementary, middle, and high school. He did well in high school and attended the University of California. After he finished college in 2004, his first job was on campus as a coordinator for a smoking prevention and cessation program.

While working on campus, Hector also began to work part time at a computer company. When the grant funding his university job ran out, he switched over to full-time work at the computer company. There, he quickly moved up from entry- to midlevel management. Things were going well for him. He was earning good money at the company and was promoted several times.

(continued)

Hector, a Guatemalan Deportee

Hector frequently traveled back to the San Fernando Valley to visit his parents and old friends. It was there that he reconnected with some people who encouraged him to join them in a credit card fraud scheme. Hector and his friends were caught forging credit cards, and he was sentenced to eighteen months in jail. After finishing his time, Hector faced automatic deportation to Guatemala.

At Hector's deportation hearing, it did not matter that he had come to the United States when he was three years old, that he was a legal permanent resident, that he had a college degree, and that he had no immediate family in Guatemala. The only consideration the judge could take into account was the fact that he had been convicted of an aggravated felony. With this conviction on his record, the judge had no choice but to order Hector deported to Guatemala, where he had to remake his life from the ground up.

Source: Golash-Boza 2012b.

TABLE 3-1
Top Ten Countries to Which Deportees Were Sent, 2014

	Number	Percent	Cumulative Percent
Mexico	275,911	66.57%	66.57%
Guatemala	54,153	13.07%	79.63%
Honduras	40,560	9.79%	89.42%
El Salvador	26,685	6.44%	95.86%
Dominican Republic	2,045	0.49%	96.35%
Ecuador	1,511	0.36%	96.71%
Colombia	1,309	0.32%	97.03%
Nicaragua	1,284	0.31%	97.34%
Jamaica	1,027	0.25%	97.59%
Brazil	931	0.22%	97.81%
Others	9,065	2.19%	100.00%

Source: U.S. Department of Homeland Security, Office of Immigration Statistics (2016).

Earlier in this chapter, we looked at the five countries of origin from which most legal permanent residents in the United States come: China, India, Mexico, the Philippines, and Vietnam. With the notable exception of Mexico, these are not the countries to which we send most deportees. The top five countries of origin of deportees in 2014 were Mexico, Honduras, Guatemala, El Salvador, and the Dominican Republic. These five countries alone accounted for over 96 percent of all people deported in 2014. Table 3-1 lists the top ten countries to which deportees were sent in 2014. These ten countries represent 97.81 percent of people deported in 2014. These data call attention to a glaring fact: Asians are prominent among immigrants overall, whereas Latin Americans and Caribbean nationals are over-represented among deportees. At this point, it will be useful to take a closer look at the numbers. As Figure 3-8 shows, even when we take into account the relative numbers of undocumented migrants in the country, Latin Americans are still much more likely to be deported than Asians.

Deportation policy also has gendered effects. About 90 percent of all deportees are men, even though only about half of all immigrants are men (Golash-Boza 2015). This disparity is due to the way criminal and immigration laws are enforced. Men are more likely than women to be in public places—driving, walking, or standing on the corner—and thus are more likely to come to the attention of the authorities. Although more men are deported than women, deportation policy does not affect only deportees—it also affects their families. When a person is deported, a family often loses a breadwinner.

FIGURE 3-8

RATIO OF UNDOCUMENTED MIGRANTS TO DEPORTEES, 2014

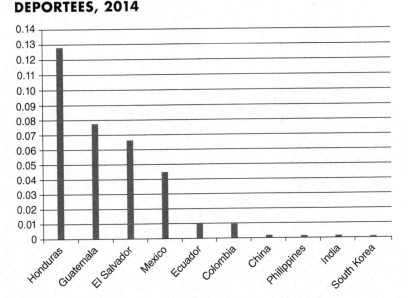

Current immigration laws, practices, and policies further enhance the extent to which our society is riddled with racism and repression. The general climate of strict enforcement of immigration laws in the post–9/11 era has further exacerbated the situation. A nationally representative survey of Hispanics found that nearly one in ten Latinx people had been stopped by authorities and asked about their immigration status, and a similar percentage had experienced discrimination in housing. Remarkably, 15 percent of all Latinx people between the ages of 18 and 29 said they had experienced some form of discrimination. It is thus no wonder that the majority of the Latinx respondents said they worry about deportation (Lopez and Minushkin 2008). These numbers indicate that the racial profiling of Latinx people is widespread and that Latinx people are targeted in immigration enforcement efforts.

The 1996 deportation laws were punitive. Moreover, they have had a disproportionate effect on people of color. This pattern is consistent with other patterns of systemic racism in this country. This point of view allows us to see that the racism embedded in immigration policy is not an isolated case but a foreseeable by-product of a society that systematically denies the dignity and humanity of people of color. The criminalization of Black men leads to the deportation of a disproportionate number of Dominicans and Jamaicans. The stereotype of Mexicans, and of those who look "Mexican," as "illegals" leads to the targeting of Mexicans and Central Americans in immigration enforcement efforts.

These practices and policies do not simply isolate and remove immigrants of color, but also have detrimental effects on their families, who are, in most cases, also people of color. Those children, spouses, and parents who witness their loved ones being mistreated and banished are also victims of this systematic denial of human rights. In light of patterns of segregation, there are whole communities of Mexicans and Mexican Americans in which children are growing up not only experiencing structural racism in terms of resource provisions, but also witnessing their mothers, fathers, brothers, sisters, neighbors, and community leaders being told they have no right to be here and, in many cases, being forcibly removed from their communities. Just as African American children often grow up knowing that Blacks are more likely than other groups to be "locked up," Mexicans and other Latin American and Caribbean people grow up knowing that people like them are being expelled from this country at the rate of nearly 1,000 people a day (Golash-Boza 2015).

THE DREAM ACT

The DREAM Act (Development, Relief, and Education for Alien Minors) was first introduced in the Senate on August 1, 2001, by Senators Dick Durbin and Orrin Hatch. As of this writing in 2022, despite widespread support, the DREAM Act still has not made it through Congress. The DREAM Act would allow undocumented youth who finish high school in the United States to apply for legalization and a path to citizenship. According to the Pew Hispanic Center, 86 percent of Latinx people in the United States believe that migrants to this country—even unauthorized ones—deserve a chance to become citizens. This belief is shared by 72 percent of all Americans. In 2012, DREAMers were able to successfully pressure President Obama into providing deferred action and work permits to undocumented youth. In June 2012, the president issued the Deferred Action for Childhood Arrivals (DACA) memorandum, which protects youth from deportation for two years. To qualify, undocumented immigrants must have been under the age of 31 on June 15, 2012; have arrived in the United States before the age of 16; and be currently enrolled either in school or in the armed forces or already have completed high school. A path to citizenship and full inclusion into the country many of them call home, however, remains elusive.

NATIVISM IN THE TWENTY-FIRST CENTURY

At the end of the twentieth century, the United States witnessed a surge in nativism not seen since the 1920s. Because this nativism was directed primarily at new immigrants—Asians and Latin Americans—it can be difficult to disentangle it from racism.

Historian George Sanchez (1997) suggests that three factors distinguish the racialized nativism of today from that of a century ago:

- The rise of extreme antipathy toward languages other than English. This is exemplified in a campaign some people have launched against having to "press 1 for English" when trying to reach customer service or townspeople's insistence that libraries not purchase books in languages other than English.
- The concern that Asian, Caribbean, and Latin American immigrants are taking advantage of affirmative action programs designed to help

native-born minorities, especially African Americans. This can be seen in conversations regarding the high numbers of West Indians entering Ivy League schools.

- The worry that immigrants are draining public resources through the overuse of welfare, education, and health care services. This sentiment persists even though laws passed in 1996 severely limit immigrants' access to welfare and health services. The Supreme Court decided in *Plyler v. Doe* in 1982 that any child in the United States has the right to an education. It is indicative of the strong sense of nativism that exists in the United States today that a politician or pundit can suggest that the children of foreigners are draining our funds by attending public schools, instead of seeing the education of children—both immigrant and native-born—as an investment in the future of this country.

The rise of nativism in the United States is closely tied to economic uncertainties. Nativism in the 1920s was connected to the country's difficult transition from a primarily agricultural economy to a massively industrialized one. At the end of the twentieth century, the United States experienced rapid deindustrialization and the rise of a service-oriented economy. These structural changes in the economy produced economic uncertainty, especially among the working class and poor. Moreover, as native-born Black, White, and Latinx people have been displaced from factory jobs, immigrants have come in to fill jobs in the service sector. As the economy has shifted, native-born workers have not always been able to retool their skill sets or displace themselves to areas of high growth. The widespread perception that immigrants are "taking our jobs" is intimately tied to the rise of nativism.

During Donald Trump's presidential campaign, he played into these fears using nativist and racist language, running his campaign on an anti-immigrant and anti-Muslim platform. He made calls to ban all Muslims from the United States. He referred to Mexicans as "rapists" and emphasized the importance of keeping out "bad hombres." Moreover, he made specific promises to revoke the rights of immigrants. Trump's rallying cry to "build a wall" played into his constituents' racialized fears related to economic and demographic changes in the United States.

Donald Trump did not invent these discourses, but he did tap into them. Despite President Obama's record-high deportations, many people in the United States argued that he was not doing enough to fix what they viewed as the immigration "problem." But Obama also issued an executive order—Deferred Action for Childhood Arrivals (DACA)—which granted reprieve from deportation and a work permit to qualified immigrants who arrived to the United States as minors. Notably, the Trump administration tried to overturn DACA, but, in June 2020, the Supreme Court ruled that DACA could stand.

During the Obama presidency, many states passed their own restrictive laws targeting immigrants. The first major state law was Arizona's Senate Bill (SB) 1070, the Support Our Law Enforcement and Safe Neighborhoods Act. This law was followed closely by Alabama's 2011 House Bill (HB) 56, the Alabama Taxpayer and Citizen Protection Act; and by Georgia's HB 87, the Illegal Immigration Reform and Enforcement Act of 2011. Many of these laws have backfired: when Alabama passed laws restricting the rights of undocumented people, the state experienced a massive outflow of immigrants. These immigrants left jobs behind that went unfilled, as immigrants in Alabama who picked tomatoes for a living could not easily be replaced by the urban unemployed. Native-born workers are unlikely to see the benefit of moving from the city to the countryside to pick tomatoes. The idea that Alabama could simply rid itself of undocumented workers and thereby fix its unemployment problem was ill conceived and riddled with nativist logic.

When Arizona SB 1070 went into effect in July 2010, it sparked national debate, protests, and boycotts. The law required local law enforcement agents to determine the immigration status of any person with whom they interacted during the course of their duties. This meant, for example, that if a police officer responded to a call for domestic violence, they would be required to check the immigration status of both the perpetrator and the victim, if they had reason to believe that either might be in the country unlawfully. SB 1070 was subsequently modified with the enactment of HB 2162 on April 30, 2010, which changed the language such that police officers would only be required to check the immigration status of people during a lawful stop, detention, or arrest. With these modified provisions, SB 1070 only required intervention in those cases in which a person was suspected of violating state laws. These modifications relieved some concerns that the law would make victims of crimes less likely to contact law enforcement officials, yet the possibility of racial profiling remained a substantial problem. According to an amicus brief filed by the American Immigration Lawyers Association (AILA) (2010, 5), "there is simply no unbiased means of implementing the term 'unlawful presence,' because as a legal status there are no observable characteristics of 'unlawful presence,' or readily available means by which a police officer could discern 'unlawful presence' in any stop, detention, or investigative encounter." In 2012, a Supreme Court decision blocked three provisions of the Arizona law, but it upheld the provision that required officers to demand papers from individuals. However, in 2016, the National Immigration Law Center and other immigrants' rights groups won a lawsuit against the state of Arizona. As a result, officers are no longer required to ask for papers during stops, although they may do so at their own discretion.

Nativism in the twenty-first century is promoted by organizations such as the Federation for Immigration Reform (FAIR) and NumbersUSA, pundits such as Lou Dobbs and Ann Coulter, and by the former president of the United States, Donald Trump. Trump's nativist statements primarily targeted undocumented immigrants and Muslims (Young 2017), although in the context of the coronavirus crisis, he also targeted Asians, referring publicly to COVID-19 as the "Chinese virus" and "Kung Flu."

One example of Trump's Islamophobia translating into law is the "Muslim ban." In January 2017, shortly after taking office, Trump signed an executive order called *Protecting the Nation from Foreign Terrorist Entry into the United States*, temporarily banning the admission of people from seven majority-Muslim countries: Iraq, Syria, Iran, Libya, Somalia, Sudan, and Yemen. The ban was implemented as flights from these countries were in midair, which caused chaos and widespread panic. An outcry on social media followed, and thousands flocked to airports to protest the ban. There was also resistance in the courts: several states and individual plaintiffs sued the federal government on the grounds that the ban was not constitutional. In February 2017, a district judge in Washington State suspended the ban nationwide with a temporary restraining order. Six days later, a district appeals court upheld that ruling. In May 2017, the Fourth Circuit Court of Appeals ruled 10 to 3 against Trump's travel ban, reaffirming the lower court's decision.

The underlying motive for the president's desire to ban the admission of people from these seven countries was Islamophobia, which manifests here as the fear that people from Muslim countries are the most likely to commit acts of terrorism against the United States. This fear is unfounded. The sum total of people killed by nationals from those seven countries between 1975 and 2015 is zero (Nowrasteh 2017). Trump's proposed Muslim ban would not have made America any safer, but it would have had harmful effects on the lives of many people, as the *Voices: The Zarour Family* story shows.

voices

The Zarour Family

The scent of black tea and rice wafts through the bare apartment the Zarour family has come to call home after fleeing Syria.

It's been three months since they arrived in El Cajon, [California,] home to the second-largest Iraqi diaspora in the United States. . . . Starting a new life has been difficult, she says, but it is better than the alternative they escaped four years ago: the crack of strafing fire from government or rebel troops in what was once the city of Homs, and explosions that left only gaping craters or rubble where bustling urban life once hummed. . . .

Zarour, her husband, and their five children are among the nearly 800 Syrian refugees who arrived in San Diego County last year and settled in El Cajon. California led the nation in resettlement of Syrian refugees in fiscal 2016, taking in 1,450 immigrants, according to the Pew Research Center. . . . Here, grocery store signs are in English and Arabic. Posters advertise realty and investment services in both languages, alongside signs for concerts headlined by Arab pop stars.

At the downtown El Cajon farmers market, resettlement agencies set up booths to explain their services and hand out ACLU pamphlets about the right to wear a hijab. Iraqi vendors work one table over, selling cilantro, turnips and herbs from a community garden maintained by immigrants and refugees. A sign hanging from their tent in Arabic asks shoppers not to haggle over vegetable prices. . . .

The stress of starting anew has been amplified in recent weeks by President Trump's executive order that placed a 120-day ban on all refugee admissions and an indefinite suspension of admission for Syrian refugees.

The travel ban is on pause after a federal judge in Seattle issued a temporary restraining order, but Zarour's husband, Ahmad, who still has family in Jordan and Syria, wonders whether the order will affect them.

"Why does he view us as terrorists? We are people looking to start a new life," he says of Trump. "We aren't like that. We are Muslims, but we are very kind." . . .

Two years after the Syrian civil war began, Zarour abandoned his small supermarket in Homs and gave up his work molding custom ceilings. The family settled in Damascus before

(continued)

voices   *continued.*

The Zarour Family

it, too, became too dangerous. They fled to the Zaatari refugee camp, a squalid, sprawling outpost near the Jordanian–Syrian border. They spent 20 days in the camp before they moved to another town....

Early in their stay in Jordan, they registered as refugees with the United Nations. Eventually, after two years of interviews, the UN High Commissioner for Refugees referred them for resettlement in the United States....

Adjusting to a new life in America has bruised the pride of a man accustomed to providing for his family.

He struggles to learn the skills taught in workshops mandated by resettlement agencies—basics such as learning English, navigating public transportation or how to open a bank account. Attending those classes is tied to the financial aid the family receives.

To fit all seven people in their small two-bedroom apartment, the five children sleep wall-to-wall in the master bedroom. He and his wife sleep in the spare room.

The three couches in his living room were donated.

Before the war in Syria, he had a home of his own, lived near his siblings, and held a government job that helped him pay the bills. As he places a glass of tea on the cardboard box he now uses as a coffee table, Zarour wonders if he will ever find a piece of the happiness he once knew.

Source: Parvini 2017.

CONCLUSION AND DISCUSSION

How far have we come since 1882, the year the U.S. Congress passed the Chinese Exclusion Act? The immigration laws passed since 1965 in the United States do not have overt racial provisions like the 1882 Chinese Exclusion Act or the 1924 Johnson–Reed Act. We also have not seen anything as egregious as the 1954 Operation Wetback. Laws with these names or provisions would be untenable in the twenty-first-century United States. Nevertheless, we continue to see both the racially uneven consequences of immigration laws and racialized sentiments directed at particular national-origin and racial groups.

U.S. immigration policy has been racialized from the beginning. At the same time, the way these policies have been racialized has changed over time, as racial ideologies have shifted. Nativism has also consistently reared its head, though in different ways over time. Harvard professor Aristide Zolberg titled his 2009 book on immigration policy *A Nation by Design*, hinting at the ways that immigration policy has been deployed with the goal of creating an ideal populace. In 1882, the Chinese Exclusion Act was passed to end the influx of Chinese laborers. The 1924 Immigration Act was designed to recruit immigrants from northern and western Europe and to exclude immigrants from the rest of the world. The 1965 Immigration and Nationality Act was passed in the name of civil rights and ostensibly to create a diverse society, and yet it ended up creating a large undocumented Mexican population. The 1986 laws were passed with the hope of ending immigration. When that did not work, the 1996 laws made life for immigrants more difficult and precarious. The current state laws are designed with the hope that immigrants will self-deport.

Each of these laws was proposed because of a vision lawmakers had for society. But the United States is a changing nation. Soon, the country will no longer have a White Anglo majority. As the United States changes, Whites can either become more accepting of differences or reject those differences more forcefully. What do you think will happen? What do you think should happen?

THE UNITED STATES has a long history of immigration from around the world and an equally long history of welcoming some immigrants while barring or discouraging others. Since the 1960s, the vast majority of immigrants to the United States have been non-White. In this context, is it possible to have laws that discriminate against immigrants without being racially discriminatory?

THINKING ABOUT RACIAL JUSTICE

Key Terms

nativism   66

Naturalization Act of 1790   69

naturalization   69

Chinese Exclusion Act   70

Immigration Act of 1917   71

Immigration Act of 1924 (Johnson–Reed Act)   71

legal permanent resident   72

bracero program   73

Operation Wetback   74

1965 Immigration and Nationality Act (Hart–Cellar Act)   75

1986 Immigration Reform and Control Act (IRCA)   85

Anti-Terrorism and Effective Death Penalty Act (AEDPA)   88

Illegal Immigration Reform and Immigrant Responsibility Act (IIRIRA)   88

Personal Responsibility and Work Opportunity Reconciliation Act (PRWORA)   88

CHECK YOUR UNDERSTANDING

3.1 Examine the racialized history of U.S. immigration policy.

Nativism and racism have been intertwined in U.S. immigration policies since the beginning of the nation's history. The first piece of immigration legislation was the Chinese Exclusion Act in 1882. Laws continued to be racialized over the course of the twentieth century.

Q What is the significance of the Chinese Exclusion Act and the court cases that stemmed from it?

Q Why was Operation Wetback important?

Q How have immigration flows and quotas changed since the 1850s?

3.2 Describe U.S. policy responses to undocumented immigration.

The passage of the 1965 Immigration and Nationality Act and subsequent 1986 Immigration Reform and Control Act created the problem of illegal immigration. Since then, more restrictive laws have been passed.

Q What were some major changes brought about by the 1965 Immigration and Nationality Act?

Q What legislative changes sparked Asian and Latin American immigration in the late twentieth century?

Q What restrictive immigration laws were passed in the late twentieth century?

3.3 Analyze the relationship between nativism and racism in the twenty-first century.

When most immigrants are people of color, racism and nativism are difficult to disentangle.

Q How has nativism changed from previous historical periods?

Critical Thinking

1. How have economic circumstances played a role in the passage of immigration laws?
2. How have U.S. colonial and imperial relationships with other countries affected migration flows?
3. Are IRCA and IIRIRA related to racialized sentiments? How so?
4. Why are Latin American immigrants the most likely to be deported?

Talking about Race

There are no statutes of limitations for illegal entry (laws specifying how long after events a case may begin), as there are for most other crimes. The next time you hear someone say something such as "What part of illegal don't you understand?" try bringing up statutes of limitations. For example, you could explain that a person who shoplifted in 2010 could not be brought to trial for it in 2019, yet an immigrant can be deported for illegal entry even decades after the original offense. Use this as an entry point for broader discussions of illegal immigration.

Learn more with this chapter's digital tools, including video clips from the author, web links, filmography, and chapter self-assessment quizzes at www.oup.com/he/golash-boza-brief3e.

4

Racism in the Media

The Spread of Ideology

AS YOU READ

4.1 How are racial stereotypes propagated in popular culture?

4.2 How have new media changed the way stereotypes are spread and countered?

4.3 How do media images and messages support the rationalization of racial inequality?

4.4 How are media representations raced, classed, and gendered?

The media feed us a constant stream of images that shape our beliefs. The media also promote and reinforce **stereotypes**— widely held but fixed and oversimplified images or ideas of types of people or things. In early American film, for example, people of color were overwhelmingly portrayed in stereotypical roles: Native Americans as silent chiefs, Arabs as mysterious or villainous desert sheikhs, Latinas as sexual objects, and African Americans as maids or buffoons. Fast-forward to the twenty-first century, and we find more nuanced depictions. Nevertheless, significant traces of these historical stereotypes remain in contemporary film, television, and new media.

Moreover, these stereotypes are not harmless: they have real and enduring consequences. Representations of Black and Latinx people as poor and lawbreaking undesirables, for example, reinforce popular notions about supposed cultural deficiencies. The pervasiveness of these images can lead to false conclusions about racial groups. In this light, it may come as no surprise that many Americans incorrectly attribute higher incarceration rates among Black and Latino men to higher criminality (P. H. Collins 2004; Feagin 2001; Priest et al. 2018). This stance ignores evidence to the contrary, as well as the racially discriminatory nature of the criminal justice system. However, it makes sense to people who constantly see media images of Black and Latino men shooting and robbing. Many media representations of people of color are essentially modern versions of past stereotypes; both historically and today, these images have been used to rationalize slavery, segregation, genocide, colonialism, and exclusion.

In this chapter, we will focus on racial ideologies propagated in the media. How do these ideologies play a role in normalizing and supporting racial inequality? Why do racial segregation and inequality remain prevalent despite laws against racial discrimination? An understanding of how the media reproduce racial stereotypes will help us answer these questions. More pointedly, this examination will show how media portrayals may partly explain why so little is being done about racial disparities in a nation that purportedly values equality and democracy.

REPRESENTATIONS IN ENTERTAINMENT

In 2020, people in the United States watched, on average, 3.1 hours of television a day, making television viewing the most common leisure activity in the country (Bureau of Labor Statistics 2021). Given that Americans spend so much time in front of screens, it is no wonder television shows and films have a great influence on how we see the world. Think, for example, of two popular shows: *Girls* and *Sex and the City*, both of which took place in New York City yet presented primarily White people in White spaces. According to the 2010 U.S. census, over one-third of the population of New York City is foreign born, and the city's population is less than half White. In these two shows, however, all of the main characters were White, and the tremendous racial and ethnic diversity of their city was largely unnoticeable, even when the characters were in public. Representations in shows such as these naturalize racial segregation. It thus seems perfectly natural to many White Americans that they themselves would live in primarily White neighborhoods and send their children to primarily White schools, even when they too live in multiracial urban areas (Orfield 2009). Racial segregation thus becomes completely normal and desirable.

Because film and television shape how we see the world, it is important to consider how various groups are represented. Media scholars Stacy Smith, Marc Choueiti, and Katherine Pieper (2016) issued a telling report on diversity of representation in American entertainment. They found that across theatrical releases and scripted series in 2014 and 2015, only 28.3 percent of all speaking characters were people of color, yet the U.S. population is 37.9 percent people of color. As previous studies have found, shows and movies are mostly Black and White: 71.7 percent of all characters were White, 12.2 percent were Black, 5.8 percent were Hispanic/Latinx, 5.1 percent were Asian, and 2.3 percent were Middle Eastern. Over half of all shows and movies featured no speaking Asian characters, and 22 percent featured no Black speaking characters. There was even more disparity at the directing level: only 13 percent of directors were people of color. Notably, out of the 414 shows and films included in the study, only two were directed by Black women.

A 2019 study examined the 100 top-grossing films each year from 2007 to 2018. Only 17 of these 1200 films had a lead or co-lead that was Latina. Notably, five of these 17 lead roles went to Cameron Diaz—a White-passing Latina. Overall, only 3 percent of the top 100 films each year had a Latinx leads or co-leads (Smith et al. 2019).

Latinxs stand out as the most underrepresented group in American entertainment, and all people of color are underrepresented as leading characters and in executive roles (Smith et al. 2016; Yuen 2016). Nancy Yuen (2016) explains that Whites are 62.6 percent of the population, yet make up 74.1 percent of all speaking roles in films, 80.7 percent of all cable TV leads, 83.3 percent of all film leads, and 93.5 percent of all broadcast TV leads. Whites also account for 81 percent of all directors and an astounding 96 percent of all television network and studio heads (see Figure 4-1).

FIGURE 4-1

UNDERREPRESENTATION OF PEOPLE OF COLOR IN AMERICAN FILM AND TELEVISION

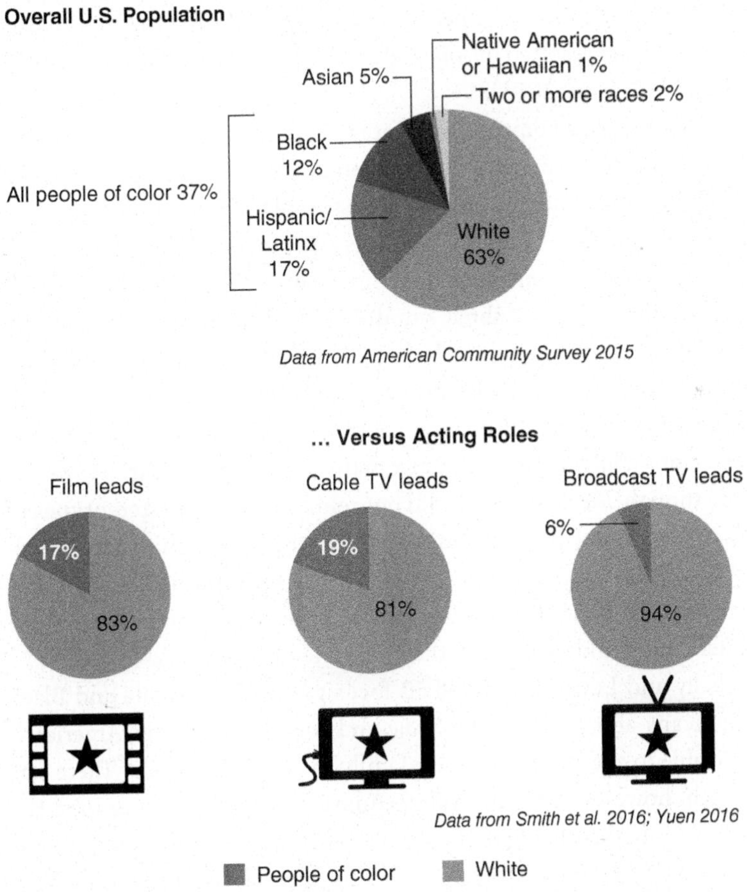

Overall U.S. Population

Native American or Hawaiian 1%

Two or more races 2%

Asian 5%

Black 12%

All people of color 37%

Hispanic/ Latinx 17%

White 63%

Data from American Community Survey 2015

... Versus Acting Roles

Film leads

17%

83%

Cable TV leads

19%

81%

Broadcast TV leads

6%

94%

Data from Smith et al. 2016; Yuen 2016

People of color   White

Source: Data from American Community Survey; Smith et al. 2016; Yuen 2016.

Portrayals of Black People

Prior to the civil rights era, portrayals of Black people on television and in popular culture were uniformly stereotypical. Shows such as *Amos 'n' Andy* featured African Americans who appeared almost exclusively as maids, cooks, con artists, or deadbeats. These representations served to legitimize the racial order of overt White dominance. The logic of the era was that African Americans were incapable of self-governance and thus were well served by the racial order of the day. Whites were reassured that while Black people were often good servants and entertainers, they were not capable of assuming the responsibilities of full citizenship. The National Association for the Advancement of Colored People (NAACP) contended that *Amos 'n' Andy* exclusively represented Black people as lazy, stupid, loud, thieving, and dishonest and promoted racial prejudice against Black people; it eventually leveled a lawsuit against CBS because of these portrayals. The lawsuit was successful and resulted in *Amos 'n' Andy* being taken off the air in 1953 (Gray 1995; Hunt 2005).

In the 1980s, a completely different kind of show became popular. Instead of presenting Black characters as deadbeats or servants, *The Cosby Show* had a central cast of successful Black characters. It reached the top of television viewers' rankings and remained there for most of its eight years on prime-time television (Hunt 2005). The show, which first aired in 1984, was about a middle-class African American family made up of Cliff Huxtable, a doctor; his wife, Clair, a lawyer; and their five children. The family lived in a spacious brownstone in New York City and were successful economically, socially, and educationally. The depictions could not be further from those of *Amos 'n' Andy*. However, even though *The Cosby Show* did not reinforce negative stereotypes of Black people, it still worked to reproduce what communications scholars Sut Jhally and Justin Lewis (1992) call **enlightened racism**: the idea that the United States is a land of opportunity and that African Americans could do better if they only tried harder.

Jhally and Lewis conducted 52 focus groups with White and Black Americans about *The Cosby Show* and found that White Americans were able to accept the Huxtable family as people like them. There was a catch, however: although White Americans were happy to have the Huxtables in their living rooms each week, the show did not reduce stereotypes about other African Americans. Instead, the depiction of successful Black characters on television reinforced "enlightened racism," as

Jhally and Lewis described it. Moreover, White Americans began to see themselves as less racist because they liked the Huxtables and other African Americans who behaved similarly. Whites attributed any negative feelings they might have had about other African Americans not to their blackness, but to how they behaved. The fact that the Huxtables never experienced racism further reinforced the idea that racism is the direct result of how African Americans behave.

In the media today, we see another seemingly positive image of African Americans: the Black athlete. African Americans dominate U.S. sports, and Americans of all hues idolize Black athletes. The idolization of Black athletes might make it seem as if the media tend to portray these athletes in a positive manner. However, scholars who analyze the portrayal of Black athletes point out that these portrayals also reinforce stereotypes and that the media portray Black and White athletes quite differently (King and Springwood 2001). For example, when Black athletes transgress moral or legal boundaries, the media are quick to home in on the stories—especially those that reinforce stereotypes. One example Fruehling and King give is of Christian Peter, a White football player, and Lawrence Phillips, a Black football player, both of whom played at the University of Nebraska. When Peter was accused of assaulting a White woman, the incident received attention only in Lincoln, Nebraska. When Phillips, however, was charged with beating his White ex-girlfriend, it received intense national coverage, including a segment on *60 Minutes*. Fruehling and King also juxtapose athletes Kobe Bryant and Drew Henson. They argue that when Kobe Bryant, who is Black, decided not to attend college full-time, the media commentary suggested that Bryant needed refinement, training, and discipline, and that this was a bad decision. In contrast, when Drew Henson, who is White, made a similar decision, the conversation in the media did not revolve around his maturity or his possibilities for upward mobility.

Stereotypical representations in sports also extend to women. David Leonard (2014) explains how portrayals of White tennis player Candace Parker differ from those of Black players Venus and Serena Williams. He argues that Parker is portrayed to represent an ideal femininity, both nurturing and sexual. In contrast, the Williams sisters are often portrayed as muscular, aggressive, and masculine. Instead of focusing on their talent, media representations of both Parker and the Williams sisters often home in on their bodies—and they do so in racialized ways.

African American women are portrayed in stereotypical ways in media more generally. A study by Melissa Harris-Perry (2011) revealed that stereotyped caricatures of Black women—as Mammies, Sapphires, and Jezebels—continue to be prominent. A **Mammy** is a stereotypical image of a Black maid, encapsulated by the "Aunt Jemima" icon and taking its name from "Mammy" in *Gone with the Wind*. **Sapphire** was one of the main characters on *Amos 'n' Andy* and is a caricature of an angry Black woman. **Jezebel** is a name with biblical origins that has come to signify an oversexed or hypersexual Black woman. Harris-Perry (2011) found that these three stereotypes about African American women have been prominent in political and popular culture since the Civil War and influence how Black women perceive themselves and are perceived by others.

Over the past few years, representations of African Americans on television have improved considerably. One example is Issa Rae's HBO series, *Insecure*, which premiered in 2016 and is based on Rae's web series hit, *Awkward Black Girl*. The comedy features a variety of protagonists, most of whom are African American, and Issa Rae stars as a version of herself. The show is set in Los Angeles, where Issa works at a youth-oriented nonprofit. The show revolves around Issa's relationships, particularly with her best friend Molly, a driven lawyer, and her boyfriend, Lawrence, who is looking for a job. With several Black protagonists, *Insecure* is able to avoid stereotypical portrayals of Black people. Additionally, the show does not shy away from dealing with racism, especially in the workplace—showing a reality many African Americans face.

voices

Why black-*ish* Is the Show We Need Right Now

Last night, black-*ish* aired an episode titled "Hope" that exemplified why diversity is so important in entertainment. Within its short 30 minutes, a tough and divisive issue was handled with intelligence and depths of which hour-long shows typically seem incapable of achieving. I submit that this was all made possible by a creator and writers who can speak from personal experience and a cast that can deliver from the same place.

The sitcom black-*ish* addresses serious issues related to race and racism.

The episode didn't stop with a surface discussion of police brutality. Instead, it delved deeper and raised discussion around "the talk" with children about brutality and protests. The genius of the episode however, was the counterpoints Dre and Rainbow took. While Rainbow took the more conservative, and hopeful position, Dre spoke for the Black anger that burns deep inside of us that we have been forced to coexist with. They were personifications of so many things: positivity and despair, old school and new school, compassion and passion.

This extended into their children, as Junior wanted to join the protests, Zoe was overcome with the frustration of it all, and the twins were just too young to even understand what was happening. Still, they were stuck in the middle between the need for self-preservation and fighting for the preservation of future generations. This is one of the most devastating aspects of blackness, often having to choose between your own health and prosperity and that of your children and those to come.

But even in all of the darkness, there was a tragic, brilliant beauty to it all. And having this displayed in such a public and truthful manner was restorative.

It was an unabashed and unbridled acknowledgment of the struggle that communicated our shared struggle nationwide. This is what good TV looks like. This is the power of diversity in entertainment. This is why representation is important. And I like to believe that, for non-minority viewers, their perception of the unrest across the nation has been shifted at least a little.

Source: Jackson 2017.

Portrayals of Latinx People

Latinx characters are both underrepresented and misrepresented in American media (Monk-Turner et al. 2010; Smith et al. 2016). In a study of prime-time television during March 2007, Monk-Turner and colleagues found that, overall, Latinx people were the group most likely to be portrayed negatively on television (2010). For example, their analyses revealed that none of the Latinx characters were depicted as articulate, whereas 25 percent of Black and 30 percent of White characters were (see Figure 4-2). Half of all African American actors were depicted as intelligent, compared with 43 percent of White and 27 percent of Latinx actors. Finally, the researchers found that only 2 percent of White actors were portrayed as immoral, compared with 18 percent of Latinx actors, and 3 percent of Whites were portrayed as despicable, compared with 18 percent of Latinx actors. In 2013, Latinxs were notably absent from significant roles in the American media. There was not a single Latinx character with a leading role in the top ten movies and scripted network TV shows.

FIGURE 4-2

REPRESENTATIONS OF BLACK, LATINX, AND WHITE PEOPLE ON TELEVISION

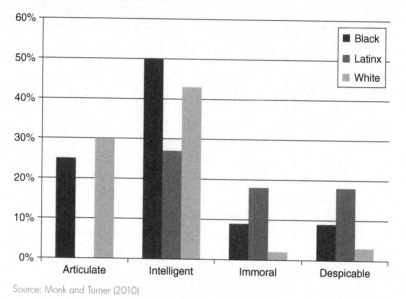

Source: Monk and Turner (2010)

There were no Latinxs among the top ten television show creators, and Latinxs constituted just 1.1 percent of producers, 2 percent of writers, and 4.1 percent of directors. Finally, only one Latinx executive ranked among the top fifty-three television, radio, and studio executives (Negrón-Muntaner 2014).

A study of the 100 highest-grossing films each year between 2007 and 2018 found that a quarter of all Latinx speaking characters were depicted as lawbreakers (Smith et al. 2019). Latino men are often stereotyped into specific roles: gangbanger, bandit, drug trafficker, police officer, janitor, gardener, and the Latin lover. Latinas are most likely to be portrayed as either hot-blooded women anxious for sexual fulfillment or maids anxious to please (Rodríguez 1997). Prime-time American television shows starring Latinx actors are few and far between, although this has been changing over the past few years. The main problem with Latinx representation in entertainment continues to be underrepresentation. Given such a limited variety of representations, it is difficult to avoid stereotypes. The main problem with Latinx representation in entertainment continues to

Jane the Virgin features a mostly Latinx cast and breaks from stereotypical portrayals.

be underrepresentation. Given such a limited variety of representations, it is difficult to avoid stereotypes.

The show *Jane the Virgin*, which debuted in 2014, breaks from some of these representational patterns. It centers on a Latinx family, made up of three generations: twenty-three-year-old Jane; her thirty-nine-year-old mother, Xiomara; and her grandmother, Alba. Nearly all of the main characters in the show are Latinx. Whereas Xiomara is cast as a sexy *Latina,* Alba performs the role of the sweet *abuelita* (grandma). Despite these (and other) tropes, the show is able to dig deeper into these roles and presents a complex view of a Latinx family. In a twist, the primary villains in the show are not Cuban cartels or the Mexican mafia, but Eastern European mobsters. *Jane the Virgin* ran for five seasons, ending in 2019.

Portrayals of Arabs and Arab Americans

Although nearly 3.7 million Americans trace their roots to an Arab country, and nearly 82 percent of Arabs in the United States are citizens (AAI 2017), Arabs are overwhelmingly portrayed on American television as foreign. Arab women are usually seen veiled or as exotic figures, and Arab men as terrorists or billionaires. In very recent years, this portrayal has begun to change, and we now occasionally see Arab Americans on prime-time television, often as the targets of racial discrimination. Evelyn Alsultany (2008) points out that in the aftermath of the September 11, 2001, terrorist attacks, some television shows took up the question of whether it was fair to discriminate against Arab or Muslim Americans in the name of national security. Alsultany contends that this representation leads to the conclusion that Americans have to choose between protecting the nation and discriminating against Arabs and Arab Americans (who are, according to the subtext, prone to being dangerous). Although more nuanced than previous representations of Arab men, this representation ultimately reinforces the idea that Arabs are terrorists and, thus, that it is legitimate to discriminate against them in the name of national security.

The trope of Muslims as terrorists continues to be prevalent in American television. In a recent article about the television series *Homeland* in Salon, Laila Al-Arian writes: "*Homeland* leaves little doubt that, regardless of the other red herring motivations of justice and psychological manipulation, it is being Muslim that makes someone dangerous." In addition to portraying most Arab or Muslim terrorists on the show as terrorists or terror suspects, *Homeland* also presents a distorted view of the Middle East. *Homeland* portrays Beirut as a backward, crumbling city when, in reality, Beirut is a modern, cosmopolitan city full of cafés, nightclubs, and clothing stores. The portrayal of the city angered Lebanese officials to the point that they threatened a lawsuit (Al-Arian 2012).

voices

Why We Hacked *Homeland*

In this excerpted blog post, three artists—Heba Amin, Caram Kapp, and Don Karl (a.k.a. Stone)—explain why they "hacked" an episode of Homeland *by painting graffiti with their own message. Their intervention was broadcast in Season 5, Episode 2.*

[*Homeland*] has garnered the reputation of being the most bigoted show on television for its inaccurate, undifferentiated and highly biased depiction of Arabs, Pakistanis, and Afghans, as well as its gross misrepresentations of the cities of Beirut,

Islamabad- and the so-called Muslim world in general. [Over several seasons], *Homeland* has maintained the dichotomy of the photogenic, mainly white, mostly American protector versus the evil and backwards Muslim threat. *The Washington Post* reacts to the racist horror of the season four promotional poster by describing it as "white Red Riding Hood lost in a forest of faceless Muslim wolves." In this forest, Red Riding Hood is permitted to display many shades of grey—bribery, drone strikes, torture, and covert assassination—to achieve her targets. She points her weapon of choice at the monochrome bad guys, who do all the things that the good guys do but with nefarious intent.

It cannot be disputed that the show looks good and is well acted and produced, as its many awards prove. But you would think that a series dealing so intensively with contemporary topics including the war on terrorism, ISIS, and ideological clashes between the US and the Middle East would not, for example, name a key terrorist character after the former real-life Pakistani ambassador to the United States. Granted, the show gets high praise from the American audience for its criticism of American government ethics, but not without dangerously feeding into the racism of the hysterical moment we find ourselves in today. Joseph Massad, Associate Professor of Modern Arab Politics and Intellectual History at Columbia University, addresses this deep-[seated] racism of American media towards the Middle East: "*Homeland* hardly deviates from this formula [of racist programming], except to add that Arabs are so dangerous that even all-American White men can be corrupted by them and become equally dangerous to America."

At the beginning of June 2015, we received a phone call from a friend who has been active in the Graffiti and Street art scene in Germany for the past 30 years and has researched graffiti in the Middle East extensively. He had been contacted by *Homeland*'s set production company who were looking for "Arabian street artists" to lend graffiti authenticity to a film set of a Syrian refugee camp on the Lebanese/ Syrian border for their new season. Given the series' reputation we were not easily convinced, until we considered what a moment of intervention could relay about our own and many

Asked to help add authenticity to the show Homeland, artists spray-painted the graffiti message above in Arabic, which translates to "Homeland is racist." The message appears in the background of a scene in Season 5.

(continued)

 *continued.*

Why We Hacked *Homeland*

others' political discontent with the series. It was our moment to make our point by subverting the message using the show itself.

In our initial meeting, we were given a set of images of pro-Assad graffiti—apparently natural in a Syrian refugee camp. Our instructions were: (1) the graffiti has to be apolitical, (2) you cannot copy the images because of copyright infringement, and (3) writing "Mohamed is the greatest, is okay of course." We would arm ourselves with slogans, with proverbs allowing for critical interpretation, and, if the chance presented itself, blatant criticism directed at the show. And so, it came to be.

Source: https://www.hebaamin.com/arabian-street-artists-bomb-homeland-why-we-hacked-an-award-winning-series/

Portrayals of Asians and Asian Americans

Darrell Hamamoto (1994) analyzed representations of Asians and Asian Americans on television between 1950 and 1990. He found that Asian men were often represented as foreign, sinister, unidimensional, effeminate characters. But whereas Asian men are often presented in U.S. media as asexual or effeminate, Asian women are often portrayed as hypersexual. Asian women are presented in two primary ways: as the **Dragon Lady** or as the **Butterfly** (Rajgopal 2010). The Dragon Lady is a sinister, crafty, destructive seductress, whereas the Butterfly is a demure, devoted, submissive wife who is eager to please Whites and men in general.

More recently, some gains have been made in the representation of Asian women on television. One example is Dr. Christina Yang, a central character in *Grey's Anatomy*. Yang is a beautiful and competent doctor. Her character has substantial depth and defies the "generic Asian" stereotype by making it clear she is both Korean American and from Beverly Hills—not Korea. However, as Rajgopal (2010) points out, Christina Yang's character does not have the feminine qualities of White characters in the show, such as Meredith Grey. She remains enigmatic and cold, showing hints of the Dragon Lady stereotype as well as the "inscrutable Oriental" stereotype. Another important example is *Fresh Off the Boat*, which premiered in 2015. Notably, it is the first prime-time American sitcom in two decades to focus on an Asian American family. Unlike previous shows featuring Asian Americans, *Fresh Off the Boat* offers a cast of characters who are dynamic, stylish, and engaging.

Fresh Off the Boat features characters who are dynamic, stylish, and engaging. It is the first prime-time American sitcom in two decades to focus on an Asian American family.

Media scholar David Stamps analyzed the television shows *Fresh Off the Boat* and *Jane the Virgin* for the proportion of racial-ethnic characters, depiction of negative stereotypes, and accuracy of cultural representation. Stamps asks: (1) Are Asian characters the largest representation of racial-ethnic groups portrayed in *Fresh Off the Boat*? (2) Is Asian cultural representation present in the broadcast show *Fresh Off the Boat*? And (3) What, if any, negative stereotypes of Asians are represented in *Fresh Off the Boat*? These same questions were asked for *Jane the Virgin*, but about Latinxs.

The content analysis of six episodes from each show reveals that even though both shows are center an Asian and Latinx family respectively, White characters still hold the most roles. Only 36 percent of characters in the six randomly selected episodes of *Fresh Off the Boat* were Asian (54 percent were White). Similarly, slightly less than half of the characters in *Jane the Virgin* were Latinx (42 percent). Stamps also found that mainstream American cultural traditions were depicted much less often than Asian or Latinx cultural traditions in both TV shows. Asian cultural representations made up 67 percent of cultural representations on *Fresh Off the Boat* and Latinx cultural representations made up 60 percent of cultural representations on *Jane the Virgin*. Cultural representation examples include the Lunar New Year and speaking Chinese for Asian culture, topics about immigration and speaking Spanish for Latinx culture, and celebrating Presidents' Day for mainstream American culture. Finally, Stamps found that both shows depict negative stereotypes of Asians and Latinxs respectively. These include: "model minority," "tiger mom," "nerdy Asian," the "sultry Latina vixen," "the snazzy entertainer," and the "bewildered immigrant."

Stamps (2019: 9) concludes: "[B]oth *Fresh Off the Boat* and *Jane the Virgin* do not adequately reflect a shift in equitable racial representation and both shows perpetuate negative stereotypes of Asians and Latinxs. Moving forward, a holistic approach regarding storytelling, appropriate representation, and authentic inclusion in television programs may benefit underrepresented audiences and society as a whole."

Portrayals of Native Americans

In the early years of the United States, when White settlers were endeavoring to take over Indian lands in the newly formed nation, the most popular depictions of Native Americans were of savages. Over time, the "captivity narrative"—in which White women and children were captured by savage natives—became a staple in American fiction throughout the eighteenth, nineteenth, and twentieth centuries. Alongside this depiction of Native Americans as primitive and savages, an alternative depiction emerged: that of the Native American wise man or medicine man. Depictions of Native American men tend to fall into either of two categories: the savage or the wise man (Kopacz and Lawton 2011a; Bird 1999; White 2012).

In popular culture in the United States, Native American men are often stereotyped into roles that serve White characters. At one end of the spectrum is the eroticized, nearly naked Native American who gives White women sexual pleasure or who is the object of White women's illicit lust. At the other end of the spectrum is the wise Native American man, who is often a stoic loner and who gives his best spiritual advice to White heroes. In both cases, sexuality and family life among Native Americans is largely invisible (Bird 1999).

Representations of Native American women also tend toward a duality: as either a princess or a lustful savage. Pocahontas is the quintessential representation of a Native American woman: she is beautiful, erotic, noble, and fully dedicated to her White lover. At the other end of the spectrum is the squaw, who has sex indiscriminately with both Whites and Indians (Kopacz and Lawton 2011a). Similar to depictions of Native American men, these portrayals are from a White point of view. Native American male and female characters often have the primary purpose of serving White interests—by providing sexual satisfaction, as well as intimate knowledge of nature and other sacred things, and by helping convince other Native Americans of the importance of assimilation (Bird 1999).

In a survey of Native American stereotypes on television, Frederick White (2012) found that television producers almost exclusively show Native Americans as shamans, wise men, sidekicks, princesses, and matriarchs. Today, Native Americans are most commonly represented on television in brief appearances on popular sitcoms. In these appearances, Native Americans are usually presented as the stereotypical wise men who offer advice to White protagonists (Tahmahkera 2008). There are very few representations of Native Americans on television as recurring main characters. Although other groups have seen breakthroughs with the success of *Jane the Virgin*, *Fresh Off the Boat*, and *Empire*, the same has not been true for Native Americans, who are notably absent from prime-time television.

NEW MEDIA REPRESENTATIONS

In 2013, the amount of time Americans spent online surpassed television viewing for the first time—the average adult spent five hours per day online (eMarketer 2013). By 2016, Americans spent an average of 10 hours and 39 minutes each day using smartphones, tablets, TV, radio, computers, or video games (Associated Press 2016). Many of the same stereotypes prevalent in television are also apparent in video games and social media.

Video Games
About 91 percent of children between the ages of two and seventeen regularly play video games (Reisinger 2011). In 2020, persons aged 15–24 spent an average of 1.9 hours a day playing games or using a computer for leisure (Bureau of Labor Statistics 2021). Moreover, instead of being passive viewers, video game players are actively engaged and thus potentially more susceptible to stereotypes. Anna Everett and S. Craig Watkins (2008) carried out a study in which they explored how youths' interactions with video games affected how they

thought about race. The researchers argue that the interactive nature of the games enhances the potential for the games not only to perpetuate stereotypes but also to counter them. Additionally, as technology has improved and permitted video games to be more realistic, game creators have been able to produce what they perceive to be more real and authentic places in video games. This increased realism has led, for example, to the creation of urban spaces that are dominated by African American and young Latino men.

Studies of video games have revealed consistent stereotyping—Latinos are overrepresented in sports games, Asians are almost exclusively portrayed in fighting games, and Arabs are typically portrayed as targets of violence (Saleem 2008; Burgess, Dill, Stermer, Burgess, and Brown 2011). A study of video games by Melinda Burgess and her colleagues (2011) revealed that Black characters were more likely to be portrayed as thugs, athletes, and gun-toting figures than White characters. Burgess and colleagues also found that Black women were largely absent from video games. Video game development is overwhelmingly White and male—73 percent of developers are White and most are male (Srauy 2019). In addition, in a study of the normative practices of game developers Srauy (2019) found that they rely on popular racial stereotypes in an effort to produce games they think are relatable.

Social Media

While corporations have the means to produce films, television, and video games, individuals can produce and consume social media. In the United States, it is easy to create a Twitter account or YouTube video. For example, in 2012, one of the students in my sociology class posted a video on YouTube called "I Am Not Trayvon Martin," which quickly went viral. Her statement is just one example of how social media allow people with low budgets and few connections to spread a message.

Social media have the power to counter stereotypes, not just reinforce them. But how often does this happen? Are people using social media to counter stereotypes, or are they simply reproducing them?

Kopacz and Lawton (2011b) conducted an analysis of YouTube videos and found that, in contrast to mainstream media, many YouTube videos in which Native Americans played central roles were depicted as both modern members of society and active agents against discrimination. Their findings indicate that user-generated videos such as those found on YouTube have the potential to counteract stereotypes. To uncover whether these videos did in fact counter stereotypes, Kopacz and Lawton (2011a) assessed audience reactions to these videos. This second study had two central findings: (1) users preferred videos that adhered to stereotypical depictions of Native Americans, such as the wise elder and the doomed warrior; and (2) viewers also favored videos that countered stereotypes and offered accurate depictions of Native American tribal diversity and activism. Whereas previous research had only shown that viewers prefer stereotypical portrayals, this study of user-generated videos found that there is also a positive audience reception to counter-stereotypical portrayals. Their study suggests that social media do have the potential to work in positive ways to counter stereotypes.

One phenomenon worthy of exploration is the racial **meme**—an idea, image, video, or phrase that spreads in a culture, particularly via social media. Memes can be an effective way to get messages across because they are easy to digest and can be widely shared across a variety of social media platforms, from Twitter to Facebook to Instagram to Snapchat. The meme shown in this section plays on stereotypes and may help people see their own biases.

Social media often afford some degree of anonymity to those who wish to propagate and validate racial stereotypes. Sociologist Jessie Daniels studies online hate speech and has found that people in the United States who have created websites with overt hate speech often go unpunished. In many cases, these website creators are protected by free speech laws and can post overtly racist messages on their own site without facing any legal troubles. Daniels (2008) has also found "cloaked" websites that seek to deceive Web users by appearing to have a neutral stance but actually give false information supporting a White supremacist outlook. One example of such a website is www.martinlutherking.org, which at first glance appears to be a tribute to civil rights leader Dr. Martin Luther King Jr. but in fact aims to undermine him and other civil rights leaders.

Twitter and other social media platforms can be used to debate racial issues. In 2012, the much-awaited film *The Hunger Games* was released, based on the novel with the same title. The movie was a box-office success and exceeded expectations. However, some viewers were surprised about the race of the characters and made their feelings public. In the book, author Suzanne Collins describes several of the main characters as having "dark brown skin." When viewers went to the premiere and saw that several of the main characters were African American—Amandla Stenberg as Rue, Lenny Kravitz as Cinna, and Dayo Okeniyi as Thresh—some were disappointed and made their views known on Twitter:

> "why does rue have to be black not gonna lie kinda ruined the movie"
> "for the record, im still pissed that rue is black"
> "rue is too black for what I pictured"
> "call me racist but when i found out rue was black her death wasn't as sad"
> "why did the producer make all the good characters black smh [shaking my head]"
> "ewwww rue is black?? I'm not watching"
> "awkward moment when Rue is some black girl and not the little blonde innocent girl you picture"

These tweets make it evident that some viewers would like to keep their heroes White. These viewers were able to share their ways of thinking via social media. However, these tweets soon caught the attention of bloggers, who called them out.

In contrast, some social media responses and campaigns can lead to positive changes, as we saw leading up to the 2017 Academy Awards. In 2015, the four acting categories included only White nominees. Activist April Reign started the hashtag #OscarsSoWhite in response, but in 2016, these four categories were again all White. This time, however, the hashtag went viral and caught the attention of Hollywood. Filmmaker Spike Lee, actress Jada Pinkett, and others announced they would be boycotting the ceremony. As a result of the outcry, in June 2016 the Academy extended 683 new membership invitations, 41 percent of which went to people of color. In 2017, the Oscar nominations and winners reflected much greater diversity—the winners of two of the four Oscars given to actors were African Americans. This represents a remarkable turn in the history of the Oscars. Additionally, Dev Patel was the first actor of Indian descent to be nominated in 13 years, and Mahershala Ali was the first Muslim actor to ever win an Oscar (The Times of India 2017).

In 2019, three of the four Oscars in acting categories went to actors of color: Rami Malek won best actor, Regina King won best supporting actress, and Mahershala Ali won best supporting actor. In 2020, however, only one actor of color was nominated across all acting categories: Cynthia Erivo for best actress. However, she lost to Renée Zellweger and, in 2020, like in most years, no actors of color won awards for acting. 2020 did bring another surprise: *Parasite* won the Best Picture Award, making it the first non-English-language film to win an award. Set in South Korea, it also had an all-Asian cast.

In 2019, people of color made up 40 percent of the U.S. population, but just 17 percent of Oscar nominees since 2016 (see Figure 4-3). A report by the *Financial Times* visualizes these trends, showing that although there have been increases in the numbers of nominees and lead actors over time, the percentages still lag behind the representation in the population. They also show how the 7,000 members of the Academy of Motion Picture Arts and Sciences continues to be primarily White and male (see Figure 4-4). Although women and people of color are added as new members each year, the Academy still has a long way to go before it is representative of the larger population—and of cinema attendees.

As another positive example of the power of social media, the previously mentioned study by Kopacz and Lawton (2011b) found that YouTube videos have the potential to counteract stereotypes. The

FIGURE 4-3

ETHNIC MINORITY SHARE OF THE U.S. POPULA-TION, LEAD FILM ACTORS AND OSCAR-NOMINATED ACTORS (%)

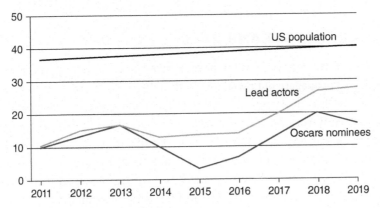

FIGURE 4-4

DIVERSITY OF THE ACADEMY ITSELF OVER TIME (%)

The Academy is growing more diverse, but progress is slow

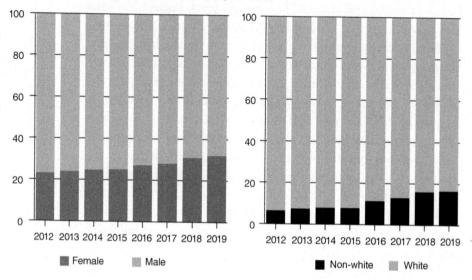

researchers assessed audience reactions to user-generated videos featuring Native Americans. Although viewers preferred videos that adhered to stereotypical depictions, they also had a positive response to videos that countered stereotypes and offered accurate depictions of Native American tribal diversity and activism. This study suggests that social media can work in positive ways to counter stereotypes. Resistance to and reproduction of racial stereotypes in new media is an emerging area of sociological inquiry, and future studies will further demonstrate how racial stereotypes are reproduced and contested in this realm.

MEDIA IMAGES AND RACIAL INEQUALITY

Pop-culture representations have evolved over time and yet continue to propagate old racial ideologies. While the seventeenth- and eighteenth-century representation of Black men as lazy served to rationalize slavery, the current representation of Black men as thugs serves to rationalize astonishingly high rates of incarceration. And while the eighteenth-century representation of Black women as sexually depraved served to rationalize rape, the current representation of Black women as promiscuous in films and other media serves to rationalize cuts in social services. Sociologist Patricia Hill Collins argues that such rationalizations rely heavily on mass media representations of African Americans. She defines and describes a new racism, one which emerged in the post–Civil Rights era.

Modern-day representations of African Americans as thugs and whores are some examples of what Collins calls **controlling images** (2004, 165), or raced, classed, and gendered media depictions of a particular racial or ethnic group. Throughout U.S. history, Black people have been represented as grotesque, physically resistant, and hypersexual. These representations create a fascination with blackness, but they also define what Whites are not. In this way, every representation of non-Whites also defines whiteness. If Black people are represented as embodying physical strength, then Whites can see themselves as embodying intelligence—brawn versus brain. The same could be said of stereotypes of other groups: for example, representations of Latinos as gangbangers and gardeners send the message that Whites are not. These stereotypical representations not only shape how Americans view one another but also fuel inequalities.

Common representations of Latinos as criminals serve to rationalize the disproportionate rates of imprisonment for Latinos. Representations of Latina women as hypersexual serve to rationalize cuts in welfare by spreading the idea that Latinas are immoral or culturally unworthy. Other common representations of Latinxs show them in some form of service to Whites, reinforcing the idea that they are of a lower class and destined for low-wage occupations. The maid and the gardener keep the well-to-do neighborhoods looking nice while fulfilling the sexual fantasies of the Whites who live there.

Representations of Arabs and Muslims often propagate Islamophobia—the systematic marginalization of Muslims—and Orientalist stereotypes, and they also work to rationalize foreign interventions. Hollywood has played an important role in portraying the Arab world as an exotic place that requires White Westerners to civilize its people and drag them into the twenty-first century. Shoba Sharad Rajgopal argues that representations of Arab women as veiled, traditional, and oppressed work to reinforce the stereotype that Western culture is "dynamic, progressive, and egalitarian," whereas Arab cultures are "backward, barbaric, and

patriarchal" (2010, 145). She further contends that these stereotypes reinforce the idea that Americans needed to go to Iraq and
Afghanistan to rescue women from themselves and, in particular,
from their brutal and oppressive Arab husbands.

Media representations often give White characters more depth and re-
deeming qualities than people of color. Such portrayals shape our perceptions and support the notion that it is somehow right or reasonable for
Whites to do better in the United States on nearly every social measure.

RACED, CLASSED, AND GENDERED MEDIA IMAGES

As we have seen increasing numbers of people of color in popular culture, we have also seen a variety of representations across class lines.
African Americans, for example, are no longer portrayed only as mammies or con artists. Instead, many are doctors and lawyers. Portrayals of
people of color on television are raced, gendered, and classed—meaning that the representations vary by race, class, and gender, and that
they influence how we think about various racial groups in this country. Patricia Hill Collins's (2004) concept of "controlling images"
argues that the media produce class- and gender-specific depictions
of people of African descent in popular culture. She further contends
that "mass media has generated class-specific images of Black women
that help rationalize and shape the new racism of desegregated,
color-blind America." Collins's analysis of the representations of Black
men and women in popular culture is useful, and I describe it in detail
later in this chapter. In addition, her idea of controlling images can be
extended to other groups, including Latinxs, Native Americans, Asians,
and Arabs.

Collins maintains that the vast majority of representations of Black
characters on television fall into the raced and classed categories presented in Table 4-1. She argues that these images influence how Black
people treat each other and how others treat them. However, this does
not mean that these images *determine* how Black people are treated.
Instead, their pervasive nature means that they affect all people in our
society. Faced with these images, we can: (1) internalize them and
accept them as reality, (2) resist them and develop our own ideas about
Black masculinity and femininity, or (3) ignore them. Any of these reactions requires some action on our part and will affect how we think
of ourselves and others.

TABLE 4-1

Raced and Classed Categories of Black Representations on Television

	Working-Class	Middle-Class
WOMEN	BITCH: Aggressive, loud, rude, and pushy BAD BITCH: Materialistic, sexualized; iconized in hip-hop culture; modern version of the Jezebel BAD BLACK MOTHER: (BBM): Mother who neglects her children; characterized by bad values; welfare queen FEMALE ATHLETE: Feminized; focuses on the family; lesbianism erased	MODERN MAMMY: Loyal female servant; focuses on work and subservience to White male boss BLACK LADY: Designed to counter images of Black women's promiscuity; focuses on the home EDUCATED BLACK BITCH: Has money, power, and job; is beautiful; success depends on her being tamed by men
MEN	ATHLETE: Physically strong; harsh temper; needs to be controlled by coaches THUG OR GANGSTA: Inherently physical and, unlike the athlete, his physicality is neither admired nor easily exploited for White gain BLACK PIMP: Involved in illegal activity; hustler; uses women for economic gain; refuses to work; promiscuous BLACK RAPIST: Hypersexual, desirous of White women	SIDEKICK: Black buddy in service to Whites; origins lie in Uncle Tom; loyal to Whites; asexual, nonviolent, safe, nonthreatening SISSY: Effeminate and derogated Black masculinity; gay characteristics, a queen; reinforces heterosexuality of others

Based on P. H. Collins 2004.

Collins restricted her analyses primarily to African Americans. The idea of controlling images can be applied to other groups, however, as it is evident that stereotypical representations vary by gender. Table 4-2 lists some examples of prominent gendered stereotypes of Arabs, Native Americans, Latinxs, and Asians. As with African Americans, these controlling images account for the vast majority of representations of these groups. Moreover, each of these depictions also defines what Whites are not. White men are not terrorists or savages; they are peaceful and civilized. White women are not exotic or hot-blooded; they are reserved and ethical.

Each of these representations is gendered. Arab women are rarely portrayed as terrorists, and men are almost always the perpetrators, not the victims, of gendered violence (Rajgopal 2010). Native American men are usually portrayed either as savages (cruel and primitive men who brutalize White people), as wise elders who use their knowledge to help Whites, or as warriors who are romanticized but know that their tribe will ultimately meet its doom. In contrast, Native American women are usually portrayed as either princesses who fall in love with a White hero or as promiscuous

TABLE 4-2
Prominent Gendered Stereotypes by Racial/Ethnic Group

	Men	Women
ARABS	Terrorist	Veiled victim
	Immoral billionaire	Exotic seductress
	Haggler	Maiden
NATIVE AMERICANS	Savage	Squaw
	Sidekick	Princess
	Wise elder	Matriarch
	Doomed warrior	
LATINXS	Latin lover	Hot-blooded Latina
	Greaser/bandito	Maid
	Gangbanger	Abuela (grandma)
	Gardener	Mexican spitfire
	Buffoon	
ASIANS	Buddy	Butterfly
	Threatening foreigner	Dragon Lady
	Martial artist	
	Corrupt businessman	

Based on Rajgopal (2010); Kopacz and Lawton (2011a, 2011b); Rodríguez (1997).

squaws (Kopacz and Lawton 2011a). When Latinos on television are not involved in urban violence as either criminals or police officers, they are most likely to be found in unskilled labor occupations such as janitor or gardener. This portrayal of Latinos as subservient is complemented by the portrayal of the Latin lover, who, despite his success in meeting the sexual desires of the Anglo woman, ends up being the "Latin loser" when his lover is in turn conquered by an Anglo man (Rodríguez 1997). Latina women, in contrast, tend to be portrayed as hot-blooded women, maids, or *abuelas* (grandmothers) who are out of touch with modern life (Berg 2002). Asian women tend to be portrayed either as Dragon Ladies or as Butterflies, both of which highlight their sexuality. In contrast, Asian men are usually desexualized and emasculated. These gendered stereotypes reinforce prevalent stereotypes about people of color in the United States and also work to define Whites as morally superior.

From "What's Wrong with Cultural Appropriation? These 9 Answers Reveal Its Harm"

by Maisha Z. Johnson

What Cultural Appropriation Is (and Isn't)

In short: Cultural appropriation is when somebody adopts aspects of a culture that's not their own.

But that's only the most basic definition.

A deeper understanding of cultural appropriation also refers to a particular *power dynamic* in which members of a dominant culture take elements from a culture of people who have been systematically oppressed *by that dominant* group.

That's why cultural appropriation is not the same as cultural exchange, when people share mutually with each other—because cultural exchange lacks that systemic power dynamic.

. . .

1. It Trivializes Violent Historical Oppression

To you, it can feel like a big deal to have to give up something you've borrowed from another culture and incorporated into your life, especially if it's meaningful to you in some way.

For example, owners and fans of the NFL team the Washington Redsk*ns have largely come to the defense of the name, pulling out every reason including "honoring Indians," "keeping to tradition," and "you're being too sensitive," in reaction to Indigenous activists calling for the end of Indian mascots.

The fans and the NFL are emotionally and financially invested in the name and don't want to take extra time and money to change it. And that makes sense.

But consider this: When violence systematically targets a group of people through genocide, slavery, or colonization, the resulting trauma lasts through generations.

So here's what's at stake for the Native people: The term "redsk*n" comes from the time when the colonial and state governments and companies paid white people to kill Native Americans and used their scalps or even genitalia (to prove their sex), a.k.a. "red skins," as proof of their "Indian kill."

Given that history, is it a surprise that so many Native people are angry about football fans who think they're "honoring" Native people with this mascot and their excuses?

(continued)

 *continued.*

From "What's Wrong with Cultural Appropriation? These 9 Answers Reveal Its Harm"

We should be ashamed of this time in our history—and we should be working to heal the damage from it.

But instead, the NFL (and other sports teams) insist on celebrating the genocide of a people for fun and profit.

. . .

3. It Makes Things "Cool" for White People—But "Too Ethnic" for People of Color

The US is a white-dominated society, and for proof of that, search no further than the way immigrants, Indigenous people, and people of color are criticized for the things that distinguish us from white Americans.

For example, standards of professionalism hold back all kinds of people who aren't white men. As a Black woman, there are many jobs that would bar me if I wore cornrows, dreadlocks, or an afro—some of the most natural ways to keep up my hair.

So for me, wearing my hair naturally is a meaningful declaration that I believe in my natural beauty. It's risky to make this declaration in a society that says I must aspire to whiteness have value.

Compare that to fashion magazines' reception of white teenager Kylie Jenner's "epic" cornrows or "edgy" dreadlocks.

When Black women have to fight for acceptance with the same styles a young white woman can be admired for, what message does that send to Black women and girls?

It says that our natural beauty isn't beautiful at all—and that our features are only appealing when they're adopted by white women.

. . .

7. It Perpetuates Racist Stereotypes

As Dr. Adrienne Keene of Native Appropriations puts it, "You are pretending to be a race that you are not, and are drawing upon stereotypes to do so."

Katy Perry, for example, said that her performance as a geisha during the 2013 American Music Awards was an homage to Japanese culture. But she completely misrepresented what she claimed to be honoring—and used a huge platform to perpetuate negative, all-too-common stereotypes about Asian women.

With her single "Unconditionally," Perry sang about undying love while playing up the image of a passive, submissive sexual object of an Asian woman.

For her, it was just a character—but this stereotypical image has real consequences for Asian women in the US. Their experiences with dating, racialized sexual harassment, and fetishization reveal that white men *actually* expect Asian women to live up to the "exotic geisha girl" stereotype of being sexually submissive and docile.

Lauren sMash described her experiences in "Yellow Fever: Dating As an Asian Woman" like this: "It is dehumanizing at best to constantly be compared to a stereotype and to have people chasing you not as a person, but as an embodiment of the stereotypes that they use to define you."

At the end of the day, Katy Perry got to take the costume off and return to the millions of dollars it helped make her and to the people who see her as a dynamic human being, and not just a demure caricature.

Asian women, on the other hand, have to deal with the racist and sexist social norms that Perry helped perpetuate, which is what happens when the only mainstream image of your sexuality is a negative stereotype reinforced constantly by cultural appropriation.

It's certainly not harmless or respectful to misrepresent people's culture and spread the toxic myths that harm them.

. . .

9. It Prioritizes the Feelings of Privileged People over Justice for Marginalized People

One of the main objections to avoiding cultural appropriation comes down to "free speech."

You should have the right to express yourself however you want to—and you do. Nobody can force you to stop taking things from other cultures. The marginalized people whose cultures are appropriated don't have the institutional power to force you to stop, even if they wanted to.

But claiming that the dominant culture has a *right* to take freely from disempowered groups sounds a lot like the lie of the "white man's burden" from the past. Colonizers used this concept to claim they had a "duty" to take land, resources, and identity from Indigenous people—trying to justify everything from slavery to genocide.

We have a lot of work to do to heal from the impact of oppression from the past through present day. Many examples of cultural appropriation may seem like not a big deal, or like we should have "more important" things to worry about.

But changing oppressive everyday norms is a huge part of the work. It's one of the ways we can help stop the way society dehumanizes, erases, and ostracizes people of color.

If the choice is between your freedom to wear a costume because it could be fun, or an ethnic group's ability to maintain the sacredness of a tradition that helps them resist harm, it's clear that skipping the costume puts you on the side of anti-oppression.

(continued)

 *continued.*

From "What's Wrong with Cultural Appropriation? These 9 Answers Reveal Its Harm"

And, hint: That's the side you want to be on.

***

I'm not saying you automatically can't enjoy Mexican food if you're not Mexican, or do a yoga-inspired practice if you're not Indian, or use any other culturally specific practice in the US.

But I *am* encouraging you to be thoughtful about using things from other cultures, to consider the context, and learn about the best practices to show respect.

Maybe you've worn a costume you didn't know had a violent history, or you had the intention of honoring a culture in a way you didn't realize was offensive. Or you learned about these oppressive histories, but you're just now realizing that what you learned wasn't even close to the entire truth.

So now, what's your next step in incorporating this information into your anti-racist work?

Challenging stereotypes? Calling out appropriation when you see it? Spreading the word about the dire need to change the inaccurate way we learn about oppressed people's struggles?

At the very least, you know you have alternatives to disrespecting cultures that aren't your own.

Don't keep making other cultures invisible under our society's "melting pot" ambitions. Make room for all of us to thrive by having fun without oppression.

Source: Johnson, Maisha Z. 2015. What's wrong with cultural appropriation? These 9 answers reveal its harm. *Everyday Feminism*, June 14. https://everydayfeminism.com/2015/06/cultural-appropriation-wrong.

CONCLUSION AND DISCUSSION

Within the television industry, debates over the representation of people of color often revolve around a sort of "chicken and egg" question: Do the media create or simply reflect popular stereotypes? For example, would a film that portrayed Black women as demure intellectuals and White women as gangbangers be unsuccessful because it would seem unrealistic?

The stereotypical portrayals we see in the media today certainly were not invented by the media. Instead, they are part of our history and were created decades or even centuries ago. In this chapter, we have seen both how these stereotypes have evolved and how they continue to be part and parcel of popular media. We have also seen some of the consequences of these stereotypes: how they work to reproduce and rationalize racial inequalities. This raises the question of whether the media have a responsibility to try to alter stereotypes.

One recurring complaint about representations of people of color in the media is that they lack the depth that White characters have. One way that this perception could change is by including more people of color as writers and producers of popular media. Shonda Rhimes, the creator of the popular series *Grey's Anatomy, Private Practice, Scandal,* and *How to Get Away with Murder,* is a prominent African American woman with a significant role in creating television shows in the United States. Rhimes's shows have garnered praise both for including more characters of color and for giving those characters more depth than we are used to seeing on other shows. Thus, with the inclusion of more people of color in Hollywood as creators of media, we will perhaps see fewer stereotypes.

One of the most prominent African American male showrunners is Tyler Perry, who is widely criticized for his use of stereotypical depictions of Black women in his works, including *House of Payne, Diary of a Mad Black Woman, Madea Goes to Jail,* and many other television shows, films, and stage plays. Although Tyler Perry has the ability to portray Black women in a nuanced fashion, he is still very much aware that the primary motive for the entertainment industry is making a profit. For Perry, it is clear that making fun of African Americans sells. In 2011, *Forbes* magazine named Tyler Perry the highest-paid man in entertainment—with five movies and two television series, he earned $130 million between May 2010 and May 2011 (Pomerantz 2011). Perry's body of work shows that simply having Black producers is not enough if the goal is to reduce stereotypes.

To return to the question of the media's responsibility for reproducing stereotypes, there are two sides to this issue. On the one hand, you could argue that the media are responsible to the public, as the public constitutes their customer base. On the other hand, you could contend that the media are simply responding to market forces and giving their customers what they desire. What do you think?

THINKING
ABOUT
RACIAL
JUSTICE
CAN YOU THINK of a positive representation of a person of color in film, television, or new media today? Describe the character and explain the extent to which they conform to the stereotypes mentioned in this chapter. To what extent do positive representations of people of color contribute to a more racially just society?

Key Terms

stereotype   105

enlightened racism   108

Mammy   110

Sapphire   110

Jezebel   110

Dragon Lady   116

Butterfly   116

meme   121

controlling images   125

CHECK YOUR UNDERSTANDING

4.1 How are racial stereotypes propagated in popular culture?
Media images shape our beliefs by creating and reinforcing stereotypes.

Q How have representations of African Americans changed since the 1950s?

Q What are some of the common stereotypes of Latinxs, Asians, and Arab Americans on television?

Q What are the historical origins of stereotypical portrayals of Native Americans?

4.2 How have new media changed the way stereotypes are spread and countered?
Old stereotypes prevail even in new media such as video games and social media, which have an increasingly important influence.

Q How do user-generated media affect the spread of stereotypes?

4.3 How do media images and messages support the rationalization of racial inequality?
Media images and messages are not harmless: they can support racial inequalities by shaping stereotypes about racial and ethnic minorities as well as about Whites.

Q In what areas have controlling images exacerbated inequalities?

4.4 How are media representations raced, classed, and gendered?

Media images vary not only by racial group but also by race and class.

🅠 What are the historical origins of the stereotype of Black women as sexually promiscuous?

Critical Thinking

1. Television shows change constantly. Do the stereotypes mentioned in this chapter apply to the shows you currently watch? Why or why not? Pick two popular shows and assess the extent to which the non-White characters fit into stereotypical roles. Are the Latinx characters portrayed as hypersexual? Are the Asians and Native Americans stoic? Describe at least two characters, and then assess the extent to which those characters fit into the controlling images for their group.

2. Do you think social media platforms can be useful in countering racial stereotypes, or do you think they simply provide an arena for the proliferation of stereotypes? Use at least one example from social media to make your case.

3. Give an example of a stereotype from the media that is used to rationalize racial inequality.

4. Why does Patricia Hill Collins argue that media representations are race-, class-, and gender-specific?

Talking about Race

The success of television shows and films is often dependent on word of mouth. If you watch a film or show that breaks away from traditional stereotypes, you can talk to your friends and family about it and encourage them to watch it. When you have that conversation, you can refer to what you learned in this chapter about stereotypes and the importance of broad representation. You can also post your thoughts on social media and play a larger role in promoting media that avoid negative stereotypes.

Learn more with this chapter's digital tools, including video clips from the author, web links, filmography, and chapter self-assessment quizzes at www.oup.com/he/golash-boza-brief3e.

5

Colorism and Skin-Color Stratification

AS YOU READ

5.1 When and how did colorism and skin-color stratification originate?
5.2 How does colorism differ across societies?
5.3 How does skin color relate to gender and beauty?

Whereas racism relies on the belief that some races are better than others, **colorism** is the idea that, within races, lighter is better. Colorism refers primarily to skin color, but it also encompasses physical characteristics that are related to skin color, such as eye color, hair color and texture, and facial features (Glenn 2009).

The prevalence of colorism has led to **skin-color stratification**, in which resources such as income and status are distributed unequally according to skin color. In the United States, lighter-skinned people generally have higher incomes and education than their darker-skinned counterparts and are more likely to own homes and marry. Darker-skinned people are more likely to be arrested, receive longer prison sentences and have lower job statuses on average than lighter-skinned people (Hochschild and Weaver 2007; Kizer 2017). Verna Keith and Cedric Herring (2001) found that lighter-skinned African Americans have advantages over their darker-skinned counterparts in terms of earnings, education, and occupations. Eduardo Bonilla-Silva and David R. Dietrich (2009) contend that the United States is a **pigmentocracy**—a society in which Black, Asian, and Latinx people have different social statuses according to their skin color.

Skin-color stratification is also evident among immigrants to the United States from Africa, Asia, and Latin America. Using data from the 2003 New Immigrant Survey, Joni Hersch (2008) found that darker-skinned immigrants generally earn less than their lighter-skinned counterparts. This nationally representative survey included interviews with people who had recently been granted legal permanent residence in the United States. Each interviewee's skin color was rated on a scale of 1 to 10, with 1 being the lightest and 10 the darkest. Overall, Hersch found that for immigrants from Africa, Asia, and Latin America, light skin color is associated with higher wages across the spectrum. There is a pay disparity of 17 percent between the lightest-skinned immigrants and the darkest-skinned immigrants, even if we account for gender, education, English-language skills, visa type, and occupation. A more recent study built on these findings, showing that dark-skinned immigrants experience less upward mobility in the United States (Han 2020). This pay disparity indicates that discrimination based on skin color likely does occur in the United States.

THE HISTORY OF COLORISM

When and how did colorism originate, not only in the United States but also around the world? Some scholars argue that the preference for light skin stems from the history of slavery and genocide in the Americas. Their argument is that the preference for light skin is fundamentally a preference for whiteness and thus that colorism has the same history as racism (Hunter 2005, 2007). For these thinkers, colorism is a modern phenomenon. Scholars who focus on Asia (Rondilla and Spickard 2007; Saraswati 2010, 2012) attribute the preference for light skin to earlier ideas that equated leisure with light skin and work with dark skin. Most scholars of colorism would agree that colorism is a global phenomenon, with a long history and distinct manifestations around the world.

The Origins of Colorism in the Americas

Colorism has existed in the United States since the colonial era. The Africans who were brought to the North American colonies as slaves were primarily dark-skinned. Soon after the arrival of Africans in the Americas, the progeny of Black and White people became a new class of mixed-race people, known as **mulattos**, who were darker than White people but lighter than Black people. At first, mulattos were officially recognized as a distinct category in the United States. In fact, the U.S. census included a mulatto category from 1850 to 1910. However, eventually both law and social custom changed, and **hypodescent**— the idea that having any amount of Black ancestry makes you Black— became more prevalent.

Each state had the authority to define which people would be classified as Black. In some states, an individual was legally Black if one of his or her grandparents was Black (i.e., if he or she was one-quarter Black). In other states, an individual was Black if his or her great-grandparents were Black. In still other states, an individual was considered Black if he or she was one-thirty-second Black. These laws were eventually abolished in the 1960s (Telles 2009). However, they have had a lasting impact in that people with relatively little African ancestry (and thus very light skin) can be considered Black. The existence of a wide color spectrum in the Black community is one factor that has enabled colorism to flourish.

Skin-color stratification was prevalent during the era of slavery: lighter-skinned slaves were more likely to work in the house instead of the fields, to be taught to read, and to be manumitted (freed). The manumission of some slaves led to a small class of freedmen who tended to be lighter in skin tone than their enslaved counterparts. These lighter-skinned Black people eventually formed the core of the Black elite in the United States; hence, skin color has been mapped onto social status in the African American community for centuries (Hunter 2005).

The association of light skin with elite status continued into the twentieth century. Jewish American anthropologist Melville Herskovits conducted a study of Black people in Harlem in the 1920s and found that the Black elite was disproportionately light-skinned and that Black men preferred light-skinned partners. His study revealed that whereas only 9 percent of the Harlem Black elites were very dark-skinned, 28.9 percent of the elites were very light-skinned. Herskovits also found that in over half of Harlem couples, wives were lighter than husbands, revealing that men often preferred lighter-skinned women and that women were able to marry higher-status darker-skinned men. Within the Black community, lighter skin was valued more highly than dark skin. Additionally, light skin became associated with elite status. Thus, the desire to be light was connected both to the idea that White was better and to the idea that light skin meant higher class.

Consequently, skin bleaches and hair straighteners were very common in Harlem in the 1920s. Skin bleaches that promised to provide women with "light skin that men can't resist" formed a substantial portion of the cosmetics products sold in Harlem at the time (Dorman 2011). The practice of skin bleaching persists today: Christopher A. D. Charles (2011) found that pharmacies and beauty supply stores in Harlem were still selling bleaching products in 2010. Moreover, the labels on these

In Harlem in the 1920s, the Black elite were disproportionately light-skinned.

products devalued Black skin by promising to help customers with "problems" associated with dark skin.

In Latin America, a skin-color hierarchy has existed for centuries. During the period that Latin American countries were Spanish colonies, the Spaniards developed an elaborate system of *castas* based on ancestry that determined one's social and legal ranking in society. By the end of the colonial period in 1821, over one hundred possible categories were memorialized in a series of *casta* paintings. The categories included *españoles* (Spaniards), *indios* (indigenous people), **mestizos** (persons with one Spanish and one indigenous parent), *castizos* (persons with one mestizo parent and one Spanish parent), and *mulattos* (persons with one African parent and one Spanish parent). The categories went on to divide people into over one hundred different possible mixtures, each with its own name. These categories were based on ancestry, not color. Nevertheless, we can say that, generally, more Spanish ancestry meant both lighter skin and more prestige. These categories are no longer used in Latin America, but the inequalities that stemmed from them persist (Telles and Steele 2012).

Brazil, in contrast to the United States and Spanish America, never had a system of official classification whereby a person with a certain amount of African ancestry would be legally considered Black. Instead, in Brazil, usually only a person who looks Black is considered Black, whereas a person who looks White is considered White, regardless of his or her actual ancestry. The Brazilian census classifies people as White, **pardo** (brown), and Black, and the term *mulato* (mulatto) is used in everyday language to describe people who are neither Black nor White. There is a certain amount of fluidity between these categories, and many families report Blacks, Whites, and *pardos* in their households on the Brazilian census. Although Brazil has never had laws that mandated racial segregation, racial inequality exists, and privilege is mapped along color lines, with lighter-skinned people generally having more education and income (Telles 2009). The presence of skin-color stratification in Brazil today is a relic of colonialism.

The Origins of Colorism in Asia and Africa

The preference for light skin in the Americas seems to have its roots in the period of colonization. In contrast, Asia has a longer history of colorism. As early as the late ninth century, the ancient Sanskrit text *Ramayana* featured light skin as ideal. Ayu Saraswati (2010) explains that in both the Indian and Indonesian versions of this text, beautiful women are described as having white faces that shine like the full moon. Aryan Indians spread their preference for white skin to the rest of South and Southeast Asia. In Indonesia, this predilection for light skin was reinforced during the Dutch colonial period in the nineteenth century. Colonial authorities granted preferential treatment to persons of mixed Dutch-Indonesian ancestry. When the Japanese became the colonial power in Indonesia in 1942, they also brought their fondness for lightness with them. And U.S. popular culture has made its mark in Indonesia through advertising, with blue-eyed blondes staring out of images in this primarily non-White country. In Indonesia today, dark-skinned people continue to be seen as unattractive and undesirable. As in other places, this social pattern has clear gendered dimensions: women feel more pressure than men do to alter their appearance and lighten their skin (Saraswati 2012).

What about preferences in Africa? Was there preference for light skin in this continent prior to the arrival of Europeans? There are people of every skin shade on the African continent, with lighter-skinned people living in the north and those with darker skin living close to the equator and in the south. Anthropologist Peter Frost (2006) has reviewed the evidence from several African tribes and found some evidence that a preference for lighter skin predates colonialism in Africa. In many tribes, women with brown or reddish skin are seen as more beautiful than those with very dark skin, and there are indications that these preferences are deeply rooted in these societies. For example, the languages of many tribes include value-laden terms that distinguish between skin colors, and early-twentieth-century anthropologists found preferences for lighter skin even among older Africans who were born before the arrival of Europeans in their communities (Frost 2006). Whether or not the preference for light skin predates colonialism is an unresolved question. However, it is clear that the obsession with light skin increased with colonization and the presence of large numbers of Europeans in Africa. In South Africa, for example, skin lighteners have been available since the 1930s (Thomas 2009).

The preference for light skin seems nearly universal. Despite varying local histories, these preferences have converged in the current era as a result of cultural globalization and the spread of transnational corporations that tend to promote whiter or lighter beauty ideals.

THE GLOBAL COLOR HIERARCHY

How does colorism differ across societies? Consider a 2016 commercial from Thailand for a product called Snowz, skin-whitening pills with the slogan "white makes you win." In the television advertisement, Cris Horwang—a 35-year-old actress, model, singer, and dance teacher—explains that the whiteness she has achieved through beauty products has brought her fame. She says: "Before I got to this point, the competition was very high. If I stop taking care of myself, everything I have worked for, the whiteness I have invested in, may be lost." As she is talking, another younger model comes onto the screen and Cris's skin slowly fades to charcoal black. She looks at her dark skin with despondence, and the narrator says "whiteness makes you win." The younger model smiles as the narrator adds that Snowz contains glutathione, derived from kiwi seeds which "helps you not return to black." After the Snowz pills appear on the screen Cris turns white again, and smiles return to her face.

Skin-whitening products are prevalent not only in Asia but also in Latin America, Africa, and the United States. They are evidence of a **global color hierarchy**, in which white (or light) skin is privileged and people—especially, but not exclusively, women—strive to become lighter. These dynamics play out differently in distinct areas of the world.

In Thailand, a 2016 commercial for a skin-whitening pill called Snowz proclaimed, "Just being white, you will win."

In this section, we will examine three areas of the world: Asia, Latin America, and Africa, as well as the **diaspora**, or dispersion, of their populations in the United States.

Asia and Asian Americans

The privileging of light skin in Asia and among Asian Americans has its roots in ancient Aryan Indian beauty ideals, Japanese and Chinese ideas of white skin as a sign of leisure, and colonial domination of India and Indonesia by European powers. Today, women from Thailand, South Korea, Vietnam, Japan, China, the Philippines, Indonesia, and India use skin-whitening creams in an effort to make their skin as light as possible, and they even undergo eyelid surgery to widen their eyes (Saraswati 2010, 2012). In India, the preference for light skin is also connected to the caste system. Although not all high-caste members (Brahmins) are light, a pattern can be seen whereby higher-caste people in India tend to be lighter than those of lower caste. In addition, the term for caste, *varna*, literally means "color," and there has been some historical association of Brahmins with whiteness and the untouchables with blackness. In India and across Asia, there are historical and present-day advantages associated with light skin, especially for women (Parameswaran and Cardoza 2009).

These preferences for light skin in Asia have carried over to Asian Americans in the United States. Research by Joanne Rondilla and Paul Spickard (2007) reveals a fascinating aspect of skin-tone discrimination among Asian Americans: the preference for light skin is omnipresent, yet Asian Americans do not want to be *too* White. The researchers tell the stories of a Vietnamese American woman who uses a destructive skin-whitening cream because she feels excluded by her ethnic group and a Filipina woman who stays out of the sun to avoid being called "dark." On the flip side, they also describe a Chinese woman whose great-grandmother was French who is excluded from social groups because her freckles and reddish hair make her look too White, as well as a woman whose mother is Japanese and father is White who struggles to feel accepted in either community. Based on these interviews and other evidence, Rondilla and Spickard argue that light skin is preferred in Asian American communities but that this does not signal a desire for whiteness.

Fair, But Not So Lovely: India's Obsession with Skin Whitening

By Neha Dixit

When I was born, my paternal grandmother wrote a letter to my maternal grandfather: "A girl is born. She is dark complexioned. You'd better prepare for her future."

It is not clear if my grandfather was offended by the doomsday prophecy for the dark-skinned me, or if he just wanted to win the upper hand. He wrote back to her, "Those who think [her future is bleak] should look at their faces in a dirty puddle." His response created a rift between my paternal and maternal family that has never healed.

I grew up in north India in the 1990s. My Brahmin family was full of government servants who were still carrying the colonial white man's burden of racial prejudices and

Satirical depiction of Indian marriage ads to highlight colorism.

Source: Illustration by Srishti Gupta Roy, appearing in Bright Magazine, July 10, 2019, edition.

superiority complexes. Growing up in the close proximity of a large extended family, I was the only dark child. "Kaali-kaluti, baigan looti / Blacky-black smeared, she robbed the color of an eggplant," my cousins would taunt when they wanted to have a laugh at my expense. I laughed along with them, eager to fit in.

My skin color was particularly concerning to my mother, since we were an upper-caste Brahmin family. Anytime someone would call me dark, my fair-skinned mother would correct them and tell them I was "wheatish," one of the many euphemisms in India for brown skin. It was her way of comforting herself that her daughter was a tad bit higher in the hierarchy than truly dark people.

During a trip to a north Indian village, an old woman walked up to me to say, "Every morning, at 5 a.m., you should drink half a cup of fresh, non-boiled cow milk. The complexion of your child-to-be will be fair." I plastered a smile on my face. I was not even pregnant. But colorism runs so deep that this was the best advice she thought to offer me.

Women have passed on similar age old "wisdom" to attain fairness for generations. "Apply gram flour, milk, and turmeric on her face daily," my mother was told when I was a kid, so I "would not look like a Madrasan anymore." Madrasan refers to a person from the southern city of Madras, now Chennai. North Indians are typically lighter-skinned than South Indians, who live in a hotter climate.

As a dark girl who did not use bleaching or fairness products, my family thought I spent my life compensating for my "unfortunate" complexion. Whether it was doing well in school, riding a heavy power scooter (unthinkable for a teenage girl in small-town India), or being the first girl in the family to pursue higher education in another city, not having to worry about protecting my skin turned out to be a blessing in disguise.

I have been able to hold a steady career as a journalist, be financially independent, and be the first girl in my extended family to choose her own life partner—all seen as ways I have made up for not being "good looking," or more accurately, light-skinned.

My dark complexion turned out to be a ticket to freedom.

Source: https://brightthemag.com/fair-but-not-so-lovely-indias-obsession-with-skin-whitening-beauty-body-image-bleaching-4d6ba9c9743d

Latin America and Latinxs

In Latin America, people of mixed ancestry have historically been considered *mulatos* (when they have African and European ancestry) or mestizos (when they have European and indigenous ancestry).

Mestizo is an official classification in Mexico, Peru, and other countries, and *pardo* (brown) is an official classification in Brazil. Within this system, only people who are very dark-skinned are considered Black, and only those who both are dark-skinned and display indigenous cultural features are considered indigenous (Golash-Boza 2011). Thus, you could find a family in which one child is considered Black, another *mulato*, and still another White. In these families, often the lighter-skinned children are given preferential treatment (Twine 1998; Hordge-Freeman 2015). Latin Americans often strategically choose romantic partners who are lighter in skin tone than themselves, with the hope that their children will be lighter and thus better positioned in society. In Spanish, this strategy is called *mejorando la raza*, or improving the race, and is common across Latin America (Sue 2009).

Latin American countries are marked by a skin-color hierarchy in which lighter-skinned people possess a disproportionate share of the resources. Because of the existence of intermediate categories, we can say that Whites are often at the top of the hierarchy, mestizos and mulattos in the middle, and Black and indigenous people at the bottom (Telles and Steele 2012).

Edward Telles and Liza Steele (2012) conducted a study in which they compared skin color and educational attainment across Latin America. They wanted to know whether or not lighter-skinned Latin Americans are more likely to complete high school and go to college than darker-skinned Latin Americans. Using a recent and innovative data set that contained information about skin color and education for nearly 40,000 people in twenty-three Latin American countries, they were able to explore the relationship between skin color and each respondent's educational attainment. These data allowed them to ask whether lighter-skinned people completed more years of schooling on average than darker-skinned people. In most Latin American and Caribbean countries, they found that lighter-skinned people were more likely to have higher educational attainment than darker-skinned people. This trend was most prominent in Andean countries such as Peru and Bolivia, where darker-skinned people receive an average of eight years of schooling, as compared to the thirteen years received by lighter-skinned people. In all the countries except four—Panama, Suriname, Belize, and Guyana—their study revealed that lighter-skinned people had more years of education than darker-skinned people. A study of 2,935 Mexican adults and adolescents in Mexico confirmed that not only do darker-skinned people have less education, but that they also have lower wages and are less likely to experience upward mobility than their darker-skinned counterparts (Campos-Vaszquez and Medina-Cortina 2019).

The prevalence of skin-color stratification in Latin America raises the question of whether this stratification is also present among Latin American immigrants in the United States. Do lighter-skinned Latinxs in the United States have more education, income, and resources? Recent studies help us to understand the extent of skin color stratification among Latinxs in the United States today.

Using a wide variety of measures, researchers have consistently found that Latinxs with darker skin tones are disadvantaged relative to their lighter-skinned counterparts. Visser (2016) found that darker-skinned Puerto Ricans experience lower job quality relative to their lighter-skinned counterparts. Alexis Rosenblum and colleagues (2016) found that Latin American immigrants with darker skin tones earn less than their lighter-skinned counterparts, even when taking into account other relevant factors such as age, education, and labor market experience. Several studies have found that Latinxs with darker skin are more likely to be stopped and arrested by police officers (White 2015; Alcalá and Montoya 2018; Finkeldey and Demuth 2019). Ekeoma Uzogara (2019) found that medium- and darker-skinned Latinas experienced more discrimination than light-skinned Latinas in Chicago. These studies all confirm that skin color matters for Latinx Americans.

Africa and the African Diaspora

Jemima Pierre (2008) describes a scene in downtown Accra, Ghana, where large billboards that feature a very light-skinned African woman to advertise *Gel Eclaircissant*—a bleaching treatment—are plastered across the town. Pierre asks how Ghana, "a proud black post-colonial African nation with an established history of Pan-Africanism," can have such blatant anti-Black advertisements. To answer this question, Pierre argues that skin-bleaching practices are a reflection of the ways that processes of racialization are alive and well in post-colonial Ghana. Thus, even though Ghana is a proud, Black nation, it is not immune to global White supremacy—a system of global power relations that includes both an ideology of White racial superiority and a set of practices that benefit White people (Beiso-De Jesús and Pierre 2020). It is through global White supremacy that Ghana and other African nations are connected to the African diaspora, where a preference for light skin is prevalent. Additionally, many African countries are marked by a hierarchy in which lighter-skinned, mixed-race people occupy more positions of power and have more economic resources than darker-skinned people (Lewis, Robkin, Gaska, and Njoki 2011).

Skin bleaching has become common throughout Africa (Sagoe et al. 2019; also see Figure 5-1). Studies have revealed that as many as 25 percent of women in Mali; 30 percent of women in Tanzania; 52 percent of women in Dakar, Senegal; 66 percent of people in Brazzaville, Congo; 75 percent of people in Lagos, Nigeria; and 60 percent of women in Zambia use skin-bleaching products (Lewis et al. 2011; Kpanake, Munoz Sastre, and Mullet 2009).

Why? In Tanzania, a team of scholars (Lewis et al. 2011) interviewed forty-two women to ask them why they used skin-bleaching products, even though these products are known to cause severe skin damage, skin cancer, and brain disease. Tanzanian women gave six primary

FIGURE 5-1

PERCENTAGE OF WOMEN IN AFRICAN COUNTRIES WHO USE SKIN-BLEACHING PRODUCTS

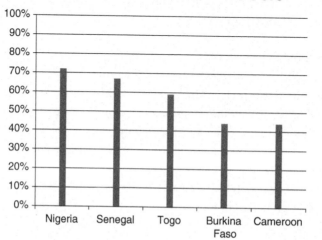

Source: Davids et al. (2016).

reasons for why they bleached their skin: (1) to remove acne, (2) to have soft skin, (3) to appear more White, (4) to remove dark patches, (5) to attract men, and (6) to impress peers. Women gave a variety of reasons for their use of these creams, but the desire to look better was at the center of all of them. For many, the desire to look better was connected to looking whiter. One woman said she started bleaching "to be beautiful and to look like Arabians or Europeans and attractive to people especially men" (33). In a similar study in Togo, Lonzozou Kpanake, María Teresa Munoz Sastre, and Etienne Mullet (2009) interviewed 300 men and women who reported using skin-bleaching creams and found that they gave a variety of reasons for doing so, including wanting to be considered important, civilized, and attractive, and to have lighter and softer skin. The prevalence of skin bleaching in a variety of African countries demonstrates that Africans continue to privilege light skin.

In a study of skin bleaching in Jamaica, Christopher A. D. Charles (2009) interviewed thirty-six women and twenty-two men who bleached their skin. He found that most of them bleached their skin either to remove facial blemishes, to lighten their skin, or to look more beautiful. Although more than 90 percent of Jamaicans are Black, light skin is viewed as socially desirable among both men and women. For this reason, people who bleached their skin often thought that having lighter skin would make them more attractive. In the United States, skin bleaching was common among African Americans in Harlem in the 1920s and 1930s. Since then, we have seen the rise of the "Black is beautiful" movement and an embrace of blackness among African Americans. Although these social movements have alleviated colorism among Black Americans, colorism has not completely dissipated.

A billboard advertising a skin-lightening product called Khess Petch in Dakar, Senegal.

A study by JeffriAnne Wilder (2010) reveals the extent to which colorism continues to be embedded in the African American community. Wilder conducted focus groups with fifty-eight African American women in which she probed them about skin-color labels and their meanings. Wilder found that a wide variety of labels are used to describe light-skinned Black people, quite a few are used to describe darker-skinned Black people, and just four are used to describe those of medium skin tone. The wide variety of labels used indicates the importance of skin tone in the African American community. Whereas the terms used to describe medium skin—brown, milk chocolate, caramel, and pecan tan—were neutral, those used to describe light and dark skin were not. Terms for light skin included "house nigga" and "pretty skin," while those for dark skin included "jigaboo" and "tar baby." The association of lightness with "pretty skin" indicates that many African Americans view light skin as more beautiful than dark skin. At the same time, use of the term *house nigga* is a reference to slavery and implies that those with light skin may be less authentically Black. Wilder found in her focus groups that many African Americans view lighter-skinned women as more beautiful, intelligent, and refined than their darker-skinned counterparts.

There is evidence that these preferences for light skin are connected to real, material rewards for being light. In the United States, historically, lighter-skinned African Americans have had more resources than darker-skinned African Americans and have tended to pass those resources down to their children. Ongoing discrimination exacerbates these inequalities. Colorism is a prominent aspect of inequality for African Americans in the criminal justice system: studies have shown that darker-skinned Black people get longer prison sentences than Black people with lighter skin and that darker-skinned Black people are more likely to receive the death penalty (Hochschild and Weaver 2007). The preference for light skin also plays out in hiring decisions: one experimental study showed that White employers were more likely to hire a lighter-skinned African American over a darker-skinned African American (Hochschild and Weaver 2007). Relatedly, Ellis Monk (2014) found that skin tone affects outcomes related to Black Americans' educational attainment, household income, occupational status, and even the skin tone and educational attainment of their spouses. Notably, lighter-skinned Black Americans have, on average, one full year more of education than darker-skinned Black Americans. In addition, Black Americans with "very dark skin" have 73 percent higher odds of having a less prestigious occupation than their lighter-skinned counterparts (Monk 2014).

Why Black People Discriminate Among Ourselves: The Toxic Legacy of Colorism

by Kaitlyn Greenidge

My grandmother was a great beauty. Everybody said so.

"Like a black Elizabeth Taylor," was the comment heard most often, because her eyes looked violet in some light. She had a perfect hourglass figure, large clear eyes, a tiny waist, long slim hands, a killer sense of dress and smooth dark skin.

The only trait I shared with her was her skin color. My mother always spoke of this with pride. It was a treasure to be kept whole through diligent care—applications of thick, pasty Eucerin lotion, which used to come in a tub, worked into the skin as it melted down and made everything smooth and shiny. My grandmother used the silkier Nivea instead—kept on the dresser in her all-white bedroom, applied throughout the day. The smell of it still reminds me of the elegance of her life.

That dark skin was the most beautiful was the logic of my family. Growing up, all my Barbies and baby dolls had skin as dark as mine. This was my mother's conscious choice. She stocked our bookshelves with black children's books, bought toys and games with black characters. She worked hard to make sure our home was a place where blackness was always celebrated. She was keenly aware, as the mother of three black girls, how the world would treat us, regardless of our varying shades.

Looking back, I think this probably had to do with her own skin color—my mother was much lighter than my grandmother, with a spray of freckles across her nose. In my grandmother's house, my mother's high school portrait sat on the mantel—it was a photograph retouched with oil. The painter had lightened my mother's skin to an anemic grayish yellow, given her green eyes, and thinned her nose. "He thought she was Italian," I remember my grandmother telling me, as explanation. My mother hated that picture, the erasure of her blackness. I haven't seen it since my grandmother died.

Growing up in the supportive environment my mother created for us, I assumed into early adulthood that colorism was a thing of the past. Colorism—the prejudice based on skin tone, usually with a marked preference for lighter-skinned people—was something I read about in novels. It seemed quaint, like pin curls or cellophane. There was a slight troubling when I would watch TV shows such as Martin or movies like Coming to America, and the love interest was always light and the girls my color were shrews—too fast, too forward, too sarcastic to be loved. But at least these were movies with people who looked like me, and it hurt less to ignore my misgivings and just enjoy seeing a woman like myself on the screen, even if she was there only for the protagonist to screw his face up at in disgust.

(continued)

Why Black People Discriminate Among Ourselves: The Toxic Legacy of Colorism

For reassurance that these scenarios were just fiction, all I had to do was look at my grandparents' marriage—my grandmother as dark as me and my grandfather, who adored her, much lighter.

It is a sad and sobering fact to realize that color—how dark or light you are perceived as being by a prospective partner, who most likely is someone of your own race—sometimes determines who in our communities is deemed deserving of romance. The question of desirability, of who we believe is worthy of love, is what led me to read more about colorism.

I went deeper into my colorism research, and what I found let me know that colorism is still alive and well. I started with the marriage market, and found out dark-skinned women are less likely to be married than lighter-skinned women. But colorism shows up in even starker ways: the difference in pay rates between darker-skinned and lighter-skinned men mirrors the differences in pay between whites and blacks. Darker-skinned women are given longer prison sentences than their light-skinned counterparts. And this discrimination starts young—if you are a dark-skinned girl, you are three times more likely to be suspended from school than your light-skinned peers.

Even more insidious, colorism even affects how we are remembered. Lighter-skinned black people are perceived to be more intelligent. Educated black people, regardless of their actual skin color, are remembered by job interviewers as having lighter skin.

The daily toll of living with colorism is inescapable. Darker-skinned people report higher experiences of microaggressions; heavier-set dark-skinned men report the highest levels of microaggressions. All of this affects our mental health and wellbeing. Darker-skinned black women report more physiological deterioration and self-report worse health than lighter-skinned women.

Wage and punishment inequity and our skewed perception by the professional world make more sense to me, because they operate on the cold logic of white supremacy. They are describing interactions with a wider, non-black world and take into account how both white and black people view skin color. But the facts around relationships and dating don't make any sense to me: given the relatively low rates of interracial marriage for black women in the US, we are talking about perceptions and prejudices within the black community—how we treat each other, our own internalized white supremacy.

I began to realize the importance of distinguishing between colorism as practiced by white power structures like courts, schools and businesses, and colorism as practiced within the black community, evidenced when we talk about marriage statistics and measurements of color.

The former seems easier for many black people to acknowledge. The latter is less explicitly talked about. To do so is to begin to unpack internalized white supremacy, something most people are unwilling to do because it can be so painful.

I am not sure how we get free from the trap of colorism, but as with most things in life, I know it begins with being able to talk about it openly. When I was a child, the love and pride my grandmother took in her color, the assumption of dignity and elegance, was an unspoken guide to how to navigate the world.

But I think the time has come to be explicit in our strategies, to have the difficult conversations, to acknowledge when they make us uncomfortable, or remind us of our own individual pain. To have your life dictated by something you are not even allowed to name is a special kind of cruelty. The way to begin to combat it is to try to speak about it.

....

Source: https://www.theguardian.com/lifeandstyle/2019/apr/09/colorism-racism-why-black-people-discriminate-among-ourselves

SKIN COLOR, GENDER, AND BEAUTY

How does skin color relate to gender and beauty? Colorism is evident in the U.S. entertainment industry, especially for women of color. Many of the most prominent Latina stars—Salma Hayek, Jennifer Lopez, Jessica Alba, Victoria Justice, and Gina Rodriguez—are very light-skinned. Light-skinned artists of color are more likely to rise to fame because light skin is associated with beauty both in the United States and around the globe. Margaret Hunter (2005) explains that beauty, like colorism, is an ideology that can be used as a tool to maintain **patriarchy**, or male dominance in a society. Beauty divides women through competition and diverts their attention to their physical appearance and away from other oppressive forces in their lives.

In the United States, light skin, long hair, light eyes, and straight noses are all associated with beauty—and with whiteness. When a woman is called "fair," this label refers both to light skin and to physical attractiveness. Thus, African American women with long, straight hair and light skin are often perceived to be more attractive than their darker-skinned counterparts. Of course, there is individual preference and variation.

Yet studies have consistently shown that dark-skinned women are de-valued both by their co-ethnics and by Whites (Hunter 2005).

Hunter (2005, 70–71) introduces the concept of a **beauty queue** to explain "how sexism and racism interact to create a queue of women from the lightest to the darkest, where the lightest get the most resources and the darkest get the least. The lightest women get access to more resources because not only are they lighter-skinned and therefore racially privileged, but their light skin is interpreted in our culture as more beautiful and therefore they are also privileged as beautiful women." For women, beauty is an asset that can lead to better jobs, better pay, and more status. Because lighter women are seen as more beautiful, they can be considered to have **skin-color privilege**, even if they belong to a disadvantaged racial group.

Siobhan Brooks (2010) uses the concept of **erotic capital** to explain how skin color relates to beauty for women of color. Doing research with strip club workers, Brooks found that White women often earned more than Latina and Black women, but that light-skinned Latina and Black women were able to use their erotic capital—their attractive-ness and sensuality—to earn more than darker-skinned Black women. Whereas lighter-skinned Latina and Black women were seen as exotic, dark-skinned Black women were perceived as hypersexual and thus devalued. Similar to Hunter (2007), Brooks found evidence of a beauty queue, in which White women earned the most, followed by lighter-skinned Black and Latina women, and then darker-skinned women. In the case of strip clubs, being whiter or lighter had material advantages.

Although there are clear advantages to being light skinned, there is also evidence that women of color do not necessarily want to be White, even if they prefer lighter skin. Dionne Stephens and Paula Fernández (2011) interviewed thirty-four Hispanic women to shed light on their perspective on the relationship between skin color and attractiveness. The researchers found that "having 'some color' was viewed as an important symbol of [the women's] 'authentic' Hispanic identity" (85). The women they interviewed specifically stated that they did not desire white skin, but that they preferred to be tan and viewed being tan as

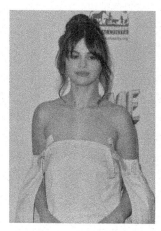

Many Latina stars, such as Selena Gomez, are very light-skinned, a trait often associated with beauty around the globe.

being attractive and sexy. Notably, the women also did not want to be "Black" or too dark.

This research is also relevant for Asian Americans. Rondilla and Spickard (2007) interviewed ninety-nine Asian Americans about their skin-color preferences. They found that respondents widely agreed that lighter skin was better in that it was associated with beauty, intelligence, and high class. Women and men recalled being told by their parents not to marry too dark so they could have light-skinned children. As part of the interview process, the researchers showed interviewees a picture of three conventionally beautiful Asian American women and asked them to make up a story about each woman. One woman had light skin, hair, and eyes; another was medium-toned and had black hair; and the third was dark-skinned. The stories about the medium-toned woman were the most positive: she was seen as smart, wealthy, and stylish. In contrast, the dark-skinned woman was seen as likely an immigrant, poor, and hardworking. The stories about the lightest woman were not positive either: interviewees saw her as confused about her identity, lazy, a partygoer, and unhappy. These findings reveal that Asian Americans have an abstract desire for whiteness but do not desire features that make them look too White. In her later work, Joanne Rondilla (2009) argues that Asian women do not use skin lighteners in an attempt to become White; instead, they use them out of a wish to become a better version of themselves.

This research has parallels with work conducted in other parts of the world. Aisha Khan (2009) argues that although there is a color hierarchy in Indo-Trinidadian society, the ultimate desire is to become light, but not White, as whiteness signifies cultural loss. Lynn Thomas (2009) points out that in South Africa, women use skin lighteners not to become White but to attain a lighter shade of black. Christina Sue (2009) contends that people in Veracruz, Mexico, use *mestizaje* as a whitening strategy to become lighter mestizos, not to become White. Evelyn Nakano Glenn (2009) argues that Filipinas associate light skin with modernity and social mobility, not necessarily with whiteness. And Ayu Saraswati (2012) finds that Indonesian women use skin whiteners to become lighter, but not to become Caucasian or to attain the light skin of Chinese women. Instead, they prefer Indonesian whiteness.

In a study of beauty pageants in Nigeria, Oluwakemi M. Balogun (2012) examined two beauty pageants: the Queen Nigeria pageant, which focuses primarily on Nigeria, and the Most Beautiful Girl in Nigeria pageant, which is geared to a more international audience and is connected to the Miss Universe and Miss World pageants. Balogun found that beauty pageant directors did not ignore skin color, nor did they give universal preference to light skin. Instead, they chose dark-skinned women when their goal was to find an authentic African woman to represent their country to the world and lighter-skinned women when they were searching for a woman with global mass appeal as a beautiful woman.

Most of these works on skin color focus on women, as colorism is a gendered dynamic. Skin-color valuations more heavily affect women's lives than men's. Jyostna Vaid (2009) highlights the increasing salience of skin color, as well as the gendered nature of judgments based on skin color, for Indians in India and the diaspora. Vaid found that Indian women are twice as likely as men to mention skin color in marriage ads, signaling that skin color is more important in marriage negotiations for women than for men. Evelyn Nakano Glenn (2009) conceptualizes light skin as a form of symbolic capital and makes the case that this form of capital is more important for women than for men. Ayu Saraswati (2012) interviewed forty-six Indonesian women about their use of skin-whitening creams and found that many of the women had experienced discrimination and denigration because of their dark skin color. Many had received comments on their skin color when they were girls and used skin-whitening creams to hide what they viewed to be a deficiency—their dark skin. Whereas dark skin can be seen as masculine, and thus appropriate, for men, Saraswati found that women in Indonesia overwhelmingly preferred light skin. Moreover, women around the world feel more pressure than men to be beautiful (Hunter 2005). A study of 149 African American women living in the United States and 168 Indian women living in India found that the extent to which women of color in these two places attempt to lighten their skin or straighten their hair is shaped by the degree to which they have internalized White beauty standards (Harper and Choma 2019).

Nevertheless, men also can experience benefits from being light-skinned and having European features. *Grey's Anatomy* star Jesse Williams, for example, explained: "To some people I might be a celebrity because I'm physically attractive. We are programmed to believe that someone is attractive because they told you that blue eyes are hot. I am not going to participate in that shit," he says. "I aim to do what I can with what I have. And I have my [looks]—you know, European beauty standards give me access to things." Williams acknowledges that his blue eyes and light skin grant him unearned privileges, yet he disparages the system that gives him these advantages (Kasperkevic 2015).

In India, it continues to be common for people to use advertisements to find spouses, and these advertisements make it clear that fair skin makes women more marriageable. Radhika Parameswaran and Kavitha Cardoza (2009) report that men are much less likely than women to report their own skin color in these advertisements and that men are much more likely to indicate a preference for light skin in a partner. These researchers consistently found ads written by men that sought a "fair" bride and even reported one advertisement by a father who lamented the fact that his daughter's skin was not fair. These preferences have generated a market for skin-lightening creams in India. In 2013, fairness products constituted 45 percent of the cosmetics and toiletries market in India (McDougall 2013). Companies that make these products also use advertising to reinforce the idea that lighter women are more marriageable. One ad for Fair & Lovely Fairness Cold Cream shows a young woman with a beaming smile. The caption reads: "This winter, I discovered the only cold cream that also made me fairer. (And *he* discovered me.)" (Parameswaran and Cardoza 2009). A consistent theme in Indian advertisements for whitening creams is that women who wish to be more beautiful can use these creams to become more fair and thus more desirable to men.

Transnational corporations have taken advantage of the widespread desire for fair skin around the world and have used it to generate immense profits. Through advertising, large transnational corporations have not only reinforced the idea that light skin is essential for success, but also have profited immensely from selling products that promise to save women from the pain and rejection associated with dark skin. Lynn Thomas (2009) underscores the importance of transnational entanglements for the global preference for lighter skin, as most companies that sell whitening products are transnational. In Indonesia, for example, transnational corporations such as Unilever, L'Oréal, and Shiseido are the main sellers of skin whiteners. And out of all the products in the cosmetics industry, it is skin-whitening products that are the most profitable in Indonesia, the fourth-most populous country in the world. (Saraswati 2012).

After #NotFairandLovely: Changing Thought Patterns Instead of Skin Tone

Namira Islam, Executive Director of the Muslim Anti-Racism Collaborative (MuslimARC), argues that by modifying our use of language, we can reshape our thinking on beauty and skin color.

The MuslimARC-launched hashtag #NotFairandLovely recently trended in London. The tweets were heart-breaking. Women shared how they were limited from going outside to play in the sun as children, their struggles to overcome an internalized hatred of a dark skin tone, and subsequent acts of self-shaming and devaluation. Some questioned whether their husband's compliments were genuine and expressed concern over the future lives of their children who may inherit their skin tone. People related stories of children judged from the day they are born by the color of their skin: a light-skinned baby is a joy . . . and a dark-skinned baby? . . .

I ask that we begin un-training ourselves from using the word "fair" to mean light. No skin tone should ever be considered unfair, nor should we settle for a world in which possession of a certain skin tone brings with it an assessment of strength of character. A "fair" world is a just world.

Second, let us remind ourselves and those around us that our words and our thoughts and our actions matter.

For example, if someone lists skin tone as [a] factor in considering whether a person is a good candidate for marriage, ask why the person's skin color is relevant to the discussion. Listen. Follow up. If you cannot end the conversation with a verbal request (i.e., to refrain from making comments valuing one skin tone over another or using skin tone to determine the worth of a person in front of you), do so in your heart. Letting people politely know that you dislike what is being said and that you are uncomfortable with it is an important starting point.

Stop adding value judgments to words in your own vocabulary. Don't use "fair" to refer to light-skinned in your thoughts, your writing, or your speech. Realize that this usage does not reflect an objective truth—this is a construction we maintain. "Fair" does not have to refer to any one particular skin tone. The human body is a miracle, skin is fascinating, and an individual is beautiful, period. Statements like "beautiful for a …" should be corrected when uttered by others and eliminated from our thinking and speech. Repeat as necessary.

Finally, realize that this entire discussion is grounded in the use of appearance as a metric of quality. Reject the notion that outward beauty dictates self-worth. Reject the idea that someone's physical beauty is the outward manifestation of their inward value. Reject the idea that your face, your skin, your hair, and your bone construction bear any connection with your strength of spirit, depth of heart, or beauty of imagination . . . .

We **must** retrain our brains to understand that **skin tone does not dictate physical beauty, and that physical beauty does not guarantee happiness**. Our words should reflect these concepts. Begin within yourself. True happiness comes from valuing the self and valuing others so that we treat ourselves well in order to better the lives of those around us.

Source: Islam 2014.

CONCLUSION AND DISCUSSION

As we have seen in this chapter, skin-color valuations have been pervasive throughout history and around the world. The preference for whiteness or lightness can be found in Africa, Asia, Latin America, and the United States. There are local variations on these preferences, yet they also have many aspects in common and are closely related to gender and sexuality. Colorism, it turns out, is a manifestation of racism that further splits fractured groups into an internal hierarchy related to color. At the same time, since race is closely tied to identity, there are costs to being perceived as too light or, especially, too White. Examining colorism around the world allows us to perceive both commonalities and differences in terms of racial stratification.

This examination also sheds light on the gendered nature of colorism: the color hierarchy has different meanings for men and women. Although some men use skin-whitening creams or pills, women are much more likely to use these products, which can be dangerous and even fatal. Darker-skinned men may find it more difficult than lighter-skinned men to find romantic partners, but this effect is more pronounced among women. And although physical attractiveness serves as capital for both men and women, patriarchy has created a situation in which women must depend more than men on their physical appearance. To the extent that light skin is viewed as more desirable around the world, this aspect of the human body more heavily influences women's lives than men's.

THINKING
ABOUT
RACIAL
JUSTICE

RACIAL JUSTICE IS the creation of a society free of racial oppression. How might a consideration of colorism affect how we think about racial justice? Explain how the presence of colorism could challenge our thinking about racial justice. Reflect on how we might overcome that challenge.

Key Terms

colorism 137
skin-color stratification 137
pigmentocracy 137
mulatto 138
hypodescent 138
mestizo 140
pardo 140

global color hierarchy 142
diaspora 143
patriarchy 153
beauty queue 154
skin-color privilege 154
erotic capital 154

CHECK YOUR UNDERSTANDING

5.1 When and how did colorism and skin-color stratification originate?

Colorism has a long history and many distinct manifestations around the world.

 What is the difference between colorism and skin-color stratification?

 How long has colorism been a factor in the African American community?

 How is skin-color stratification in Brazil related to colonialism?

 What is the history of colorism in Asia and Africa?

5.2 How does colorism differ across societies?
Skin-whitening creams, which are evidence of a global color hierarchy, can be found from the United States to Asia to Latin America to Africa.

 What are some indicators of colorism and skin-color stratification in the United States, Asia, Latin America, and Africa?

5.3 How does skin color relate to gender and beauty?
Skin-color stratification and colorism are more prominent for women than men, and this disparity is largely related to beauty norms.

 What is a "beauty queue"?
 How does skin-color privilege vary by racial group?

Critical Thinking

1. Why might it be important to understand whether colorism predates colonialism?
2. What are some distinctions between a desire to be White and a desire to have light skin?
3. In what ways is colorism "gendered"?

> ### *Talking about Race*
>
> How would you respond if a friend or relative implied that you are a better (or worse) person because of your skin color or hair texture? You might first ask your friend for an explanation of what this comment means, then listen to any justification offered, and, finally, use the knowledge you have gained in this chapter to respond accordingly. For example, you might demonstrate to your friend how remarks that devalue dark skin are harmful, or you could explain the connections between colorism and racism.

Learn more with this chapter's digital tools, including video clips from the author, web links, filmography, and chapter self-assessment quizzes at www.oup.com/he/golash-boza-brief3e.

6

Educational Inequality

AS YOU READ

6.1 What are the dimensions of racial inequality in our educational system?

6.2 How does the legacy of inequality affect contemporary educational opportunities and outcomes?

6.3 How can we explain continuing racial disparities in educational achievement?

E ducation is meant to be the great equalizer. Every child in the United States, regardless of race, gender, or citizenship status, has the right to attend free public school up until the twelfth grade. With these educational opportunities, any child should be able to be successful. Nevertheless, there are tremendous gaps in educational achievement in the United States. And these gaps fall along racial and ethnic lines.

Historically, educational opportunities in this country have not been equal. Enslaved Africans and their children were forbidden to learn how to read or write. Chinese immigrants were banned from public schools. African American, Asian American, and Mexican American children were relegated to separate and unequal schools. Prior to 1954, U.S. laws prevented many non-White children from accessing the best educational opportunities.

Today, nearly seven decades later, some things have changed. There are no longer any all-White universities in the United States, and the number of all-White high schools has decreased. The best colleges and universities now seek out a diverse student body, and many offer scholarships to students who can contribute to campus diversity. Elite private high schools offer similar incentives to attract students who are neither White nor from privileged backgrounds. Yet non-White children still do not have equal access to the opportunities available to their White counterparts.

In this chapter, we will look at the history and current state of educational inequality in the United States. We will see how far we have come and how far we must go to achieve equality in educational opportunities and outcomes for all children in the United States.

THE HISTORY OF EDUCATIONAL INEQUALITY

In the United States, the idea of equal opportunity holds great weight, even as the reality has fallen short of the ideal. Before the *Brown v. Board of Education* decision of 1954, children who were not White were systematically prevented from attending White schools under a doctrine called "separate but equal."

During slavery, most African Americans were prevented from learning to read and write, sometimes by law. Free Black people were not permitted to enroll in the few public schools that existed in southern states. With emancipation came the freedom to learn and to teach.

African Americans across the South started schools wherever they could—in fields, in one-room schoolhouses, and in people's homes. Southern Black people who managed to learn to read and write taught others in their community. They also recruited Northerners as teachers. By the end of the nineteenth century, states across the South offered free public schooling for all children (Span 2002).

Beginning in the early twentieth century, racial tensions heightened. African Americans lost the right to vote in several southern states. In this context, school segregation was implemented and enforced in both the North and the South. With segregation, Black children were often left with few educational resources. Their communities often had to make do with one-room schoolhouses provided by the state, or else they had to pool their own funds to build better schools. Community-established schools provided some of the first educational opportunities to Black children in the South, but they were gravely underresourced (Span 2002).

Official segregation in public schools persisted until 1954. Whereas many African American, Asian American, and Mexican American children were obliged to attend segregated schools in their home communities, many Native American children were sent to Indian boarding schools. The history of segregated and unequal schools in this country stretches over many decades and continues to have implications today.

Indian Schools

In the late nineteenth and early twentieth centuries, U.S. government officials enacted policies to ensure that Native Americans would leave behind their traditional ways and assimilate into American society. One of the measures aimed at obliterating indigenous cultures was the creation of Indian schools, as these institutions were called in the early twentieth century.

The three main types of schools designed for Native Americans were (1) boarding schools located outside of reservations, (2) boarding schools located on reservations, and (3) day schools on reservations. In addition, starting in 1819, there were federally subsidized mission schools, which focused on teaching Native American children about Christianity. These schools were designed to assimilate Native Americans into mainstream society (Watras 2004).

In 1877, there were 3,598 Native American children enrolled in 150 Indian Schools. By 1900, there were 307 Indian Schools, with a total enrollment of 21,568 children. The majority of these children (17,708) were in boarding schools (Martinez-Cola 2019). One of the earliest boarding schools was the Carlisle Indian School in Pennsylvania, established in 1879. The philosophy of the school's founder, Richard Henry Pratt, was that by fostering assimilation, the school could "kill the Indian and save the man." By 1926, about 70,000 of the 84,000 Native American children in the United States were attending a government-created school (Watras 2004). In 1930, there were 707 Indian schools across the United States, with 52 in Montana alone (Noel 2002).

Some Native American children attended boarding schools by choice, often with the hope that they would be provided for materially and would learn skills that would help them survive in mainstream society. Many children, however, were forced or coerced to attend these schools (Noel 2002). Once there, students who tried to run away were often harshly punished. At Chemawa School in Oregon, for example, there were forty-six runaway attempts in 1921 and seventy in 1922. At this school, runaways, called deserters, were forced to stand in the hallway with their arms and legs tied. If they tumbled over because they fell asleep, the matron would whip them and make them stand again (Marr n.d.). At Haskell Indian School in Kansas, there were fifty-three runaways in September 1910, and another thirty-five in October. If runaways were returned to the school, they would face physical punishment for their transgression (Stout 2012).

When children arrived at these schools, they were often renamed. A young man named Raining Bird, for example, was renamed Arthur Raining Bird. If the boys had long hair, it was cut. Native American children were forbidden from speaking in their native language and from practicing their own religions. Children who spoke in their native languages were often physically punished if the teacher overheard them. Native languages, dress, and hairstyles were forbidden in order to inculcate Native American children in the ways of White Americans (Noel 2002).

The children spent half of the day in classes learning English, reading, and mathematics, and the other half of the day doing industrial, agricultural, or domestic chores, which were framed as "productive activities." The girls were assigned to kitchen duties, sewing, laundry, ironing, and cleaning, while the boys were required to do farm labor, gardening, grounds keeping, and carpentry (Noel 2002). In some cases, once Native American girls learned how to keep house, they were sent to local White homes to work as servants (Trennert 1983).

Students in cadet uniforms at the Carlisle Indian School, CA. 1880.

Native American children who went to boarding schools were often underfed at the schools, and many became ill or died. In 1926, a comprehensive study of Indian schools showed that the boarding schools' budget for feeding children was only eleven cents a day—$1.41 a day in today's currency, and not nearly enough to provide a reasonable diet. Because of undernourishment, the children often succumbed to diseases such as tuberculosis (Watras 2004). Many boarding schools across the United States today have burial grounds for Native American children who died while at school.

Following the official end of assimilation programs in 1993, these boarding schools were either reformed or closed. The repercussions of these institutions, however, continue to be felt. Genevieve Williams, who was born in 1922, went to an Indian school as a young girl. She remembers being forced to scrub floors on her hands and knees and being beaten for speaking in her native language. She recalls girls being flogged for wetting the bed. When she returned home at age fourteen, she no longer recognized her mother. Having never bonded with her own mother, Williams found it hard to nurture her own children. Her husband had been physically abused at school, and this also affected his ability to raise their children (King 2008). Lynne Eagle Feather's mother dropped her off at the Saint Francis Mission School in the early 1960s. Lynne Eagle Feather was six years old. Her grandfather had attended Carlisle Indian School in the 1880s. Ms. Eagle Feather recounts being hit on the head by her teacher, a nun, with a pair of scissors. After boarding school, she was sent to foster care, where she was forced to work as well as experienced sexual assault. When Lynne Eagle Feather had her own children, she found herself unable to take care of them and sent them to a boarding school in Oklahoma. Her son, Paul Castaway, was shot and killed by the police in Denver, Colorado in July 2015. The effects of Indian schools are felt across generations as the children of Native Americans like Genevieve Williams and Lynne Eagle Feather continue to suffer from intergenerational trauma.

voices

Mary Tape

Mary and Joseph Tape lived with their four children in a middle-class home in San Francisco. In 1884, they tried to enroll their 8-year-old daughter, Mamie, in Spring Valley Primary School. She was not allowed to enter the schoolhouse because she was Chinese. The Tapes took their case to court. In 1885, the court decided in *Tape v Hurley* that Chinese American children should be allowed access to schools. The city responded by opening a segregated school and obliging Mamie Tape to attend the newly created Chinese Primary School (Ngai 2010). Mary Tape responded on April 16, 1885, with the following letter in the *Daily Alta California*.

To the Board of Education—Dear Sirs:

I see that you are going to make all sorts of excuses to keep my child out of the Public schools. Dear sirs, Will you please to tell me! Is it a disgrace to be Born a Chinese? Didn't God make us all!!! What right have you to bar my children out of the school because she is a chinese Decend. They is no other worldly reason that you could keep her out, except that. I suppose, you all goes to churches on Sundays! Do you call that a Christian act to compel my little children to go so far to a school that is made in purpose for them. My children don't dress like the other Chinese. They look just as phunny amongst them as the Chinese dress in Chinese look amongst you Caucasians. Besides, if I had any wish to send them to a chinese school I could have sent them two years ago without going to all this trouble. You have expended a lot of the Public money foolishly, all because of a one poor little Child. Her playmates is all Caucasians ever since she could toddle around. If she is good enough to play with them! Then is she not good enough to be in the same room and studie with them? You had better

(continued)

voices *continued.*

Mary Tape

come and see for yourselves. See if the Tape's is not same as other Caucasians, except in features. It seems no matter how a Chinese may live and dress so long as you know they Chinese. Then they are hated as one. There is not any right or justice for them.

You have seen my husband and child. You told him it wasn't Mamie Tape you object to. If it were not Mamie Tape you object to, then why didn't you let her attend the school nearest her home! Instead of first making one pretense Then another pretense of some kind to keep her out? It seems to me Mr. Moulder has a grudge against this Eight-year-old Mamie Tape. I know they is no other child I mean Chinese child! care to go to your public Chinese school. May you Mr. Moulder, never be persecuted like the way you have persecuted little Mamie Tape. Mamie Tape will never attend any of the Chinese schools of your making! Never!!! I will let the world see sir What justice there is When it is govern by the Race prejudice men! Just because she is of the Chinese decend, not because she don't dress like you because she does. Just because she is decended of Chinese parents I guess she is more of a American then a good many of you that is going to prevent her being Educated.

Mrs. M. Tape.

Source: "Chinese Mother's Letter," *Daily Alta California*, April 16, 1885, 1. Available online via California Digital Newspaper Collection (https://cdnc.ucr.edu/?a=d&d=DAC18850416.2.3).

Segregation and Landmark Court Cases

Between 1896 and 1954, it was legal for states to deny African Americans, Mexican Americans, Native Americans, and Asian Americans access to public schools and other facilities designated for Whites (Wollenberg 1974). The 1896 court decision in *Plessy v. Ferguson* was used to justify the existence of separate educational facilities for White and non-White students. By 1931, more than three-quarters of the school districts in California practiced segregation (Wollenberg 1974). At that same time, 90 percent of the schools in Texas were racially and ethnically segregated (Godfrey 2008).

The schools established for non-Whites were inferior in many ways to those that served Whites. Schools for Mexican American children were designed to "Americanize" them through instruction in cooking, hygiene, English, and civics. In these segregated schools, children were punished for speaking Spanish, and girls were taught home economics so that they could work in the homes of Whites (Wollenberg 1974). People took to the courts to address these educational inequalities. There were over 100 different court cases brought against legal segregation. Most of these cases involved African American plaintiffs. However, two involved Mexican American schools, four involved Chinese American schools, and five had Native American plaintiffs (Martinez-Cola 2019).

In 1924, Pike and Annie Piper filed a lawsuit on behalf of their daughter, Alice, after she had been denied admission to the White school. Pike and Annie Piper were members of the Paiute Tribe of Inyo County, California. Their lawyers argued that Alice had adopted civilized ways and that she was a citizen of both California and the United States under the recently passed Dawes Act. The judge ruled in their favor and the following year, Alice Piper and her fellow Paiute plaintiffs enrolled in Big Pine school along with the local White children (Martinez-Cola 2019).

In the 1930s and 1940s, Mexican Americans in Texas and California initiated protests against separate and inferior schools for Mexican American children. In Texas, the League of United Latin American Citizens (LULAC), founded in 1929, led the protests. The first case brought by LULAC was *Salvatierra v. Del Rio Independent School District*, in 1930. The court decided that segregation was permissible, reasoning that it was not based on race but on language and academic abilities. Over the next two decades, advocates of educational equality in Texas continued to be unsuccessful through a series of similar court cases.

One of the first victories for Mexican Americans came in 1947 with the case of *Mendez v. Westminster*, when a federal circuit court in California ruled that the segregation of children of Mexican and Latin American descent was unconstitutional. The *Mendez* case was a critical forerunner to the landmark 1954 Supreme Court decision in the case of *Brown v. Board of Education*, which overturned the *Plessy v. Ferguson* ruling. *Mendez* began when Gonzalo Mendez, a Mexican American naturalized U.S. citizen, and his Puerto Rican wife, Felicítas, attempted to enroll their three children in the 17th Street Elementary School in Orange County, California. Although Gonzalo Mendez had attended the school himself as a boy, his children were turned away because the school no longer allowed Mexican Americans to attend. Following failed attempts to win over the school board, he and 5,000 other people filed suit against several Orange County school districts in 1945. Their court case was successful, and the Supreme Court ruled that segregation based on a Spanish surname was unconstitutional (Ruiz 2001).

For African Americans, the landmark case regarding educational segregation was *Brown v. Board of Education* in 1954, which was a compilation of four separate cases from four different towns. It involved two rural communities—Clarendon County, South Carolina, and Prince Edward County, Virginia—and two urban districts—Topeka, Kansas, and Wilmington, Delaware. African Americans in each of these communities perceived that the education their children received in segregated schools was inferior to that given to White children. Indeed, local governments spent less money on the education of Black children. Nationally, prior to 1950, the average expenditure for Black students was less than two-thirds of that for White students (Siddle Walker 2000). In 1951, in Clarendon County, for example, the annual average expenditure was $44.32 per Black student, compared with an average of $166.45 per White student. Additionally, White children did not have to pay for their school materials, whereas Black students did (Anderson and Byrne 2004). These unequal expenditures meant that African Americans had access to fewer educational resources (Siddle Walker 2000). Parents in Clarendon County got together to protest this tremendous inequality, and their case became one of the four cases heard in *Brown v. Board of Education*.

Despite tremendous obstacles, African Americans in the pre–civil rights era worked hard to ensure that their children had educational opportunities. Parents often provided equipment and spaces when they could. Communities mobilized to ensure educational opportunities. At exemplary high schools for Black students such as Dunbar High School in Washington, DC, 60 percent of graduates went on to attend college in the 1950s. At this same high school, several of the teachers had doctorates from elite institutions (Siddle Walker 2000).

The rulings in *Mendez v. Westminster* and *Brown v. Board of Education* were only the beginning of the long process of school desegregation. In Prince Edward County, Virginia, for example, the *Brown* decision led to the closing of all public schools so that White students would not have to integrate. In 1964, a Supreme Court decision—*Griffin v. County School Board of Prince Edward County*—forced the county to reopen public schools (Orfield and Lee 2004).

The Persistence of Racial Segregation in the Educational System

Educational institutions are no longer allowed to prevent non-White children from attending. Nevertheless, segregation persists, in part because school districts are not required to promote integration. In a landmark civil rights case, *Swann v. Charlotte-Mecklenburg Board of Ed*, the U.S. Supreme Court ruled that federal courts could order school districts to rezone schools and bus students to achieve school desegregation. School districts that were ordered to desegregate did so and schools were successfully integrated. These measures also led to positive outcomes for Black students in integrated schools—their graduation rates increased as did their postsecondary school earnings, and their incarceration rates fell (Liebowitz 2018). However, once schools achieved integration, proponents of neighborhood schools took their cases to court and argued schools should be released from court-ordered desegregation. In 1991, in *Dowell v. Oklahoma City*, the Supreme Court decided that school districts that had achieved desegregation could be released from court orders. Figure 6-1 shows that schools released from court order rapidly resegregated.

FIGURE 6-1

THE RETURN OF SEGREGATION AFTER RELEASE FROM COURT OVERSIGHT

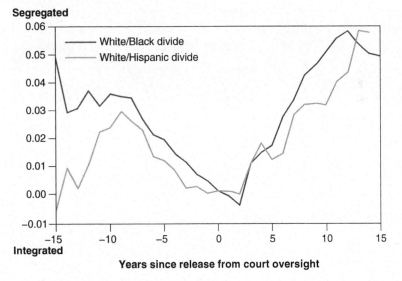

Note: Stanford researchers used a "dissimilarity index" to measure segregation, from 0 (balanced integration) to 1 (complete segregation).

Source: PBS Frontline (2014)/Stanford Center for Education Policy Analysis (2012)

Although 1988 was a high point of desegregation for Black students, the *Dowell* decision reversed that trend. Since 1991, we have seen increasingly high rates of segregation, as measured by the percentage of schools that are over 90 percent non-White—nearly one in five by 2013 (Orfield, Ee, Frankenberg, and Siegel-Hawley 2016). In 2017, 70 percent of Black students attended a school that was majority students of color, as compared to 13 percent of White students (García 2020).

This high level of racial segregation is often associated with poverty: in 2017, 72.4 percent of Black eighth-graders attended a high-poverty school, as compared to 31.3 percent of White students. In that same year, only 3 percent of Black eighth-graders attended a school that was low-poverty and mostly White, as compared to nearly a quarter of White eighth-graders (García 2020). There is a direct relationship between the percentage of Black and Latinx students in a school and the percentage of poor students (Orfield and Frankenberg 2014). Segregation also affects school performance: Black students in high-poverty schools with mostly students of color scored 20 points lower on the mathematics assessment than did Black students in low-poverty and mostly White schools (García 2020).

TABLE 6-1

Relationship between Segregation and Poverty, 2011–2012

% Poor in Schools	Percent Black and Latinx Students in Schools									
	0–10	11–20	21–30	31–40	41–50	51–60	61–70	71–80	81–90	91–100
0–10	11.4	10.0	3.6	1.9	2.2	2.2	2.1	2.9	2.1	2.2
11–20	11.8	16.2	11.3	4.2	2.8	1.9	1.8	1.6	1.5	1.3
21–30	13.4	14.7	14.4	10.1	5.2	3.7	2.5	2.2	1.7	1.5
31–40	16.1	15.0	15.2	14.8	10.7	7.2	4.8	2.7	2.2	1.8
41–50	16.3	14.3	15.5	16.5	15.1	12.7	8.6	4.9	3.0	2.4
51–60	13.4	12.7	14.9	17.1	16.7	16.9	13.4	8.0	4.6	3.5
61–70	9.0	9.3	12.5	15.7	19.1	17.8	18.5	15.5	9.2	5.4
71–80	4.7	4.7	7.7	11.3	16.0	18.8	20.8	22.0	18.3	10.5
81–90	2.0	1.9	3.4	5.7	8.7	13.2	17.5	23.2	29.3	20.6
91–100	1.9	1.2	1.5	2.6	3.4	5.6	10.0	17.0	28.0	50.8
Total	100	100	100	100	100	100	100	100	100	
% U. S. schools	33.2	13.9	9.0	6.9	5.9	4.9	4.4	4.2	5.0	12.7

Source: Adapted from Orfield and Frankenberg (2014).

Affirmative Action in Higher Education

Racial diversity in schools is a contentious issue at the university level as well. Title VI of the 1968 Civil Rights Act enabled colleges and universities to take **affirmative action** to enhance racial diversity on campus. Affirmative action encompasses policies and procedures designed to combat ongoing discrimination in schools and in the workplace. In higher education, it has meant giving preferential treatment to people who are members of historically disadvantaged groups. In schools with affirmative action programs, admissions committees can consider the racial and ethnic background of applicants as one factor in their decision to admit a student to a university.

In 1965, only 2 percent of medical students in the country were African American. In response to this underrepresentation, the University of California at Davis Medical School set aside sixteen of its one hundred admission slots for underrepresented minority students. In 1978, a White applicant named Allan Bakke was denied admission to the medical school. Bakke believed that in the absence of these racial quotas, he would have been admitted. He therefore filed a class-action lawsuit alleging that UC Davis had discriminated against him based on his race. In the *Regents of the University of California v. Bakke* (1978) case, the Supreme Court ruled that the preferential racial quotas did deny equal protection to White students and thus were unconstitutional. However, the Supreme Court also ruled that race could still be used as one factor in determining admission. With this ruling, racial quotas were no longer permissible, but diversity could continue to be used as a factor in determining admission. The *Bakke* decision thus ended the relatively short history of racial quotas in university admissions, leaving us today with more ambiguous options for promoting diversity. The University of California system, for example, can argue that a student or job candidate would contribute to the diversity of the campus, but it cannot say that it did or did not offer a position because of racial or ethnic identity (Yosso, Parker, Solorzano, and Lynn 2004).

After the *Bakke* decision, affirmative action programs continued to come under attack across the United States. In 1996, California voters passed Proposition 209, which banned the consideration of race in higher education admissions. Consequently, admission rates of Black, Latinx, and Native American students to the University of California system fell dramatically. Between 1997 and 1998—the year the ban took effect—admissions of underrepresented students fell 61 percent at UC Berkeley and 36 percent at UCLA. These disparities continue today: Black, Latinx, and Native American students made up 54 percent of all California high school graduates in 2012 but just 27 percent of all UC freshmen in that same year (Murphy 2013).

In June 2016, in *Fisher v. The University of Texas*, the Supreme Court reaffirmed the right of the University of Texas to take racial status into consideration in university admissions. This factor is one of many considered, including grades, test scores, extracurricular activities, hardship, and other personal characteristics. The case came to the Supreme Court after applicant Abigail Fisher, who is White, filed a lawsuit alleging that her denial of admission to the University of Texas was due to her race. Fisher was not in the top 10 percent of her high school graduating class, and she thus was not able to enroll at the University of Texas through the program that guarantees admission to top students in Texas. Instead, she was competing for a relatively small pool of spots for students not in the top 10 percent. University officials argued that, with an SAT score of 1180 and a 3.59 GPA, Fisher's record simply did not qualify her for admission. The Supreme Court agreed that Fisher had not faced discrimination based on her Whiteness (Hannah-Jones 2016).

Demonstrators in support of affirmative action in schools gather outside the U.S. Supreme Court in 2015.

EDUCATIONAL INEQUALITY TODAY

At all levels of schooling, educational achievements in the United States vary by racial or ethnic group, affecting earning potential. If we look at high school completion rates for people aged 25 to 29 in the United States, we will see that, by 2018, nearly all White and Asian people had a high school degree, as compared to 92 percent of Black people, and 85.2 percent of Hispanic people. However, it is also notable that, between 2008 and 2018, the percentage of Latinxs in this age category who completed high school increased from 68.3 percent to 85.2 percent. The disparities are starker once we consider college completion rates. In 2018, 70 percent of Asians aged 25 to 29 had completed college, as had 43.5 percent of Whites in the US. In contrasts, only 22.6 percent of Black people and 20.7 percent of Latinxs had completed college (Snyder, de Brey, and Dillow 2019). Notably, the rates of college completion increased for every group except Black students between 1996 and 2010 (see Figure 6-2). College completion rates are critical for lifetime earnings: in 2017, men with at least a bachelor's

FIGURE 6-2

SHARE OF STUDENTS WHO GRADUATE FROM FOUR-YEAR UNIVERSITIES WITHIN SIX YEARS, BY YEAR THEY ENTERED COLLEGE

Colleges are failing most black students

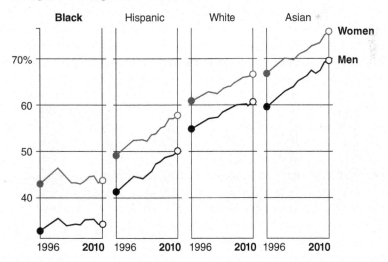

Source: Snyder, T.D., de Brey, C., and Dillow, S.A. (2019). Digest of Education Statistics 2018 (NCES 2020-009).

degree earned an average of $71,990, as compared to $42,440 for men with a high school degree (Snyder, de Brey, and Dillow 2019). And, in 2018, high school dropouts were three times as likely to be unemployed as people who had completed college (Snyder, de Brey, and Dillow 2019).

Although disparities in educational outcomes persist, it is undeniable that they have lessened over the course of the past hundred years in the United States. Legal segregation has been banished, Native American children are no longer forced to attend boarding schools, standard curricula now include multicultural components, nearly all youth have achieved literacy, and high school graduation rates for all racial groups are converging. Between 1971 and 1996, the gap in reading test scores between Black and White students shrank by almost one-half (Kao and Thompson 2003). There are still some significant disparities among racial groups, but they are not as pronounced as they were at the beginning of the twenty-first century, when 28 percent of Hispanic/Latinx youth dropped out of high school, compared with only 12 percent in 2014 (Fry and Taylor 2013; Krogstad 2016).

In aggregate data, it becomes apparent that Asian students are outperforming all other students in test scores and high school and college completion rates (see Figure 6-3). These achievements have led to a **"model minority" myth**, according to which Asians are widely perceived as the racial minority group that has succeeded in

FIGURE 6-3

EDUCATIONAL DISPARITIES BY RACE AND ETHNICITY, 2015

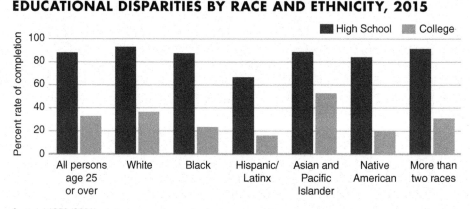

Source: NCES (2016).

the United States. As we saw earlier, Asians have not always been viewed as a model minority. In fact, as already noted, they were prevented from attending public schools in California in the late nineteenth century. The current stereotype did not become prevalent until the late twentieth century, after large numbers of highly-educated and professional Asians migrated to the United States (Wing 2007). And today, even though Asians perform better on average than other groups, it is not the case that every single Asian student is an overachiever. Additionally, when we break the Asian population down into groups by national origin, we can see a more complex story (Ngo and Lee 2007). For example, only about 14 percent of Hmong, Laotian, or Cambodian adults in the United States have college degrees, compared with about half of all Chinese, Filipino, and Pakistani adults. Indian adults have the highest rate of college graduation, at 70 percent (Piccorossi 2012).

Disparities in college attendance and completion are continuing, although these disparities have changed over the years. In 2012, Asians were the most likely racial or ethnic group to attend college, with 84 percent of Asian recent high school graduates enrolled in college. Of these students, 79 percent were enrolled at a four-year college or university, and 91 percent were enrolled full time (Fry and Taylor 2013). In 2012, 69 percent of Latinx high school graduates enrolled in college, compared with 67 percent of White high school graduates, 84 percent of Asian high school graduates and 63 percent of Black high school graduates. Latinxs, however, were less likely to attend a four-year college than White students. In 2012, 56 percent of Latinx college students were at a four-year college, compared with 72 percent of White students. In addition, Latinxs were less likely than Whites to attend a selective college, to be enrolled in college full time, and to complete a four-year degree (Fry and Taylor 2013).

Educational disparities among racial and ethnic groups are evident at each level of the educational system. In the next section, we will explore these disparities in more detail and look at the various explanations sociologists offer for them. Before we proceed with sociological explanations, pause to think about why Black, Latinx, and Native American students are faring less well than White and Asian students in the educational system. What have we learned so far that might inform your explanations?

THE ACHIEVEMENT GAP: SOCIOLOGICAL EXPLANATIONS FOR PERSISTENT INEQUALITY

What explains persistent disparities in educational outcomes by race and ethnicity? Sociologists describe the disparate educational outcomes of White, Asian, Black, Latinx, and Native Americans as the **achievement gap**. A variety of sociological explanations have been offered for this gap, and we will explore a few of them in this section.

The first observation to make when discussing educational disparities is that public education in the United States depends heavily on local property taxes. Inequalities in housing values translate into inequalities in schools.

Parental Socioeconomic Status

In the United States, parental education, income, and wealth are not distributed evenly. A major factor that can help us understand racial and ethnic inequality in education is overall socioeconomic inequality. For example, one study tracked the college completion rates of youth who were sophomores in high school in 1980. Over half of the youth whose family incomes were in the top 25 percent had earned a college degree by 1992, compared with only 7 percent of those whose family incomes were in the lowest 25 percent. The higher-income group therefore had seven times higher chances of completing college than the lower-income group. Overall, differences in family income can explain about one-third of the test score gap between Black and White students and nearly all of the differences in college completion rates (Gamoran 2001).

In addition to family income, parental education matters. Children whose parents have college degrees, for example, are much more likely to attend college than children whose parents have not completed high school. Parental education is one factor that explains Asians' relatively high educational attainment. In 1990, 65 percent of immigrants from India had college degrees, as did 63 percent of immigrants from Taiwan. However, it is important to recognize the variety in the Asian American experience: less than 5 percent of Cambodian and Laotian immigrants had a college degree in 1990 (Kao and Thompson 2003). The reason for these differences is related to immigration policy: most Taiwanese and Indian immigrants came on skill-based visas, which required high levels of education, whereas most Cambodians and Laotians came as refugees.

In their 2015 book, Jennifer Lee and Min Zhou explored the factors that have led to Asian Americans' educational success in the United

States (Lee and Zhou 2015). One factor they focus on is the *hyperselectivity* of Chinese and Vietnamese immigrants—a pattern whereby these immigrants have much higher rates of educational attainment than the general population in their countries of origin. In China, for example, only about 4 percent of adults hold a bachelor's degree or higher. In contrast, 50 percent of Chinese immigrants to the United States hold a bachelor's degree or higher. Chinese immigration to the United States is thus hyperselective in terms of college education. Selectivity works very differently in the case of Mexicans. People in Mexico are much more likely to have college degrees than people in China—17 percent versus 4 percent. Only 5 percent of Mexican immigrants to the United States, however, have bachelor's degrees or higher. For Mexican immigrants, then, we witness negative educational selectivity, when compared with the general population in Mexico.

Children from working-class backgrounds tend to fare less well in school than children from middle-class or wealthy families. In 2013, these differences in test scores persisted, both by socioeconomic status and by race/ethnicity (Kena et al. 2016; Figures 6-4 and 6-5). In another national study, Paschall, Gershoff, and Kuhfeld (2018) found that gaps in reading and math test scores between White children and their Black and Latinx counterparts persist. They also found that

FIGURE 6-4

AVERAGE SCIENCE SCALE SCORES, K–2ND GRADE, BY FAMILY SOCIOECONOMIC STATUS (SEES), 2011–2013

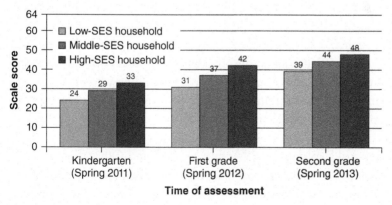

Source: Snyder, T.D., de Brey, C., and Dillow, S.A. (2019). Digest of Education Statistics 2018 (NCES 2020-009).

FIGURE 6-5

AVERAGE NAEP READING SCALE SCORES, 4TH-8TH GRADE, BY RACE/ETHNICITY

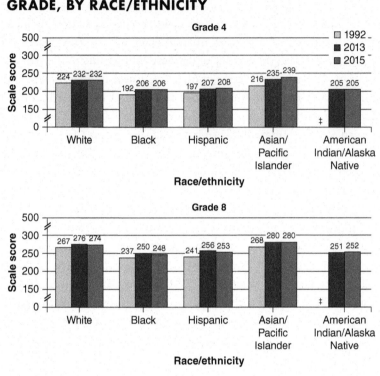

Source: Kena et al. (2016).

the achievement gap between White children of low socioeconomic status and their poor Black and Hispanic counterparts has grown. In an earlier study, sociologists Vincent Roscigno and James Ainsworth-Darnell (1999) found that family socioeconomic status could explain about half of the difference between the test scores of Black and White children. What explains the other half? Why do Black and Latinx children fare less well in school than White children who have the same family structure and income levels? Sociologists offer a few explanations, which we will consider next.

Cultural Explanations: "Acting White" and Other Theories

Sociologists and other social scientists have long conducted research on the role of culture in the achievement gap. Culture is a broad analytical concept and can refer to a wide variety of factors, often revealing disconnects among students, parents, and teachers.

Scholars of education have spent much ink trying to understand why Black students perform more poorly in school and have lower test scores than White students. One explanation that gained currency in the 1980s and 1990s is the **oppositional culture** thesis. Anthropologists Signithia Fordham and John Ogbu (1986) are credited with proposing this thesis, which has two basic components: (1) African American children don't do well in school because they equate school success with "**acting White**," and (2) African American children have responded to widespread discrimination by developing an identity in opposition to dominant White culture, and thus in opposition to school success. The basis of this argument is that Black children receive signals from both the White and Black communities that lead them to reject schooling as a route to success. Fordham and Ogbu contend that the experiences of Black students and their parents with discrimination cause them to distrust White authority figures and institutions. Additionally, they argue that Black students develop anti-achievement attitudes to avoid peer sanctions. They found that Black students equate "working hard to get good grades in school" (186) with acting White. Fordham and Ogbu's thesis is based on a study with only thirty-three students, yet it gained an inordinate amount of media attention.

The idea that Black students do not do well in school because they have antischool attitudes was widely accepted and publicized because it resonated with the popular belief that Black people do not value education. However, a series of subsequent studies have shown that it is simply not true that Black students consciously underachieve or equate academic success with acting White. For example, using a nationally representative sample of nearly 17,000 students, James Ainsworth-Darnell and Douglas Downey (1998) found that Black students had more positive attitudes toward school than White students. They also found that Black students reported being more popular when they did better in school, refuting the claim that Black students experience peer pressure to reject school. They did not find support for the claim that Black students perceive lower returns from education than White students; instead, Black students were more likely than White students to agree with the statement that education is important to getting a job.

In a qualitative study of seventy-two Black students from the southeastern United States, Karolyn Tyson (2002) found that Black third and fourth graders were consistently very excited about school and about learning. In her study, students were proud when they excelled and disappointed when they got answers wrong or were not allowed to participate in classroom activities. Instead of experiencing high achievement as a burden, as Fordham and Ogbu (1986) have argued, Tyson (2002, 1174) found that Black youth experienced a "burden of low achievement," in which they felt emotional distress when they did not do well.

In a national study of over 6,000 high school students that compared college-going behaviors by race, Blake (2018) found that, once we consider socioeconomic status and school-related variables, Black students are the most likely to take the ACT/SAT, contact school sources about college, and submit college applications. Blake's (2018) analyses revealed that Black students not only actively pursue college at higher rates than White students, but they also follow through and attend college at higher rates when academic performance is accounted for. Blake's findings push back against the claim that Black students are not interested in doing well in school because excellent performance is associated with "acting White."

Tracking

Even when schools are supposedly integrated, there is often internal segregation. In her well-known book titled *Why Are All the Black Kids Sitting Together in the Cafeteria?* (2003), Beverly Daniel Tatum provides many answers to this question. One response is that schools are internally segregated, with White students being the most likely to be in the more advanced classes. When children are in different classes, it is not surprising that they do not spend time together during social hours (Tatum 2003).

From elementary to high school, students in U.S. schools are placed in different classes based on ability groups, or "tracks." Many studies have found that non-White children are more likely to be placed in low-ability groups, beginning in elementary school, whereas White children are more likely to be placed in college-bound tracks in high school. Kao and Thompson (2003) discuss data from 1997 which reveals that nearly half of Whites and Asians were in college preparatory tracks, compared with about a third of Latinx and Asian students and less than a quarter of Native American students. Another study, based on 1998 data, found that White students were twice as likely as Black students to be in advanced mathematics courses. This study, however, found that the differences could be explained by accounting for test scores, grades, prior track placement, and socioeconomic status (Kelly 2009). A more recent nationally representative study found that African Americans and Latinxs were underrepresented in advanced sophomore math classes in a large number of schools. Moreover, Black and Latinx students at those schools had lower average GPAs and rates of university enrollment (Muller et al. 2010).

In addition to within-school differences, there are also disparities between schools. Schools that are predominantly White are more likely to have advanced placement (AP) classes than primarily Black and Latinx schools. The different opportunities of Black, Latinx, and Native American students to take advanced classes have important impacts on their overall academic achievement and college success rates (Kao and Thompson 2003).

Social and Cultural Capital and Schooling

Sociologists of education also often turn to social and cultural capital as explanations for the achievement gap. **Social capital** refers to relationships and networks, whereas **cultural capital** describes available cultural resources. Put simply, social capital is *who* you know, whereas cultural capital is *what* you know. Students who know many people who have had educational success—parents, uncles, aunts, and cousins with college degrees—will have more information and resources at their disposal than students whose social networks primarily include high school dropouts or people with no schooling at all. This social capital

Why are schools often internally segregated?

will play a role in a student's ability to succeed. In a similar fashion, students with access to dominant cultural capital—the norms, values, and cultural knowledge of the school—will have more chances for success than students whose families are not part of the dominant culture.

Based on their research with Mexican-origin students in the Bay Area, sociologists Ricardo Stanton-Salazar and Sanford M. Dornbusch (1995) argue that to be successful in school, adolescents require supportive ties with institutional agents. An **institutional agent** is a person who occupies a position of power and is able to access or negotiate resources for students. These institutional agents can be family or community members as well as school personnel. An institutional agent can be a high school counselor who helps a student obtain financial aid, an alumnus of a local college who serves as a mentor to a student and helps him or her fill out college applications, or a high school teacher who writes a college recommendation for a student. These institutional agents constitute a form of social capital that permits students to reach their educational goals. Working-class youth have less access to this necessary form of social capital, which makes reaching their educational goals more difficult.

Most schools in the United States make some effort to recognize the multicultural nature of the nation. Nevertheless, people whose culture and experiences are part of the dominant culture are in charge of most schools. Children whose families are part of the dominant culture thus have an inherent advantage, as they do not have to learn the codes and norms of the dominant culture to be successful in school. Moreover, the school does not devalue their experiences and culture.

The concept of cultural capital draws from the work of French sociologist Pierre Bourdieu (1984), who argued that the dominant group in a society makes its preferences, tastes, and norms appear to be superior to those of the nondominant group. He describes the power of the dominant group to do this as **symbolic violence**, as the dominant group creates a context in which the norms, values, and tastes of other groups are labeled as inferior. An example of this symbolic violence in the United States is the idea that the standard form of English spoken by middle-class White Americans is an indication of intelligence and eloquence, whereas the forms of English that working-class African Americans speak to one another is an indication of ignorance. The dominant group—middle-class Whites—sets the standards.

What all this means for education is that children who grow up in homes where Standard English is spoken can speak this language in school and receive praise for their intelligence and eloquence. Meanwhile, children raised in homes where other forms of English or other languages are spoken must learn new languages and accents in school, and their teachers may tell them not to speak the way their parents do at home. The act of telling children that the way their parents speak is inferior and unacceptable in a school environment can amount to symbolic violence.

Scholars such as Michèle Lamont and Annette Lareau (1988, 164) define cultural capital as "widely shared, legitimate culture made up of high-status cultural signals (attitudes, preferences, behaviors, and goods) used in direct or indirect social and cultural exclusion." Other scholars, however, contend that all people have cultural capital, not solely those who belong to the dominant group. Sociologist Prudence Carter (2003) explains that nondominant cultural capital refers to those cultural resources and tastes that people who do not belong to the dominant group use to gain authenticity as members of their group. For example, African American youth may use nondominant cultural capital such as knowledge of the latest underground hip-hop music to signify their cultural authenticity. In this way, nondominant cultural capital also has an instrumental use—even though that use may not gain the youth very much in terms of the dominant society.

In a 2003 study, Prudence Carter interviewed African American youth in New York, who explained to her that they used different ways of talking at home and at school because they knew that speaking Standard English would be valued in a school setting. Carter's interviewees pointed to dress, musical, and speech styles as the most salient cultural indicators of what it means to be authentically Black. Carter, however, found that a certain amount of tension was involved in these students' navigation of their home and school identities. Students told her that they could easily navigate the different cultural markers and language of the two environments. However, in some cases, the youth "sensed that their cultural presentations of selves negatively influenced teachers' evaluations" (150). Black youth who wish to maintain cultural authenticity have to work hard to maintain an appropriate balance. However, middle-class White youth whose families and communities value dominant cultural capital do not have to worry about this balancing act. As Carter explains, the Black youth she worked with

> perceived that teachers evaluated them as deficient based on the teachers' and the schools' standards of cultural decorum. They

understood that most Whites with whom they came into contact used Standard English primarily, the language that facilitates success in U.S. schools (although it is not a sufficient condition by itself). At the same time, they did not believe their own speech styles to be incompatible with school success. (151)

Although most teachers have good intentions, the reality is that teachers are members of our society and, like all of us, they are inundated with media images that reinforce stereotypes. The prevalence of stereotypes about Black men and criminality, for example, influences how teachers respond to Black boys who misbehave. This, in turn, affects Black boys' schooling outcomes. Ann Arnett Ferguson (2001) offers a poignant example from a school in California where a White teacher compared Black children who didn't return library books to "looters." Instead of seeing the children as careless or forgetful, the teacher resorted to racialized stereotypes of Black men as thieves. Ferguson argues that cultural representations of Black men as criminals serve to **adultify** Black boys in the eyes of teachers. Thus, instead of seeing Black boys as "just being boys" when they misbehave, teachers were inclined to say things such as "that boy has a jail cell with his name on it."

voices

Andrew Yang's Problematic Reinforcement of the Model Minority Myth

By Jenn Fang

Tonight, Silicon Valley entrepreneur Andrew Yang joined the nine other top Democratic presidential candidates on the debate stage at Texas Southern University. A noteworthy moment for Asian Americans, Yang remains one of the first Asian Americans in history to run a national campaign for the presidency.

That's why it is all the more problematic that Yang routinely leans upon Model Minority stereotypes of Asian Americans to advance his candidacy. As early as last year, Yang routinely framed himself as qualified to be president because he is a "smart Asian" who is "good at math"—a classic Model Minority trope reminiscent of the infamous *Time* magazine cover that popularized model minority stereotypes for a generation of Americans. . . .

Model minority stereotypes of Asian Americans first crystalized in 1966 with sociologist William Petersen's article "Success Story, Japanese-American style", published in *The New York Times*. In his article, Petersen explicitly contrasted high-achieving, persevering, and "law-abiding" Japanese Americans against those he labeled to be "problem minorities"—that is, Blacks fighting for civil rights in response to historic oppression. Later articles by other writers similarly profiled other "successful" Asian American groups, birthing the modern "Model Minority" stereotype of Asian Americans.

Today, the Model Minority Myth has changed little from the 1960s when it arose as direct repudiation of Black liberation efforts. Asian Americans are touted as wealthy, highly-educated, and hard-working success stories—a testament to how our system selectively rewards well-behaved model minorities at the expense of those Petersen described as "problem minorities." The Myth pits communities of colour against one another, suggests we ignore the scars of systemic racism, and encourages us to bootstrap our way into racial acceptance—as if that were even possible.

Model minority stereotypes are not fun, good-natured flattery. They are ugly, demeaning, racist caricatures that co-opt the Asian American identity into the service of assaulting Black civil rights.

The Model Minority Myth is, of course, based on a myth. Time and time again, proponents of the Myths will rechristen themselves amateur sociologists to declare that the Myth is based in fact. Asian Americans actually *are* smarter, they declare. We actually *are* all doctors. We actually all *do* love math.

Certainly, there are some Asian Americans who may embody characteristics consistent with model minority stereotypes. In any community, there will be smart folks, nerdy folks, apolitical folks, and folks who like math. The problem is not that these folks exist, but that when it comes to Asian Americans, the Model Minority Myth asserts these individuals to be meek, intelligent, and industrious *because* they are Asian.

Model minority stereotypes obscure the real diversity of the Asian American community. Whereas some Asian Americans enjoy above-average median household incomes and better access to higher education, they are a subset of Asian Americans and it is concerning and unhelpful to consider them representative of the community as a whole.

Every time the Model Minority Myth is misrepresented as fact, we render invisible the real facts about Asian Americans. We fail to see the staggering wealth gap among Asian Americans, which leaves more than 10 percent of Asian Americans living below the poverty line. We ignore evidence that the poverty rate is several times higher for some Asian American ethnic groups, whose members also struggle with greatly reduced access to college.

. . .

The Model Minority Myth hurts Asian Americans because it erases the many ways in which some Asian Americans struggle, and how they depend on public assistance to

(continued)

continued.

Andrew Yang's Problematic Reinforcement of the Model Minority Myth

survive. The perniciousness of the Model Minority Myth has cemented decades of Asian American marginalization in conversations of who gets—and who deserves—social services and civil rights.

. . .

We deserve, at the very least, an Asian American presidential candidate who is up-to-date with the current discourse around the Model Minority Myth's inherent racism—a discourse that most anti-racist Asian Americans are already familiar with. We deserve, at the very least, a candidate who has the pulse of Asian American identity politics; not one who sees anti-Asian stereotypes as a chance to grab a cheap punchline.

Again, I have to wonder: if Yang is joking, who's laughing?

Source: Jenn Fang. http://reappropriate.co/2019/09/
andrew-yangs-problematic-reinforcement-of-the-model-minority-myth/#more-27158

Hidden Curricula and the School-to-Prison Pipeline

Schools are sites of socialization and learning: it is in schools that students learn to become members of society and develop the skills necessary to be successful. The official curricula of schools include subjects such as math, science, history, and, increasingly, test-taking skills. Schools are also meant to function as sorting mechanisms: students who work hard and perform well will become the future leaders of society. Some education scholars argue that there is also a **hidden curriculum**: that is, the school curriculum is designed to reflect the cultural hegemony and to ensure the class interests of the dominant group. From this perspective, schools also function as sorting mechanisms, but not in a meritocratic fashion. Instead, schools reproduce the status quo.

One way in which schools reproduce racial inequality is through rules and punishment. Students are evaluated not only on their achievement, but also on their ability to conform to rules. Punishment for rule breaking becomes a mechanism of social differentiation and normalization. The disciplinary techniques used by schools label children as "good," "bad," "gifted," and "troublemakers," and children are judged on their ability to conform to school rules (Ferguson 2001, 52).

In her book *Bad Boys: Public Schools in the Making of Black Masculinity*, Ann Arnett Ferguson argues that teachers are more likely to interpret the behavior of African American boys as defiant or inappropriately expressive (2001). As a result of this interpretation and labeling, these students are more likely to receive punishment. There is a certain circularity here: since punishment often involves exclusion from the classroom, these students fall further behind.

This circularity is a crucial part of what some scholars call the **school-to-prison pipeline**—a set of practices that leads to children being funneled from public schools into the juvenile and criminal justice system. Factors contributing to this pipeline include a rise in suspension rates across the country and increased policing of and arrests within schools. These practices build up over the course of a child's educational career and have harmful effects on Black and Native American youth in particular. Across all age groups, starting with preschool, Black students are three times more likely than White students to be suspended from school, and Native American students, twice as likely. Relatedly, Black and Native American students are also twice as likely as other students to be subject to school-related arrest (U.S. Department of Education, Office for Civil Rights, 2014).

CONCLUSION AND DISCUSSION

In the United States, one-third of adults over the age of twenty-five have a bachelor's degree. With the changing labor market and growing inequality, postsecondary education has become increasingly important. Opportunities for financial stability increasingly depend on completing college.

In this chapter, we have explored various dimensions of educational inequality. Sociologists offer a range of explanations for why Native Americans, Latinx Americans, and African Americans are less likely than White adults to have a college degree. Some of these reasons are historical; the parents of many people of color did not have college degrees because of extreme barriers to higher education in the past. Other reasons are socioeconomic. For example, it is more difficult to attend college if you are in a financially precarious situation, and Whites have, on average, higher incomes than other groups. There are also structural and cultural explanations for racial disparities in educational outcomes.

What do we do with all of this information? Many top-tier public schools across the country continue to be primarily or exclusively White. Meanwhile, many underresourced and even dangerous schools serve primarily Black, Latinx, and Native American youth. What are the implications of failing to provide truly equal opportunities to children from disadvantaged backgrounds?

THINKING ABOUT RACIAL JUSTICE HOW HAS YOUR cultural capital affected your educational experience? Reflect on the extent to which you have had access to dominant versus nondominant cultural capital and how that has shaped your education. Drawing from the readings and your own experiences, describe an idea for how youth without access to dominant cultural capital could excel academically.

Key Terms

affirmative action 173

"model minority" myth 176

achievement gap 178

oppositional culture 181

acting White 181

social capital 183

cultural capital 183

institutional agent 184

symbolic violence 184

adultify 186

hidden curriculum 188

school-to-prison pipeline 189

CHECK YOUR UNDERSTANDING

6.1 What are the dimensions of racial inequality in our educational system?

The United States has a long history of educational inequality. In the early twentieth century, Native American, African American, and Mexican American children were relegated to separate and inferior schools. Segregation was outlawed in 1954, yet it has produced lingering effects.

 How has educational attainment across racial and ethnic groups changed over time?

 What are Indian schools, and what were the conditions like in those schools?

Q On what basis could plaintiffs in the *Brown v. Board of Education* case argue that schools were not "separate but equal"?

Q Why did it take so long for schools to become integrated after the 1954 *Brown v. Board of Education* decision?

6.2 How does the legacy of inequality affect contemporary educational opportunities and outcomes?

Asian and White students tend to do better on tests, have higher GPAs, and have higher rates of college completion than African American, Native American, and Latinx students.

Q What is the relationship between school segregation and poverty?

Q Why have schools begun to resegregate since 1991?

6.3 How can we explain continuing racial disparities in educational achievement?

Sociologists offer several explanations for disparate educational outcomes, including oppositional culture, tracking, social and cultural capital, and hidden curricula.

Q Give examples of the theoretical explanations sociologists offer for the achievement gap.

Q What is the difference between social and cultural capital? How are social and cultural capital related to educational success?

Critical Thinking

1. What are some lingering effects of forced school segregation?
2. How might the concept of intergenerational trauma help us understand racial inequalities today?
3. Why is there so much variation in the educational success rates among Asian American students of different nationalities?
4. Explain and reflect on the tension some youth face between maintaining cultural authenticity and being perceived as serious students. To what extent have you observed or experienced this tension personally?
5. How do racial ideologies play a role in reproducing racial inequalities within the school system? Explain how specific ideologies are connected to inequality.

6. Which explanation for the achievement gap do you find most convincing? Why?

7. To what extent do you think Black children do less well in school than White children to avoid being perceived as "acting White"? On what empirical basis do you make your arguments?

8. How are social capital and cultural capital important for school success? Reflect on their importance in your own educational experiences.

Talking about Race

Have you ever heard someone say that Asians are naturally good at math? Based on what you have read in this chapter, what are some ways you could respond to such a statement? Could you talk about the variation in Asian American rates of success? Could you talk about hyperselectivity? What other factors can help us unravel the "model minority" myth?

Learn more with this chapter's digital tools, including video clips from the author, web links, filmography, and chapter self-assessment quizzes at www.oup.com/he/golash-boza-brief3e.

Income and Labor Market Inequality

AS YOU READ

7.1 What is the extent of income inequality, and how does it vary by race, ethnicity, and gender?

7.2 What are some dimensions of labor market inequality?

7.3 How do sociologists explain labor market inequality?

7.4 Can affirmative action be an appropriate remedy for labor market discrimination?

7.5 What is the relationship between self-employment and labor market inequality?

After World War II, quality of life for those in the working and middle classes improved each year until 1973, when the average income began to fall. Meanwhile, the income of the upper classes began to skyrocket. Today, the United States is one of the most unequal countries in the Western Hemisphere (Johnston 2015). Moreover, inequality is mapped along race and gender lines, with African Americans and Latinxs earning substantially less than Whites. We see this racial inequality not just in income but also in the labor market as a whole. In this chapter, we will take a closer look at income and labor market inequality and develop a deeper understanding of racial inequality in the United States today.

Studies of labor market discrimination and income inequality clearly show that men earn more than women and that White workers earn more than non-White workers, even accounting for differences in education, skills, years on the job, and productivity (Pager, Western, and Bonikowski 2009; Georgetown University Center on Education and the Workforce 2019). Why are employers willing to pay a premium for White male workers? It seems as if in a capitalist society, employers should want to get the best worker they can for the lowest price. Yet the evidence suggests that employers routinely pass over highly qualified Black and Latinx candidates and offer raises and promotions to White candidates (Pager and Shepard 2008). Why do you think this is the case? Why are employers less likely to hire Black and Latinx candidates? Why are highly qualified Asians paid less than their White counterparts?

INCOME INEQUALITY BY RACE, ETHNICITY, AND GENDER

Before delving into inequalities among racial and ethnic groups, it is worth pointing out that in the United States, the difference in earnings between the richest and the poorest people has widened over the past few decades. Income inequality among Americans has increased in large part because of tremendous growth in the incomes of the highest earners and stagnation or decline in the incomes of the lowest earners. Although the average national household income was about $64,500 in 2000, which was 60 percent more than it had been in 1980 (in constant 2014 dollars), the average income of the bottom 50 percent of earners was only $16,000—the same as it was in 1980. By 2014, the top

50 percent of earners were taking in 88 percent of all income, up from about 80 percent in 1980. The top 1 percent alone took in 20 percent of all income. In fact, the average income of the top 1 percent rose from $420,000 in 1980 to $1.3 million in 2014—81 times more than the average income of the bottom 50 percent (Piketty, Saez, and Zucman 2016). By 2018, the top 10 percent of earners in the United States were earning 12.6 times that of the bottom 10 percent—up from 9.1 times in 1980 (Horowitz, Igielnik, and Kochhar 2020). These disparities are even sharper when we take wealth into consideration: by 2016, the top 10 percent of the population controlled 77 percent of the wealth in the U.S. and the bottom 50 percent only controlled 1.1 percent (Kuhn, Schularick, and Steins 2020).

You may recall the slogans of the "Occupy Wall Street" movement referring to this income (and wealth) disparity, such as: "We are the 99%." Tensions over inequality in the United States have risen in recent years in response to rising inequality. The United States has become one of the most unequal advanced economies in the world, with a Gini coefficient of 0.48 (see Figure 7-1). The **Gini coefficient** is a measure from 0 to 1, with 0 representing perfect equality (i.e., everyone earning exactly the same amount) and 1 representing perfect inequality (i.e., a single person having all the earnings) (International Labour Organization 2016). The high level of inequality in the U.S. is

FIGURE 7-1

GINI COEFFICIENTS IN THE AMERICAS, 2017

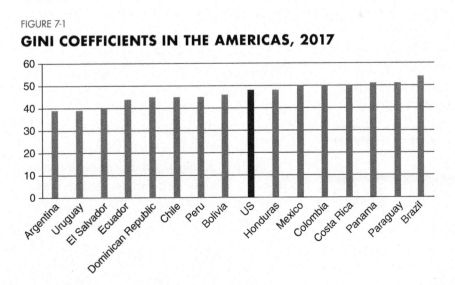

problematic both because it means that the United States has an increasingly large poor population and because inequality is related to a host of health and social problems, including high rates of low birth weight, homicide, mental illness, and violent crime (Wilkinson and Pickett 2009). Among the thirty-five member states of the Organization for Economic Cooperation and Development (OECD) countries, the Gini coefficient for the United States is the fourth highest, after Turkey, Mexico, and Chile. The U.S. has higher inequality than the other thirty-one countries—including Australia, Germany, Sweden, and Iceland. The Slovak Republic has the lowest Gini coefficient—at .241 in 2016 (OECD 2020).

Compared with similar nations, the United States is the most unequal on a variety of other measures as well. In addition to having the highest Gini coefficient, it also ranks last in child poverty rates, has the largest ratio between the richest 10 percent and the poorest 10 percent, and has the highest percentage of people living below 50 percent of the median income (Internationalcomparisons.org 2014).

Overall inequality is exacerbated by inequality distributed along racial and ethnic lines. Black and Latino families in the United States own just nine cents of wealth for each dollar White families own (Kuhn, Schularick, and Steins 2020). In terms of income, Asians have the highest median earnings, followed by White and then Black and Latinx earners (Figure 7-2). The median income of White workers in the United States has been higher than that of Black workers for as long as income data have been tracked. Such differences in earnings by group are called the **earnings gap**. Sociologists provide a wide array of explanations for this gap, many of which we will analyze later in this chapter.

How does income inequality by race and ethnicity further break down by gender? As we see in Figure 7-3, the largest difference in income is between Asian men—whose median weekly earnings were $1,383 in 2020—and Latina women—whose median weekly earnings were $702 per week. We don't have complete data on Native American earnings. However, we do know that only 19 percent of Native Americans

FIGURE 7-2

MEDIAN WEEKLY EARNINGS BY RACE/ ETHNICITY, 2020

Median weekly earnings by race/ethnicity, 2020
Workers over the age of 25 employed full time

Asian	White	Black	Hispanic/
$1242	$1023	$811	Latino
			$759

U.S. Bureau of Labor Statistics, 2020

Source: Bureau of Labor Statistics, 2015.

earned more than $1,200 per week, as compared to 50 percent of Asians (Allard and Brundage 2019).

In addition to the earnings gap, sociologists have identified a **wage gap**, which refers to differences in hourly earnings among groups. Whereas the earnings gap refers to overall income regardless of hours worked, the wage gap refers only to the difference in the amount earned per hour worked. To understand earnings and wage gaps by group, we need to account for broader forces at work in the labor market.

FIGURE 7-3

MEDIAN WEEKLY EARNINGS BY RACE/ETHNICITY AND GENDER, 2020

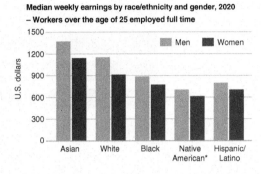

Median weekly earnings by race/ethnicity and gender, 2020 – Workers over the age of 25 employed full time

*Median earnings for Native American men and women are from the 2015 American Community Survey.

Source: U.S. Bureau of Labor Statistics, 2020.

DIMENSIONS OF RACIAL DISPARITIES IN THE LABOR MARKET

Disparities in earnings and wages are tied to many facets of the labor market, including unemployment rates, promotion practices, and employment stability. For example, Black women are at a higher risk of unemployment than White women, meaning they are even more economically disadvantaged than the wage gap suggests (Pettit and Ewert 2009).

Is it harder for people from some racial or ethnic groups to obtain jobs? Are some groups less likely to be promoted? Are some groups less likely to be in stable employment? All of these factors are relevant to understanding the extent of labor market disparities.

Disparities among Women

First, let's look at the role that gender plays. There is a wage gap between men and women in the United States: women earn, on average, 82 cents an hour for each dollar that men earn (Bleiweis 2020). Moreover, earnings differences by gender within and across racial and ethnic groups can be striking. White women earn 79 cents for each dollar that White men make. However, Black women make only 62 cents for each dollar that White men make, and Native American women only 57 cents (Bleiweis 2020; Figure 7-4). Thus, analyses of racial inequality

FIGURE 7-4

WOMEN'S HOURLY EARNINGS ON THE DOLLAR VERSUS MEN'S BY RACE/ETHNICITY

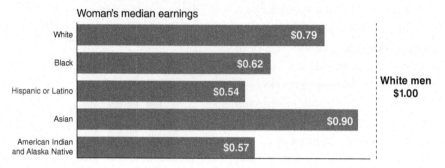

Source: Bureau of Labor Statistics, 2013. http://www.bls.gov/news.release/pdf/wkyeng.pdf

in the labor market that do not take gender into account provide an incomplete picture (Browne and Misra 2003).

A study by Raine Dozier (2010) helps us understand how labor market forces affect the earnings gap between Black and White women. Her study found that both groups experienced wage gains during the 1980s and 1990s, but White women gained more. Dozier explains that this disparity developed because White and Black women were not equally represented in the job sectors that had the most earnings growth. Between 1980 and 2002, more women entered the labor force and more highly paid professional positions became available to them. White women were more likely to attain these highly paid positions and thus gain more than their Black counterparts.

Completing college, for most people, leads to higher income. But, the gains in income varies by race and gender. White women who attend college will earn 24.4 percent more in their lifetime than their counterparts who don't attend college whereas Black men and women will only earn about 19 percent more in their lifetime. When we compare across races, we see different disparities: college-educated White men earn an average of $88,700 in retirement, as compared to $69,000 for Black and White women and $64,500 for Black men (Cosic 2019).

Most studies of labor market inequality focus on earnings. In a recent article, Tali, Cohen and Novot (2018) turn their attention to inequalities in employer-provided benefits—which account for 25 percent of total compensation. They found that, whereas women overall are more likely to have jobs with benefits such as employer-provided health insurance and retirement accounts, Black and Latinx people are less likely. For example, Hispanic men earned 63 cents for every dollar that White men earned, but only 48 cents for every dollar that White men obtained in employer-provided benefits. When we take total compensation into account, the earnings gap by race and ethnicity widens.

In the United States, women earn an average of 82 cents for each dollar men earn. This pay gap was one of the reasons for the 2017 Women's March on Washington.

COVID-19 and Racial Economic Disparities

There is a saying in the Black community: "When America catches a cold, Black people get pneumonia." The economic effects of the COVID-19 pandemic on Black Americans were in line with this saying. By April 2020, only 48.8 percent of Black adults were gainfully employed (see Figure 7-5). The labor force participation of Black Americans had not dropped below 50 percent since the early 1980s (Long and Van Dam 2020). In the early months of the COVID-19 pandemic, nearly 1 in 5 Black and Latinx people experienced food and housing insecurity, and over half had lost income since March 2020 (Long and Van Dam 2020).

Black Americans were particularly hard hit by the economic crisis caused by COVID-19 in large part because of their precarious economic position at the start of the start of the pandemic. Figure 7-6 shows how the median income of all racial groups fell between 2000

FIGURE 7-5

U.S. BLACK EMPLOYMENT AS A SHARE OF THE BLACK ADULT POPULATION

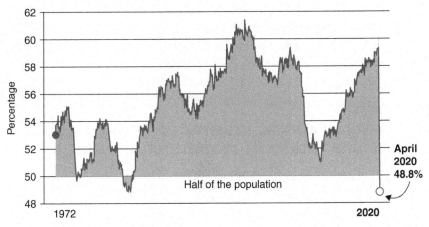

Source: Labor Department via FRED

FIGURE 7-6

CHANGE IN MEDIAN INCOME SINCE THE YEAR 2000, ADJUSTED FOR INFLATION

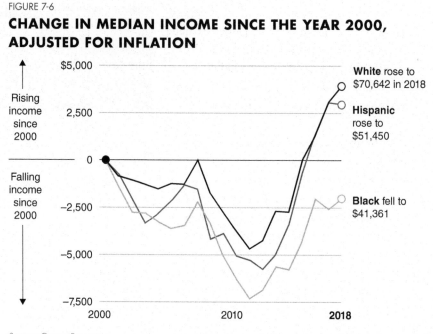

Source: Census Bureau

and 2011. During the economic recovery between 2011 and 2018, income rose for all groups. However, whereas income for Whites and Latinxs rose well above the medians from 2000, Black Americans, on average, were doing worse in 2018 than they were in 2000. By 2018, the median income for Whites was $70,642, for Latinxs it was $51,450 and for Blacks it was $41,361 (Long and Van Dam 2020).

Disparities among Asian Americans

Given the tremendous diversity within the Asian American population, it can be helpful to break these groups down by national origin when analyzing economic disparities. There is a lot of variation in household income among Asian Americans of different national origins (Figure 7-7). Whereas the average annual household income for

FIGURE 7-7

MEDIAN ANNUAL HOUSEHOLD INCOME AMONG ASIAN AMERICANS BY NATIONAL ORIGIN, 2015

Source: Pew Research Center (2017).

Indians in 2015 was $100,000, it was only $48,000 for Hmong house-holds. Taking a close look at the average earnings of different national origins among Asians is even more instructive because the average household income could include one, two, three, or more earners. In contrast, when we look at hourly earnings, we get a better sense of indi-vidual-level outcomes. In 2014, the median annual hourly earnings for Indian men was nearly $40 per hour, as compared to just less than $30 for Indian women. In contrast, the average earnings for Hmong men and women were both less than $15 per hour (Figure 7-8). These results

FIGURE 7-8

WAGE GAPS FOR ASIAN AMERICAN AND PACIFIC ISLANDER WOMEN BY SUBGROUP

Wage Gaps for Asian American and Pacific Islander Women by Subgroup					
Wage gaps among subgroups of AAPI women compared to white, non-Hispanic and AAPI men					
Self-Reported Ancestry or Ethnicity	Total Number in the United States	Median Wages for Women	Annual Wage Gap Compared to White, Non-Hispanic Men	Cents-on-the-Dollar versus White, Non-Hispanic Men	Cents-on-the-Dollar versus AAPI Men's Wages (Within subgroup)
Nepalese	167,468	$30,000	$30,000	50	81
Burmese	178,490	$31,000	$29,000	52	103
Fijian	39,103	$33,000	$27,000	55	59
Cambodian	240,379	$34,000	$26,000	57	85
Bangladeshi	203,845	$36,000	$24,000	60	86
Hmong	305,323	$36,800	$23,200	61	97
Samoan	110,606	$37,100	$22,900	62	84
Hawaiian	186,996	$38,000	$22,000	63	95
Guamanian/Chamorro	104,219	$39,500	$20,500	66	92
Laotian	203,494	$40,000	$20,000	67	100
Thai	218,514	$40,000	$20,000	67	80
Vietnamese	1,862,395	$40,000	$20,000	67	80
Tongan	40,538	$45,000	$15,000	75	125
Indonesian	70,851	$47,300	$12,700	79	79
Filipino	2,920,160	$50,000	$10,000	83	96
Pakistani	487,937	$53,000	$7,000	88	88
Korean	1,468,279	$54,000	$6,000	90	86
Sri Lankan	52,183	$54,000	$6,000	90	68
Japanese	782,776	$55,000	$5,000	92	73
Chinese	4,217,892	$60,000	$0	100	83
Indian	4,161,088	$72,000	−$12,000	120	73
Taiwanese	178,020	$74,000	−$14,000	123	100
Malaysian	20,599	$75,000	−$15,000	125	75

Source: Freeman 2011 and Bureau of Labor Statistics

show that it is not the case that race and gender are additive factors in the labor market. Instead, racism and sexism operate in distinct ways for different ethnic and racial groups.

Asian American men have the highest average earnings in the United States. Does this mean they do not face discrimination? Not necessarily. Many sociologists have pointed out that Asians earn more than Whites, but that their average earnings should actually be even higher because Asians have higher average educational attainment than Whites. Because of how our labor market distributes rewards, we should expect people with more education to earn more than their less educated counterparts, not the same or less. One study, for example, found that over half of Asians born in the United States complete college, compared with less than a third of Whites. Asians are also more likely than other groups to major in areas that have higher pay, such as science and engineering (Kim and Sakamoto 2010).

ChangHwan Kim and Arthur Sakamoto (2010) evaluated whether Asian American men experience labor market discrimination. Their study included only men who were college graduates. They found that Asian American men who are college graduates do earn more than their White counterparts. However, once you take into account the region where they live, their field of study, and their college type, native-born Asian American men have an 8 percent earnings disadvantage. In other words, if an Asian American man and a White man both live in New York, both went to selective universities, and both studied engineering, we could expect that the Asian man would earn, on average, 8 percent less than the White man. In contrast, Kim and Sakamoto found that Asian American men born abroad who went to school and now work in the United States do not experience a labor market disadvantage relative to White men.

Kim and Sakamoto's 2010 study included only college-educated men. However, in a follow-up study published in 2014, the researchers revealed that Asian American men without a college degree earn substantially less than their White counterparts. Kim and Sakamoto explain that the model-minority myth can have negative effects for Asians who do not achieve a certain level of educational success. The follow-up study showed particularly striking results for Asian American male high school dropouts, who earned significantly less than White male dropouts (Kim and Sakamoto 2014).

Underemployment, Unemployment, and Joblessness

Earnings inequality is compounded by unemployment rates. Earnings data do not factor in unemployed people, who may not be taking home any income. It is thus important to consider the effects of unemployment and underemployment on the bigger picture. These rates vary significantly by race and ethnicity, as shown in Figure 7-9. Since 1970, the unemployment rate for Black people has been about twice that for White people.

Wage differentials in the labor force provide a limited view of overall inequality, as analyses of the earnings gap account only for people who are actually working. Thus, as we will see, the finding that the earnings gap between White and Black workers has decreased since 1980 may not be as promising as it seems in terms of racial equality. The Bureau of Labor Statistics counts people as unemployed when they do not have a job and have actively looked for work in the previous month. Insofar as many people do not work and have given up looking for work, the unemployment rate is only one measure of joblessness (University of California Berkeley Labor Center 2013).

The labor market prospects of Black and Latinx workers also look bleak when we take underemployment into account. The **underemployment** category includes jobless workers actively seeking work, people who are working part time yet are available to work full time, and those who have looked for work in the past year but are not

FIGURE 7-9

UNEMPLOYMENT RATE BY RACE/ETHNICITY, 1973–2013

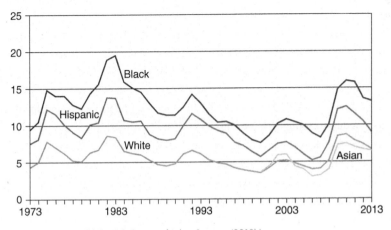

Sources: Freeman (2011); U.S. Bureau of Labor Statistics (2013b).

actively seeking employment. In 2017, 15 percent of Latinx workers and 13 percent of Black workers met this definition of underemployed, compared with 8 percent of White workers. For all workers, these rates had improved since 2010, when 25 percent of Black and Latinx workers and 15 percent of White workers were underemployed (Bureau of Labor Statistics 2017). Notably, these disparities are greater in rural areas—where 17 percent of White workers are underemployed, as compared to 23 percent of Latinx workers, and 33 percent of Black workers (Slack, Thiede, and Jensen 2019).

voices

Foraging on the Margins of the Labor Market

by Kelsey Drotning

Finding a job is hard no matter who you are. But some people face more barriers to obtaining employment than others, including racial minorities and those with criminal records who have to "check the box." In *American Journal of Sociology*, Naomi F. Sugie shows how the latter group of men navigate reentry into labor markets after incarceration.

As part of the Newark SmartPhone Reentry Project, Sugie collected smartphone data from 133 men recently released from prison in Newark, NJ. The men were asked to participate for a period of three months, after which they could keep the provided smartphone. Sugie learned that the majority of respondents engaged in "foraging behavior"—taking on short-term jobs in a variety of industries as a way to make ends meet.

Initially, most participants spent about half of their time searching for long-term work, but almost half stopped searching after the first month. But their decreases in job search days were not linked to an increase in working days. Rarely did the men spend more than two days in the same job or even work the same job week to week during the three-month study period. Even those who found relatively consistent work still had less stability than people working Monday to Friday jobs. And among the typically older respondents who continued searching after the first month, foraging was necessary to meet day-to-day financial needs.

Workers who forage often lack the social integration and job protection associated with long-term employment. While this study looked at one group on the margins of the labor market, Sugie believes foraging may be prevalent among other groups that struggle to obtain traditional entry into America's workforce.

Source: https://contexts.org/articles/foraging-on-the-margins-of-the-labor-market/

The 2 million people in the criminal justice system are also mostly outside the labor force, yet they are not included in the official counts of the unemployed. As many as 1 in 10 Black men age 20–34 are in prison or jail on any given day, as compared to 1 in 100 members of the general population (Pettit and Sykes 2015). High rates of incarceration for young Black men exacerbate their rates of joblessness. As one example of how the incarceration rate affects the jobless rate, we can consider a study by Western and Pettit (2002) that looked at the percentages of Black and White high school dropouts with jobs. The study found that without taking the incarcerated population into account, 50 percent of Black high school dropouts aged twenty-two to thirty had jobs, compared with 80 percent of White high school dropouts. After factoring in the incarcerated population, however, this percentage dropped to less than 30 percent for Black male high school dropouts, compared with over 60 percent for their White counterparts (Western and Pettit 2002).

Western and Pettit (2005) found that the gains in Black men's wages between 1980 and 1999 must be assessed in light of the large numbers of Black men who went to prison and became jobless during that same time period. Incarceration is an important factor in assessing labor market inequality for Black men. If we look at labor market inequality without taking into account incarceration rates, we will have an incomplete picture because large numbers of Black men are effectively taken out of the labor market by imprisonment. As Western and Pettit (2002) explained, when we take into account the incarcerated population, less than a third of Black male high school dropouts are employed.

One in three Black men born in the twenty-first century can expect to spend time in prison during his lifetime (Mauer and King 2007). While incarcerated, people are either unemployed or employed at extremely low wages, as the minimum wage does not apply to prison labor. Moreover, the effects of imprisonment endure after incarceration. People who spend time in prison often have trouble finding work once released because of the stigma of a criminal record (Pager 2007). They also are likely to earn less than people who have not been to prison, as their time in prison takes them out of the labor market, rendering them incapable of gaining work experience during this time. Over a quarter of formerly incarcerated people are unemployed, and these disparities are even starker by race. Whereas 6.4 percent of Black men aged 35-44 were unemployed in 2008, 35.2 percent of Black men aged 35-44 who had been released from prison in the past four years were unemployed. Formerly incarcerated Black women also faced very high unemployment rates (43.6 percent) as did Latinas (39.4 percent) (Couloute and Kopf 2018).

SOCIOLOGICAL EXPLANATIONS FOR INCOME AND LABOR MARKET INEQUALITY

One question that arises from these disparities is whether the gaps in earnings and employment are due to differences in human capital, labor market discrimination, or other factors. **Human capital** refers to educational attainment, skills, and job experience. Scholars who study labor market disparities often measure earnings gaps while taking into account human capital differences. The idea is that an individual's earnings should be based on his or her qualifications. If disparities remain once we take into account human capital differences, we can argue that labor market discrimination plays a role in the earnings gap. Studies of the earnings gap consistently show that about 10 to 20 percent of this gap cannot be explained by human capital differences. Sociologists often consider the unexplained gap to be an indicator of labor market discrimination (Pager et al. 2009).

The existence of an earnings gap tells us that labor market discrimination is likely at play. Field research or audit studies provide further evidence of labor market discrimination, particularly in terms of hiring. In these studies (e.g., Pager et al. 2009), researchers send out people with similar qualifications but different racial and ethnic identities to apply for existing jobs to find out if racial identity plays a role in employers' hiring decisions.

The lower earnings of African Americans and Latinxs can be attributed in part to individual factors such as discrimination and lower levels of human capital. But lower earnings are also attributable to structural factors such as changes in the labor market. During the 1980s, for example, wages increased for high-skilled jobs, government sector work declined, many unionized jobs went overseas, and part-time and temporary work rose. These structural changes affected labor market disparities. Of course, individual and structural factors also work together. For example, Black people have, on average, lower educational attainment than Asian Americans. This disparity has disadvantaged Black people in recent years because of the diminished opportunities for low-skill work that has resulted from outsourcing. This section considers both individual-level and structural explanations for labor market inequality.

Individual-Level Explanations

One way to explain the earnings gap among different racial groups in the United States is on an individual level. Some scholars argue that the earnings gap is due to individual human capital differences; for example, if Asian Americans have higher levels of education than Black people, we can expect them to have higher incomes.

In 2016, 87.4 percent of Asians, 70.6 percent of Latinxs, 70.5 percent of Whites, 56.5 percent of Blacks, and 18.8 percent of Native Americans who graduated from high school immediately enrolled in college (Espinosa, Turk, Taylor, and Chessman 2019). Higher levels of education among Asians are part of the reason they earn more than other racial groups. But to what extent does educational attainment explain overall patterns of income inequality?

According to a study published by the Federal Reserve Bank of San Francisco, in 2016, the average Black male worker earned $18 an hour, compared to the average White male worker, who earned $25 an hour. The authors used a statistical method called regression to figure out what factors explain this average difference of $7 per hour—which, by the way, adds up to about $14,000 a year. For example, the fact that Black and White men work in different types of jobs accounts for just over $2 of the earnings gap. The fact that White men have higher levels of education accounts for just over $1 of the earnings gap. The differences between Black and White men in age, part-time status, and state of residence account for less than $1. The remaining difference, which amounts to just over $3 per hour is unexplained by differences between Black and White men in age, education, occupation, and other factors relevant to the labor market.

When differences in earnings cannot be explained fully by relevant labor market characteristics such as age, education, or occupation, many scholars argue that the remaining earnings gap can be explained by discrimination. Racial discrimination in the labor market occurs when racial status plays a role in an employer's decision to deny a person a job, promotion, or raise. Studies have found that employers admit they are hesitant to hire Black workers (Pager and Shepherd 2008).

voices

Latina Professionals as Racialized Tokens: Lisa's Story

Glenda Flores argues that Latina professionals are "racialized tokens." When they are numerical minorities in White-collar occupations, they experience a series of uncomfortable situations rooted in racial conflict. Flores's work on Latina doctors introduces us to Lisa, a thirty-four-year-old family medicine physician born in El Salvador. Lisa moved to the United States with her family as an infant and settled in the Pico Union District in downtown Los Angeles.

Lisa explained that her college-educated, White-collar parents experienced downward mobility upon arrival. As undocumented immigrants, they found work in the garment industry. Lisa overcame obstacles associated with her parents' low socioeconomic status and earned her medical degree from the University of California at Davis.

Despite experiencing intergenerational upward mobility and securing a prestigious profession that paid over $100,000 a year, Lisa shared that she frequently experienced gendered and racial inequities in her interactions with colleagues and patients, both co-ethnics and non-Latinxs. In an interview, Lisa recounted a situation with a White physician:

> I ended up doing way more [work] than that [White] doctor. That doctor slowed me down because his Spanish was broken and he did not know anything about medical Spanish, which I have been studying. So they were using me to interpret [for him] and I was really mad . . . I'm like "why am I doing that?" . . . I am okay doing it but it was just funny that [another] Latino [doctor], a Peruvian guy, was putting him [the White doctor] on a pedestal because he is male, White, and older and I am the opposite.

Later, Lisa, who had a very slight accent indicative of a native Spanish speaker, explained how racial/ethnic inequality influenced how patients interacted with her during office visits:

> There was an intern who was an Asian [male] and had seen this patient. I am understanding it was [an instance rooted in] race because this is what the [White] patient said. . . . I am talking [to the patient] in English and he is like "I don't understand you. Bring back the Asian doctor. I don't understand you." [I say] "Sir, I am speaking English!" He says, "no but I don't understand *your*

English." . . . the Caucasian [patients] are the ones that [it has happened with] at least in two situations. It is more race and language because I do have an accent and I realize that but I can communicate.

While Lisa felt she was culturally competent to aid patients of various social and economic backgrounds, she was aware that her race/ethnicity and gender meant that both physicians and patients undermined her medical expertise, favoring medical interns who held a lesser rank or less competent White doctors over her.

White women also face gender discrimination in male-dominated jobs. However, the experience is different for professional Latina who encounter gendered racism. Inequality in the professions manifests itself in different ways, and bilingual Latina working in the "token" context often find themselves doing additional work—such as translations—that others performing the same job are not asked to do.

Source: Glenda Flores, University of California at Irvine.

One way of measuring labor market discrimination is to use statistics to identify systematic disparities between different groups. For example, if we compare the earnings of thirty-five-year-old college-educated White men to similarly situated Black men and find a disparity, we can conclude that labor market discrimination plays a role in the earnings disparity. As previously mentioned, another method for uncovering discrimination involves the use of field experiments or audit studies in which researchers send equally qualified individuals out to apply for jobs and calculate the extent to which race or ethnicity affects employers' hiring practices. Each of these methodologies has revealed labor market discrimination (Pager and Shepherd 2008).

Marianne Bertrand and Sendhil Mullainathan (2004) conducted an extensive audit study to find out if employers discriminate against African Americans. They created four résumés—two high-skill and two low-skill—to send to over 1,300 job ads in Chicago and Boston. To isolate the effect they were studying, they randomly assigned either an African American–sounding name (such as Lakisha Washington or Jamal Jones) or a White-sounding name (such as Emily Walsh or Greg Baker) to each résumé. They found that applicants with White-sounding names needed to send out about ten résumés to get a callback, whereas applicants with African American–sounding names needed to send about fifteen. This audit study shows that African Americans have a harder time securing interviews that lead to employment than Whites in part because employers often prefer White employees. This preference may reflect conscious or unconscious bias.

Researchers who study **implicit bias** explain that we all have biases at a subconscious level. Owing to stereotypes, for example, a potential employer may exhibit bias in evaluating the same résumé from "Lakisha Washington" versus "Emily Walsh" without even being aware that they are doing so.

A clear example of implicit bias comes from a study of lawyers. A group of researchers crafted a fictitious legal research memo and asked sixty law firm partners to evaluate the memo. The memo contained seven deliberate spelling and grammatical errors. The partners (which included twenty-three women, thirty-seven men, twenty-one racial/ethnic minorities, and thirty-nine Caucasians) all received the same memo. However, half were told the author was Black, and the other half were told the author was White. The partners were asked to find the errors in the memo. Evaluators who were told that the author was Black found more of the embedded errors and rated the memo as lower quality than did those partners who were told the author was White. Specifically, they found an average of 2.9 spelling or grammar errors in the memo allegedly written by the White attorney, as compared with 5.8 spelling/grammar errors in the one supposedly written by the Black attorney. The author of the study explains: "We see more errors when we expect to see errors, and we see fewer errors when we do not expect to see errors" (Reeves 2014, 6).

The evaluators in the lawyer study were not people who think of themselves as racist or who hold a low opinion of African Americans. Instead, their implicit biases led them to find more errors when they thought the author of the memo was Black. Understanding these biases helps us understand some ways that African Americans are disadvantaged in the labor market.

Lincoln Quillian, Devah Pager, Ole Hexel, and Arnfinn Midtbøen (2017) conducted a meta-analysis—a research method that examines the results of existing research studies on the same research question to look for overarching patterns in the findings and study design. They examined field experiments in hiring discrimination as measured by the ratio of "callbacks" or invitations to interview. They looked at every research study available since 1989, which totaled twenty-eight studies. Combining the twenty-eight studies, the researchers looked for patterns in 55,842 submitted applications for 26,326 job openings. Their analyses found no change in racial discrimination in callbacks for African Americans and only a modest decline in discrimination against Latinxs. The authors (2017: pp. 10870) write: "Since 1989, Whites receive on average 36% more callbacks than African Americans, and 24% more callbacks than Latinos." This meta-analysis provides ample evidence of labor market discrimination.

Structural Explanations

Some scholars have looked beyond individuals to explain the disparities between social groups in terms of larger structures. One prominent explanation for earnings disparities between Black and White men points to the changing nature of U.S. cities, where the decline in manufacturing has meant the disappearance of work. This shift in the labor market has affected Black men in particular because of their concentration in the manufacturing sectors of many major cities.

Deindustrialization, the shift from a manufacturing to a service economy, has affected working-class people in all racial and ethnic groups in the United States. After World War II, working families in the United States experienced newfound prosperity as the U.S. economy grew rapidly with the production of automobiles and steel. These manufacturing jobs often paid well and came with benefits. Mostly men worked in these jobs, and many earned a family wage—an income sufficient to support their wives and children (Milkman 1997; Sugrue 2014). Between 1950 and 1960, average incomes in the United States increased steadily. However, these increases began to level off, and by the 1970s, incomes for the working poor had stopped increasing. The average income for people with less than a high school diploma actually decreased from about $30,000 in 1967 to about $25,000 in 2014 (in constant 2014 dollars; Cahalan and Perna 2015).

One reason for the decreases in the average pay for low-skilled workers is deindustrialization. In 1950, 40 percent of all jobs involved the production of goods. By 1997, less than 20 percent of all jobs were goods-producing (see Figure 7-9). Whereas, historically, manufacturing jobs often offered stable employment and a family wage, service-sector jobs are often temporary and part time, and offer lower wages. Between 1979 and 1985, the United States lost 10 percent of its manufacturing jobs. These losses were concentrated in certain geographical areas, thereby amplifying their localized effects. The Midwest lost over a million jobs, and the Northeast lost 800,000. By contrast, the West gained 53,000 manufacturing jobs (Sassen 1989). Detroit was one of the cities hit hardest by global economic restructuring: it lost 70 percent of its manufacturing jobs between 1969 and 1989. By the end of the 1980s, over a third of all African Americans in Detroit lived in poverty, as did half of Detroit's African American children (Kodras 1997).

The decline in manufacturing was also accompanied by a decline in unionized jobs: In 1954, 35 percent of the nation's workforce was unionized. By the early 1980s, this figure had dropped to 20 percent (see Figure 7-10). And, by 2021, the unionization rate was 10.3 percent (Bureau of Labor Statistics 2022). In that same year, non-union workers had median weekly earnings of $975 compared to union workers' median weekly earnings of $1,169. States like North and South Carolina that have right-to-work laws had exceptionally low rates of unionization—at 1.7 and 2.6 percent, respectively (Bureau of Labor Statistics 2022).

FIGURE 7-10

PERCENTAGE OF U.S. LABOR FORCE IN MANUFACTURING, 1939–2016

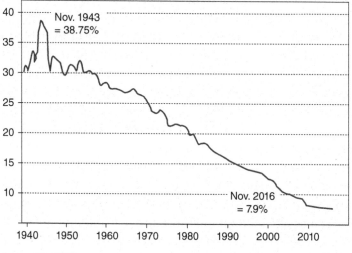

Source: BLS (2015)

In the 1950s, many urban African American families lived in poverty, but they were among the working poor. For example, in 1960, 69 percent of men over the age of fourteen who lived in the Black Belt region of the city of Chicago were regularly employed. By 1990, only 37 percent of men sixteen or over were regularly employed (Wilson 1996). This figure is even smaller if we take into account the incarcerated population, as discussed previously.

Until the 1980s, many Black men were employed in manufacturing jobs, which provided benefits and a family wage, permitting families to attain comfortable standards of living. Once these factories began to close, these comfortable lifestyles went with them. Black men were the hardest hit by this economic restructuring: Oliver and Shapiro (2006, 26) write that "from 1979 to 1984 one-half of Black males in durable-goods manufacturing in five Great Lakes cities lost their jobs."

When the economic crisis hit Detroit and other cities, White residents often fled, whereas African American residents rarely had this option. As a result, by the end of the 1980s, urban areas were much less White and much more impoverished than they had been a decade earlier. The unemployment rates of African American men in these urban areas rose to extraordinarily high rates—by 1990, only 37 percent of males sixteen or over who lived in the Black Belt in Chicago were regularly employed (Wilson 1996).

African American men in Detroit were hit particularly hard by deindustrialization. This is due in part to the fact that, in 1970, 94 percent of employed Black men in Detroit had blue-collar jobs, the sector that experienced the greatest decline (Sugrue 2014). This deindustrialization trend that started in the 1950s continued for five decades: between 1972 and 1992, three out of four production jobs disappeared from Detroit (Boyle 2001). As the availability of manufacturing jobs declined, Black men began to have difficulty finding work (Farley, Danziger, and Hozer 2000).

The prevalence of Black unemployment in deindustrializing urban areas such as Detroit and Chicago is better understood by examining both the skills mismatch and the spatial mismatch that deindustrialization has created. The **skills mismatch hypothesis** suggests that many African American men in particular often do not have the skills required to secure work in the current economy. Although employment sectors that require a college degree have experienced growth, many African American men do not have the qualifications for these jobs.

The **spatial mismatch hypothesis** sheds further light on these trends, as it explains that African American families have been excluded from buying homes in the suburbs where much of the job growth has occurred. This exclusion has created a disconnect between where African Americans live and where the jobs are concentrated. In Detroit, for example, the city is 80 percent Black, whereas the Detroit metropolitan area (including the suburbs) is 22 percent Black. The city is much poorer than the suburbs and has fewer well-paying jobs. Over half of city residents live in areas where the poverty rate is over 40 percent. Over 100,000 people who live in Detroit commute to the suburbs for work—and 36 percent of them earn less than $15,000 a year. Less than a third of employed Detroit residents both live and work in Detroit. In sum, Detroit's overwhelming Black population has a spatial disadvantage in the labor market due to a spatial mismatch between where they live and the jobs available to them (Abello 2017).

AFFIRMATIVE ACTION IN EMPLOYMENT

In a profit-based economic system, wages should be determined by competition, and the most qualified people should get the available jobs. If there are lots of people with a certain skill set, wages will be lower for that job. In contrast, if there are fewer people with the requisite skills, then wages should be higher. However, prior to the civil rights era, employers practiced overt discrimination: they refused to hire African Americans and paid them less than Whites when they did hire them.

Edna Bonacich (1976) explains that historic disparities between Blacks and Whites are due to a **split labor market**, which refers to a difference in the price of labor for two or more groups of laborers. For example, in 1927 in Virginia, the average daily pay rate for White brick-layers was $11.00, whereas it was $9.60 for Blacks. Similarly, White cement workers earned an average of $6.33 per day, whereas Blacks earned an average of $4.42. While many companies paid African Americans less, others refused to hire them at all. This seems somewhat illogical, as we would expect employers to hire the lowest-paid workers they could find. However, often racial discrimination is not based on logic.

One story from the late 1950s is that of Thomas Bailey, a skilled brickmason who had trouble finding steady work. When he applied for jobs, foremen often told him that he had to be a member of a union to work there. Yet, when he applied for membership in the union, the business agent told him he could only be a member if he was actively working. Bailey, an African American, was caught in a bind. He had trouble getting steady work because the unions often refused to allow Black men to join, and the unions controlled access to construction employment. When this issue came to the attention of local civil rights leaders, they pressured the union to allow Bailey to join. He eventually was let in but faced intimidation by other union members. Because of the widespread nature of cases like Bailey's, national leaders began to push for more systemic changes. The construction industry was one of the first targets because it relied on federal contracts. The federal government had the power to require these companies to obey anti-discrimination laws as a condition of their contracts (Golland 2011).

One of the proposed solutions to labor market discrimination came to be known as *affirmative action*. This term was first used in 1935 in the National Labor Relations Act, which specified that employers could not discriminate against union members or organizers. If they did, they would have to take affirmative action to remedy the effects of that discrimination (Skrentny 1996). Three decades later, President Lyndon Johnson used the term in Executive Order 11246 (1965). In this order, Johnson called for federal contractors to "take affirmative action to ensure that applicants are employed, and that employees are treated during employment without regard to their race, color, religion, sex or national origin."

Because of this order and other civil rights legislation and rules, by the 1960s, federal contractors had to sign pre-award affirmative action agreements ensuring active recruitment of a diverse workforce. Contractors also had to agree to sponsor non-White workers for apprenticeships and training. In this way, in towns and cities across the nation, African Americans and Latinxs were able to secure employment in what had been a primarily White employment sector (Golland 2011).

Today, affirmative action refers to policies and procedures designed to combat ongoing discrimination in the workplace and in schools (see Chapter 6). Affirmative action policies aim to prevent discrimination by requiring employers to be proactive in their attempts to diversify their workforce. In addition, affirmative action policies require employers to be conscious of the racial and ethnic makeup of their employees to ensure a more diverse workforce (Skrentny 1996). The overarching goal of affirmative action in employment is to decrease the influence of racial discrimination on the employment prospects of people of color.

Government orders for contractors are one of four kinds of affirmative action in the United States:

1. Government orders regulating government contractors and subcontractors
2. Regulations requiring affirmation action by public employers
3. Court orders based on antidiscrimination law
4. Employers' voluntary human resources policies

Since 1965, companies that do business with the federal government have been required to meet affirmative action requirements. The U.S. Department of Labor website (U.S. Department of Labor, n.d.) indicates that "for federal contractors and subcontractors, affirmative action must be taken by covered employers to recruit and advance qualified minorities, women, persons with disabilities, and covered veterans. Affirmative actions include training programs, outreach efforts, and other positive steps." In other words, any company that works with the federal government has to show that it is taking positive steps to maintain or increase the diversity of its workforce. One example is the promotion of broad recruitment strategies: posting a job advertisement for at least thirty days, advertising in a range of venues, and using objective evaluation criteria to review the applicants. Contrary to popular belief, affirmative action does not mean giving preference to minority candidates. Instead, it just means that companies must show they made an effort to hire people of color —in other words, took affirmative actions.

In 1972, the Equal Opportunity Act created a provision mandating that employers found guilty of discrimination must implement affirmative action policies. Since 1965, hundreds of employers have implemented affirmative action voluntarily in their hiring and promotion strategies. It is clearly not enough: despite fifty years of affirmative action, African Americans, Latinx, and Asian Americans continue to experience labor market discrimination.

ENTREPRENEURSHIP AND SELF-EMPLOYMENT

Given the unequal conditions of the formal labor market, many racial and ethnic minorities turn to self-employment as a means to achieve the American Dream and to be their own boss. Self-employment rates vary significantly among groups. In 2010, 13.5 percent of White men were self-employed, compared with 6.2 percent of African Americans,

34 percent of Israelis, 27 percent of Koreans, 10 percent of Mexicans, and 9 percent of Dominicans. Most sociologists explain these disparities in self-employment rates by pointing to differences in social and ethnic networks and human capital (Portes and Yiu 2013).

The self-employment strategy has worked better for some groups than for others. Chinese and Cuban small-business owners, for example, tend to do better than their counterparts who are not self-employed. However, African American, Korean, and Mexican small-business owners often experience severe setbacks. The work of both Adia Harvey Wingfield (2008) and Zulema Valdez (2008a, 2011) adds complexity to traditional understandings of the **ethnic enclave economy**, which refers to clusters of small businesses that primarily serve people of the same ethnicity and work to facilitate the success of co-ethnics. The ethnic enclave economy has helped immigrants of certain national origins, such as Cubans, attain economic success in the United States. According to this framework, immigrants such as the Chinese, Cubans, Greeks, and Koreans have attained success in small-business ownership because of their high human capital, social networks, and close-knit ethnic communities. However, both Wingfield and Valdez have criticized scholarship that focuses solely on ethnicity and culture. They argue that it is critical to understand how race, class, and gender—in addition to ethnicity and culture—play a role in the success of small businesses.

Wingfield (2008) draws on the concept of a **racial enclave economy**, in which a business's success is both shaped and limited by the racial group membership of the business owner. She uses the example of Black female owners of hair salons to elaborate on this concept. Valdez (2011) draws from interviews with restaurant owners of different ethnic origins to explain how race, class, and gender play a role in shaping the success of local businesses. To explain disparities in the success of small businesses, she uses the concept of an **embedded market**—a market economy embedded within interlocking systems of oppression and privilege, such as "capitalism, patriarchy, and White supremacy" (37). These systems of oppression affect an individual's possibilities for success as an entrepreneur. Whereas previous scholarship on ethnic enclaves might presume that Mexicans have similar options in the restaurant industry, Valdez explains that an upper-class male Mexican may be able to open a highly profitable Italian restaurant in a wealthy neighborhood, whereas a poor female Mexican may be limited to opening a taqueria in the barrio.

Valdez (2008b) conducted a national study in which she looked at four groups of entrepreneurs: White, Korean, Mexican, and Black men.

She found that 40 percent of the White owners earned over $75,000 a year, as did 25 percent of the Koreans, 20 percent of the Mexicans, and 17 percent of the Black business owners. In contrast, nearly half of the Black business owners earned less than $25,000 a year, as did 41 percent of the Mexicans, 33 percent of the Koreans, and 24 percent of the White male business owners. Her study found that this disparity can be explained in part by the fact that Korean and White small-business owners are more likely to have higher educational levels than the Mexican and Black business owners. Black and Mexican business owners with higher levels of education and more access to bank loans are able to do much better with their businesses. Nevertheless, as Wingfield (2008) notes, some African American women without college educations are able to do well for themselves in certain racial enclave economies, such as hair salons. She further points out, however, that the enclave places limits on the success of Black female hair salon owners: they are able to do well, but their profits tend to plateau after about five years.

The 2015 *State of Women-Owned Businesses Report* emphasizes that the number of women-owned minority businesses has grown substantially over the past twenty years. However, it also shows that revenues from minority-owned businesses continue to lag behind those of White-owned businesses. The average revenue for businesses owned by Black women in 2015, for example, was just $39,893, compared with an average of $155,477 for all women-owned firms (*The State of Women-Owned Businesses Report*, 2015, 7). As shown in Figure 7-11, Whites own 79.3 percent of all firms but take in 90.7 percent of all revenue. In contrast, African Americans own 9.4 percent of firms but take in only 1.3 percent of all revenue.

Small businesses owned by people of color are also likely to be particularly hard hit during a crisis. In the first few weeks of the COVID-19 pandemic, two out of five Black small businesses and self-employed businesses

FIGURE 7-11

SHARE OF BUSINESS REVENUE BY GENDER AND RACE/ETHNICITY

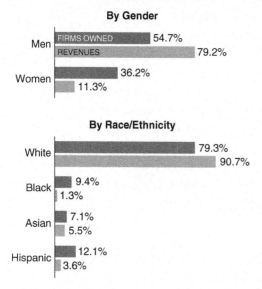

Note: Among those firms whose ownership can be classified by gender and race/ethnicity. Hispanics/Latinxs can be of any race; White, Black, and Asian figures include Hispanics/Latinxs.

Source: Desilver, Drew. 2015, Septmber 1. Business owned by women, minorities lag in revenue share.

were forced to temporarily close—and many were never able to reopen. Nearly 40 percent of Black self-employed people and small-business owners were not working in April 2020 (Long and Van Dam 2020).

CONCLUSION AND DISCUSSION

Despite fifty years of affirmative action and scores of antidiscrimination laws and lawsuits, non-Whites continue to be disadvantaged in the labor market. There are many reasons for this discrimination.

One reason is that it is difficult, or even impossible, to legislate away discrimination. Some employers may discriminate against non-Whites and women unconsciously. Racial ideologies are often ingrained in our individual perceptions. A White hiring manager may not be aware that because of entrenched stereotypes and implicit biases, he thinks of a White man as a "natural leader." He also may not realize that he presumes a Black man is irresponsible or a Latina woman is incapable of being professional. Labor market discrimination will not disappear until racial stereotypes do.

Another set of reasons for the earnings gap is structural: growth in certain industries and contraction in others are due to global forces that are beyond the control of a single government. Nevertheless, a government can provide training programs to get people up to speed and to work in emerging fields. This is an example of a race-neutral program that may help reduce racial disparities.

A related reason for this gap is that the labor market and the small-business market are structured by deeply entrenched inequalities, patriarchy, and racial divisions. Racial segregation in housing and schools, for example, leads to racially segregated social networks, which themselves reproduce preexisting inequalities. As the United States becomes increasingly unequal, it is critical to work toward ameliorating overall inequality while striving to reduce disparities among racial groups.

IMAGINE THAT EVERYONE in the United States, regardless of racial status, had an equal chance of being rich, middle class, or poor. Imagine further that the overall level of inequality remained the same. Would that be racial justice? Keep in mind that, in that scenario, with so many poor people in the United States, millions of people of color would continue to be poor. Reflect on the extent to which racial justice is tied to economic justice.

THINKING ABOUT RACIAL JUSTICE

Key Terms

Gini coefficient 195

earnings gap 196

wage gap 197

underemployment 203

human capital 206

implicit bias 210

deindustrialization 211

skills mismatch hypothesis 213

spatial mismatch hypothesis 214

split labor market 214

ethnic enclave economy 217

racial enclave economy 217

embedded market 217

CHECK YOUR UNDERSTANDING

7.1   What is the extent of income inequality, and how does it vary by race, ethnicity, and gender?

Overall income inequality in the United States is at a historic high. This inequality is exacerbated when we take racial, ethnic, and gender disparities into account.

 How has inequality changed over the course of the twentieth and twenty-first centuries?

 How unequal is the United States compared with other countries?

What is the difference between the wage gap and the earnings gap?

7.2   What are some dimensions of labor market inequality?

A complete understanding of racial disparities in the labor market requires a consideration of gender, national-origin differences, incarceration rates, and unemployment rates.

 Why is it important to take human capital into account when measuring earnings disparities?

How do racism and sexism operate differently in the labor market?

7.3   How do sociologists explain labor market inequality?

Sociologists offer various explanations for labor market disparities, ranging from human capital disparities to employer discrimination and structural changes in the overall economy.

 To what extent are Asian Americans advantaged or disadvantaged in the U.S. labor market?

 How do the individual-level explanations for labor market disparities differ from the structural explanations? To what extent could these explanations work together?

7.4 Can affirmative action be an appropriate remedy for labor market discrimination?

Few employers have affirmative action policies in place. Those that do are required to take positive steps to ensure that their company does not practice racial discrimination and has a diverse workforce that reflects the working-age population of the United States.

 How has affirmative action been implemented in the United States?

7.5 What is the relationship between self-employment and labor market inequality?

Self-employment and entrepreneurship have worked well for some racial minority groups but not for others.

 In owning successful small businesses, what barriers do women and racial minorities face in particular?

Critical Thinking

1. How do the wage and earnings gaps represent different facets of inequality?
2. Why has earnings inequality increased over the past fifty years?
3. Of the explanations provided, which do you find most convincing for explaining the earnings disparities between Black men and White men? Why?
4. Why does the author argue that the incarcerated population should be included in counts of the unemployed?
5. Are audit studies a useful way to measure discrimination? Why or why not? What are the weaknesses and strengths of this approach?
6. Why is it important to take gender into account when studying racial inequality?
7. What strategies do you think could be implemented to reduce the earnings penalty for non-White workers?
8. Can people of color avoid discrimination by becoming entrepreneurs? Why or why not?
9. How is an embedded market related to ethnic and racial enclaves? Evaluate how the embedded market affects minority-owned businesses.

Talking about Race

Income inequality has increased overall in the United States since the 1970s: the rich have become richer while the poor have become poorer. Think of ways to use what you have learned in this chapter to talk with people close to you about inequality. What is the relationship between overall inequality and inequality between racial groups? How could a decrease in overall inequality lead to a decrease in racial inequality? Do you think there could be room for interracial solidarity in discussions about income inequality?

Learn more with this chapter's digital tools, including video clips from the author, web links, filmography, and chapter self-assessment quizzes at www.oup.com/he/golash-boza-brief3e.

8

Inequality in Housing and Wealth

AS YOU READ

8.1 What are some historical reasons for housing and wealth inequalities in the United States?

8.2 When and how did residential segregation become a characteristic of U.S. cities?

8.3 What is the extent of wealth inequalities today in homeownership and beyond?

8.4 What factors are sustaining and exacerbating wealth inequalities?

nequalities in housing and wealth are deeply rooted in American history. In this chapter, we will learn about wealth inequality—both overall inequality and inequality among racial and ethnic groups. **Wealth** is the sum total of a person's **assets**—cash in the bank and the value of all property, not only land but houses, cars, stocks and bonds, and retirement savings—minus debt. It is something built up over a lifetime and passed on to the next generation through inheritances.

Wealth inequality in the United States is staggering: 1 percent of Americans own nearly half of the wealth in the country (Norton and Ariely 2011). Despite this tremendous inequality, the idea persists that if you work hard, you will succeed. This ideology is deeply rooted in the American psyche and sustained through popular media and folklore. Yet many people work hard all of their lives and die with no assets. As writer and activist George Monbiot (2011) put it, "If wealth was the inevitable result of hard work and enterprise, every woman in Africa would be a millionaire."

In Chapter 7, we learned about income inequality. Wealth inequality, as we will see, is both more entrenched and more severe. Most Americans think wealth should be distributed more equally—even as they underestimate the true extent of inequality. Most believe a fair distribution would mean a substantial amount of wealth for the middle class. The reality, however, is very different, with the middle class holding very little or no wealth and the poor having no wealth at all. These proportions—broken down into ideal, perceived, and actual distributions—are shown in Figure 8-1. As this figure shows, the United States is a highly unequal society in terms of wealth and is even more unequal than most of us realize. The top 20 percent of the population controls over 80 percent of the wealth (Norton and Ariely 2011). More recent data shows these inequalities have sharpened: by 2016, the top 10 percent of the population controlled 77 percent of the wealth in the US and the bottom 50 percent only controlled 1.1 percent (Kuhn, Schularick, and Steins 2020).

When we add race into the equation, the numbers get starker. Black and Latinx families in the United States own just nine cents of wealth for each dollar White families own (Kuhn, Schularick, and Steins 2020). How do we explain such racial disparities in wealth?

As we will see, the reasons for these disparities run deeper than those for income disparities. Wealth inequality is related to income

FIGURE 8-1

IDEAL, PERCEIVED, AND ACTUAL WEALTH DISTRIBUTION IN THE UNITED STATES

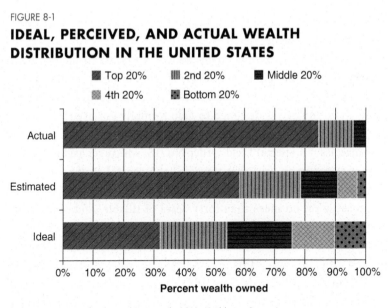

Source: Norton, Michael I. and Dan Ariely 2011. "Building a Better America—One Wealth Quintile at a Time." Perspectives on Psychological Science 6: 9 DOI: 10.1177/1745691610393524

inequality, but wealth and income inequality function differently. The wealth inequality between White and Black people, for example, is a result of historically embedded inequalities that go back to the time of slavery, the Jim Crow era, and early-twentieth-century housing policies. Today, these disparities are perpetuated and even exacerbated by inequalities in homeownership, college attendance, inheritance, and unemployment rates. Homeownership, often considered the cornerstone of the American Dream, is one of the primary driving forces behind racial disparities in wealth. In this chapter, we will take a close look at the historical roots of wealth inequality, as well as contemporary trends, through the lens of race.

LAND OWNERSHIP AFTER SLAVERY

At the end of the Civil War, African-descended people who had been enslaved for generations were freed. Slaves had cleared the forests and made the land productive, generating wealth for southern landowners. They ceased to be the property of Whites, yet had no property of their own. Enslaved Africans played a tremendous role in creating prosperity for the United States, but their enslavement prevented them from accumulating any wealth.

Slaves were, by definition, unable to own any type of property. With freedom came limited possibilities for land ownership. In 1865, Congress established the Freedman's Bureau and the Freedman's Savings Bank—two initiatives designed to help formerly enslaved people establish financial independence. In that same year, General William Sherman issued Special Field Order No. 15, which set aside land for former slaves in an area that traversed the coastal regions of South Carolina and Florida. Sherman's order specified that Black families could settle on no more than forty acres of tillable land. The order, however, stopped short of conferring titles to the land. In less than a year, 40,000 formerly enslaved people had settled on 400,000 acres of land. The success of this program was short-lived: by the end of 1865, President Johnson had ordered the removal of formerly enslaved people from the lands they had settled and returned the lands to their former owners (Darity 2008; Cimbala 1989).

In 1866, formerly enslaved people were given another opportunity to acquire land: the Southern Homestead Act (SHA) reopened the door for former slaves to apply for land. The SHA allocated 46 million acres of public lands for homesteading in five southern states: Alabama, Arkansas, Florida, Louisiana, and Mississippi. Both Blacks and Whites were permitted to apply for this land, much of which was not productive (Canaday, Reback, and Stowe n.d.). In 1872, Congress dismantled the Freedman's Bureau. And, in 1874, the Freedman's bank failed because its all-White trustees issued speculative loans to White investors and corporations. The 60,000 Black people who had deposited more than $1 million (over $20 million in today's dollars) into this bank lost most of their savings (Lee 2019). By 1900, only one-quarter of southern Black farmers owned their land (Oliver and Shapiro 2006). The rest eked out a living working for others or eventually made their way north to seek their fortunes.

Although some Black Americans found economic opportunities in northern cities, they were not able to reap the same advantages over time as their White counterparts. One of the main reasons for the inability of Black people to build wealth has been the creation of housing segregation within U.S. cities. **Residential segregation** happens when different groups of people are sorted into distinct neighborhoods.

RESIDENTIAL SEGREGATION

Today, most U.S. cities are heavily segregated, yet this was not the case during the nineteenth century. Urban residential segregation in the United States was created in the early twentieth century and has had harmful consequences for the wealth portfolios of Black Americans.

The century following emancipation saw dramatic changes in the demographics of the United States. In 1870, 80 percent of Black Americans lived in the rural South. By 1970, this figure had reversed: 80 percent of Black Americans had come to live in cities, equally divided between the North and the South. During the same period that Black Americans were migrating to the North, European immigrants were arriving in U.S. cities.

At first, Black residents of urban areas lived in proximity to White residents. Yet between 1900 and 1940, U.S. cities were transformed from having very little residential segregation to having high levels of it. In Kansas City, for example, residential segregation tripled between 1900 and 1930. By 1930, the typical Black Chicagoan lived in a neighborhood that was over two-thirds Black. In effect, the urban ghetto in the United States was created in the first two decades of the twentieth century (Massey and Denton 1993). How did this happen?

Part of the explanation is that African Americans moved into cities that had previously had small numbers of non-Whites. The rise of segregation, however, was not an organic process: White residents created segregation and ensured that it persisted.

The Creation of Residential Segregation

A combination of three forces led to residential segregation: collective racial violence carried out by Whites, practices created and reinforced by the emerging real estate industry, and federal housing programs that were made available almost exclusively to Whites.

The first factor that contributed to residential segregation was that throughout the twentieth century, White residents used racial violence to keep Black people out of primarily White neighborhoods (Gotham 2000; Lipsitz 2006). Whites engaged in cross burning and window breaking, and joined organized mobs in nearly every major northern city. Hundreds of incidents of racial violence intended to prevent Black people from moving into White neighborhoods took place in Chicago,

Detroit, Philadelphia, and other cities. In most cases, these violent actions went unpunished (Sugrue 2008).

The second factor was the creation of **racially restrictive covenants**—contractual agreements that prevent the sale or lease of property within an area to non-Whites—originated and reinforced by the real estate industry. By the 1920s, deeds in nearly every new housing development in the northern United States prevented the ownership or rental of houses in the development by anyone who was not White. From the 1930s until the 1960s, the guidelines of the National Association of Real Estate Boards prevented realtors from selling homes to non-Whites in White areas (Sugrue 2008). Kevin Gotham (2000) argues that the primary motive for these covenants was economic: real estate investors wanted to ensure their profits, and they believed that racially stable and all-White neighborhoods were the most likely to increase in value over time.

In 1948, the Supreme Court declared these covenants unenforceable. And in 1968, the passage of the Fair Housing Act made these covenants illegal. Once covenants became illegal, real estate agents developed new tactics to preserve residential segregation. One of the most common activities was **steering**, in which real estate agents would show homes in White neighborhoods only to White buyers and homes in Black neighborhoods only to Black buyers. For these and other reasons, over sixty years after passage of the Fair Housing Act, we still have high levels of residential segregation, which in turn exacerbate wealth inequality.

The final reason for residential segregation is the nature of federal housing programs and policies. The early twentieth century was a time when the color line for White immigrants was in flux. Federal housing policies in the 1930s would solidify the line between Whites and non-Whites for decades to come.

The **Federal Housing Administration** (FHA) was established in 1934 with the purpose of bolstering the economy and, in particular, the construction industry. The FHA encouraged the building of new homes for people living in crowded tenements in inner cities by creating a new, government-backed mortgage system. Prior to the creation of the FHA, people had to come up with as much as half the value of a home before purchasing it. The FHA created the conditions under which banks could loan people money to purchase homes with small down payments and at reasonable interest rates. The vast majority of

One real estate developer built a half-mile-long wall in Detroit in 1940 to separate the Black and White communities. Today, because of White flight, the wall separates one Black community from another.

new homes were built in city suburbs, where suburban living was enabled by the simultaneous construction of highways and the development of suburban services (Oliver and Shapiro 2006).

Banks used FHA guidelines to decide who should be permitted to borrow money. The 1938 *Underwriting Manual* of the FHA stated that "if a neighborhood is to retain stability, it is necessary that properties shall continue to be occupied by the same social and racial classes." The *Manual* further recommended the implementation of restrictive covenants, which remained in place until they were outlawed in 1948 (quoted in Oliver and Shapiro 2006).

Between 1933 and 1978, U.S. government policies enabled over 35 million families to increase their wealth through housing equity. As homeowners, millions of Americans were able to begin to accumulate the tax savings, home equity, economic stability, and other benefits associated with homeownership. White Americans benefited disproportionately from this shift for two primary reasons: (1) it was easier for White people to purchase homes, and (2) the homes that White people bought increased in value more rapidly than those purchased by Black people because of the perceived desirability of all-White neighborhoods. In addition, few women were able to benefit directly from these policies, as they did not have the financial stability to purchase homes on their own. Because of racial endogamy in marriages (marrying within one's race), White women benefited because their White husbands purchased homes, whereas Black women reaped either the same paltry benefits as their husbands or hardly any at all if they were single (Oliver and Shapiro 2006).

voices

How America's Vast Racial Wealth Gap Grew: By Plunder

By Trymaine Lee

Elmore Bolling, whose brothers called him Buddy, was a kind of one-man economy in Lowndesboro, Ala. He leased a plantation, where he had a general store with a gas station out front and a catering business; he grew cotton, corn and sugar cane. He also owned a small fleet of trucks that ran livestock and made deliveries between Lowndesboro and Montgomery. At his peak, Bolling employed as many as forty people, all of them Black like him.

One December day in 1947, a group of White men showed up along a stretch of Highway 80 just yards from Bolling's home and store, where he lived with his wife, Bertha Mae, and their seven young children. The men confronted him on a section of road he had helped lay and shot him seven times—six times with a pistol and once with a shotgun blast to the back. His family rushed from the store to find him lying dead in a ditch.

The shooters didn't even cover their faces; they didn't need to. Everyone knew who had done it and why. "He was too successful to be a Negro," someone who knew Bolling told a newspaper at the time. When Bolling was killed, his family estimates he had as much as $40,000 in the bank and more than $5,000 in assets, about $500,000 in today's dollars. But within months of his murder nearly all of it would be gone. White creditors and people posing as creditors took the money the family got from the sale of their trucks and cattle. They even staked claims on what was left of the family's savings. The jobs that he provided were gone, too. Almost overnight the Bollings went from prosperity to poverty. Bertha Mae found work at a dry cleaner. The older children dropped out of school to help support the family. Within two years, the Bollings fled Lowndes County, fearing for their lives.

The period that followed the Civil War was one of economic terror and wealth-stripping that has left Black people at lasting economic disadvantage. . . .

The fate suffered by Elmore Bolling and his family was not unique to them, or to Jim Crow Alabama. It was part of a much broader social and political campaign. . . .

"The origins of the racial wealth gap start with the failure to provide the formerly enslaved with the land grants of forty acres," says William A. Darity Jr., a professor of public policy and African American studies at Duke University. Any financial progress that Black people made was regarded as an affront to White supremacy. After a decade of Black gains under Reconstruction, a much longer period of racial violence would wipe nearly all of it away.

To assuage Southern White people, the federal government pulled out the Union troops who were stationed in the South to keep order. During this period of so-called Redemption, lawmakers throughout the South enacted Black Codes and Jim Crow laws that stripped Black people of many of their freedoms and property. Other White people, often aided by law enforcement, waged a campaign of violence against Black people that would rob them of an incalculable amount of wealth.

Armed White people stormed prosperous majority-Black Wilmington, NC, in 1898 to murder dozens of Black people, force 2,000 others off their property and overthrow the city government. In the Red Summer of 1919, at least 240 Black people were murdered across the country. And in 1921, in one of the bloodiest racial attacks in United States history, Greenwood, a prosperous Black neighborhood in Tulsa, OK, was burned and looted. It is estimated that as many as 300 Black people were murdered and 10,000 were rendered homeless. Thirty-five square blocks were destroyed. No one was ever convicted in any of these acts of racist violence.

"You have limited opportunity to accumulate wealth, and then you have a process where that wealth is destroyed or taken away," Darity says. "And all of that is prior to the effects of restrictive covenants — redlining, the discriminatory application of the G.I. Bill and other federal programs."

The post-Reconstruction plundering of Black wealth was not just a product of spontaneous violence, but etched in law and public policy. Through the first half of the twentieth

(continued)

 *continued.*

How America's Vast Racial Wealth Gap Grew: By Plunder

century, the federal government actively excluded Black people from government wealth-building programs. In the 1930s, President Franklin Roosevelt's New Deal helped build a solid middle class through sweeping social programs, including Social Security and the minimum wage. But a majority of Black people at the time were agricultural laborers or domestic workers, occupations that were ineligible for these benefits. The establishment of the Home Owners Loan Corporation in 1933 helped save the collapsing housing market, but it largely excluded Black neighborhoods from government-insured loans. Those neighborhoods were deemed "hazardous" and colored in with red on maps, a practice that came to be known as "redlining."

The G.I. Bill is often hailed as one of Roosevelt's most enduring legacies. It helped usher millions of working-class veterans through college and into new homes and the middle class. But it discriminatorily benefited White people. While the bill didn't explicitly exclude Black veterans, the way it was administered often did. The bill gave veterans access to mortgages with no down payments, but the Veterans Administration adopted the same racially restrictive policies as the Federal Housing Administration, which guaranteed bank loans only to developers who wouldn't sell to Black people. "The major way in which people have an opportunity to accumulate wealth is contingent on the wealth positions of their parents and their grandparents," Darity says. "To the extent that Blacks have the capacity to accumulate wealth, we have not had the ability to transfer the same kinds of resources across generations."

Seventy years later, the effects of Bolling's murder are still felt by his children and their children. "There was no inheritance, nothing for my father to pass down, because it was all taken away," says Josephine Bolling McCall, the only one of Bolling's children to get a college degree. Of the seven siblings, those with more education fared best; the men struggled most, primarily working as low-paid laborers. Of Elmore and Bertha Mae's twenty-five grandchildren, only six graduated from college; of those, two are McCall's children. The rest are unemployed or underemployed. They have never known anything like the prosperity of their grandparents.

Trymaine Lee is a Pulitzer Prize- and Emmy Award-winning journalist and a correspondent for MSNBC. He covers social-justice issues and the role of race in politics and law enforcement.

Source: Trymaine Lee, *The New York Times*, August 14, 2019 at https://www.nytimes.com/interactive/ 2019/08/14/magazine/racial-wealth-gap.html

One hundred years after slavery ended, these policies and practices related to housing became one of the primary factors responsible for inequality in the wealth portfolios of Black and White families in the United States. Racial violence against Black people who tried to move into White neighborhoods continued well after the civil rights movement of the 1960s. Today, real estate agents continue to practice steering, and the wealth generated by the properties purchased by Whites who benefited from the federal housing policies of the 1930s continues to be passed down to those individuals' children and grandchildren.

For example, in 1948, houses in Levittown, New York, were available only to White families. A White couple born in the 1920s could purchase a brand-new home there for $8,000, with no down payment, by taking advantage of the federal housing programs. In the 1960s, that family could use the home equity built up in that property to take out loans to pay for their children's college tuition. And if the couple passed away in the first decade of the twentieth century, their children would inherit the home, in a neighborhood still 98 percent White, valued at $400,000. The opportunity to accumulate that kind of wealth was denied to Black families, who were not permitted to purchase homes in Levittown. Eugene Burnett, for example, is a Black Army veteran who tried to purchase a home in Levittown in 1949. When he put in an application, the agent told him that "the owners of this development have not as yet decided whether they're going to sell these homes to Negroes" (Lambert 1997). Those Black families who were able to purchase homes did not see their real estate values climb in the same way. The average home value in nearby, primarily non-White Central Islip is about a third of the value of a home in primarily White Levittown.

These exclusion processes played out across the nation. In Washington, DC, racially restrictive covenants made it difficult for African Americans to purchase homes outside of the areas into which Black people were crowded, yet this did not stop them from trying. In October 1944, an Italian American real estate agent helped Black homebuyer James Hurd purchase 116 Bryant Street, NW, in Bloomingdale—a central city neighborhood. Hurd's White neighbors filed suit, arguing the sale violated the racially restrictive covenant in place for homes on Bryant Street. The DC Court upheld the covenant and the appeals court struck down the appeal. Then, the Supreme Court agreed to hear the case. And, in 1948, the Supreme Court ruled that the covenants were in violation of the Civil Rights Act of 1866 (Shoenfeld and Cherkasky 2017).

Discriminatory and Predatory Lending Practices

Even though the FHA's discriminatory housing programs have been discontinued, Black and Latinx families have continued to face disadvantages through contemporary discriminatory lending practices. On average, Black borrowers are 2.7 times more likely than White borrowers to be denied mortgages. Prospective homeowners who are denied mortgages have to either forgo the opportunity to accumulate wealth through homeownership or seek out a less favorable loan with a higher interest rate. In fact, Black homeowners pay 0.54 percent higher interest rates than Whites. This half-point differential adds up to tens of thousands of dollars over the course of a loan. Thus, the racial disparity in lending practices has far-reaching consequences. Bankers often claim that Black borrowers are more often denied loans because they do not have the same creditworthiness as White borrowers. Yet, a study by the Federal Reserve Bank of Boston revealed that even when credit scores were taken into account, Black and Latinx mortgage applicants were still 60 percent more likely to be turned down than Whites (Oliver and Shapiro 2006). Continued discrimination in home loans perpetuates the wealth inequality that was solidified with the FHA programs of the 1930s (Oliver and Shapiro 2006).

In the 1990s and early 2000s, bank lending became more predatory, particularly for Black and Latinx people. **Predatory lenders** traditionally include pawnshops, payday lenders, and check cashing services that charge very high fees and interest rates. Following changes in lending laws, the late 1990s saw the rise of another type of predatory financial practice: **subprime loans**, or high-interest loans to people at high risk of defaulting. Black and Latinx homeowners were much more likely than Whites to receive loans with unfavorable conditions such as prepayment penalties and high interest rates. Between 1993 and 2000, the percentage of subprime mortgages in Black and Latinx neighborhoods rose from 2 to 18 percent. Overall, Black and Latinx families were about twice as likely to receive subprime loans as White families. By 2009, over 15 percent of subprime loans were in foreclosure (Dymski, Hernandez, and Mohanty 2013; Rugh and Massey 2010).

Segregation exacerbated the effects of the economic crisis for Black families. Metropolitan areas with higher degrees of racial segregation had higher rates of foreclosure. Additionally, Black families in highly segregated cities had been more likely to get subprime loans than their counterparts in less segregated cities. The subprime loan rate in segregated cities was higher partly because unregulated mortgage brokers targeted Black neighborhoods where regulated banks were less likely to have branches. Notably, more than half of all subprime loans made in the first decade of the twentieth century were for refinancing instead of purchasing new homes. When those homes in primarily Black neighborhoods failed to appreciate in value as expected or decreased in value, families who had borrowed at high interest rates found themselves in financial trouble (Dymksi et al. 2013; Rugh and Massey 2010).

Neighborhood Segregation Today

Even though the housing policies that contributed to residential segregation have been repealed, neighborhood segregation persists today. How do we quantify it? One measure is the **dissimilarity index**, which describes the extent to which two groups—such as Black and White residents—are found in equal proportions in all neighborhoods. We can interpret this measure as the percentage of individuals in either group who would have to move to achieve perfect integration. Another tool for measuring segregation is the **isolation index**, which compares a neighborhood's demographics against citywide demographics. If, for example, a city is 30 percent Black, yet Black people live in neighborhoods that are 50 percent Black, the isolation index would be the difference, 20 percent.

Black–White segregation continues to have the highest national dissimilarity index. In 2010, Milwaukee had the highest Black–White **segregation index** at 81.5. In contrast, the segregation index for Hispanics/Latinxs in Milwaukee was 57.0. The city with the highest Hispanic/Latinx–White segregation index was Springfield, Massachusetts, at 63.4. Los Angeles had the second highest, at 62.2 (Michigan Population Studies Center, n.d.). The Black–White segregation index is consistently high in cities with large Black populations, such as Detroit and Chicago. This index in 2010 was 80 for Detroit and 76 for Chicago. The average Detroit Black resident lives in a neighborhood that is 81 percent Black, and the average Black person in Chicago lives in a neighborhood that is 67 percent Black. Latinx and Asian Americans have remained somewhat less segregated from Whites, with dissimilarity indexes of 48 and 41, respectively, in 2010 (Logan and Stults 2011).

FIGURE 8-2

DIVERSITY EXPERIENCED IN EACH GROUP'S TYPICAL NEIGHBORHOOD, BY RACE/ETHNICITY, 2010

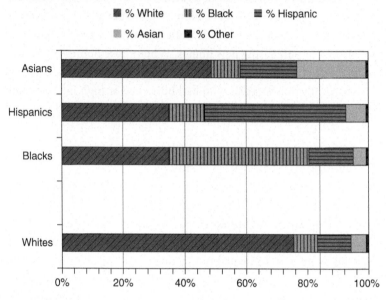

Source: John R. Logan and Brian Stults, 2011. "The Persistence of Segregation in the Metropolis: New Findings from the 2010 Census" Census Brief prepared for Project US2010. http://www.s4.brown.edu/us2010

Segregation is high in the United States, but it is not absolute: many people share neighborhoods with people of different races. According to data from the 2010 census, the average White American in a metropolitan area lives in a neighborhood that is 75 percent White, whereas the average African American lives in a neighborhood that is 45 percent White and 45 percent Black. The average Latinx lives in a neighborhood that is 35 percent White, and the average Asian American lives in a neighborhood that is 49 percent White (see Figure 8-2). The only group that, on average, lives in a primarily White neighborhood is Whites (Logan and Stults 2011).

Scholars sometimes refer to African Americans in urban areas as **hypersegregated** because of the high levels of segregation in these neighborhoods. In contrast, other racial and ethnic minorities tend not to experience such high levels of segregation. Studies show relatively low levels of Native American segregation in urban areas, especially compared to the levels experienced by African Americans (Wilkes and Iceland 2004). In 2000, 1.4 million Native Americans lived in rural areas—accounting for about a third of all Native Americans. Most of these rural Native Americans lived on Indian reservations, effectively separated from non–Native Americans. Outside of reservations, however, rural Native Americans have relatively low levels of segregation (Lichter, Parisi, Grice, and Taquino 2007).

Racial segregation poses a problem not just because people of different races have little contact with one another but because it exacerbates existing inequalities. Black and Latinx families of all economic statuses are more likely than White families to live in neighborhoods with high poverty rates. Even affluent Blacks and Latinxs live in neighborhoods with fewer resources than those inhabited by poor Whites (Logan 2013). Racial segregation often means concentrated poverty, which in turn leads to underresourced neighborhoods with poor public schools, high levels of crime, and high unemployment rates. High levels of racial segregation mean that Black and Latinx families are more likely than White families to live in neighborhoods that are inhospitable to their success. Children who grow up in segregated, high-poverty neighborhoods are much less likely to finish high school and to secure employment. They are more likely to experience violence growing up and to have children out of wedlock. Residential segregation limits opportunities for both middle-class and poor Black families (Charles 2003). One of the most longstanding consequences of segregation is the inability of Black families in Black neighborhoods to build up home equity, therefore causing them to lag far behind White families in wealth accumulation.

As we have seen, racial segregation in housing is driven by formal and informal policies and practices. It is also affected by Whites' preferences to live in primarily White neighborhoods. Most White Americans balk at the idea of living in a neighborhood with more than a few Black families. Contrary to popular perceptions, residential segregation is not due to Black Americans' preferences for living exclusively among other Black Americans. Sociologists Maria Krysan and Reynolds Farley (2002) analyzed survey data from 2,000 Black families in several cities and found that African Americans prefer racially diverse neighborhoods. In the study, the interviewers showed respondents fictional representations of five neighborhoods, ranging from all Black to all White, and asked them to rank the neighborhoods in order of preference. They also asked respondents if they would not want to live in one of the fictional neighborhoods. Half of the Black respondents chose the neighborhood that was evenly split between Black and White as their most preferred neighborhood. Only 20 percent of the Black respondents chose the neighborhood that was all Black. African Americans in this survey expressed a strong preference for mixed neighborhoods. Although only 35 percent of African Americans were willing to be the first Black family to move into a White neighborhood, nearly all of the respondents expressed willingness to move into a neighborhood if it was primarily White, as long as there were one or two other Black families living there. In contrast, less than a third of White respondents indicated they were willing to move into a neighborhood that was evenly split between Black and White families.

Racial segregation is also encouraged by real estate agents. A recent study in Long Island used undercover paired-tests to evaluate racial discrimination by real estate agents. Two undercover testers (either one White and one Black; or one White and one Latinx; or one White and one Asian) would approach real estate agents with identical financial profiles and neighborhood preferences. In 19 percent of the instances, Asians experienced discrimination. For Latinxs, this percentage went up to 39 percent, and half of the Black testers experienced discrimination. Examples of the kinds of discrimination they experienced included providing prospective White buyers with more listings or making different comments about neighborhoods to the testers, based on race. In one example, a realtor commented to a Black customer about how "excited" he gets when there is a new house listing for Brentwood because "they are the nicest people." Meanwhile the same realtor warned the paired White prospective buyer, "please kindly do some research on the gang related events in that area for safety." In other cases, agents refused to provide house listings or home tours for people of color unless they met their financial qualifications— although they did not impose these same financial qualifications to Whites. The researchers highlight that the findings are even more chilling, as this "happened in one of the most educated, most liberal regions of the country" (Choi, Winslow, and Browne 2019).

WEALTH INEQUALITIES

Racial segregation in housing is one of the driving factors behind wealth disparities among racial groups. On average, African Americans and Latinxs have less than 9 percent of the wealth of Whites (Figure 8-3; Pew Research Center 2014). The disparities between the wealth portfolios of Whites and Latinxs and between those of Whites and Blacks are about twice as large today as they were prior to the recession that began in 2007, primarily as a result of residual effects from the related crisis in the housing market. The housing crisis wiped out all of the gains in wealth made by Black and Latinx families compared to Whites since 1984, when the United States first began to track wealth inequality. In 2009, one-third of Black and Latinx households had zero or negative wealth (Kochhar et al., 2011). By 2016, the median Black household had about 12 percent the wealth of the median White household (Kuhn et al. 2020).

Let's briefly review the differences between income and wealth. Americans primarily use their income to live on a day-to-day basis: to pay the rent or mortgage, to buy food and other necessities, to pay for school, and to pay bills. Income differentials often translate into differences in standards of living. Wealth, by contrast, has a different functionality. Wealth includes an individual's accumulated assets, such as savings, home equity, stocks, and business ownership. People don't use wealth to pay for daily expenses (except in financial emergencies). Instead, wealth grants financial stability and is often used to ensure the financial success of future generations through inheritances. Oliver and Shapiro (2006, 175) contend that "wealth is money that is not typically used to purchase milk, shoes, or other necessities. . . . It is used to create opportunities, secure a desired stature and standard of living, or pass along a class status already obtained to a new generation." The vast discrepancies between Black and White wealth, then, translate into the solidification of racial inequality across generations.

FIGURE 8-3

MEDIAN NET WORTH OF HOUSEHOLDS BY RACE/ETHNICITY

Median net worth of households, in 2013 dollars

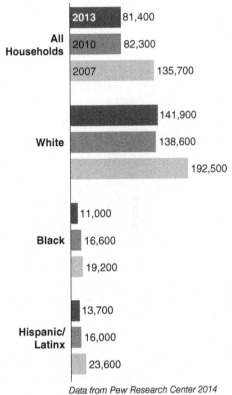

Data from Pew Research Center 2014

Source: Data from Pew Research Center, 2014.

FIGURE 8-4

AVERAGE WEALTH OF FAMILIES BY RACE/ETHNICITY BEFORE AND AFTER THE HOUSING CRISIS—IN 2005 AND 2009

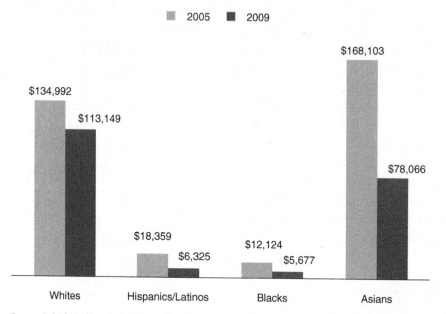

Source: Rakesh Kochhar, Richard Fry and Paul Taylor. "Wealth Gaps Rise to Record Highs Between Blacks, Whites, Hispanics." Pew Research Center, Washington, D.C. (July 26, 2011). http://www.pewsocialtrends. org/2011/07/26/wealth-gaps-rise-to-record-highs-between-whites-blacks-hispanics/, accessed on January 17, 2014.

Many factors affect wealth inequality. One of the main factors is inequality in home values and homeownership. In 2005, Black and Latino families derived much greater proportions of their wealth from their homes than Whites. Looking at the loss in average wealth for families between 2005 and 2009, we clearly see that nearly all of the losses for all families came from losses in home equity (Figure 8-4). Since Black and Latinx families had almost no other wealth—an average of $479 for Latinx families and $626 for Black families—these households lost nearly all of their wealth as a result of the housing crisis (Kochhar et al., 2011).

In 2000, Native Americans were the racial group in the United States with the lowest average incomes. Although relatively little data is available on their wealth holdings, Jay Zagorsky (2006) was able to use data from the National Longitudinal Study of Youth to assess their wealth. He found that in 2000, the average Native American born between 1957 and 1965 had only $5,700 in wealth, compared with the $65,500 amassed by their White counterpart. He also found that only 43 percent of the Native Americans in this age group had bank accounts, compared with 65 percent of baby boomers overall. Only a third of Native American baby boomers owned homes, compared with 57 percent overall. Zagorsky (2006) found that Native Americans own fewer businesses, have lower rates of homeownership, and reside in homes with lower values than the average person living in the United States.

In a study of wealth inequalities in Washington, DC, Kijakazi and colleagues (2016) found that White households have, on average, a net worth that is eighty-one times greater than that of Black households. The nation's capital is 47.7 percent Black, 35.7 percent White, 10.4 percent Latinx, and 3.7 percent Asian. The study found substantial wealth disparities by race and ethnicity. The median net worth—the sum of all assets less the value of debts—for White households was $284,000, compared with $13,000 for Latinx households, $3,500 for U.S. Black households, and $3,000 for African households. Korean, Asian Indian, and Vietnamese households all had a median net worth of over $400,000, higher than that of the average White household.

Kijakazi and colleagues (2016) found that even highly educated Black families have less wealth on average than White families. For White households headed by an individual with a high school diploma or less, the average net worth was $265,000, compared with $130,000 for Black households headed by an individual with a graduate degree. Whereas net worth for Whites varies relatively little between those who have a high school diploma or less and those with a bachelor's degree, for Latinx households the difference is substantial: $5,500 versus $53,000. For Black households, the largest gain is between a BA degree (–$19,000) and a graduate degree ($130,000). At all educational levels, however, net worth for Blacks lags behind that for Whites (Figure 8-5).

Inequality in Homeownership and Home Values

Using the 2001 American Housing Survey, Lauren Krivo and Robert Kaufman (2004) found that over 70 percent of White households owned their homes, compared with 46 percent of Black households, 49 percent of Latinx households, and 55 percent of Asian households. In addition, they found that White homeowners have more home

FIGURE 8-5

MEDIAN NET WORTH BY EDUCATIONAL ATTAINMENT AND RACE/ETHNICITY IN WASHINGTON, DC, 2016

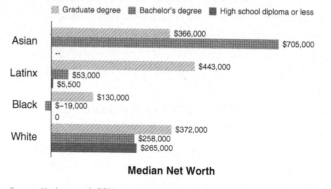

Median Net Worth

Source: Kijakazi et al. 2016.

equity than do Black and Latinx homeowners. The median value of home equity for Blacks was $52,882, and for Latinxs it was $60,000. In contrast, the median home equity value for Whites was $80,000. At $111,100, Asians had the highest average home equity. Moreover, Blacks and Latinxs were the most likely to have high-interest mortgages: 4 percent of Whites had an interest rate higher than 9 percent, compared with nearly 11 percent of Black homeowners and 7 percent of Latinx homeowners. Asians were the least likely to have this kind of mortgage, with only 1.5 percent reporting high interest rates.

Between 2007 and 2009, Black and Latinx homeowners were twice as likely as White homeowners to experience foreclosures (Kochhar et al. 2011). Analyses of home loans made between 2005 and 2008 reveals that 790 African Americans experienced a foreclosure by 2009 for each 10,000 loans, compared with 769 Hispanics and 452 Whites. By 2010, 17 percent of Latinx homeowners, 11 percent of African American homeowners, and 7 percent of non-Hispanic White homeowners had lost or were at imminent risk of losing their homes (Gruenstein Bocian, Li, and Ernst 2010). The housing crisis thus exacerbated preexisting inequalities in homeownership and home values.

Wealth Inequality Beyond Homeownership

Families can have negative wealth if the total of their debts exceeds the total value of their assets. This situation has become increasingly common with the expansion of home equity loans, falling housing prices, and rising student debt.

Wealth includes factors beyond homeownership, such as stock holdings. When stock prices plummeted in 2007, Black and Latinx families lost the largest shares of their holdings. Latinxs who owned stocks and mutual funds saw a 32 percent decline in their value between 2005 and 2009, and Blacks saw a 71 percent decline in the same period. The stocks owned by Whites fell only 9 percent, and those owned by Asians actually increased 19 percent during this same period (Kochhar et al. 2011). In 2013, only 3.3 percent of Black households owned stocks, compared with 17.2 percent of White households (Herring and Henderson 2016).

High levels of debt also help explain wealth inequality. In 2002, over a quarter of Black and Latinx households had negative net worth, compared with 13 percent of White households. The numbers are even starker when we consider gender: nearly half of all Latina and Black women had zero or negative wealth in 2007 (Kochhar et al., 2011). In 2013, over half (54 percent) of young Black households (aged twenty-five to forty) had student debt, compared with 39 percent of young White households. Relatedly, these young Black households had a median wealth of $3,600, compared with young White households' median wealth of $35,800 (Huelsman et al., 2015).

EXPLAINING THE WIDENING WEALTH GAP

Rather than decreasing over time, inequalities among Whites, Blacks, and Latinxs are increasing. The wealth gap between Blacks and Whites tripled between 1984 and 2009. In 2013, Thomas Shapiro, Tatjana Meschede, and Sam Osoro published a study that sought to explain why. Based on their study of 1,700 households, these analysts attributed the wealth gap to five factors:

1. Years of homeownership
2. Household income
3. Years of unemployment
4. College education
5. Inheritances or financial support from family members

Notably, Shapiro and colleagues did not find the wealth gap to be a consequence of behavioral differences, such as consumption patterns or the propensity to build savings. It is also not solely a function of income differentials. Instead, the researchers were able to explain two-thirds of the wealth gap using these five factors. Years of homeownership accounted for 27 percent of the difference, household income for 20 percent, unemployment for 9 percent, and college education and inheritances for 5 percent each (Shapiro, Meschede, and Osoro 2013).

Figure 8-6 presents an explanation of the gap between Black and White wealth. Many people would expect household income to account for the differences in wealth. However, as we have seen, income differences can explain only a portion of wealth inequalities. And although it is true that college education makes it easier to build up wealth, the fact that Whites are more likely to be college educated accounts for only 5 percent of the differences in wealth between White and Black households.

In a follow-up study, Amy Traub et al. (2017) found that racial wealth inequality was not attributable to factors such as educational attainment and out-of-wedlock birth. White adults with less than a high school education who had children but were not married and

FIGURE 8-6

HOW DO WE EXPLAIN THE BLACK/WHITE WEALTH GAP TODAY?

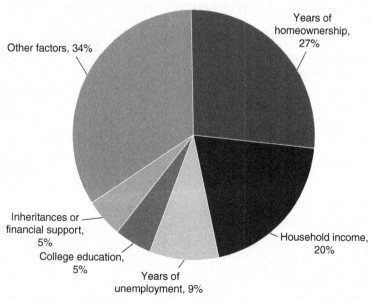

Source: Shapiro, Meschede, and Osoro (2013).

who did not work full time had more wealth on average than Black and Latinx adults who were married, completed higher levels of education, or worked longer hours. For example, among households under age fifty-five, the median White high school dropout has a similar amount of wealth to the median Black or Latinx adult who graduated from high school and attended some college. Additionally, White adults who attended college have 7.2 times more wealth than their African American counterparts and 3.9 times more than their Latinx counterparts (Figure 8-7).

Years of homeownership accounted for the largest portion of the differences in wealth between White and Black families. African American families tend to purchase homes later in life because they face more obstacles in home buying than Whites. Further, Black homeowners are less likely to build up equity over the years because of residential segregation, and White families are more likely to receive financial assistance in purchasing a home from their family members. Even though homeownership accounts for, on average, 53 percent of the Black families' wealth, compared with 39 percent for Whites, the return on investment in housing turns out to be far greater for White than for Black households (Shapiro et al. 2013). Black families who are able to purchase homes face outright discrimination by real estate agents who continue to steer them to Black neighborhoods and

FIGURE 8-7

MEDIAN WEALTH BY EDUCATIONAL ATTAINMENT AND RACE/ETHNICITY (WORKING HOUSEHOLDS UNDER AGE 55), 2017

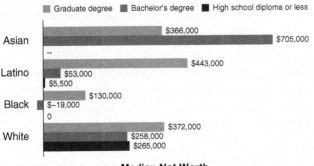

Median Net Worth

Source: *The Color of Wealth in the Nation's Capital,* Urban Institute, 2016.

by lenders who quote them higher interest rates. The limited market potential for homes in primarily Black neighborhoods inhibits the possibility for the value of these homes to increase, and the higher interest rates make it more difficult for Black people to pay off their mortgages quickly. These factors work together to reduce the home equity of Black homeowners, thereby enhancing the wealth gap (Krivo and Kaufman 2004).

The foreclosure crisis of 2007–2009 further decimated Black and Latinx wealth portfolios. A study by the Center for Responsible Lending (Bocian, Li, and Ernst 2010) found that among recent borrowers, nearly 8 percent of Black and Latinx homeowners had lost their homes, compared with 4.5 percent of Whites. Nearly two-thirds of all foreclosures between 2005 and 2008 were on homes mortgaged using subprime loans; that is, people with subprime loans were three times as likely to experience a foreclosure than people with conventional or government loans. And Black and Latinx borrowers were the most likely to obtain subprime loans with unfavorable conditions (Bocian et al. 2010).

Whites and Blacks at similar income levels tend to have vastly different wealth portfolios. One reason is that Whites are more likely to have jobs with benefits. Whites are therefore less likely to dip into their savings for medical emergencies, and their employers are more likely to be contributing to a retirement plan (Shapiro et al. 2013). Black people also tend to be in more precarious employment situations and are more likely to lose their jobs. When unemployment rose from 5.0 percent in December 2007 to 9.5 percent in June 2009, Latinx and Black earners were hit the hardest, with Black unemployment rates peaking at 15.6 percent and the Latinx rate at 12.6 percent in 2009 (Kochhar et al. 2011).

The 2013 study by Shapiro and his colleagues found that 36 percent of White households inherited some money over the twenty-five-year period under study, compared with only 7 percent of Black households. Moreover, the inheritances Black households received were, on average, only about 10 percent of the amount inherited by White households. Inheritances are thus another important part of the legacy of inequality in the United States.

Wealth researchers such as john powell (2008) and Melvin Oliver and Thomas Shapiro (2006) make a case for **asset-based social policies** that are designed to help narrow the wealth gap. These researchers contend that the FHA policies of the early twentieth century set the stage for the wealth gap and that now the United States has the responsibility of reversing that trend by setting up proactive policies. These policies could include individual-level assistance in buying homes as well as larger-scale efforts such as improvements to transportation and investments in neighborhoods. For example, if the local, state, or federal government invested money in a working-class Black neighborhood by building a transportation hub, transforming empty lots into parks, and revitalizing the business district, this investment would increase property values and provide job opportunities for the local community, thereby enhancing their wealth portfolios. It would take enormous investments to reverse the trend, but that is primarily because of the decades of investment the federal government has put into White communities.

CONCLUSION AND DISCUSSION

In this chapter, we have seen how wealth inequalities are entrenched and complex. Married White couples with college educations are well positioned to accumulate wealth over the course of their lives. However, married Black couples with the same levels of education consistently earn less money and have much less wealth. Wealth provides a safety net for emergencies, such as serious medical issues or the loss of a job. This means that comfortably middle-class Black families are at a much greater risk of descending into poverty than similarly placed White families. Not all White families have wealth, but historical racial disparities in the United States, as well as ongoing discriminatory practices, ensure that White families are more likely to accumulate wealth than Black and Latinx families.

Wealth also provides opportunities and allows families to invest in their future and to take risks. Families with substantial home equity can use this asset to finance their children's college educations. Families with significant savings and a wide social net can use them to take risks and invest in business opportunities. In these and other ways, wealth begets more wealth. For these reasons, wealth inequality is hard to overcome.

Between 1933 and 1978, federal government policies enabled over 35 million families to purchase homes in new suburban areas. As a direct consequence of these policies, these families will pass on trillions of dollars of wealth to their children through accumulated home equity. Nearly all these families are White because non-White Americans were locked out of this tremendous wealth-generating federal program. Today, most Black families have no wealth to pass on to their children. For this reason, many activists contend that it is time for the federal government to enact new wealth-generating programs that, unlike past programs, are not exclusive to White Americans (Oliver and Shapiro 2006).

**THINKING
ABOUT
RACIAL
JUSTICE**

SOME SCHOLARS ARGUE that programs such as the Federal Housing Administration and Veterans Affairs bills formed the basis of the Black–White wealth gap. Can you imagine federal programs that would be capable of helping close this gap?

Key Terms

wealth 224
assets 224
residential segregation 226
racially restrictive covenants 228
steering 228
Federal Housing Administration
  (FHA) 228

predatory lender 234
subprime loan 234
dissimilarity index 235
isolation index 235
segregation index 235
hypersegregation 236
asset-based social policy 246

CHECK YOUR UNDERSTANDING

8.1 What are some historical reasons for housing and wealth inequalities in the United States?
Enslaved African Americans were unable to accumulate wealth. Once freed, their opportunities for land ownership were limited.

Q What does slavery have to do with contemporary wealth inequalities?

8.2 When and how did residential segregation become a characteristic of U.S. cities?
Today, most U.S. cities are segregated, but this has not always been the case. Residential segregation was created in the early twentieth century by White residents' desire for homogeneous neighborhoods,

by the real estate industry's profit seeking, and by federal housing programs that were available exclusively to Whites. Whites are the only group that, on average, lives in primarily White neighborhoods. Black families are the most likely group to be hypersegregated.

 What factors contributed to the creation of residential segregation?

 How is residential segregation related to the racial wealth gap?

8.3 What is the extent of wealth inequality today in homeownership and beyond?

On average, African Americans and Latinxs have less than 9 percent of the wealth of Whites. The 2007–2009 housing crisis exacerbated racial inequalities in wealth.

 What is the difference between wealth and income? Why is this difference important in studies of racial inequality?

 Why and how did the wealth gap between Whites and other groups change between 2005 and 2009?

8.4 What factors are sustaining and exacerbating wealth inequalities?

Black families with incomes similar to those of White families have substantially less wealth. This is because wealth is not solely a function of income differentials. The disparity is also attributable to years of homeownership, years of unemployment, college education, and inheritances.

 What programs and policies have contributed to the racial wealth gap, and in what ways?

 What other factors have exacerbated the wealth gap in the twenty-first century? Give examples.

Critical Thinking

1. In the United States, why does the idea endure that if you work hard, you will get ahead? Why might this not be true, especially for people of color?
2. How have race, class, and immigration history played a role in the amount of your family's wealth? Consider factors such as Veterans Administration or Federal Housing Authority loans.

3. Why is racial segregation problematic? Suggest at least three reasons.

4. What distinct social challenges stem from overall wealth inequality and the racial wealth gap?

5. To what extent would narrowing the racial income gap contribute to narrowing the racial wealth gap?

6. How would asset-based social policies work in practice? Could they work?

Talking about Race

The overall wealth inequality between White families and African American or Latinx families is staggering. Citing this issue is one way to broach the topic of racial inequality. After reading this chapter, have a discussion with family and friends, mentioning that White families have, on average, over ten times the wealth of African American or Latinx families. Highlight historical reasons for this disparity. How would you respond to potential comments or questions about African Americans' or Latinxs' spending habits or educational levels?

Learn more with this chapter's digital tools, including video clips from the author, web links, filmography, and chapter self-assessment quizzes at www.oup.com/he/golash-boza-brief3e.

9

Racism and the Criminal Legal System

AS YOU READ

9.1 What factors explain the rise of mass incarceration in the United States?
9.2 How are disparities in the criminal legal system reflective of institutional racism?
9.3 How is the rise of mass incarceration tied to large-scale economic trends?
9.4 What are the collateral consequences of mass incarceration?

Writing at the turn of the twentieth century, W. E. B. Du Bois likened the prison system to "slavery in private hands" (Du Bois 1904, 2). He explained that with the end of slavery, the number of Black convicts in the South rose substantially, in large part because of vagrancy laws passed in the aftermath of emancipation. Police officers often used vagrancy laws to arrest African Americans whom they perceived to be vagrants or drifters. African Americans' testimonies in courts were largely ignored, and any accusation by Whites could result in conviction. Southern states, however, were not able to build prisons fast enough to house these new convicts. Thus, a convict-lease system was born, whereby convicts could be leased to the highest bidder to work as slaves. This practice was legal because the Thirteenth Amendment allows forced labor as a punishment for crime. Notably, in our present system, prisons still can (and do) force prisoners to work for little or no pay.

Convict leasing was a system of both forced labor and social control. Today, prisons do not function to the same extent as a source of unpaid labor, yet the element of social control persists. One place we can see this is in the lifelong stigma attached to being labeled a felon. As Michelle Alexander (2010) explains, this stigma makes various forms of racial discrimination legal. Felons face discrimination in housing, employment, and access to social services.

This chapter elaborates on these and other ways mass incarceration is a tool of social control, and how this crime control strategy has disproportionately affected people of color. The evidence presented makes it clear that mass incarceration not only is ineffective at preventing crime, but also has been particularly detrimental to communities of color across the United States. This chapter begins with a discussion of mass incarceration and then moves to an analysis of institutionalized racism in the criminal legal system. It concludes with a consideration of the economic and collateral consequences of mass incarceration.

The United States has more people in prison than any other country in the world and today incarcerates people at a higher rate than at any other time in history. Our crime rate, however, is not higher than that of other countries or than it has been historically. Why, then, are so many Americans behind bars? The answer lies in the United States' use of mass incarceration as a strategy to reduce crime even though mass incarceration has not been effective at reducing crime. It has, however, destroyed families and communities and exacerbated racial inequality because the primary victims of intensified law enforcement efforts have been people of color.

MASS INCARCERATION IN THE UNITED STATES

An understanding of the racially disparate consequences of the criminal legal system in the United States must begin with an exploration of the uniqueness of this system. The United States is distinctive among wealthier nations in its liberal use of the prison system. Strict drug enforcement, repeat offender laws, and mandatory sentencing have meant that in the United States, many people spend years behind bars for nonviolent crimes. Because of the racially disparate implementation and character of these laws, their impact is most visible in Black and Latinx communities.

The Rise of Mass Incarceration

Mass incarceration is a relatively new phenomenon in the United States and marks a divergence from the attitudes and practices of the mid-twentieth century. At that time, Americans tended to view

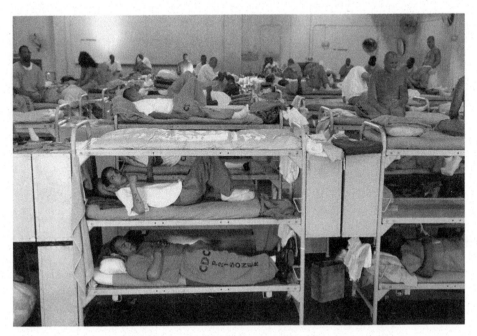

In the United States, prisons are crowded with nonviolent offenders.

incarceration as an ineffective means of controlling crime and searched for other solutions to make communities safer. Prison was seen as a last resort, and, accordingly, the Federal Bureau of Prisons planned to close large prisons in Kansas, Washington, and Georgia. In 1970, Congress voted to eliminate nearly all federal mandatory minimum sentences for drug offenders, as most Americans viewed drug addiction as a problem of public health, not criminal justice (Alexander 2010).

Just ten years later, this mindset—that drugs are a public health problem and that prisons are barbaric—was pushed to the margins as a policy of mass incarceration took off. Many scholars attribute the start of this change to the Omnibus Crime Control and Safe Streets Act, signed by President Lyndon B. Johnson in 1968. This law was the convergence of liberal and conservative anticrime agendas, as both parties realized that anticrime rhetoric could help win elections. Parties began to compete with one another as to which could be tougher on crime, and this competition contributed to a surge in incarceration rates (Gottschalk 2015; Murakawa 2014).

The U.S. incarceration rate was about 1 per 1,000 residents for almost the entire twentieth century until the 1970s. That rate doubled between 1972 and 1984, and again between 1984 and 1994. By the end of the twentieth century, the United States had an unprecedented number of inmates: over 2 million, more than ten times the number of U.S. inmates at any time prior to the 1970s. Today, the American criminal justice system holds almost 2.3 million people in 1,833 state prisons, 110 federal prisons, 1,772 juvenile correctional facilities, 3,134 local jails, 218 immigration detention facilities, and 80 Indian Country jails as well as in military prisons, civil commitment centers, state psychiatric hospitals, and prisons in the U.S. territories (Sawyer and Wagner 2020). The increase in incarceration cannot be explained by a rise in crime, as crime rates have fluctuated independently of incarceration rates (Wacquant 2009; Gottschalk 2015). Incarceration rates soared because the laws changed, making a wider variety of crimes punishable by incarceration and lengthening sentences for those incarcerated. Recently, incarceration rates began to decline slowly. By the end of 2016, 6,613,500 people were under correctional supervision in the United States, and 2,262,400 were incarcerated (Kaeble and Cowhig 2018). (Figures 9-1 and 9-2). Although the current incarceration rate is about 1 in 38 adults, it is the lowest since 1993 (Kaeble and Cowhig 2018).

FIGURE 9-1

TOTAL U.S. ADULT CORRECTIONAL POPULATION, 2015

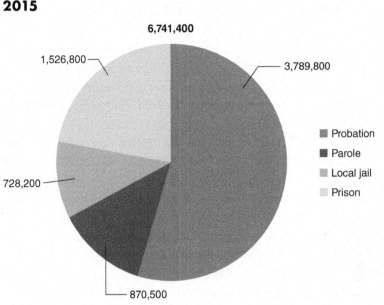

6,741,400

1,526,800 — 3,789,800

Probation
Parole
Local jail
Prison

728,200 —

870,500

Source: Data from BJS, 2016.

FIGURE 9-2

TOTAL U.S. ADULT INCARCERATED POPULATION, 1980–2015

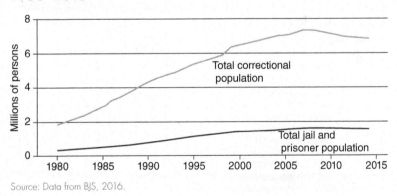

Total correctional
population

Total jail and
prisoner population

Source: Data from BJS, 2016.

Mass Incarceration in a Global Context

The United States stands alone in its rate of incarceration. In 2017, 666 of every 100,000 U.S. residents were incarcerated—a rate nearly 8 times that of western Europe's average rate of 84 per 100,000 residents (Walmsley 2017; and see Figure 9-3). The U.S. prison population also dwarfs that of other, larger, countries, including China, in terms of sheer numbers. According to the World Prison Brief (2022), the United States had 2,068,800 people behind bars. The next largest incarcerated population was in China, with 1,690,000 prisoners, followed by Brazil (811,707) and India, with 488,511 prisoners. No other country incarcerated more than a half a million people. Iceland, for example, had only 106 people behind bars.

The so-called War on Drugs in the United States accounts for much of this disparity. In the United States, a moral panic erupted in the 1980s surrounding the emergence of crack cocaine, which led to harsh laws against selling or possessing crack and other narcotics. These laws in turn resulted in historically and globally unprecedented rates of imprisonment for drug sales and possession (Gottschalk 2016). In most other developed countries, a first-time drug offense leads to no more than six months in jail, and rehabilitation is more common than criminalization. In the United States, the typical mandatory minimum sentence in federal court for a first-time drug offense is five or ten years (Alexander 2010). At the state level, there are even more extreme examples: in Florida,

FIGURE 9-3

INTERNATIONAL COMPARISON OF INCARCERATION RATES (PER 100,000), 2017

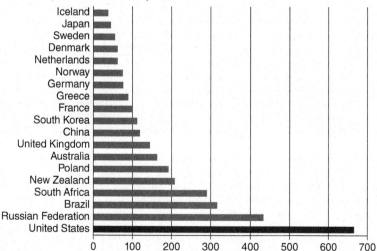

Source: World Prison Brief (2021). Data from Institute for Crime & Justice Policy Research, https://www.prisonstudies.org/highest-to-lowest/prison_population_rate?field_region_taxonomy_tid=All

illegal possession of 100 grams or more of the painkiller hydroco-
done (one of the most frequently prescribed drugs in the United
States) leads to a twenty-five-year mandatory minimum sentence
(Riggs 2014).

Race and Mass Incarceration

When we consider racial disparities in the U.S. incarceration rate,
the picture becomes even more unsettling. Although 13 percent of
the population of the United States is Black, Black people make up
30 percent of those imprisoned. Hispanics account for about 18 percent of the U.S. population, but represent 22 percent of the nation's
prison population (Kovera 2019). At year-end 2017, the imprisonment rate of Black males was 2,336 per every 100,000 in the population, as compared to 397 per 100,000 White males. Black males
were six times as likely to be incarcerated as White males by the end
of 2017 (Bronson and Carson 2019). Figure 9-4 shows these rates by
race and gender.

   Much of the racial disparity is due to imprisonment for drug crimes,
even though people of all races use and sell drugs at similar rates (Alexander 2010). This disparity has increased over time. In 1975, the ratio
of Black to White arrests for drug crimes was two to one. By 1990,
the ratio was five to one, even though there is no evidence that Black
people began to use or sell drugs at higher rates than White people
during this period (Wacquant 2009).

FIGURE 9-4

RATE OF INCARCERATION* PER 100,000 U.S. RESIDENTS, 2015, BY GENDER AND RACE/ETHNICITY

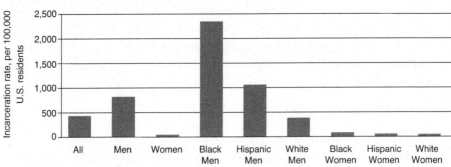

Source: Data from BJS, 2016.

voices

How Can We Reconcile Prison Abolition With #MeToo?

The past 17 years have seen an increase in prison abolition groups and organizing. In stark contrast to prison reform advocates, who push to improve prison conditions but posit that prisons are ultimately necessary for societal safety, prison abolitionists charge that prisons themselves are sites of violence and can never be adequately reformed. Instead, prisons must be eliminated; so too must the conditions that send people to prison, including racism, poverty and root causes of violence.

Conspicuous by its absence in many of the conversations about prison abolition, however, is how to address gender-based violence and harm without relying on police and prisons.

At the same time, many of the most prominent organizations and movements fighting domestic and sexual violence continue to rely on policing and prisons. In the aftermath of the six-month prison sentence imposed upon Brock Turner, the White Stanford student convicted of sexually assaulting an unconscious woman, feminist groups and activists expressed outrage at the shortness of the sentence and called for the ouster of his sentencing judge.

Harsher punishments and lengthier sentences have always fallen hardest upon—and devastated—people and communities of color, while providing little safety or prevention from gender violence.

Similarly, as accusations against celebrities like Harvey Weinstein and Bill Cosby mounted, calls for justice centered arrest and prison. The most vocal calls for "justice" failed to recognize that harsher punishments and lengthier sentences have always fallen hardest upon—and devastated—people and communities of color, while providing little safety or prevention [sic] from gender violence.

This reliance on criminalization reinforces state violence, which is not only perpetrated against overwhelmingly Black and brown and poor men, but also upholds a system punishing women (cisgender and trans), trans men, gender non-conforming and intersex people, even when they themselves are victimized by violence. We've seen this in the case of Marissa Alexander, the Florida mother initially sentenced to twenty years in prison after firing a warning shot to stop her abusive husband's assault. We've seen this in the case of Ky Peterson, a Black trans man currently serving a 20-year prison sentence after fatally shooting the man who raped him.

How did we get to this divide?

In 1994, Congress passed the Violence Against Women Act (VAWA), which pushed police to respond to complaints of domestic violence, sexual assault and other gender-based violence. The act was the result of years of lawsuits and organizing by many feminists to force law enforcement to respond to gender-based violence rather than dismissing it as an interpersonal issue. In many jurisdictions, VAWA resulted in mandatory arrest laws and more punitive prison sentences. It also led to policies such as dual arrests, in which police arrested both people. Some jurisdictions jail victims as material witnesses or impose fines and threaten a survivor with arrest if they do not cooperate with prosecution. (The city of Columbus, Georgia, changed its policy of non-cooperation fines and arrests after a lawsuit by abuse survivor Cleopatra Harrison and the Southern Center for Human Rights.)

Carceral feminism is the term often used to describe this reliance on increased policing, prosecution and imprisonment as the primary solution to gender-based violence. By and large, carceral feminism views solutions to gender-based violence through a White middle-class lens, one which ignores the ways in which intersecting identities, such as race, class, gender identity and immigration status, leave certain women more vulnerable to violence, including state violence.

. . .

It's still also true that nearly 90 percent of incarcerated people are men (or classified as men). But not every feminist and anti-violence activist espouses a carceral solution. For years, anti-violence activists and organizations, such as Beth Richie and INCITE!, have argued that increased criminalization replaces abuse by an individual with abuse by law enforcement, courts and prisons while doing nothing to address the root causes of violence against women. We've seen this with Marisa Alexander, Ky Peterson, and countless other women and trans people.

. . .

I've interviewed numerous adult survivors of domestic violence imprisoned for defending themselves. Again and again, they tell me that they turned to the police and legal system, both of which failed to protect them. Perhaps the police took their abuser away for a few days, but that didn't stop the violence. Perhaps the courts issued an order of protection, a piece of paper that their abuser flagrantly ignored. Perhaps the police did nothing. Perhaps their abuser was the police. This same legal system that failed to protect them then punished them for their survival. In prison, many are subject to violence—at the hands of other incarcerated people, staff members or the day-to-day practices.

At the same time, much prison abolition organizing continues to reflect larger society's failure to consider the societal and cultural shifts needed to end gender-based violence or to develop concrete ways to prevent and address domestic and sexual violence in daily life.

. . .

Transformative Justice

One way to address interpersonal violence without relying on state violence is through transformative justice. Transformative justice refers to a community process that addresses not only the needs of the person who was harmed, but also the conditions that enabled this

(continued)

voices   *continued.*

How Can We Reconcile Prison Abolition With #MeToo?

harm. In other words, instead of looking at the act(s) of violence in a vacuum, transformative justice processes ask, "What else needs to change so that this never happens again? What needs to happen so that the survivor can heal?" There's no right or wrong set of footprints to follow in transformative justice; instead, each process depends on the people and circumstances.

... [P]rocesses of community accountability are messy and rarely follow a uniform path. They often, however, mix and match from a distinct set of alternative tools that include actions for both organizations and individuals. Counseling for the person who caused harm, removal from leadership positions, admission of guilt, public or private apologies, workshops and trainings, and specific behavioral changes are just some of the demands that communities can make. Regardless of what forms they take, continuing to explore alternatives to state violence in response to gender-based violence is an essential piece of the movements to end both.

Source: By Victoria Law, September 25, 2018. https://filtermag.org/how-can-we-reconcile-prison-abolition-with-metoo/

FIGURE 9-5

PERCENTAGE OF MALE POPULATION IN PRISON BY RACE/ETHNICITY, 2015

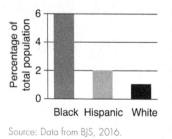

Source: Data from BJS, 2016.

By the end of the twentieth century, Black men were seven times more likely than White men to go to prison (Figure 9-5). Over the course of a Black man's life, he is more likely to go to prison than to get a bachelor's degree or join the military. Whereas a White man is ten times more likely to get a college degree than to go to prison, a Black man is nearly twice as likely to end up in prison than to finish college. Imprisonment has become an expected life outcome for some Black men: one in every three Black males in the United States will be in prison at some point in his life, compared with one in every six Latino males, and one in every seventeen White males (The Sentencing Project 2013). The number of incarcerated women has also increased over the past few decades—at a rate 50 percent higher than that of men since 1980 (The Sentencing Project 2016).

The Inefficacy of Mass Incarceration

Incarceration has emerged as the most popular crime control strategy in the United States. However, according to state-level incarceration trends, there is limited evidence that incarceration is an effective strategy to control crime. Between 1998 and 2003, some states greatly increased the number of people they sent to prison, while other states did not. The average decrease in crime rates in these states, however, was similar. Additionally, the states with higher increases in incarceration did not experience more substantial declines in their crime rates (King, Mauer, and Young 2005).

Incarceration has had a limited impact on crime rates for two reasons. First, it is just one of many factors that influence crime rates: changes in the economy, fluctuations in the drug market, and community-level responses often have more pronounced effects. Second, there are diminishing returns from incarceration: incarcerating repeat violent offenders takes them off the streets and thus reduces crime, whereas incarcerating nonviolent offenders has a minimal effect on crime rates (King et al. 2005).

The rates of incarceration began to increase in the 1970s, during a time when violent and property crime rates were high. Even though crime rates began to fall in 1993, incarceration rates and populations continued to rise for another decade. Some of the most draconian laws were passed in the mid-1990s, after crime rates had started falling. Figures 9-6 and 9-7 provide a visual representation of how violent crime and property crime rates have decreased since 1993.

FIGURE 9-6

PROPERTY VICTIMIZATION RATE, 1993–2015

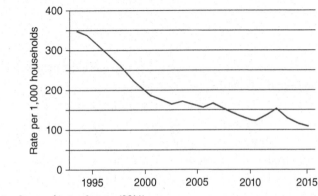

Source: Bureau of Justice Statistics (2016)

FIGURE 9-7

VIOLENT VICTIMIZATION RATE, 1993–2015

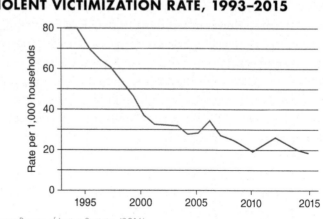

Source: Bureau of Justice Statistics (2016)

FIGURE 9-8

U.S. INCARCERATION RATE, 1980–2015

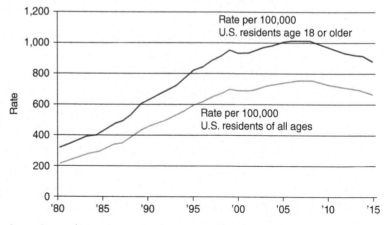

Source: Bureau of Justice Statistics, Key Statistics, www.bjs.gov, 2017.

Despite the low efficacy of imprisoning nonviolent offenders, this is the segment of the prison population that has grown the fastest. Between 1970 and 2000, incarceration rates in the United States increased five-fold, in large part because of legislation designed to fight drugs (see Figure 9-8). As a result of the War on Drugs, the number of people incarcerated for drug offenses in the U.S. skyrocketed from 40,900 in 1980 to 452,964 in 2017 (The Sentencing Project 2022). The irony is that the incarceration of drug offenders is a highly ineffective way to reduce the amount of illegal drugs sold in the United States. When street-level drug sellers are incarcerated, they are quickly replaced by other sellers, since what drives the drug market is demand for drugs. Incarcerating large numbers of drug offenders has not ameliorated the drug problem in the United States (King et al. 2005).

Despite the lack of evidence that increased incarceration rates lead to decreased crime (Lynch 1999), we continue to build prisons and imprison more people (Gilmore 2007). We have not changed our policies in response to substantial evidence that being tough on crime does not lead to safer communities. Politicians who direct money to the criminal legal system can claim to their constituents that they are serious about law enforcement. This strategy, creating the impression that they have the crime victims' interests at heart, has become essential for winning electoral campaigns (Simon 2007). In 1998, political activist and scholar Angela Davis pointed out: "Mass incarceration is not a solution to unemployment, nor is it a solution to the vast array of social problems that are hidden away in a rapidly growing network of prisons and jails. However, the great majority of people have been tricked into believing in the efficacy of imprisonment, even though the historical record clearly demonstrates that prisons do not work" (1998, 3). The emergence of mass incarceration as a solution to social ills can be attributed primarily to the War on Drugs, as we will see.

Mass Incarceration and the War on Drugs

Whereas only 41,000 people were behind bars for a drug offense in 1980, the figure had risen astronomically to about half a million in 2010 (Alexander 2010). Many people are incarcerated for low-level drug crimes. Between 1993 and 2011, thirty million people were arrested for drug crimes. About 85 percent of these arrests were for drug possession, and only 15 percent were for drug sales (Sawyer and Wagner 2020; Figure 9-9).

Zealous enforcement of drug laws disproportionately affects people of color, even though Whites are more likely to use and sell drugs. In the United States, Black men are sent to prison on drug charges at thirteen times the rate of White men, yet five times

FIGURE 9-9

DRUG SALES VERSUS DRUG POSSESSION ARRESTS, 2018

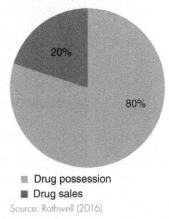

20%

80%

- Drug possession
- Drug sales

Source: Rothwell (2016)

as many White as Black people use illegal drugs (Alexander 2010). According to results from the National Household Survey on Drug Abuse, White youth aged twelve to seventeen are more likely than Black youth to have sold illegal drugs (Alexander 2010). These data are based on self-reports, yet they are confirmed by more objective data: White youth are about three times as likely as their African American counterparts to end up in an emergency room for drug-related emergencies. White users most often buy their drugs from White sellers, just as Black users buy from Black sellers (Alexander 2010).

Law enforcement agents cannot fully enforce drug laws because drug use and selling are too widespread. More than half of the people in the United States have violated drug laws at some point in their lives, yet relatively few have been punished for it. In any given year, about 10 percent of American adults violate drug laws. As law enforcement agents have neither the resources nor the mandate to prosecute every lawbreaker, they must be strategic with their resources and enforcement tactics. Because of stereotypes that drug law violators are Black, combined with the relatively weak political power of poor Black communities, law enforcement agents have targeted open-air drug markets in poor Black communities instead of the places where Whites use and sell drugs (Alexander 2010).

Crack cocaine was often portrayed as public enemy number one in the War on Drugs. Yet crack did not hit the streets until 1985—three years after President Ronald Regan prioritized the War on Drugs (an initiative President Richard Nixon had declared in 1971). In 1982, less than 2 percent of Americans viewed drugs as the most important problem facing the nation. Public opinion changed drastically after Reagan greatly expanded the drug war's reach in 1982, however, and crack cocaine became an urban problem in 1985. A media frenzy broke out over the problems of crackheads and crack babies. The media often racialized the crack problem as a Black problem by showing images of Black people in connection with stories about crack cocaine (Alexander 2010).

The penalties that emerged for possession and sale of crack cocaine were the harshest drug penalties in U.S. history. When the Anti-Drug Abuse Act was passed in 1988, it meted out a five-year mandatory minimum sentence for simple possession of crack. This was unprecedented: prior to this legislation, one year of imprisonment was the maximum sentence one could receive for possession of any amount of any drug (Alexander 2010). Along with the federal laws, states began to pass stricter laws, including "three strikes," "truth in sentencing," and "zero tolerance" legislation, which led to a huge upswing in incarceration rates. By 1996, nearly three-quarters of all people admitted to state prisons were nonviolent offenders with relatively minor convictions (Ladipo 2001).

At the federal level, three major laws were passed in 1984, 1986, and 1988 that marked the beginning of a new era in the criminal legal system:

- The **1984 Crime Control Act** established mandatory minimum sentences and eliminated federal parole.
- The **Anti-Drug Abuse Act of 1986** imposed even more mandatory minimum sentences. Most significantly, it set a five-year mandatory minimum sentence for offenses involving 100 grams of heroin, 500 grams of cocaine, or 5 grams of crack cocaine.
- The **Anti-Drug Abuse Act of 1988** included a five-year mandatory minimum sentence for simple possession of crack cocaine, with no evidence of intent to sell. Prior to 1988, one year of imprisonment had been the maximum penalty for possession of any amount of any drug.

Race, Class, Gender, and Mass Incarceration

Mass incarceration has led to the filling of jails with Black and Latino working-class and poor men. Mass incarceration is thus evidently raced, classed, and gendered. However, an intersectional analysis requires consideration not only of the numbers of Black people, Latinx people, and men behind bars, but also of how mass incarceration affects people in distinct social locations differently. When we look at women, for example, it becomes clear that mass incarceration has directly affected women in three distinct ways from men:

1. Very few women were behind bars prior to 1970, so incarceration is a relatively new phenomenon for women. Incarceration rates for women rose dramatically in the context of the War on Drugs. Between 1970 and 1997, the population of women in prison rose more than twelve-fold, from 5,600 to 75,000. With the addition of 35,000 more women in jails, there were about 100,000 women incarcerated by the late 1990s (Covington and Bloom 2003). By 2017, 105,033 women were behind bars (Bronson and Carson 2019). Similar to

men, women of color are incarcerated at a higher rate than White women. In 2017, Black women were twice as likely as White women to be incarcerated, and Latina women were 34 percent more likely (Bureau of Justice Statistics).

2. Women are more likely than men to have been the primary caregivers prior to being incarcerated. This means that the incarceration of women often has a more direct and immediate effect on their children.

3. Women are more likely than men to have experienced physical or sexual abuse. One study found that nearly 80 percent of women prisoners had experienced some form of abuse in their lives. Many of the women serving time for violent crimes are in jail for retaliating against their abuser (Covington and Bloom 2003).

INSTITUTIONAL RACISM IN THE CRIMINAL LEGAL SYSTEM

Racial disparities in incarceration rates are a classic example of institutional racism. As discussed in Chapter 2, institutional racism is the creation of racial disparities as a result of institutional practices and policies that distribute resources, power, and advantages to Whites. Racial inequalities in law enforcement are institutionalized at every level of the criminal legal process, from stops to arrests to charges to sentencing to release. Black and Latinx people are more likely to be arrested than Whites. They are more likely to be charged, more likely to be convicted, more likely to be given a longer sentence, and more likely to face the death penalty. The cumulative effect of these disparities at each stage of the process creates a situation in which Black men are seven times more likely than White men to be put behind bars.

Racial Profiling

Racial profiling is the use of race or ethnicity as grounds for suspicion. In the United States, Black and Latinx drivers are more likely than White drivers to be stopped by police (Baumgartner et al. 2017). In the early 1990s, statistician John Lamberth (1994) conducted a detailed investigation that provided convincing evidence of racial profiling. Lamberth's study revealed that only 13 percent of all cars on the New Jersey Turnpike had a Black driver or passenger but that 35 percent of those stopped on the turnpike were Black, and 73.2 percent of those arrested were Black. Black drivers were much more likely than White drivers to be stopped, even though Black and White drivers violated traffic laws at almost exactly the same rate. Studies in other states have revealed similar results: police officers are more likely to pull over African American drivers than White drivers. In Maryland, an American Civil Liberties Union (ACLU) study found that 75 percent of drivers along Interstate 95 were White, but between January 1995 and September 1996, 73 percent of the motorists whom Maryland state police searched were Black (Harris 1999). Racial profiling also extends to Hispanics: a study in Volusia County in Florida, for example, revealed that Black and Hispanic drivers were more likely to be pulled over and much more likely to be searched once pulled over than Whites (Mauer 1999).

In response to these findings that police officers engage in racial profiling, state legislatures began to mandate that police departments collect more data. Frank R. Baumgartner, Leah Christiani, Derek A. Epp, Kevin Roach, and Kelsey Shoub (2017) were thus able to analyze publicly available information about racial profiling from hundreds of police agencies across thirteen states. Baumgartner and his colleagues focused their analysis on police searches following a traffic stop. They wanted to know the likelihood that a motorist would be searched by the police after being pulled over and how that likelihood varies depending on the race of the driver. After analyzing 55 million stops and 1.9 million searches, they found that police officers search an average of 3.2 percent of White drivers whom they stop, compared with 7.6 percent of Black drivers and 8.7 percent of Hispanic or Latinx drivers. The Evanston (Illinois) Police Department had the greatest disparity in its stops of Black and White drivers: it was seven times more likely to search a Black driver than a White driver. The Cook County (Chicago metropolitan area) Sheriff's Department had the single largest racial disparity: its police officers were eighteen times more likely to search a Hispanic or Latinx driver than a White driver. Of the 132 agencies surveyed, only 9 of them were less likely to search Black drivers than White drivers.

Racial profiling happens on street corners as well as highways, where police officers stop and frisk Black and Latinx pedestrians much more frequently than they do White pedestrians. African Americans make up 13 percent of the U.S. population and 14 percent of illegal drug users in this country. However, they account for 37 percent of the people arrested for drug offenses, in part because they are more likely to be stopped and frisked than Whites (Mauer 2009). In New York City, for example, one study found that Blacks account for half of all people stopped by the police, even though they are only a quarter of the New York City population (Gelman, Fagan, and Kiss 2007). Once stopped, New York police officers are more likely to frisk Blacks and Latinxs than Whites. According to data provided by the New York Police Department (NYPD), between 1998 and 2008, NYPD officers frisked 85 percent of Blacks and Latinxs whom they stopped, compared with only 8 percent of Whites (New York City Bar 2013). A study in Seattle revealed similar results. Seventy percent of people in Seattle are White, and the majority of those who sell and use drugs in Seattle are White. However, Black people represent nearly two-thirds of all those arrested for drug offenses (Barnes and Chang 2012). This is primarily because police officers tend to target predominantly Black neighborhoods in criminal law enforcement operations.

Racial profiling leads to disparate treatment of Whites, Blacks, and Latinxs by police agencies and vigilantes. It also can have deadly consequences, as in several high-profile cases. The **Black Lives Matter** movement arose in 2013 as part of a broad campaign against this type of racial violence. The associated hashtag—created by Alicia

Racial profiling leads to disparate treatment of White, Black, and Latinx people by police agencies.

Garza, Patrisse Cullors, and Opal Tometi—channeled reactions on social media following the outcome of *Florida v. George Zimmerman*. Zimmerman, a self-appointed neighborhood watchman, fatally shot unarmed teenager Trayvon Martin in 2012 yet was acquitted of all charges. In 2014–2015, Black Lives Matter gained momentum in response to a series of police-related deaths, including those of Eric Garner in New York City; Michael Brown in Ferguson, Missouri; Walter Scott in North Charleston, South Carolina; Freddie Gray in Baltimore, Maryland; and Sandra Bland in Waller County, Texas. Sandra Bland, whose story is told in the Voices sidebar in this section, was pulled over after she failed to use her turn signal.

voices

Sandra Bland

Sandra Annette Bland—who went by Sandy—was born in 1987, in Chicago. After completing high school, she received a music scholarship at Prairie View A&M University, a historically Black university in Waller County, Texas. She graduated in 2009 with a degree in animal science.

Sandy secured a low-paying job in nearby Houston after graduating. Driving around Houston, she racked up a series of traffic tickets. When she was unable to pay them, a warrant was issued for her arrest. She later was arrested for marijuana possession and was sentenced to thirty days in jail. She did that time in addition to several days for the traffic tickets.

A protestor holds a sign in remembrance of Sandra Bland.

After that experience, Sandy moved back to Illinois, where she worked in several low-paying jobs. While in Illinois, she battled depression, yet managed to hold on to work most of the time.

(continued)

voices *continued.*

Sandy Bland

In July 2015, Sandy applied for a job at Prairie View A&M University. When she was called for an interview, she left her job in Chicago and drove down to Texas. On July 10, she signed the papers for her new job. On her way home, Texas state trooper Brian Encinia pulled her over.

Encinia claims that he pulled Sandy over because she had failed to use her turn signal. Sandy claims she was trying to move out of the way so that he could pass.

As Encinia was writing her ticket, he asked her to put out her cigarette. Sandy, annoyed that she was getting a ticket for such a minor traffic offense, insisted that she did not have to put out her cigarette as she was in her own car.

At that point, Encinia asked her to get out of her car. She refused, saying that he did not have the right. Encinia opened her car door and told her that if she did not step out, he would remove her. He then began to use force against her while Sandy insisted that he did not have the right to remove her from her car. Encinia then stated she was under arrest. When she asked what for, he did not respond but pulled a gun and yelled that she had to get out of the car. At that point, she stepped out.

Sandy was arrested and taken to jail. As she did not have funds for bail, she remained there. Three days later, she was found dead in her cell, and her death was labeled a suicide.

Encinia was indicted for perjury because a grand jury decided he had lied when he said he forced Sandy to get out of the car to conduct a safe traffic investigation. He was fired by the Texas Department of Public Safety after the indictment.

The family of Sandra Bland settled a wrongful death lawsuit against officials in Waller County for $1.9 million.

Sources: Chammah 2016; *Chicago Tribune* 2016; Nathan 2016.

Sentencing Disparities

Black and Latinx people are more likely to be arrested than White people. An arrest is just the first point of entry into the criminal legal system, where Black and Latinx defendants are likely to continue to find the odds stacked against them. A study of federal offenders, for example, found that Blacks and Latinxs are more likely to be sentenced to longer prison terms than Whites, even after taking into account the severity of the charges. In contrast, Whites are more likely than Blacks to get no prison time when that option is available. This study also found that the disparities between sentences for Whites and non-Whites is most evident in drug-trafficking cases (Mustard 2001).

Although more Whites than Blacks are convicted of drug felonies, more Blacks are admitted to prison. This disparity is related to the differing severity of sentences that Blacks and Whites receive in courts of law. Overall, Black people are sent to prison on drug charges at nearly twelve times the rate of Whites, even though, as mentioned previously, Blacks and Whites use and sell drugs at about the same rates (Alexander 2010). One of the main reasons for this disparity is that police officers target open-air drug markets in Black neighborhoods and yet often ignore the widespread usage of narcotics in primarily White suburban areas and on college campuses. Because Whites are less likely to be arrested for drug offenses, they are less likely to be charged, convicted, or sentenced to prison for drug offenses. This means that harsh penalties for drug offenses have had a disproportionate impact on people of color.

As the War on Drugs advanced in the 1980s, discretionary power was increasingly taken away from judges out of fear they might be soft on crime. One of the trends in sentencing reform has been the introduction of mandatory minimum sentences and mandatory guidelines for calculating prison sentences (Simon 2007). The implementation of mandatory prison terms for certain drug crimes has had a disproportionate impact on African Americans. The 1986 Anti-Drug Abuse Act established mandatory prison terms of five years for possession or sale of 5 grams of crack cocaine or 500 grams of powder cocaine. This sentencing disparity is emblematic of how drug law enforcement has meted out different sentences to Black and White people.

Between 1986 and 2006, more than 80 percent of people sentenced to prison for crack cocaine were Black (Mauer 2007). This statistic is especially remarkable when we consider that two-thirds of regular crack cocaine users are either White or Latinxs (Mauer 2009). The 1986 act is one of many pieces of legislation that set mandatory minimum sentences, which have disproportionately affected African Americans. Blacks are 21 percent more likely than Whites to receive a mandatory minimum sentence when facing an eligible charge, and Black drug defendants are 20 percent more likely than White drug defendants to be sentenced to prison (Mauer 2009).

The Ultimate Sentence: Racial Disparities in the Death Penalty
A study conducted in California found that people accused of killing Whites are over three times more likely to be sentenced to death than those who kill African Americans (American Civil Liberties Union 2003). Another study examined all death penalty cases since 1977, when the death penalty was reinstated, and found that although Whites accounted for about half of all murder victims, 80 percent of all death penalty cases involved White victims (American Civil Liberties Union 2003). In addition, between 1976 and 2002, only twelve people were executed for crimes in which the defendant was White and the victim Black, compared with the 178 Black defendants who were executed after having been convicted of killing a White person (American Civil Liberties Union 2003). Between 1976 and 2017, over 75 percent of murder victims in death penalty cases were White, even though only about half of all murder victims are White. In that same period, more than 1,400 people were executed in the United States, and 34 percent of them were African American. Remarkably, more than 155 people were released from death row in that period after being found innocent (Death Penalty Information Center, 2017).

In recent years, the death penalty has come under increasing scrutiny. New Mexico and New Jersey have abolished the death penalty, and death sentences have decreased since their peak in the 1990s. In addition, the U.S. Supreme Court has abolished the death penalty for minors and people with intellectual disabilities (Amnesty International 2010).

THE ECONOMICS OF MASS INCARCERATION

Mass incarceration is a consequence of laws passed at both the state and federal levels. Before the election of Ronald Reagan as president, however, keeping street crime in check had traditionally been the responsibility of state and local law enforcement. To fulfill Reagan's campaign promise to fight crime, his administration poured money into federal law enforcement agencies, and Congress passed federal laws that enhanced the punishments for drug-related offenses.

California led the states in prison buildup. Between 1977 and 2007, the California State Assembly passed more than 1,000 laws extending and toughening prison sentences (Wacquant 2009). The California state prison population increased five-fold between 1982 and 2000, even though the crime rate peaked in 1980 and declined thereafter (Gilmore 2007). Notably, California's incarceration rate increased *after* the crime rate had begun to decrease. California had built only twelve prisons between 1852 and 1964, yet it built twenty-three major new prisons between 1984 and 2004 (Gilmore 2007). What happened? Why did California engage in this massive prison-building project? Why did the legislature pass so many anticrime laws?

The answers to these questions can be found through a consideration of the economic restructuring that California underwent leading up to this period. During World War II, much of California's prosperity had been tied directly to defense contracts: people from across the country flocked to California to secure well-paying jobs building defense machinery. After the war, California invested in education and technology to ensure that defense contracts would continue, and it endeavored to make itself uniquely able to provide research, development, and manufacturing for the Department of Defense (DoD). DoD contracts continued to come in until the 1980s, but they contributed to splitting the labor market into high-skilled, well-paid technology jobs on one hand and low-skilled, poorly paid jobs on the other (Gilmore 2007).

The restructuring of California's economy led to increases in unemployment, poverty, and inequality. By the 1980s, California was a highly unequal state, with high poverty rates, high housing costs, and high unemployment rates while also being home to some of the wealthiest people in the nation. Over the next fifteen years, its economy continued to change, with increasing numbers of low-paid manufacturing and service jobs and fewer high-paid manufacturing jobs. Childhood poverty rates had increased 25 percent between 1969 and 1979, and they continued to soar over the next decade, increasing another 67 percent between 1980 and 1995, so that by the end of the twentieth century, one in four children in California lived in poverty (Gilmore 2007). Beset with social problems, the California legislature attempted to use mass incarceration as a solution to poverty, unemployment, and inequality. Prisons serve the double purpose of providing employment to tens of thousands of Californians and locking away a good proportion of the surplus labor force.

The economic restructuring in California mirrored that of the rest of the country, as did cuts in government spending. When Ronald Reagan took office in 1980, he implemented **Reaganomics**, a set of economic policies that involved heavy cuts to a wide variety of social programs across the country. Christian Parenti (1999, 40–41) explains: "In 1982 alone, Reagan cut the real value of welfare by 24 percent, slashed the budget for child nutrition by 34 percent, reduced funding for school milk programs by 78 percent, urban development action grants by 35 percent, and educational block grants by 38 percent." These enormous cuts in social spending disproportionately affected low-wage people of color in urban areas.

While states were cutting spending on education and social services, all but two states (Massachusetts and New Hampshire) increased spending on incarceration. Nationwide, spending on state and local corrections outpaced spending on PK–12 education three-fold from 1979–1980 to 2012–2013 (Figure 9-10). Public school expenditures increased by 107 percent (from $258 to $534 billion), while total state and local corrections expenditures increased by 324 percent (from $17 to $71 billion). The magnitude of this increase varied considerably from state to state. In New Mexico and Wyoming, incarceration spending outpaced education spending eight-fold (Stullich, Morgan, and Schak 2016).

FIGURE 9-10

PERCENTAGE CHANGE IN EDUCATION EXPENDITURES (PK-12) VERSUS STATE AND LOCAL CORRECTIONS EXPENDITURES FROM 1979–1980 TO 2012–2013

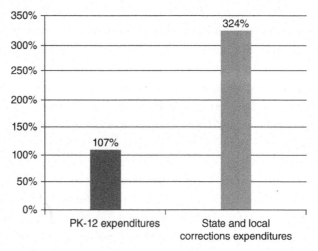

Neoliberalism is a label for the ideology stating that open markets, liberalized trade, and privatization are the keys to economic success. It is based on the idea that the government's primary role is to protect property rights, free markets, and free trade, and not to hand out social services to its citizens. Under this ideology, the government does not provide any social assistance, and the needs of the poor are left to the market. Although neoliberalism demands that the government cut back its social services, there is one area that tends to grow when these policies are implemented: its coercive arm (i.e., the police force and the military). Insofar as neoliberalism diminishes opportunities and services for the poor, the government must ensure that working-class and poor people do not pose a threat to the rich. Government cutbacks in social services often lead to dissent and increases in crime. The government responds by strengthening the police force and the military. Under neoliberalism, "in the United States, incarceration became a key state strategy to deal with problems arising among discarded workers and marginalized populations. The coercive arm of the state is augmented to protect corporate interests and, if necessary, to repress dissent" (Harvey 2005, 77).

At the same time as the government began to cut social spending, companies began to **outsource** manufacturing, moving jobs once held by Americans overseas, where cheaper labor could be found. This practice, part of the larger process of **deindustrialization**, led to the impoverishment of cities such as Chicago and Detroit. Detroit was hit particularly hard: it lost half of its population in the 1980s. In Detroit as well as other cities across the country, the War on Drugs kicked off at the same time that inner-city communities were experiencing a dramatic economic crisis. As discussed in Chapter 7, well-paying, stable blue-collar jobs disappeared, leaving unemployment, as well as social unrest, in their wake (Alexander 2010). This social unrest in turn led to the expansion of the criminal legal system, which was designed to manage and contain the underclass created by neoliberal economic policies.

When we tie economics into an analysis of the criminal legal system, however, it also becomes clear that the Great Recession (2007–2008) finally gave elected leaders the political will to make cuts to the prison system. In 2009, after thirty years of prison building, California found itself with a massive prison system it was no longer able to finance, and it began to release some prisoners to cut costs. Nationwide, the number of prisoners decreased for the first time in thirty-seven years (Aviram 2015). By 2011, one-fourth of states had closed or planned to close a prison (Clear and Frost 2015). In 2010, then-president Barack Obama signed the Fair Sentencing Act, which repealed the five-year mandatory sentence for first-time offenders and for repeat offenders with less than 28 grams of cocaine. The change also involved reducing the 100-to-1 sentencing disparity between crack and powder cocaine convictions to 18-to-1, in response to decades of activism (Murakawa 2014). And in 2016, Obama announced that the federal government would be ending its contracts with private prisons that held federal prisoners. When Donald Trump took office in 2017, he decided not to honor that agreement.

Private Prisons

Private prisons in the United States date back to 1984, when the Corrections Corporation of America (CCA) was awarded its first government contract. During the 1990s, the CCA began to see substantial profits, and by 1998 its stock prices had hit $44 a share. The CCA was doing so well that at the end of the twentieth century, the company began to build speculative prisons—"excess prison space for inmates who did not yet exist" (Wood 2007, 232)—with the expectation that the prison population would continue to grow.

At the beginning of the twenty-first century, however, rates of incarceration leveled off, and the CCA faced serious problems. Its stock values fell from $44 in 1998 to a mere $0.18 in December 2000. By 2001, the CCA had 8,500 empty beds and was over a billion dollars in debt (Wood 2007). Its rival, Wackenhut, also saw its stock lose a third of its value between 1998 and 2001 (Berestein 2008). Both companies had reinvested their immense profits in new prisons that were now sitting empty, and funding options seemed bleak.

Because states had cut back funding for prisons, the CCA looked to the federal government. Its federal lobbying expenses increased from $410,000 in 2000 to $3 million in 2004, and these efforts appear to have paid off. Not only has the CCA been awarded lucrative federal contracts in recent years to build new prisons, but the government has increased its rate of immigrant detention, leaving no doubt that newly built prisons can be kept full (Golash-Boza 2012a). There was a slight decline in CCA stock prices when Obama announced that the Department of Justice would not be using private prisons, but their stock rebounded a few months later when Donald Trump—who had campaigned on a promise of mass deportation—was elected. The day after Trump's victory was announced, shares of the two largest private prison companies—the CCA and the GEO Group—increased 43 and 21 percent, respectively (Takei and Egan 2017).

The CCA has been able to obtain favorable government contracts in part because of its ties to current and former elected officials. The former head of the Federal Bureau of Prisons, J. Michael Quinlan, is one of the CCA's top executives. Both the CCA and its competitor Wackenhut have dominated the private prison sector because of their political influence. As Phillip Wood notes, "both benefit from extensive and intimate connections with state and local politics and the public corrections sector as well as from the usual interlocking directorships with other corporations in prison services, construction, the media and finance" (Wood 2007, 231). The enormous public and private investment in the criminal legal system has led some scholars to argue that we now have a prison-industrial complex.

The Prison-Industrial Complex

The **prison-industrial complex (PIC)** refers to the vast network of prisons, jails, courts, police officers, and other elements that purport to reduce the amount of criminal activity in our society. The PIC is a "self-perpetuating machine": the enormous investment in prisons, jails, and law enforcement, combined with the perceived political benefits of crime control, has led to policies such as mandatory minimum sentences that ensure that more people are sentenced to prison, thereby creating the need for more prison beds (Brewer and Heitzeg 2008, 637). A core feature of the idea of the PIC is that prisons are not built solely to house criminals; instead, a confluence of interests has led to building more prisons, enacting harsher laws, and mass incarcerating poor people. The constituencies with interests in mass incarceration include the media, private contractors, politicians, state bureaucracies, and private prisons (Davis 1998; Gilmore 2007; Schlosser 1998; Do Valle, Huang, and Spira 2006).

Ideas of racial otherness play an important role in the demonization of criminals. This otherization allows politicians to play on public fears and portray these groups as threatening public safety. As Michael Welch argues, the punitive drug control legislation passed in the last decades of the twentieth century to control crime and immigration is "not only poorly formulated, but also unjust and discriminatory against the poor and people of color" (Welch 2002, 14). Welch further contends that these laws are passed in the context of a "moral panic, a turbulent and exaggerated response to a putative social problem" (8).

The PIC relies on the production of criminals through repressive laws and the policing of communities to fill the prisons it builds (Richie 2005). The creation of increasingly strict crime laws is partly due to campaign tactics used by politicians who aim to play on fears regarding crime to capture more votes. One of the most famous examples of a politician using the fear of crime as a campaign tactic is the Willie Horton case. In the 1988 presidential race, George H. W. Bush's campaign played on White Americans' fear of crime and racial prejudices against Black people through use of an ad that featured Willie Horton, a young Black man who had escaped from prison while on a weekend pass. Horton then "kidnapped and brutally assaulted a White couple in their home, raping the woman and stabbing the man" (Mendelberg 1997). An ad that featured this story and a mugshot of Horton were used by the Bush campaign to portray the opposing party as being lax on crime. This ad was part of Bush's successful campaign to keep the presidency in Republican hands. It is just one of many examples of politicians using fears about crime for political gain. Notably, the Willie Horton case used both the fear of crime and the fear of Black men to push forward a political agenda.

The PIC has come into being because it serves the interests of powerful groups in our society. Politicians have used a tough-on-crime approach to gain votes. The mass media have highlighted local crime to attract viewers (Chermak 1994). Rural areas have turned to building prisons to boost local economic development. For example, over two-thirds of the prisons built in California between 1982 and 1998 were built on formerly irrigated agricultural land that had ceased production (Gilmore 2007, 105–106). Finally, private prisons have cashed in on growing rates of incarceration (Brewer and Heitzeg 2008; Schlosser 1998; Do Valle et al. 2006). For these reasons, not because of excessive rates of criminality, we now have over 2 million people behind bars in the United States, over ten times as many as we did prior to the 1970s. Mass incarceration of poor people has generated profits for private prisons and political capital for politicians, yet it has not made this country any safer (Hattery and Smith 2006).

BEYOND INCARCERATION: COLLATERAL CONSEQUENCES

Incarceration most directly affects the 2 million people behind bars. It also has a great impact on the 7 million people under criminal legal supervision. Because of the lifelong stigma associated with a felony, mass incarceration also affects the 12 million felons in the United States long after they have been released from prison. Incarceration not only influences the lives of these 19 million people who have been directly involved in the criminal legal system; it also has wide-ranging collateral consequences for their children, spouses, and communities.

The Impact of Mass Incarceration on Families and Children

Over half of all inmates—more than 120,000 mothers and 1.1 million fathers behind bars—have minor children (Pew Charitable Trusts 2010). Often, when a family member is incarcerated, people who have no criminal conviction have to change their behavior, expectations, and living arrangements in response to the loss of a family member or friend. They also may suffer emotional or health-related consequences (Comfort 2007). Children are the most obvious victims of adult incarceration. More than 5 million American children, a staggering 7 percent (1 in 14), have had a parent incarcerated at some point in their lives (Annie E. Casey Foundation 2016). Nearly one-third of the residents of the United States—113 million people—have an immediate family member who has spent time in prison or jail (Sawyer and Wagner 2020).

Parental imprisonment deepens racial inequality insofar as Black and Latinx families are disproportionately affected (Wildeman 2009). Black and Latinx children face trauma and disadvantage because of parental incarceration more often than do White children (Wildeman 2009). The incarceration of a parent—usually a father—often has financial consequences for a household. This is particularly the case when the father was working, as men often are the primary or only breadwinner in a family unit. Families with an incarcerated member often have to change residence because of the loss of an income. Relocating affects family members' access to neighborhood support networks, and children may be forced to change schools (Geller, Garfinkel, Cooper, and Mincy 2009).

Over half of all inmates have minor children, who suffer the collateral consequences of mass incarceration.

Some mothers choose to maintain a relationship with the incarcerated fathers of their children. However, doing so requires resources and often puts a financial strain on families, especially if they are poor (Woldoff and Washington 2008). The loss of a parent has economic costs, but there may be other costs as well. When one parent is incarcerated, the other parent may have less time and money to invest in his or her children. In addition, older siblings may find themselves with new responsibilities, ranging from care of younger siblings to housework to the need to seek outside employment (Foster and Hagan 2009). The stigma associated with the incarceration of parents may also be a source of shame for children (Foster and Hagan 2009).

A study of nearly 2000 women in Mexico found that Mexican women with an incarcerated family member had significantly higher levels of stress than women without an incarcerated family member (Connors et al. 2020). Studies conducted in the United States have found that the imprisonment of a family member negatively affects family communication, mental health, physical health, finances, and educational outcomes (DeHart and Clone 2018; Shaw 2019). Marcus Shaw (2019) explains that "the mass incarceration of marginalized groups plays a key role in sustaining inequality through limited intergenerational educational success" (286).

Although women are less likely to be incarcerated than men, female prisoners are more likely to have been primary caregivers for their children. Thus, the incarceration of women often means that children's lives are drastically altered, as they frequently find themselves in a new home, either with their father for the first time or with their grandparents. In the absence of any willing relative, many of these children end up in foster homes. When children are placed in foster care, parents face losing their children permanently. The 1997 Adoption and Safe Families Act (ASFA) mandates the termination of parental rights once a child has spent more than fifteen months in foster care (Covington and Bloom 2003).

Children with incarcerated parents have been found to suffer mental health problems such as depression, anxiety, and aggressiveness. Some even exhibit symptoms of posttraumatic stress disorder. These problems are exacerbated when a parent is incarcerated because of child or spousal abuse (Comfort 2007). Foster and Hagan (2009, 191) have "found strong evidence that the imprisonment of fathers has negative causal consequences for children." They further contend that economic disadvantages are only one of many that children of the incarcerated face: children also suffer educational and emotional disadvantages when their parents are incarcerated.

The Lifelong Stigma of a Felony: "The New Jim Crow"

In the 2016 presidential election, over six million adults in the United States were prevented from voting because of laws restricting voting rights for those convicted of felony-level crimes (The Sentencing Project 2016). Voting restrictions are just one way that former inmates face legalized exclusion. When a person is released from prison, he or she must not only figure out how to start anew with few resources, but also deal with life as a felon. In the United States, it is illegal to discriminate against people because of race, color, or national origin. However, it is perfectly legal to discriminate against a person because of a felony record. Felons can be excluded from employment, housing, voting, public benefits, and jury service. In many major cities, three-quarters of African American men have criminal records and are subject to legalized discrimination (Alexander 2010). Legal scholar Michelle Alexander (2010, 38) argues, "Today a criminal freed from prison has scarcely more rights, and arguably less respect, than a freed slave or a Black person living 'free' in Mississippi at the height of Jim Crow."

CONCLUSION AND DISCUSSION

Legal scholar Michelle Alexander (2010) has made the case that mass incarceration is the civil rights issue of the twenty-first century. She contends that because incarceration has become a common life event for African Americans, and because it is legal to discriminate against felons, our criminal legal system systematically denies rights and opportunities to African Americans, effectively replacing openly racist policies of the past. According to Alexander, "today it is perfectly legal to discriminate against criminals in nearly all the ways that it was once legal to discriminate against African Americans. Once you're labeled a felon, the old forms of discrimination—employment discrimination, housing discrimination, denial of the right to vote, denial of educational opportunity, denial of food stamps and other public benefits, and exclusion from jury service—are suddenly legal" (2010, 2). As discussed previously, she even goes so far as to contend that "today a criminal freed from prison has scarcely more rights, and arguably less respect, than a freed slave or a Black person living 'free' in Mississippi at the height of Jim Crow" (138). What do you think? Is mass incarceration the "new Jim Crow"?

Mass incarceration has been condoned by American voters because crime control is considered a crucial element of a safe society. However, the evidence presented in this chapter makes it clear that mass incarceration is not an effective crime control strategy. Moreover, the consequences of zealous law enforcement have been felt more deeply in already-disadvantaged communities. What if, instead of creating a safer society, mass incarceration has been the root cause of poverty, violence, and instability in U.S. cities?

The incarceration rate appears to have leveled off in recent years, largely because the global economic crisis has required states to cut back on expenditures—the highest of which are related to the criminal legal system. In short, states do not have the budgets to incarcerate more people. But the question of whether we will witness yet another turn in the history of criminal legal system is an open one.

THINKING
ABOUT
RACIAL
JUSTICE

THE UNITED STATES has the largest prison population in the world, and Black men are dramatically overrepresented in our prisons. What role does racism play in this process? More broadly, what would prisons look like in a racially just society? Does the devaluation of Black lives make it possible for the United States to have the largest prison system in the world? Or is our society punitive independent of racial ideologies?

Key Terms

1984 Crime Control Act   265
Anti-Drug Abuse Act of
   1986   265
Anti-Drug Abuse Act of
   1988   265
racial profiling   266
Black Lives Matter   268

Reaganomics   273
neoliberalism   275
outsourcing   275
deindustrialization   275
prison-industrial complex
   (PIC)   277

CHECK YOUR UNDERSTANDING

9.1   What factors explain the rise of mass incarceration in the United States?

The United States has one of the highest incarceration rates in the world. Moreover, Black and Latino men are disproportionately affected by harsh crime control policies.

Q What is the difference between crime rates and incarceration rates?

Q Explain the trends in property crime and violent crime rates between 1970 and 2000. Compare these trends to incarceration rates. What differences do you see?

Q How do incarceration rates in the United States compare to those of other developed countries?

Q Why does the author argue that the United States is in the midst of an era of mass incarceration?

9.2   How are disparities in the criminal legal system reflective of institutional racism?

The high rates of incarceration for Black and Latino men can be traced to racial profiling and sentencing disparities. Racial ideologies of Black male criminality have serious implications for the lives of African American men.

Q How does racial profiling affect incarceration rates?

Q What roles do individual racism and institutionalized racism play in maintaining the high rates of incarceration for African Americans?

Q What are three reasons African American men are seven times more likely than White men to be incarcerated?

9.3   How is the rise of mass incarceration tied to large-scale economic trends?

Mass incarceration came about at the same time that inner cities began to lose jobs. There are profit motivations behind private prisons, and certain groups have benefited economically from mass incarceration.

 How is economic restructuring related to incarceration and crime rates?

 What is the prison-industrial complex? How did the Great Recession affect incarceration rates?

9.4   What are the collateral consequences of mass incarceration?

Mass incarceration affects the 2 million people behind bars and the 7 million people under criminal legal supervision. It also affects millions of felons in the United States and their families and children.

 What are some of the ways that mass incarceration affects men and women differently?

 What parallels does Michelle Alexander draw between the Jim Crow era and the present era?

 How are children affected when their parents are incarcerated?

Critical Thinking

1. What unique features of the United States might play a role in its high incarceration rates?
2. How has the War on Drugs affected mass incarceration?
3. Why do you think police officers are more likely to conduct drug raids in low-income, Black neighborhoods than in wealthier, primarily White neighborhoods?
4. What role might individual discrimination play in maintaining the high incarceration rates for African Americans?
5. Evaluate the evidence presented in this chapter for the connection between economic trends and mass incarceration.
6. Evaluate the human cost of incarceration: in what ways, beyond financially, does the United States pay for mass incarceration?

Talking about Race

The United States has the highest incarceration rate in the world. In a discussion, consider why incarceration rates in the United States continued to increase in the 1990s even as crime rates fell. How are our distinctively high incarceration rates related to ideas about race? For a contemporary example, you may be able to compare responses to the current heroin epidemic versus the crack epidemic of the 1980s.

Learn more with this chapter's digital tools, including video clips from the author, web links, filmography, and chapter self-assessment quizzes at www.oup.com/he/golash-boza-brief3e.

10

Health Inequalities, Environmental Racism, and Environmental Justice

AS YOU READ

10.1 What is the racial history of health disparities in the United States?

10.2 How do health disparities in the United States today vary by race and ethnicity?

10.3 What are the effects of environmental racism?

10.4 What are some community movements for environmental justice?

Thus far, we have examined racial inequalities in education, the labor market, housing, and the criminal justice system. But the accumulated disadvantages for people of color, what Joe Feagin (2001) calls "systemic racism," are also found in the areas of health and the environment. Racial inequalities in the United States not only diminish opportunities but shorten lifespans and have profound effects on quality of life.

In this chapter, we will explore the complexities of racial inequalities in health and the environment. This discussion will shed light on why some people of color have lower life expectancies than White people, as well as a host of other facts related to health disparities. We will continue to consider the effects of racial ideologies by asking, "How have unequal health outcomes been explained in the past, and how do these explanations relate to changing racial ideologies over time?"

THE HISTORY OF HEALTH DISPARITIES IN THE UNITED STATES

Disparities in life expectancy for Black and White people in the United States are not new. Medical treatment of African Americans during and since slavery has been at best subpar and at worst deadly. It is not difficult to imagine that the lives of people of African descent were devalued in the past, but a look into the history of health disparities and medical care also gives us insight into present-day inequalities.

Involuntary Experimentation on African Americans
During slavery in the United States, medical care was brutal and ineffective for most people. Slaves in particular suffered in innumerable ways under the care of physicians, and they had no option to refuse treatment. The accounts that remain about the treatment of slaves by southern doctors provide a window into some of the brutality slaves endured. One account is that of John Brown, who escaped from slavery and lived to tell his story.

In 1847, a formerly enslaved person who had been known as "Fed" escaped to England, where he took on the name John Brown. In his memoir, Brown describes how he was subjected to medical experimentation in Georgia in the 1820s and 1830s. Dr. Thomas Hamilton had cured Brown's former master of an illness and, in exchange, asked to perform experiments on an enslaved person. John Brown describes several sets of experiments Dr. Hamilton performed on him. The first was to subject him to extreme levels of heat in order to find a treatment for sunstroke. The next set involved letting him bleed every day. Then Dr. Hamilton burned Brown in an effort to see how deep his Black skin went. Brown explained that Dr. Hamilton "also tried experiments upon me, which I cannot dwell upon" (quoted in Washington 2006, 54).

Dr. Hamilton's tactics, unfortunately, were not an isolated case. The famed American doctor James Marion Sims (1813–1883) is sometimes called the father of American gynecology. A lesser-known fact about Dr. Sims is that he used involuntary subjects—many of them enslaved African Americans—for experiments. During the nineteenth century, vesicovaginal fistulas (abnormal passages connecting the bladder and the vagina that often develop as a result of childbirth) were a serious problem for women of all races. In developing a cure for the fistulas, Dr. Sims carried out a series of painful operations on enslaved women.

Sims convinced the owners of eleven female slaves with the condition to lend the women to him for treatment. It took Dr. Sims scores of experimental operations to arrive at his cure: silver sutures to prevent infection. One of the slaves, named Anarcha, was seventeen when she came under his care in 1844. She developed a fistula and a torn vagina after a forceps-induced birth to a stillborn baby. Sims repeatedly sewed up Anarcha's vagina, yet it became infected every time, and he had to painfully reopen the wounds. Sims knew about anesthesia but refused to administer it to Anarcha or to the ten other women. When Sims began his experiments, he worked with several other doctors who helped him hold down the women as he performed the surgeries. Within a year, however, all the other doctors left, as they could not bear to hear the screams of the women. From then on, the enslaved women had to hold one another down as Sims operated without anesthesia. In 1849, Sims at last announced that he had found the cure and succeeded in repairing Anarcha's fistula. It remains unclear whether he repaired the fistulae of the other ten enslaved experimental subjects. This example is one of many situations in which treatments that would primarily benefit Whites who could afford a doctor were first tried in an experimental fashion on slaves (Washington 2006).

The practice of using involuntary Black experimental subjects continued after slavery and involved both live and dead bodies. In 1989, construction workers in Augusta, Georgia, uncovered nearly 10,000 human bones and skulls beneath what was once the Medical College of Georgia. This discovery led to an appalling finding: in the nineteenth century, doctors at the Medical College of Georgia had ordered porters at the college to remove bodies from nearby cemeteries for medical dissection. Most were removed from an African American burial ground. Overall, 75 percent of the bones belonged to African Americans, even though Black people made up less than half of the local population. When Harriet Washington (2006) researched the grave-robbing, she discovered that faculty at the Medical College had sent a slave called Grandison Harris to pull bodies from graves. Harris continued to work at the Medical College and to rob African American graves after emancipation until his death in 1911.

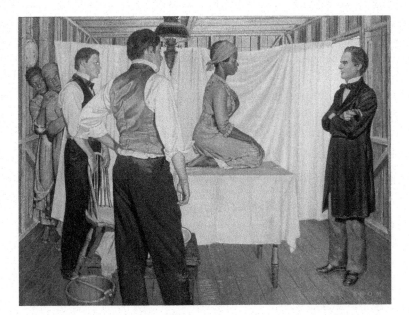

Dr. James Marion Sims carried out horrific operations on enslaved women without their consent.

Involuntary experimentation continued well into the twentieth century. One infamous example is the **Tuskegee syphilis experiment**. In 1932, the Public Health Service (PHS) and the Tuskegee Institute in Alabama recruited nearly 400 poor Black men for a study of the long-term effects of syphilis. They determined that the men had syphilis but did not give them this diagnosis, instead telling them they would be treated for "bad blood," a nonspecific, nonmedical term. Unable to afford health care, these men agreed to participate in the study in exchange for free medical exams, free meals, and burial insurance. Rather than treating the men for syphilis, however, the PHS doctors used the study to determine what untreated syphilis would do to the body. When it finally came to an end in 1972, the unethical study had involved a total of 624 participants and lasted for four decades (Reverby 2009).

Another area of research in which Black people were disproportionately affected is the experimental use of radiation. In 1945, an African American truck driver named Ebb Cade was in a serious accident. When he arrived at the hospital in Oak Ridge, Tennessee, doctors determined that he would not survive his injuries. Unbeknownst to Cade, the doctors were under contract with the U.S. Atomic Energy Commission and had been waiting for a moribund patient so that they could test the effects of plutonium, a radioactive element used in nuclear weapons and reactors. Without Cade's consent, they injected him with plutonium. The doctors' expectation was that Cade would soon die, but they hoped to keep him alive long enough to see the effects of the high dose of radiation on his body. In order to do so, they extracted bone chips and pulled fifteen of his teeth. Cade recovered, however, and escaped from the hospital six months later. He returned to his home in Greensboro, North Carolina, where he died in 1953 of heart disease, unrelated to his injection (Washington 2006).

In 1953, the U.S. Department of Defense adopted the **Nuremberg Code**. Under this policy, any research subject has to be provided with information about the nature, duration, and purpose of the research before participating in it. Subjects also have to be informed that their participation in any research project is voluntary. Despite this order, approximately fifty more experimental radiation treatments on uninformed subjects occurred during the 1960s and 1970s (Washington 2006).

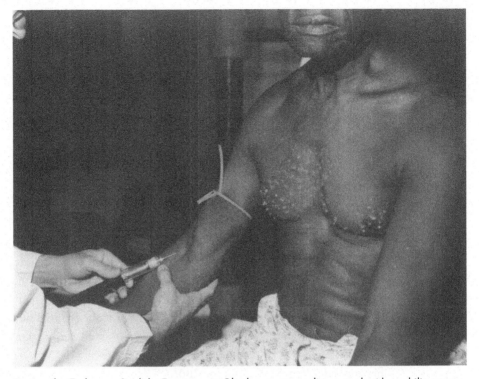

During the Tuskegee Syphilis Experiment, Black men were diagnosed with syphilis, yet were neither treated for it nor told they had it.

Free Black People as Mentally and Physically Unfit

The 1840 U.S. census indicated that free Black people suffered from far worse mental health than either White people or enslaved Black people, reporting that whereas only 1 in 1,558 (enslaved) Black people in the South were "idiot or insane," 1 in 144 (free) Black people in the North fell into this category. People who defended slavery used these numbers to argue that Black people were incapable of self-government. These writers portrayed slavery as necessary to protect White people from mentally unstable Black people as well as to protect Black people from themselves (Washington 2006).

A few statisticians took it upon themselves to review the 1840 census data and found enormous statistical errors. For example, they found towns that reported having a total of only three Black people but six insane Black residents. Once these errors were made public, the U.S. Congress ordered a review. However, William A. Weaver, the originator of the census, was the person appointed to examine it; he of course declared the census to be error-free (Washington 2006).

Whites used pseudoscience to justify slavery on the basis that Black people were physically stronger than White people and that Black people would suffer mentally if they were freed. Yet "scientific" studies were also used during the postslavery era to argue that Black people were physically weak. Many pundits predicted the eventual demise of the Black race based on physical unfitness. It was true that Black people were more likely to suffer from diseases. However, instead of blaming poor living conditions, lack of sanitation, and poverty for their illnesses, scientists often chose to blame Black people's presumed inherent defects.

One of the most pernicious consequences of the widespread belief that Black people were physically unfit was compulsory surgical sterilization. In the early to mid-twentieth century, hundreds of thousands of Black girls and women were subjected to involuntary sterilization. Women who went to the doctor for other reasons, such as an appendectomy, would later discover that they had been sterilized without their permission. In some areas of the South, involuntary sterilization of Black women was so common that it became known as a "Mississippi appendectomy" (Washington 2006).

Sterilization was not unique to African Americans, and it continues to the present day. Thomas Volscho (2010) offers the concept of **sterilization racism**, which he defines as those health care policies and practices that attempt to control the reproductive capacities of women of color. Volscho argues that Native American, Latina, and Black women are more likely to be sterilized than White women because health care providers see these women as incapable of controlling their own reproductive capacities. Volscho found that over a third of American Indian women had undergone a tubal sterilization in 2004, as did 30 percent of African American women. In contrast, only 19 percent of White women had undergone this procedure. Moreover, Volscho found that Black and Native American women are more likely to undergo sterilization than White women, even when the women in the cohort had similar characteristics, including marital status, income, education, and health insurance. Both Volscho (2010) and Elena Gutiérrez (2008) argue that these women are more likely to be sterilized because of stereotypes about non-White women as breeders and unfit mothers.

When we look back in history and then at our medical care system today, it is clear that disparities between Whites and non-Whites persist. How we decide to explain these disparities is a matter of racial ideology. Is the low life expectancy of Black people a result of their genetic makeup, or is it a result of social factors such as poverty and isolation? Is it a result of direct racial discrimination by doctors, or is it a result of institutional racism? The facts of racial inequalities are clear. For sociologists, the task is to explain them.

EXPLAINING HEALTH DISPARITIES BY RACE AND ETHNICITY TODAY

African Americans at every age are more likely than any other racial group to die (Figure 10-1). They are twice as likely as White people to die of diabetes, almost eight times as likely to die of homicide, and almost nine times as likely to die of AIDS. Overall, Black people have a 17 percent higher age-adjusted death rate than White people for all causes and can expect to live about four years less than Whites (Centers for Disease Control and Prevention 2019). Sociologists have offered a range of theories to explain these and other health disparities by race and ethnicity, as we will explore in this section.

Socioeconomic Status and Health Disparities by Race/Ethnicity

First, we should note that health disparities are clearly linked to socio-economic status. These disparities are evident in our earliest records and have been found in every country where they have been examined:

FIGURE 10-1

AGE-ADJUSTED DEATH RATE BY RACE/ETHNICITY, 2015

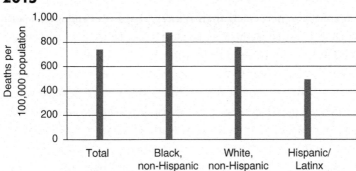

Source: Data from MMWR, 2017.

people with higher incomes live longer, healthier lives. Moreover, it is not just poverty that affects health—relative poverty is also important. One way this relationship can be seen is through a comparison of life expectancies in Japan and Great Britain. In 1970, these two countries had similar life expectancies and similar levels of inequality. Over the next two decades, inequality increased dramatically in Great Britain while it narrowed in Japan. By 1990, Japan had the highest life expectancy in the world, while Great Britain's had declined (Williams and Collins 1995).

Every step up in income and wealth translates into an increased likelihood of having good health. However, once we begin to parse these outcomes by race, a different story emerges. African Americans do not experience the same health gains as Whites do by virtue of an increase in socioeconomic status—though they do experience some health gains. There is clearly a relationship between health and socioeconomic status, but these factors work in different ways across racial and ethnic lines.

Black/White disparities do not disappear as African Americans gain more education and income. In California in 2014, 6.7 percent of babies were born with low birth weight. Black women were twice as likely to have low birth weight babies as White women. Over 10 percent of babies born to Black women with a college degree had low birth weight, as compared to 8 percent of babies born to White women without a high school degree. At all levels of education, Black women have the highest prevalence of low-birthweight babies (Ratnasiri, Parry, Arief, et al. 2018).

Babies born with low birthweight are at a higher risk for death, making birthweight an important factor for health scholars to consider. As shown in Figure 10-2, African American mothers with college degrees are more likely than Whites, Hispanics, and Asians with less than a high school education to have low-birthweight babies (Centers for Disease Control and Prevention 2011).

Researchers continue to investigate why African American women have poorer birth outcomes than White women. Furthermore, why is it the case that health outcomes for African Americans do not improve with higher levels of income and education? If socioeconomic status alone does not explain these disparate outcomes by race and ethnicity, what does? Sociologists and public health scholars have offered several different explanations, which we will consider next.

FIGURE 10-2

LOW BIRTHWEIGHT AMONG MOTHERS 20 YEARS OF AGE OR OLDER, BY RACE/ETHNICITY AND EDUCATION OF MOTHER, 2008

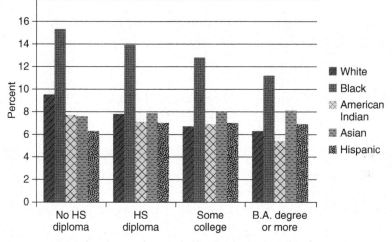

Source: CDC 2011, http://www.cdc.gov/nchs/data/hus/2011/010.pdf

voices

I'm Sick of Asking the Children of Flint to Be Resilient

By Mona Hanna-Attisha

A baby born in Flint, where I am a pediatrician, is likely to live almost 20 fewer years than a child born elsewhere in the same county. ... Some of the babies I care for have the bad luck to be born into neighborhoods where life expectancy is just over sixty-four years. Only a few miles away, in a more-affluent community, the average life span is eighty-four years. The ravages of COVID-19, which disproportionately affect low-income families and people of color, are surely widening this gap even further.

Throughout the United States, geography defines and describes inequities in health, wealth, mobility, and longevity. The reasons for this are both visible and hidden. Life in a distressed neighborhood means limited access to health care and healthy food. It means living with violence, racism, poverty, and uncertainty. It means bearing the brunt of environmental injustice—not having safe and affordable water, as Flint knows too well, or living in the shadow of a polluting factory. More air pollution increases rates of respiratory disease

(continued)

I'm Sick of Asking the Children of Flint to Be Resilient

and reduces student achievement as well as life span. We are also beginning to understand the interplay of water access and air quality with COVID-19 severity.

These disparities between neighborhoods are rarely accidental; they are the product of purposeful policies and practices that have widened gaps in income, opportunity, and equality. Over the decades, city inhabitants have been battered by deindustrialization; racist banking and real estate practices; White flight and population loss; austerity cuts to public education, public health, and safety net programs; the corporate-driven weakening of unions; dilution of environmental regulations; housing and nutrition insecurity; and racially driven mass incarceration. And so much more.

Science tells us that children exposed to multiple adversities, both in their home and in their neighborhood, have a far greater likelihood of challenges later in life. From addiction to eviction, these constant pressures change children on smolecular, cellular, and behavioral levels—and make them sick. The effects of toxic stress can be as disruptive as environmental pollution on their bodies and brains, increasing risk for chronic diseases like asthma and hypertension, and lowering life expectancy. Exposure to six or more adverse childhood experiences can cut a life short by as much as twenty years.

The pandemic hot spots in Michigan follow this pattern: Outside of metropolitan Detroit, the troubled Flint area has been hardest hit. In Flint, we just marked the sixth anniversary of the water crisis, when poisonous, lead-laced water was used to fill baby bottles and sippy cups of unsuspecting Flint kids who just happened to be born in the wrong city. Now we're being ravaged by another preventable public health emergency. With over 200 deaths, the county where Flint is has more COVID-19 fatalities than 19 statesto date.

All of us who live or work in this beleaguered community know somebody who has died from the disease caused by the coronavirus. There's Wendell Quinn, the gentle giant of a hospital public safety officer who always gave me a warm smile and a nod when I walked into work; and , the dedicated United Auto Workers leader; and Nathel Burtley, the first Black superintendent of Flint schools; and Karen Dozier, the kind and loving custodian at the early child care center. And bringing a level of grief that is difficult to comprehend, Calvin Munerlyn, a Family Dollar store security guard and devoted father of six, was recently shot and killed after telling a shopper to wear a mask. The epidemic of gun violence has compounded tragedy upon tragedy.

At a multigenerational level of loss, there are the Jones and Brown families. Within weeks, a Flint elementary school principal, Kevelin B. Jones II, lost his father, Pastor Kevelin B. Jones; his uncle Freddie Brown Jr.; and his cousin Freddie Brown III. At the combined burial for her husband and only child, Sandy Brown waved to the parade of cars that drove by quietly as she stood alone next to two freshly dug graves. Reflecting on the difficult losses, a church elder, Keimba Knowlin, spoke on resilience, a quality that I've long observed and admired in the people of Flint. "We're going to rise above this and get past this," he said.

The will to survive and endure can be the deciding factor between a child who overcomes adversity and thrives and a child who never makes it to adulthood. But how long can we ask people born in the wrong ZIP code to "rise above" and persevere in circumstances beyond their control, no matter how central the idea of overcoming is to our archetypal American identity? When Hazim Hardeman, a 2019 Rhodes scholar, was asked about his journey from public housing in North Philadelphia, where many of his friends were shot or stabbed to death, he spoke a truth that we all need to hear: "Don't be happy for me that I overcame these barriers. Be mad as hell that they exist in the first place."

Surviving life's hardest blows should not be celebrated—or expected. Recovery and reconciliation require reparations and resources. To expect resilience without justice is simply to indifferently accept the status quo.

Just as the New Deal sprang from the Great Depression and public health best practices were born in response to a previous plague, we need to embrace the bold innovations that are certain to arise.

To begin with, we need to establish policies and practices rooted in science. And science tells us that where you live matters. For children raised in places replete with the stresses of misfortune, these adversities rooted in historic and systemic bias are scarring. Just as new COVID-19 cases can represent a time lag from infection two weeks earlier, adversities in early childhood play out later, filling our hospital beds and deteriorating the public's health.

As this pandemic makes painfully visible, medicine alone—ventilators, pharmaceuticals, defibrillators, ICUs—will not save us. It's always an ego-deflating moment for my medical residents when they learn that medical care contributes only 10 percent to 20 percent to positive health outcomes. Our medical interventions are largely reactive measures—and happen too late. Addressing the upstream root causes is the only answer.

This means mandating universal basic income and living wages, for a start, and enhancing health and safety protections, along with benefits like paid parental and sick leave. This means establishing desegregated and well-funded public education, starting with child care, as a fundamental right. Universal health care needs to be untethered from employment and free of racial disparities. And environmental health regulations need to be strengthened and enforced so that all children—no matter the ZIP code—can breathe clean air and drink safe water.

These big and bold ideas are not new. They are measures proved to improve health, quality of life and longevity—standards that most developed countries already employ. And to

(continued)

voices   *continued.*

I'm Sick of Asking the Children of Flint to Be Resilient

ensure we are moving in the same direction together, the pathogens of divisiveness and bigotry need to be treated as the deadly, life-shortening contagions they truly are.

This is how we begin to transform the concept of resilience from an individual trait to one that describes a community—and society—that cares for everyone. Rather than hoping a child is tough enough to endure the insurmountable, we must build resilient places—healthier, safer, more nurturing and just—where all children can thrive. This is where prevention and healing begin.

Dr. Hanna-Attisha is a pediatrician and professor at Michigan State University College of Human Medicine.

Source: Mona Hanna-Attisha, *The New York Times*, https://nyti.ms/2Zb42vC

Segregation and Health

David Williams and Chiquita Collins (2001) argue that racial residential segregation is the primary cause of Black/White health disparities because it affects the educational opportunities of children, concentrates poverty and resources, and forces many African Americans to live in environments that are unhealthy on a variety of levels. Williams and Collins suggest that segregation has adverse health outcomes for Black people because it creates "pathogenic residential conditions"— unsafe streets where people are scared to exercise, have few opportunities to buy fresh produce, see more advertisements for alcohol and tobacco, and live with higher rates of violent crime. One study in Baltimore, for example, found that neighborhoods with a high percentage of African Americans are more likely to have liquor stores than are White communities (LaVeist and Wallace 2000). People living in disadvantaged neighborhoods also have higher incidences of heart disease, diabetes, obesity, tuberculosis, infant mortality, and hypertension.

Availability of healthy food is one way that segregation can affect health outcomes. A study in New York compared East Harlem, which is 6 percent White, with the Upper East Side, which is 84 percent White. East Harlem has the highest prevalence of diabetes and obesity in New York City, whereas the Upper East Side has the lowest. The researchers who carried out the study wanted to know if stores in these neighborhoods carried foods that doctors recommend for people with diabetes. They surveyed stores to find if they had diet soda, 1 percent or fat-free milk, high-fiber bread, fresh fruit, and fresh vegetables. They found that Upper East Side stores were three times as likely to carry all of the recommended food items as East Harlem stores (Horowitz, Colson, Hebert, and Lancaster 2004). The lack of access to healthy food in poor neighborhoods is a national problem (Ghosh-Dastidar et al. 2014).

Black, Latinx, and low socioeconomic status people all have higher obesity rates than the general population. One possible explanation for this disparity has to do with the resources available in the neighborhoods where they reside. Public health scholars have found that people who live close to supermarkets and have safe places to exercise are less likely to be obese. Low-income and non-White people are more likely to live far from supermarkets with healthy produce and closer to fast-food outlets and convenience stores. They are also more likely to live in areas where crime is higher, making it less safe to walk around the neighborhoods. By concentrating poverty and people of color, segregation can contribute to higher levels of obesity in these groups (Lovasi, Hutson, Guerra, and Neckerman 2009).

American Indians, African Americans, and Hispanics are about twice as likely as Whites to die from diabetes (Kochanek et al 2019). These disparities are closely related to diet. What people eat is a result of their personal food preferences as well as what food is available where they live. The Tohono O'odham and Pima Indians of southern Arizona have the highest rate of type 2 diabetes in the world—nearly 50 percent of the people in their community have diabetes. A century ago, there were almost no cases of diabetes among these American Indian tribes. What happened? The film *Bad Sugar* explains that the Tohono O'odham diet changed when the government cut off their irrigation water supply, preventing them from growing their own food. Instead of growing and eating the food they had eaten for centuries, they consumed food from the U.S. Commodity Supplemental Food Program (Adelman 2008). Prior to 1999, this program included no fresh produce. When the Tohono O'odham people began to consume large amounts of white flour, shortening, sugar, and canned foods, their diabetes rate skyrocketed. We see similar patterns, though not as drastic, in Black and Latinx neighborhoods, which have high concentrations of fast-food restaurants and corner stores selling many more packaged, processed foods than fresh produce. Diet is influenced by what food is available, and what we eat affects our health outcomes.

The Effects of Individual Racism on African American Health

To explain why African Americans have the worst health outcomes on nearly every measure, some scholars point to perceived discrimination. They argue that African Americans are disproportionately exposed to racial discrimination, that discrimination can produce stress, and that stress can lead to negative health outcomes. When African Americans experience discrimination, their responses may include anger, resentment, fear, frustration, and other stress responses. Scientists have found that these responses cause the adrenal gland to produce hormones that inhibit immune responses and increase vulnerability to disease (Clark, Anderson, Clark, and Williams 1999).

Although African Americans have higher levels of most physical ailments, Patricia Louie and Blair Wheaton (2019) found that they have lower levels of mental illness (Louie and Wheaton 2019). The relatively low rates of mental illness among African Americans are noteworthy because Black youth are much more likely to have experienced traumatic events such as death of a relative, parental divorce, witnessing domestic violence, seeing someone get murdered, being mugged or threatened with a weapon, going to prison, or failing a grade in school than White adolescents (Umberson 2017; Louie and Wheaton 2019). Louie and Wheaton (2019) also found that Black youth have higher levels of self-esteem than White youth and that these higher levels of self-esteem help Black youth deal with these traumatic events and reduce the likelihood that they will develop depression or other mood disorders. Public health scholar James Jackson and his colleagues (Jackson, Knight, and Rafferty 2010) offer an explanation for this finding. They contend that African Americans have developed coping strategies that enable them to deal with stress (such as that related to individual racism), but that these same coping strategies ultimately have negative physical health outcomes. For example, many African Americans are confronted with stressful conditions such as poverty, crime, poor housing, and racial discrimination. In response, many engage in unhealthy behaviors such as smoking, alcohol use, and overeating of fatty foods to alleviate stress. Jackson and his colleagues found that African Americans are likely to eat comfort foods to deal with stress because fatty foods inhibit the release of certain hormones and do provide short-term stress relief. However, the consumption of these foods leads to long-term health problems, obesity, stroke, and cardiovascular disease. They argue that the consumption of comfort foods does help reduce stress in the short term, thus leading to lower levels of mental illness, but has long-term physical effects.

About half of all African American women are obese; the rate for White women, by contrast, is 30 percent. Christie Malpede and her colleagues (2007) explored the extent to which weight-related beliefs and attitudes are linked to obesity among Black and White women. When the researchers asked Black women how being Black affected their weight, the most common responses included the consumption of unhealthy foods and lack of exercise. In contrast, White women responded that being a White woman meant that they had distorted expectations of body type, that they thought their success depended on being thin and beautiful, and that they had negative body images. Overall, when asked about their weight-related beliefs, Black women talked more about food choices, and White women talked more about body image.

The majority of the research on racism and health focuses on African Americans (Williams and Mohammed 2013). However, a few recent studies have shown similar patterns for other people of color. For example, Paradies et al. (2015) found a stronger association between poor mental health and racism for Asian Americans and Latinx Americans than for African Americans, whereas the association between racism and poor physical health is strongest for African Americans. In another study, Diane Lauderdale (2006) found that Arab women who gave birth in the six months following the terrorist attacks of September 11, 2001, had a higher risk of poor birth outcomes than those who gave birth before 9/11. She attributes this higher risk to heightened discrimination against Arabs in the aftermath of 9/11. Another study found that infants born to Latina mothers had a 24 percent higher risk of low birth weight after a traumatic immigration raid happened in Postville, Iowa (Novak, Geronimus, Martinez-Cardoso 2017). A study of emergency room care providers found implicit biases against Native American adults and children, which are likely to affect their care in these settings (Puumala et al. 2016). Ongoing research in the area of racism and health will help us better understand these nuances; yet the current research demonstrates that racial discrimination continues to be prevalent in our society and leads to negative health outcomes for people of color.

Life-Course Perspectives

Health inequality increases with age across a range of outcomes. For example, older African Americans have significantly higher levels of daily function limitations and disability than do older Whites. Because of this type of health disparity, scholars have offered **life-course perspectives**, which focus on how health outcomes change over the life course. Two of the most accepted life-course explanations are the **cumulative disadvantage perspective** and the **weathering hypothesis**. The first explanation focuses on how disadvantages accumulate over the life course, and the second focuses on how constant exposure to stress accelerates health decline for Black people (Thorpe and Kelley-Moore 2012).

The cumulative disadvantage perspective provides a framework to explain the increasing divergence between Black and White health outcomes. It focuses on the fact that many health conditions are related to stressors that accumulate over the life course. These stressors include poor nutrition, discrimination, and living in disadvantaged neighborhoods (Thorpe and Kelley-Moore 2012).

Scholars who adopt the weathering perspective contend that the health status of Black people declines more quickly than that of White people as a consequence of long-term exposure to unhealthy conditions. According to this perspective, Black Americans age more quickly than Whites because of the social, economic, and environmental conditions they face. The focus in this perspective is on the effects of sustained stressors—constant discrimination, financial stress, family crises, and fear—which can wear down the body in tangible ways (Thorpe and Kelley-Moore 2012).

Jan Warren-Findlow (2006) interviewed Black women with early-stage heart disease to better understand how the weathering perspective could be applied to their lives. She found that two-thirds of the women she interviewed were taking antidepressants or anti-anxiety medication as a response to high levels of stress. All of the women talked about being stressed for reasons such as family problems, neighborhood violence, and financial strain. One woman explained that the stress of living "one paycheck away from homelessness" was "killing" her. Warren-Findlow argues that high levels of stress over the life course of these African American women contributed to their development of heart disease and the worsening of their condition.

A recent study found that although African and Mexican Americans have worse health outcomes than White Americans overall, Mexican Americans do not experience cumulative disadvantage or weathering in the same way that African Americans do. Instead, Mexican Americans' higher likelihood of having serious medical conditions does not increase with age (Brown, O'Rand, and Adkins 2012).

Culture and Health

Is simply being or becoming an American bad for your health? The United States ranks fairly low for a country in the developed world on a wide range of health indicators. Moreover, immigrants often have better health than their native-born counterparts. In the United States, foreign-born women have substantially better pregnancy outcomes than women born in the United States. Gopal Singh and Stella Yu (1996) found that foreign-born women have lower infant mortality rates, lower rates of low birthweight, and lower rates of teenage births than their counterparts born in the United States. However, their study found some important variations. The reduced risk for infant mortality is most pronounced among Cuban immigrants—compared with Cubans born in the United States, they have a 39 percent lower risk. Black immigrants also are 25 percent less likely to experience infant mortality than native-born Blacks. Overall, foreign-born Blacks, Cubans, Mexicans, and Chinese have lower risks for infant mortality and low birthweight than their native-born counterparts.

In a phenomenon scholars call the **Hispanic Paradox**, health outcomes for Latinxs compare favorably with those of other groups on a wide variety of measures (recall Figure 10-1). In 2013, the age-adjusted death rate for Latinxs was lower than that of all groups except Asians, and Latinxs had the lowest rates of low-birthweight babies (Centers for Disease Control and Prevention 2016). And even though Latinxs have, on average, a lower socioeconomic status than Whites, they have comparable infant mortality rates (Lara, Gamboa, Kahramanian, Morales, and Bautista 2005).

One hypothesis to explain the Hispanic Paradox is that many Hispanics are immigrants and have better health behaviors than native-born Americans. There is some support for this explanation, but the results are mixed. Mariaelena Lara and her colleagues (2005), for example, found that Latinxs who are more acculturated into U.S. society are more likely to engage in unhealthy behaviors such as eating unhealthy foods, smoking, and drinking alcohol. In contrast, there were positive factors associated with **acculturation**, or the process by which immigrants adopt the behaviors and preferences of the host society: more acculturated Latinxs were more likely to go to the doctor, get preventive care, be screened for cancer, and have health insurance. Overall, the researchers found that acculturation has negative effects in terms of health behaviors, but positive effects in terms of health care usage and access.

Research by Edna Viruell-Fuentes (2007), however, challenges these findings on acculturation. Viruell-Fuentes acknowledges that Mexican immigrants often have better health outcomes than Mexican Americans. Yet, she argues that this is because Mexican Americans are more attuned to racial discrimination in the United States and that this discrimination leads to stress, which has negative effects on their health. Viruell-Fuentes's interviews with Mexican immigrants and Mexican Americans shed light on the differences between these two groups. Mexican immigrants are likely to live in ethnic enclaves, where they have few interactions with non-Mexicans and thus are less likely to experience discrimination. In contrast, Mexican Americans experience persistent discrimination, exclusion, and "othering" beginning in elementary school. Mexican Americans recounted to Viruell-Fuentes that they grew up feeling angry about being excluded by White Americans. This exclusion was alienating and psychologically straining. Viruell-Fuentes argues that these stressors—not acculturation—can explain why Mexican Americans have worse health outcomes than Mexican immigrants.

Most of the research on acculturation and health has focused on Latinxs. However, there may be similar patterns for other groups. A recent study (Al Dahir et al. 2013) investigated the relationship between acculturation and diabetes risk among Arab Americans in southeastern Louisiana—a group that has higher than average rates of diabetes and other chronic diseases. The findings were mixed: men who were less acculturated to U.S. society had lower risk for diabetes, whereas women who were less acculturated had a higher risk. Across groups, immigrants tend to have worse health outcomes the longer they stay in the United States. Research continues on why this is the case—and how to change it (Oza-Frank, Stephenson, and Narayan 2011).

Genetics, Race, and Health

Although most social scientists accept that there is no biological basis for dividing humans into distinct racial groups, it can be hard to fully divorce ourselves from the idea that there are races and that they are distinct. One area in which there is a lot of discussion of racial differences in in health disparities—as there are often stark differences between racial groups.

Asthma is the most common chronic childhood disease in the United States. Black and Latinx children are more likely to suffer from asthma than White children and are more likely to visit the emergency room due to an asthma attack. Black and Latinx children are also three times more likely to die from asthma than White children. Prior to 1980, these racial disparities in asthma prevalence did not exist. In the late 1980s, we began to see a disparity in asthma prevalence rates and by 2010, twice as many Black and Latinx children had asthma as White children.

It is certainly true that Black and Latinx children are more likely to suffer from asthma than White children. Most scholars, however, would attribute that disparity to the fact that Black and Latinx children are more likely to be exposed to toxins. Asthma is triggered by exposure to indoor toxins such as dust mites, cigarette smoke, mold, pet dander, cockroaches, and rodents as well as outdoor toxins such as traffic pollution, ozone and particulate matter, and toxic waste. Children who live in unhealthy environments are more likely to suffer from asthma.

A 2007 report entitled *Toxic Wastes and Race at Twenty—1987–2007: Grassroots Struggles to Dismantle Environmental Racism in the United States* (Bullard 2007) used 2000 census data and databases of hazardous waste facilities to find out if there were racial disparities in the location of toxic waste facilities. The authors discovered that "people of color make up the majority of those living in neighborhoods within two miles of hazardous waste facilities, and toxic neighborhoods have twice the percentage of minorities as nontoxic neighborhoods."

Black and Latinx children are more likely to live in segregated, inner-city areas with poor living conditions where they are exposed to indoor contaminants such as mold, rodents, and cockroaches. They are also more likely to live in areas with high rates of air pollution and near hazardous waste facilities. These living conditions increase the likelihood of asthma attacks.

Despite substantial evidence linking asthma to exposure to unhealthy living conditions, some scientists search for genetic explanations for racial disparities in asthma prevalence. What could their motive be? If there were a genetic basis for racial disparities in asthma prevalence, it would be unusual to see a change in the disparities in such a short time span, as evolution happens at a much slower pace. Nevertheless, some medical researchers seek out genetic explanations for racial disparities in asthma rates.

In *Fatal Invention*, Dorothy Roberts (Roberts 2012) explains that a primary motive for seeking genetic explanations is profit potential. If diseases have genetic causes, corporations can design personalized medicine to cure them, and then sell these cures to people who can afford them. In contrast, there is no profit to be found in addressing deep structural inequalities that contribute to health disparities.

In the case of asthma, researchers have found that Puerto Ricans are more susceptible to asthma than Mexicans. Medical researcher Esteban Burchard attributes this disparity to the prevalence of African ancestry among Puerto Ricans and has thus spent his career searching for a genetic basis for this disparity. His goal is to create personalized medicine for people who suffer from asthma so that doctors can prescribe medicine based on a person's genetic makeup (Burchard 2022).

While researchers such as Burchard seek out genetic explanations, community activist groups advocate for better living conditions and a healthy environment for all children. After completing a community-based study of asthma disparities, a community group called "We Act" concluded that a comprehensive approach is required to address asthma disparities, one that takes into account the stress, poverty, poor housing, and lack of access to quality health care that many children of color face.

Myths that "Black" diseases exist may also motivate some researchers to seek genetic explanations for racial disparities in health. Many people, for example, believe that sickle cell disease is a Black disease, but this is not true. Sickle cell disease is common wherever malaria is common. Thus, you can find sickle cell disease in parts of Africa as well as in parts of Europe, Oceania, India, and the Middle East—all regions where malaria is common (Figure 10-2). In contrast, large swaths of Africa are unaffected by both malaria and sickle cell disease. If doctors were to look for sickle cell disease only in Black patients, they would risk the lives of many other patients who also are vulnerable to the disease. Sickle cell disease is more common among African Americans than other groups in the United States because the ancestors of many African Americans were from parts of Africa where malaria is common. African Americans whose ancestors came from other parts of Africa, however, are at much lower risk of sickle cell disease than people from Saudi Arabia, where malaria is also common.

Advances in genomic mapping have made it possible to identify associations between genes and certain disease. For example, genomic mapping studies have found an association between the APOL1 gene and the propensity to develop end-stage renal disease. Notably, this association is not the same as causation—less than 15 percent of people with the APOL1 gene will develop end-stage renal disease, and many people without the APOL1 gene will also develop end-stage renal disease. The APOL1 gene has been traced to genetic mutations in certain populations in Africa about 60,000 years ago that granted protection against trypanosomal infection (sleeping sickness). About 15 percent of African Americans have the APOL1 gene, and it is non-existent among other groups (Reidy, Hjorten and Parekh 2018). Current research thus indicates that the APOL1 gene is exclusive to the African-descended population. However, 85 percent of the African American population does not have the APOL1 gene as it is exclusive to those parts of Africa where sleeping sickness is prevalent. And, although Black people are at higher risk of end-stage renal disease, this illness is neither exclusive to Black people nor to those with the APOL1 gene (Assari 2016).

The simple facts that Black people are more likely to have sickle cell disease or end-stage renal disease or that there are genetic variants associated with these diseases does not mean that there is any scientific evidence for genetic variation between racial groups. Scientists discovered decades ago that most genetic variation occurs within—not between—racial groups. And, these findings continue to hold up as genomic mapping becomes more advanced.

In health sciences, race is often used as a stand-in for a more precise genetic explanation. Neither sickle cell anemia nor end-stage renal disease are "Black diseases." Instead, they are diseases more prevalent among people with ancestry in certain regions of the world, and these regions do not map neatly onto race. In other cases, racial associations are unrelated to genetics. For example, if researchers find that a certain glaucoma drug works better for Black patients, the most likely explanation is that the drug actually works better for people with dark eyes and thus could be harmful for Black patients with light eyes. Or a drug found to require a low dose for Asians could be related to weight, not to Asian ancestry. When scientists find that drugs work better for some races than for others, or in different doses depending on race, these racial explanations are most likely explained by another factor. Racial dosing and racial prescribing are imprecise and potentially harmful because race is always a stand-in for a better explanation (Roberts 2012).

ENVIRONMENTAL RACISM

As discussed earlier, African Americans and Latinxs are more likely to live in neighborhoods where they have less access to fresh produce, parks, jogging trails, and healthy foods. In addition, people of color and poor people are also more likely to live close to places that can directly damage their health—toxic waste dumps, highly polluted freeways, and other environmental hazards. In this way, health disparities can be linked directly to **environmental racism**: institutional policies and practices that differentially affect the health outcomes or living conditions of people and communities based on race or color. The disparities between the living conditions of White and non-White communities are clear.

In the United States, poor people and people of color are more likely to be exposed to environmental hazards. Black children are five times more likely than White children to have lead poisoning. More than 68 percent of African Americans live within thirty miles of a coal-fired power plant, compared with 56 percent of White Americans. In 2000, neighborhoods with hazardous waste facilities were, on average, 56 percent non-White, and neighborhoods without such facilities were 30 percent non-White. In the southeastern region of the United States—the area once dominated by slaves and slaveowners—three out of four of the largest hazardous waste landfills can be found in majority-Black areas (Checker 2006). Commercial hazardous waste treatment, storage, and disposal facilities sited between 1966 and 1955 were placed in locations that were disproportionately poor and non-White at the time of siting; not surprisingly, those neighborhoods have become poorer and more non-White over time (Mohai and Saha 2015). As shown in Figure 10-3, neighborhoods with hazardous waste facilities—called host areas—have, on average, higher percentages of people of color than nonhost areas.

FIGURE 10-3

PERCENTAGES OF PEOPLE OF COLOR LIVING IN NEIGHBORHOODS WITH AND WITHOUT TOXIC WASTE FACILITIES, IN STATES WITH THE LARGEST DISCREPANCIES, 2007

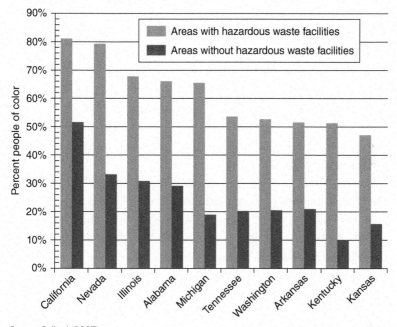

Source: Bullard (2007).

The placement of hazardous waste facilities affects community health. The lack of basic plumbing also has serious consequences and renders communities vulnerable to a host of diseases. In 1950, 27 percent of houses in the United States lacked complete plumbing facilities. By 2000, this percentage had dropped to 0.64 percent—a great improvement. However, nearly 700,000 households, representing 1.7 million people in the United States, continued to live without complete plumbing facilities in 2000, and a half a million households in 2014 still were without plumbing (Byrne 2015). The lack of plumbing continues to disproportionately affect non-Whites. In 2000, 0.47 percent of Whites lived without plumbing, compared with 1.1 percent of Blacks; 1.47 percent of Hispanics; and 4.41 percent of American Indians and Alaska Natives, primarily concentrated on reservations (Rural Community Assistance Partnership n.d.).

Latin American immigrants are also disproportionately exposed to toxins and their concomitant risks. Camila Alvarez and Kathryn Norton-Smith (2018) measured estimated cancer risk from air toxins in immigrant communities. They found that the destinations to which Latin American immigrants were moving had higher than average estimated cancer risks from air toxins. They further found that rates of estimated cancer risk from air toxins were highest in those places where Latinxs have lived the longest—what they call "early new destination counties." The implications of the discrepancy in estimated cancer risk from air toxins are likely exacerbated in new immigrant destinations because these places tend to lack the infrastructure (government and non-profit institutional support) for helping marginalized immigrant groups.

Faced with these disparities, communities across the United States have fought to have their communities cleaned up and to gain better access to clean air, water, and soil. These struggles can be contentious, and the possible outcomes are not always clear. What does a community do when it realizes that a toxic waste dump is in its backyard? Should everyone leave? They can't, in good conscience, sell their properties, so are they stuck?

ENVIRONMENTAL JUSTICE

The movement for **environmental justice** focuses on the right to live in nontoxic neighborhoods. Many scholars locate the beginning of the environmental justice movement in the 1980s, when primarily non-White communities began to come together and insist on their right to live in nontoxic neighborhoods. Melissa Checker (2006) traces this activism back to earlier struggles to get city services in low-income and primarily Black communities. Dorceta Taylor (2009) agrees and argues that Blacks' fights for lead screening, Chicanos' and Filipinos' struggles against the use of pesticides in agriculture, and Native Americans' battles for fishing rights in the 1950s and 1960s are all part of the movement for environmental justice. Environmental justice movements fight for causes ranging from the creation of parks and open spaces, to lobbying toxic waste producers to clean up their byproducts, to clean air and water and other initiatives to improve the health and quality of life in neighborhoods.

voices

The Fight Against the Dakota Access Pipeline

In 2016, a Native American tribe engaged in a long fight against the Dakota Access Pipe-line—a construction project that could endanger the lives and well-being of people in and around North Dakota. North Dakota has recently undergone an oil boom, in part owing to a new technology called fracking, which allows oil to be drilled from beneath the earth. One issue oil companies face is getting the oil from North Dakota to the rest of the country. Pipelines allow for crude oil to be transported underground.

In 2015, a coalition of business interests known as Energy Transfer Partners began the process of constructing a pipeline to transport crude oil from North Dakota to Illinois. When the Standing Rock Tribe learned the pipeline would pass through their reservation, they requested a full archaeological investigation, which never took place (Sammon 2016). Although North Dakota has experienced economic growth thanks to the oil boom, the Standing Rock Sioux reservation sits in one of the poorest counties in the nation. Nearly 40 percent of the residents of the reservation live below the poverty line, and the unemploy-ment rate is 86 percent. They do not stand to benefit economically from construction of the pipeline, yet they will face consequences if the pipeline bursts.

Members of the Standing Rock Sioux feared the pipeline could burst and contaminate the Missouri River. For this reason, they mounted a protest in opposition to the pipeline. On April 1, 2015, members of the tribe launched a prayer camp to protest the pipeline. They called on other tribes to join them. Over 300 tribes came together in solidarity in an effort to shut down construction of the pipeline (Democracy Now 2016).

Energy Transfer Partners began construction in May 2016. In July 2016, the Army Corps of Engineers granted permits for the pipeline to cross beneath the Missouri and Cannon Ball Rivers. Although this pipeline would pass through tribal lands, the Army Corps of Engineers did not seek approval from the Standing Rock Sioux Tribe. As a result, the Standing Rock Sioux Tribe filed a lawsuit against the Army Corps of Engineers on July 27, 2016, and asked them to stop construction immediately (Earth-Justice 2016).

On September 3, 2016, bulldozers came to prepare the ground to install the pipeline. Hundreds of protestors gathered to protest the construction. When the protestors went through the fence, the result was violent confrontation. Security guards hit and pushed protestors, unleashed dogs on them, and discharged pepper spray into protestors' faces. Eventually, the protestors were able to stop the construction for that day (Democracy Now 2016).

(continued)

 *continued.*

The Fight Against the Dakota Access Pipeline

Over the next couple of months, thousands of people gathered at Standing Rock to protest the pipeline. By December 2016, there were 7,000 people camping at Standing Rock in solidarity with the Standing Rock Sioux Tribe. Even though authorities deployed pepper spray, rubber bullets, and water cannons at the protestors, and even though temperatures were well below freezing, the protestors persisted (Mele 2016). However, on January 24, shortly after taking office, President Donald Trump signed a memorandum ordering the Secretary of the Army to expedite approval of the Dakota Access Pipeline. And, on February 22, 2017, state officials ordered the protestors to evacuate. Just before the final evacuation, protestors set fire to the camp.

Melissa Checker (2006) conducted an in-depth study of Hyde Park, a Black community near Augusta, Georgia, that has long struggled for environmental justice. In 1970, Hyde Park residents won a two-year struggle to get sewage, paved roads, and running water in their community. In many ways, this was both an environmental battle and a battle against racism, as the conditions in the neighborhood during heavy rains were toxic, and the White neighborhoods had long had adequate city services.

In Hyde Park, the struggle for environmental justice is clearly linked to the fight for civil rights. In the late 1960s, residents of Hyde Park, a small community of 250 people, formed an organization called the Hyde Park and Aragon Park Improvement Committee (HPAPIC) to fight for better services for their neighborhood. This same organization survived over many decades and evolved into a movement for environmental justice during the 1990s, when it became clear that many of the nearby factories were emitting toxic chemicals and poisoning the community. Residents of Hyde Park became increasingly incensed as a junkyard in their neighborhood continued to expand—at times practically into their backyards—and when dust from a ceramics factory left White powder sprinkled on their cars and caused smelly water to fill their ditches during heavy rains.

Residents began to tie these environmental hazards to high rates of disease and death in their community. For Hyde Park residents, the environmental hazards were evident: whereas they once were able to grow bountiful gardens, their plots became less productive after the factories and junkyards moved in. In 1991, researchers from the University of Georgia confirmed their suspicions when they found elevated levels of arsenic and chromium in the local soil and produce and warned residents not to eat the produce from their gardens.

Around that same time, residents of the neighboring Virginia subdivision filed a lawsuit against Southern Wood Piedmont—the local wood-processing plant—for contamination. Although the neighborhoods are very close and the same water travels between them, the primarily White residents of the Virginia subdivision did not include Hyde Park residents in their lawsuit.

Hyde Park residents decided to file their own lawsuit in 1991. When the Environmental Protection Agency (EPA) tested the air, water, and soil in Hyde Park, they found weak evidence of contamination. However, when HPAPIC commissioned its own studies, a neuropsychologist found a high degree of neurological abnormalities among residents, and a dermatologist found a high rate of arsenical keratosis. For Hyde Park residents, it was clear that they had a high number of health issues and that their neighborhoods were toxic and filled with smelly air and water. EPA testers, however, were unable to find conclusive evidence of a connection between contamination and their illnesses. In all, Hyde Park residents filed three separate lawsuits between 1991 and 1995. One was dismissed, and nearly three decades later, the other two were still pending. At the end of the twentieth century, Hyde Park residents were finally able to secure government grants to clean up the toxic waste near their

Residents of Hyde Park Near Augusta, Georgia, faced a long struggle for environmental justice as factories and junkyards polluted their community.

neighborhood and to clear out a junkyard. The struggle for a clean environment, however, continues (Checker 2006).

How is the fight for environmental justice in Hyde Park tied to race? Many of the residents of Hyde Park interpret their experiences through a racial lens: the failure of the local, state, and federal governments to respond to their need is part of a history of exclusion that African Americans have faced since slavery. Additionally, African Americans are more likely to live in toxic neighborhoods than Whites—meaning that we can tie their plight to structural racism in the United States insofar as environmental rules, laws, and policies reproduce historical racial disparities.

The struggle in Hyde Park is decidedly local: residents of this Georgia community experienced the direct effects of the emission of toxins by industrial facilities that were right in their community. They won a small victory when some of the toxic waste was cleaned up. But where did that waste go? It is conceivable that it went to another country. Ninety percent of the hazardous waste in the world is produced in industrialized nations such as the United States, Japan, and European countries. Much of it is eventually shipped to Latin America, the Caribbean, South and Southeast Asia, and Africa. In some cases, environmental clean-up in the United States can have detrimental effects on poor countries that accept the hazardous waste in exchange for much-needed cash (Pellow 2007).

The United States has only 5 percent of the world's population, yet generates 19 percent of the world's waste. The waste output of residents of the United States is the highest in the world (Pellow 2007). Within the United States, there is continued controversy over what to do with the waste. One solution is to incinerate it. However, this produces incinerator ashes, which also must be disposed of.

In 1986, the mayor of Philadelphia found himself with 15,000 tons of incinerator ash, and nowhere to dump it. Local environmental activists had succeeded in closing the Kinsley landfill, but there was nowhere to dispose of the ash it had produced. The city contracted a local company to get rid of the ash; that company in turn handed it over to Amalgamated Shipping, a company headquartered in the Bahamas. The shipping company loaded the ashes onto the *Khian Sea*, and the ship set sail for the Bahamas on September 5, 1986. However, officials in the Bahamas refused to accept the toxic waste, which then traveled to the Dominican Republic, Honduras, Guinea-Bissau, Puerto Rico, Bermuda, and the

Dutch Antilles. Each port refused to accept the waste. Finally, in December 1987, the boat landed at Gonaives, Haiti, where the captain was able to work out an agreement with the military regime, in part because he told them the ash was fertilizer. The crew succeeded in unloading 3,700 tons of ash onto the beach before local activists and authorities became suspicious and were able to stop the dumping. The ship left Haiti, leaving the ashes on the beach. The *Khian Sea* continued its journey, unable to get rid of the remaining waste. The ship's captain later admitted he dumped the ashes in the middle of the Indian Ocean several months later. But the 3,700 tons of ash dumped on the beaches of Gonaives still remained. It took years of local and international activism before the toxic ash was finally removed from Haiti in April 2000.

The story of the *Khian Sea* is part of a story of global environmental injustice. Wealthier countries consume more resources than poorer ones and thus produce more waste. This global inequality is exacerbated when wealthy countries dump their waste in poorer countries. These inequalities are also drawn along racial lines: Western European countries and the United States attempt to dump their waste in Africa and the Caribbean.

voices

The Flint Water Crisis

In March 2016, the Flint Water Advisory Task Force Report found that the residents of Flint, Michigan, a majority-Black and overwhelmingly poor city, had been exposed to environmental and health hazards because of water-supply decisions made by city officials. The report also showed that these decisions were made with outright disregard for the lives and health of the residents of Flint, Michigan.

Residents of Flint pick up bottled water and water filters from Red Cross Disaster Relief volunteers.

(continued)

voices   *continued.*

The Flint Water Crisis

For nearly five decades, Flint had obtained clean drinking water from Lake Huron, the third-largest body of fresh water in the world. Beginning in June 2012, however, in an effort to save money, Flint city officials began to seek out alternative water sources. At the time, Flint was on the verge of financial collapse, and the city was being run by a governor-appointed emergency manager, Darnell Earley. City officials calculated that Flint could save $200 million over twenty-five years if it built its own pipeline to derive water from the Karegnondi Water Authority (KWA). However, by 2014, it became clear that the transition to the KWA would be delayed. Officials then decided to connect a temporary pipeline to obtain water from the Flint River, beginning in April 2014.

City officials received advice that they should add an anticorrosive element to the water, but they decided not to do this because it would cost $100 a day. The Flint River water was highly corrosive, however, and shortly after the switch to it, residents began to complain about the water's smell and color. In August 2014, test of the water revealed the presence of *E. coli* and total coliform bacteria. Residents were advised to boil their water before consuming it. They began to complain of skin rashes and hair loss, among other issues, as they became ill due to the water. City officials ignored nearly all complaints. In fall 2014, only one complaint was finally answered—that of General Motors.

The owners of the General Motors factory in Flint had become concerned about the water quality, as it was causing their car parts to corrode. In October 2014, they complained to Governor Rick Snyder, who used $440,000 of state funds to reconnect the factory to the Lake Huron pipeline. Nevertheless, the other residents of Flint remained connected to the contaminated Flint River water.

In January 2015, Flint was found to be in violation of the Safe Drinking Water Act. A month later, the water was found to contain extremely high levels of lead, a highly toxic element. In September, a local study reported that following the switch to the Flint River water, twice as many children under the age of five had elevated levels of lead in their blood.

In October 2015, Flint switched back to the Lake Huron water supply, but the corroded, lead-tainted pipes were still in use. One year later, in 2016, many residents continued to distrust the city's government and to doubt the water's safety. Three years later, in 2018, Flint still did not have clean water.

As of June 2021, 10,000 pipes had been replaced and the city claimed they were in the final stages of replacing all the pipes. Nevertheless, many residents will never trust the water again.

Sources: Bosman, Davey, and Smith 2016; Kennedy 2016; *New York Times* 2016; Sanburn 2017; Blakely 2021.

CONCLUSION AND DISCUSSION

During slavery, medical professionals had no qualms about using slaves as involuntary subjects in medical experiments. We no longer live in such brutal times, but we can't ignore our legacy. One hundred and fifty years after the abolition of slavery, Whites continue to receive better medical care than Blacks. Moreover, it is hard to say that White and Black lives are equally valued when Black life expectancy continues to be years lower than that of Whites.

The ability to breathe clean air, eat healthy food, have access to good medical care, and spend time outside in green spaces all lead to better health outcomes. In this way, the movement for environmental justice is intimately tied to the fight against health disparities.

Outright disregard for people of color informed the decisions made by industry and local leaders in the early twentieth century to place toxic waste facilities in primarily non-White neighborhoods. These same sentiments meant that non-White neighborhoods and towns were often the last to receive sewage infrastructure and piped water in their homes. By 2000, most communities had clean water, but non-White households continue to be the most likely to lack basic services.

Social scientists and public health scholars have provided the data we need to see the persistence of these disparities. These scientific studies leave little room for doubt that White Americans, on average, have better access to clean air and water and healthy communities than do non-White Americans. People of color in the United States and around the world are the most likely to have to contend with the health and environmental consequences of toxic dumping.

How do we explain these disparities? In each chapter, we have seen how racial ideologies help explain and justify inequalities. When looking at health and the environment, we can also uncover ideologies that serve this purpose, such as the misconception that African Americans are not interested in healthy eating and exercise. Such ideologies blame African Americans for their high prevalence of heart disease and diabetes while overlooking the structural reasons for health disparities, such as the lack of fresh vegetables and safe places to exercise in Black neighborhoods.

One of the United States' core values is the right of every person to have an equal opportunity to flourish. How does the ideology of equal opportunity coexist with the reality that non-Whites have less access than Whites to education, to jobs, and to services and circumstances that promote health? How is this discord related to racial ideologies?

THINKING
ABOUT
RACIAL
JUSTICE

WORLDWIDE, PEOPLE WITH higher standards of living have longer and healthier lives. In the United States, African Americans are on average not as healthy as Whites with similar incomes. How do we think about racial justice given this context? What would racial justice look like in terms of our health and environment?

Key Terms

CHECK YOUR UNDERSTANDING

10.1   What is the racial history of health disparities in the United States?

During and even following slavery, African Americans were subjected to involuntary experimentation that was often brutal and had no therapeutic effects.

 What is involuntary experimentation?

 Why was the Nuremberg Code important?

10.2   How do health disparities in the United States today vary by race and ethnicity?

African Americans have lower life expectancies than Whites, and racial disparities in health can be found from the womb to the deathbed. Many of these disparities are due to structural and individual-level discrimination.

 Describe the differences in infant mortality rates for Black and White women.

 How are health disparities related to segregation?

Q Why has diabetes become a problem for Native Americans?

Q How can racial discrimination affect health?

Q What is a life-course perspective on health disparities?

Q What is the Hispanic Paradox?

10.3 What are the effects of environmental racism?

Black and Latinx neighborhoods are more likely to host toxic waste facilities than White neighborhoods. These facilities have negative health outcomes for the residents.

Q How prevalent is environmental racism?

10.4 What are some community movements for environmental justice?

The fight for clean neighborhoods has come to be called the environmental justice movement.

Q How did the environmental justice movement get started?

Critical Thinking

1. Why is it important to understand the history of health injustice in the United States?
2. What factors led doctors to conduct cruel experiments on African Americans?
3. How does our understanding of health disparities change when we take into account both race and socioeconomic status?
4. Is segregation at the root of health disparities? Or are there more deeply rooted causes? Explain your position.
5. What role do you think acculturation plays in explaining the Hispanic Paradox?
6. What are some reasons that genetic explanations for health disparities may be problematic?
7. How is the fight against toxins in Hyde Park related to race and racism?

Talking about Race

In light of this chapter's data on racial disparities in health outcomes, consider the findings most relevant to your own experiences. What information in this chapter could you draw from to have a conversation about health disparities and environmental racism in your community? For example, does your family live in a neighborhood with access to healthy food and green spaces? What structural explanations might explain why or why not? How are racial ideologies used to explain persistent health disparities?

Learn more with this chapter's digital tools, including video clips from the author, web links, filmography, and chapter self-assessment quizzes at www.oup.com/he/golash-boza-brief3e.

Glossary

1965 Immigration and Nationality Act Legislation that put an end to the racially biased quotas set forth in the 1924 Oriental Exclusion Act and the Immigration Act of 1924. It set a universal quota of 20,000 immigrants for every country in the world.

1984 Crime Control Act An act that established mandatory minimum sentences and eliminated federal parole.

1986 Immigration Reform and Control Act (IRCA) A series of immigration provisions that (1) offered a legalization option for undocumented workers living in the United States and (2) imposed sanctions on employers who hired undocumented workers.

abstract liberalism The first of Bonilla-Silva's "frames" of color-blind racism. It involves using liberal ideas such as equality of opportunity or freedom of choice to explain or justify racial inequality.

acculturation A process by which immigrants adopt the behaviors and preferences of the host society.

achievement gap The disparate educational outcomes of Whites, Asians, Blacks, Latinxs, and Native Americans.

acting White A term used to refer to non-Whites who are perceived as behaving in ways associated with White people.

adultify When a teacher or other authority figure interprets children's behavior as if they were adults.

affirmative action Policies and procedures designed to combat ongoing discrimination in schools and the workplace.

Anti–Drug Abuse Act of 1986 Legislation that imposed even more mandatory minimum sentences. Most significantly, it set a five-year mandatory minimum sentence for offenses involving 100 grams of heroin, 500 grams of cocaine, or 5 grams of crack cocaine.

Anti–Drug Abuse Act of 1988 Act that included a five-year mandatory minimum sentence for simple possession of crack cocaine, with no evidence of intent to sell.

Anti-Terrorism and Effective Death Penalty Act (AEDPA) 1996 legislation that, among other provisions, eliminated judicial review of some deportation orders and required mandatory detention for many noncitizens.

asset-based social policy Proactive policy, at either the individual or structural level, designed to help narrow the wealth gap.

assets Cash in the bank and the value of all property, not only land but also houses, cars, stocks and bonds, and retirement savings.

beauty queue A concept explaining how sexism and racism interact to create a queue of women ranging from the lightest to the darkest, in which the lightest get the most resources.

biological racism The idea that Whites are genetically superior to non-Whites.

Black Lives Matter A hashtag and movement aimed at ending anti-Black racism and violence in all its permutations.

bracero program A U.S. government program that brought in temporary workers from Mexico between 1942 and 1964.

Butterfly A stereotype of an Asian woman who is a demure, devoted, and submissive wife.

Chinese Exclusion Act Legislation that denied Chinese laborers entry to the United States.

colonialism The practice of acquiring political control over another country, occupying it with settlers, and exploiting it economically.

color-blind racism An ideology in which race is not explicitly acknowledged, but individual prejudices, acts of racial discrimination, and structures of inequality work to benefit Whites.

colorism The idea that, within races, lighter is better.

controlling images Raced, gendered, and classed depictions in the media that shape people's ideas of what African Americans are and are not.

craniometry the measurement of cranial capacity.

critical race theory a theory of race and racism that centers the voices of people of color, focuses on the eradication of racist oppression, and uses reflexive thinking

cultural capital Cultural resources that offer social and other benefits.

cultural racism (Bonilla-Silva) The third of Bonilla-Silva's "frames" of color-blind racism, relying on culturally based explanations such as the idea that Blacks live in poor neighborhoods because they don't work hard enough to get out of the ghetto.

cultural racism A way of thinking that attributes disadvantaged racial groups' lack of prosperity to their behavior and culture, rather than to structural factors.

cumulative disadvantage perspective A framework used to explain the increasing divergence between Black and White health outcomes that focuses on how disadvantages accumulate over the life course.

deindustrialization (1) The process of decline in industrial activity in a region or economy that involves a shift from a manufacturing to a service economy. (2) The process of decline in industrial activity in a region or economy.

diaspora A dispersion of people from their original homeland.

discrimination The practice of treating people differently.

dissimilarity index Measure that describes the extent to which two groups—such as Blacks and Whites—are found in equal proportions in all neighborhoods.

Dragon Lady A stereotype of an Asian woman as a sinister, crafty, and destructive seductress.

earnings gap Differences in annual earnings among groups.

embedded market A market economy embedded within interlocking systems of oppression and privilege.

enlightened racism The idea that the United States is a land of opportunity and that African Americans could do better if they only tried harder.

environmental justice Efforts to ensure the right to live in nontoxic neighborhoods, regardless of race.

environmental racism Institutional policies and practices that differentially affect the health outcomes or living conditions of people and communities based on race or color.

erotic capital A concept linking the attractiveness and sensuality of a woman to her skin color.

ethnic enclave economy Clusters of small businesses that primarily serve people of the same ethnicity and work to facilitate the success of co-ethnics.

ethnicity Group identity based on notions of similar and shared history, culture, and kinship.

eugenics The practice of controlled breeding to increase the occurrence of desirable characteristics in a population.

Federal Housing Administration (FHA) Government agency established in 1934 with the purpose of bolstering the economy and, in particular, the construction industry.

genocide The mass killing of a group of people, especially those of a particular ethnic or racial group.

Gini coefficient A measure of inequality, with 0 representing perfect equality and 100 representing perfect inequality.

global color hierarchy A worldwide system in which White (or light) skin is privileged and people—especially women—strive to become lighter.

hegemony When racial ideologies become so widely accepted that they become common sense.

hidden curriculum Underlying curriculum designed to reflect and promote the interests of the dominant class.

"Hispanic Paradox" The observation that even though Latinxs have, on average, a lower socioeconomic status than Whites, they have comparable health outcomes to Whites.

human capital Educational attainment, skills, and job experience.

hypersegregation Instances of notably high levels of segregation.

hypodescent The idea that having any amount of Black ancestry makes you Black.

ideology A set of principles and ideas that benefit the dominant group.

Illegal Immigration Reform and Immigrant Responsibility Act (IIRIRA) 1996 legislation under which legal permanent residents face mandatory deportation if they are convicted of "aggravated felonies."

Immigration Act of 1917 Legislation expanding the 1882 Chinese Exclusion Act and denying entry to the United States for anyone coming from the "Asiatic Barred Zone," which included India, Burma, the Malay States, Arabia, and Afghanistan.

Immigration Act of 1924 (Johnson-Reed Act) Legislation that greatly reduced U.S. immigration from southern and eastern Europe by introducing quotas, or limits on the number of people from these countries who were allowed entry.

implicit bias Unreasoned judgmental inclinations that operate without our conscious awareness.

Indian Removal Act of 1830 Act that enabled the administration of U.S. president Andrew Jackson to use military power to displace at least 70,000 Native Americans, killing tens of thousands in the process.

individual racism When one person discriminates against another on the basis of race or ethnicity.

institutional agent A person who occupies a position of power and is able to access or negotiate resources for others.

institutional racism Policies, laws, and institutions that reproduce racial inequalities.

intelligence testing The attempt to quantify intellectual ability using scientific measures.

intersectionality A simultaneous look at multiple forms of oppression, such as race, ethnicity, class, and gender oppression.

Islamophobia The systematic marginalization of Muslims.

isolation index Measure that compares a neighborhood's demographics against citywide demographics.

Jezebel A name with biblical origins that has come to signify a stereotypically oversexed or hypersexual Black woman.

Jim Crow laws A system of laws passed in the late 1800s denying non-Whites equality.

legal permanent resident A foreign national who is granted the right to remain in the United States and who will be eligible for naturalization after a period of three to five years.

life-course perspective A framework used to explain how health outcomes change over the life course.

Mammy A stereotypical image of a Black maid.

meme An idea, image, video, or phrase that spreads in a culture.

mestizo A Latin American classification of people of European and indigenous ancestry.

"model minority" myth The stereotype that Asians are the racial minority group that has "made it" in the United States.

mulatto The progeny of Blacks and Whites; a class of mixed-race people who are darker than Whites but lighter than Blacks.

nativism The presumed superiority of native-born citizens, favoring the allocation of resources to them over immigrants and promoting a fear of foreign cultures.

naturalization The process whereby people become citizens of a country where they do not have birthright citizenship.

naturalization (Bonilla-Silva) The second "frame" of color-blind racism, which permits people to explain racial phenomena as if they were natural.

Naturalization Law of 1790 The first piece of U.S. legislation relating to the foreign-born, stating that only free White persons who had lived in the United States for at least two years were eligible for citizenship.

neoliberalism The ideology that open markets, liberalized trade, and privatization are the keys to economic success.

new racism An ideology in which it is not acceptable to make overtly racist statements, yet racial inequality persists.

Nuremberg Code Policy adopted by the U.S. Department of Defense in 1953 under which research subjects have to be informed that participation is voluntary and be provided with information about the nature, duration, and purpose of the research.

Operation Wetback Massive roundups of Mexicans by the U.S. Border Patrol from 1950 to 1954.

oppositional culture Signithia Fordham and John Ogbu's (1986) thesis that Black children receive signals from both the White and Black communities that lead them to reject schooling as a route to success.

outsourcing The practice of moving jobs once held by Americans overseas, where cheaper labor can be found.

pardo A Brazilian census category meaning "brown."

patriarchy A system of oppression that ensures male dominance in terms of power and property.

Personal Responsibility and Work Opportunity Reconciliation Act (PRWORA) 1996 legislation that denied government services and benefits to legally present migrants.

pigmentocracy A society in which Blacks, Asians, and Latinxs have different social statuses according to their skin color.

predatory lender A pawnshop, payday lender, or check cashing service that charges very high fees and interest rates.

prejudice The belief that people belong to distinct racial groups with innate hierarchical differences that can be measured and judged.

prison-industrial complex (PIC) The vast network of prisons, jails, courts, police officers, and other elements that purport to reduce the amount of criminal activity in our society.

race A social construction to describe a group of people who share physical and cultural traits as well as a common ancestry.

racial capitalism As defined by Jordanna Matlon (2016), an economic system that organizes and justifies exploitation by racial classification.

racial enclave economy An economy in which a business's success is both shaped and limited by the racial group membership of the business owner.

racial formation As defined by Michael Omi and Howard Winant (1994), "the sociohistorical process by which racial categories are created, inhabited, transformed, and destroyed."

racial ideology A set of principles and ideas that (1) divides people into racial groups and (2) serves the interests of one group.

racial microaggression Daily, commonplace insults and racial slights that cumulatively affect the psychological well-being of people of color.

racial profiling The use of race or ethnicity as grounds for suspicion.

racial project As defined by Michael Omi and Howard Winant (1994), a way of giving meaning to racial categories through cultural representations and social structures.

racialized social systems Societies in which economic, political, social, and ideological benefits are partially structured by the placement of actors in racial categories.

racially restrictive covenants Contractual agreements that prevent the sale or lease of property within an area to non-Whites.

racism (1) The belief that races are populations of people whose physical differences are linked to significant cultural and social differences and that these innate hierarchical differences can be measured and judged. (2) The practice of subordinating races believed to be inferior.

Reaganomics The economic policies of former U.S. president Ronald Reagan, involving heavy cuts to a wide variety of social programs across the country.

residential segregation The separation of different groups of people into distinct neighborhoods.

rhetorical strategy Way of expressing racist ideas without being labeled as racist.

Sapphire One of the main characters on the television show *Amos 'n' Andy*; the caricature of an angry Black woman.

school-to-prison pipeline A set of practices that lead to children being funneled from public schools into the juvenile and criminal justice system.

scientific racism The use of science or pseudoscience to reproduce and/or justify racial inequalities.

segregation index Measure that describes the percentage of 88 percent non-Whites who would have to move in order for the city to be fully residentially integrated.

skills mismatch hypothesis The hypothesis that African American men in particular often do not have the skills required to secure work in the current economy.

skin-color privilege The privilege of being considered more beautiful, intelligent, or otherwise superior as a result of having lighter skin.

skin-color stratification A system in which resources such as income and status are distributed unequally according to skin color.

slave codes Laws enacted in the 1660s that clearly spelled out the differences between African slaves and European indentured servants.

social capital Relationships and networks that offer social and other benefits.

social construction An idea or way of viewing people based not on biological differences but on social perceptions.

sociological theory of racism Sociological explanation for how racial inequality is created and reproduced.

spatial mismatch hypothesis Hypothesis that African American families have been excluded from buying homes in the suburbs where much of the job growth has occurred, thereby creating a disconnect between where African Americans live and where the jobs are concentrated.

split labor market A difference in the price of labor for two or more groups of laborers.

steering A practice by which real estate agents show homes in White neighborhoods only to Whites and homes in Black neighborhoods only to Blacks.

stereotype A widely held but fixed and oversimplified image or idea of a type of person or thing.

sterilization racism Racist health care policies and practices that attempt to control the reproductive capacities of women of color.

structural racism Interinstitutional interactions across time and space that reproduce racial inequality.

subprime loan High-interest loan to someone at high risk of defaulting.

symbolic violence As described by Pierre Bourdieu (1984), the power of a socially dominant group to make its preferences, tastes, and norms appear to be superior to those of the nondominant group.

systemic racism As defined by Joe Feagin (2001), a diverse assortment of racist practices, encompassing daily microaggressions, deep-seated inequalities, historical inequalities, and anti-Black ideologies.

Trails of Tears The forced displacement of the Cherokee of Georgia, the Apalachicola of Florida, the Peoria of Illinois, the Shawnee of Ohio, and a host of other tribes.

underemployment A category including jobless workers actively seeking work, people who are working part time yet are available to work full time, and those who have looked for work in the past year and yet are not actively seeking employment.

wage gap Differences in hourly earnings (wages) among racial groups.

wage of Whiteness As defined by W. E. B. DuBois in 1936, psychological benefits that White workers received by aligning with the dominant group, their White bosses, as opposed to developing working-class solidarity with recently freed Black slaves.

wealth The sum total of a person's assets minus debt. Wealth is built up over a lifetime and passed on to the next generation through inheritances.

weathering hypothesis A framework used to explain the increasing divergence between Black and White health outcomes that focuses on how constant exposure to stress accelerates health decline for Blacks.

White privilege The advantages inherent in being categorized as White.

References

Abello, Oscar Perry. 2017 (August). "These Detroit Commuting Numbers Show Stark Inequality." *Next City*. nextcity.org/daily/entry/new-report-detroit-jobs-numbers-pay-commute.

Adelman, L. 2008. *Unnatural Causes: Is Inequality Making Us Sick? [Television Series]*. PBS. https://www.pbs.org/unnaturalcauses/production_team_advisors.htm

Ainsworth-Darnell, James, and Douglas Downey. 1998. "Assessing the Oppositional Culture Explanation for Racial/Ethnic Differences in School Performance." *American Sociological Review* 63 (4): 536–53.

Al-Arian, Laila. 2012, December 12. "*Homeland*, TV's Most Islamophobic Show." http://www.alternet.org/homeland-tvs-most-islamophobic-show.

Alcalá, Héctor E., and Mónica FL Montoya. 2018. "Association of Skin Color and Generation on Arrests among Mexican-Origin Latinos." *Race and Justice* 8 (2): 178–93.

Al-Dahir, Sara, Fatima Brakta, Alaa Khalil, Mustafa Benrahla, Leonard Jack Jr, and Kathleen Kennedy. 2013. "The Impact of Acculturation on Diabetes Risk among Arab Americans in Southeastern Louisiana." *Journal of Health Care for the Poor and Underserved* 24 (1): 47–63.

Alexander, Michelle. 2010. *The New Jim Crow*. New York: New Press.

Allen, Theodore. 1994. *The Invention of the White Race*. New York: Verso.

Allard, M.D. and V. Brundage Jr. 2019. "American Indians and Alaska Natives in the US Labor Force." *Monthly Labor Review* 142: 1.

Alsultany, Evelyn. 2008. The Prime-Time Plight of Arab Muslim Americans After 9/11. In *Race and Arab Americans Before and After 9/11: From Invisible Citizens to Visible Subjects*, edited by Amaney A. Jamal and Nadine Christine Naber, 204–27. Syracuse, NY: Syracuse University Press.

Alvarez, Camila H. and Kathryn G. Norton-Smith. 2018. "Environmental Inequality in Latino Destinations: Estimated Cancer Risk from Air Toxics in Latino Traditional and New Destinations." *Socius* 4: 1–11.

Alvarez, R. Michael, and Tara L. Butterfield. 2000. "The Resurgence of Nativism in California? The Case of Proposition 187 and Illegal Immigration." *Social Science Quarterly* 81 (1): 167–79.

American Civil Liberties Union (ACLU). 2003. *Race and the Death Penalty*. https://www.aclu.org/capital-punishment/race-and-death-penalty.

American Immigration Lawyers Association (AILA). 2010. *Case No. Civ-10-1061-Srb*. http://www.aila.org/content/default.aspx?docid=32246.

Amnesty International. 2010, October 8. USA Increasingly Isolated as the World Turns Against Death Penalty. https://www.amnesty.org/en/latest/news/2010/10/19094/

Anderson, James, and Dara N. Byrne. 2004. *The Unfinished Agenda of Brown v. Board of Education*. Diverse: Issues in Higher Education. Hoboken, NJ: John Wiley and Sons.

Annie E. Casey Foundation. 2016, April. *A Shared Sentence*. http://www.aecf.org/m/resource-doc/aecf-asharedsentence-2016.pdf.

Arab American Institute (AAI). 2017. http://www.aaiusa.org/demographics.

Assari, S. 2016. Racial Disparities in Chronic Kidney Diseases in the United States: A Pressing Public Health Challenge with Social, Behavioral and Medical Causes. *Journal of Nephropharmacology* 5 (1): 4–6.

Associated Press. 2016. Media Use in America Up a Full Hour over Just Last Year. https://www.cbsnews.com/news/media-use-in-america-up-a-full-hour-over-just-last-year/

Auspurg, Katrin, Andreas Schneck, and Thomas Hinz. 2019. Closed Doors Everywhere? A Meta-Analysis of Field Experiments on Ethnic Discrimination in Rental Housing Markets. *Journal of Ethnic and Migration Studies* 45 (1): 95–114.

Ávila, José Luis, Carlos Fuentes, and Rodolfo Tuirán. 2000. "Migración Temporal De Adolescentes Y Jóvenes, 1993–1997." *México-Estados Unidos: Continuidad y cambios.* Mexico City: Consejo Nacional de Poblacion.

Aviram, Hadar. 2015. *Cheap on Crime: Recession-Era Politics and the Transformation of American Punishment.* University of California Press.

Ballinas, Jorge. 2017. Where Are You From and Why Are You Here? Microaggressions, Racialization, and Mexican College Students in A New Destination. *Sociological Inquiry* 87 (2): 385–410.

Balogun, Oluwakemi M. 2012. Cultural and Cosmopolitan: Idealized Femininity and Embodied Nationalism in Nigerian Beauty Pageants. *Gender and Society* 26 (3): 357–81.

Barnes, Mario, and Robert Chang. 2012. Analyzing Stops, Citations, and Searches in Washington and Beyond. *Seattle University Law Review* 25: 673.

Baugh, Ryan. 2019. *U.S. Lawful Permanent Residents: 2018.* Office of Immigration Statistics. Department of Homeland Security.

Baugh, Ryan, and Kathryn Wistman. 2017. *U.S. Lawful Permanent Residents, 2015.* U.S. Department of Homeland Security, Office of Immigration Statistics. https://www.dhsgov/sites/default/files/publications/Lawful_Permanent_Residents_2015.pdf.

Baumgartner, Frank, Leah Christiani, Derek A. Epp, Kevin Roach, and Kelsey Shoub. 2017. Racial Disparities in Traffic Stop Outcomes. *Duke Forum for Law and Social Change.* 21–53. Available at: https://scholarship.law.duke.edu/dflsc/vol9/iss1/2

Beliso-De Jesús, Aisha M., and Jemima Pierre. 2020. "Anthropology of White Supremacy." *American Anthropologist* 122 (1): 65–75.

Berestein, Leslie. 2008, May 4. "Detention Dollars: Tougher Immigration Laws Turn the Ailing Private Prison Sector into A Revenue Maker." *San Diego Tribune.*

Berg, Charles Ramírez. 2002. *Latino Images in Film: Stereotypes, Subversion, and Resistance.* University of Texas Press.

Berger, B. 2009. "Red: Racism and the American Indian." *UCLA Law Review* 56: 591–656.

Bertrand, Marianne, and Sendhil Mullainathan. 2004. Are Emily and Greg More Employable Than Lakisha and Jamal? A Field Experiment on Labor Market Discrimination. *American Economic Review* 94 (4): 991–1013.

Bird, Elizabeth. 1999. "Gendered Construction of the American Indian in Popular Media." *Journal of Communication* 49 (3): 61–83.

Bischoff, Kendra, and Sean F. Reardon. 2014. "Residential Segregation by Income, 1970–2009." In *Diversity and Disparities: America Enters a New Century,* edited by J. Logan. New York: Russell Sage Foundation.

Blake M.K. 2018. "All Talk and No Action? Racial Differences in College Behaviors and Attendance." *Sociological Perspectives* 61 (4): 553–72.

Blakely, N. 2021. "Seven Years On: The Flint Water Crisis Has Yet to Conclude." https://www.greatlakesnow.org/2021/10/seven-years-flint-water-crisis/

Bleiweis, Robin. 2020. "*Quick Facts about the Gender Wage Gap.*" Center for American Progress.

Bocian, Debbie Gruenstein, Wei Li, and Keith S. Ernst. 2010. "Foreclosures by Race and Ethnicity." *Center for Responsible Lending*: 4–6. https://www.responsiblelending.org/mortgage-lending/research-analysis/foreclosures-by-race-and-ethnicity.pdf

Bonacich, Edna. 1976. "Advanced Capitalism and Black/White Race Relations in the United States: A Split Labor Market Interpretation." *American Sociological Review* 41: 34–51.

Bonilla-Silva, Eduardo. 2013. *Racism Without Racists: Color-Blind Racism and the Persistence of Racial Inequality in America*. Lanham, MD: Rowman & Littlefield.

Bonilla-Silva, Eduardo. 1997. "Rethinking Racism: Toward A Structural Interpretation." *American Sociological Review* 62 (3): 465–80.

Bonilla-Silva, Eduardo, and David R. Dietrich. 2009. "The Latin Americanization of US Race Relations: A New Pigmentocracy." In *Shades of Difference: Why Skin Color Matters*, edited by E.N. Glenn, 40–60. Stanford, CA: Stanford University Press.

Bosman, Julie, Monica Davey, and Mitch Smith. 2016, January 20. "As Water Problems Grew, Officials Belittled Complaints from Flint." *The New York Times*. https://www.nytimes.com/2016/01/21/us/flint-michigan-lead-water-crisis.html.

Bourdieu, Pierre. 1984. *Distinction: A Social Critique of the Judgment of Taste*. New York: Routledge.

Bowser, F. P. 1974. *The African Slave in Colonial Peru, 1524–1650*. Stanford, CA: Stanford University Press.

Boyle, Kevin. 2001. "The Ruins of Detroit: Exploring the Urban Crisis in the Motor City." *The Michigan Historical Review* 27 (1): 109–127.

Brewer, Rose M., and Nancy Heitzeg. 2008. "The Racialization of Crime and Punishment: Criminal Justice, Color-Blind Racism, and the Political Economy of the Prison Industrial Complex." *American Behavioral Scientist* 51 (5): 625–44.

Brodkin, Karen. 1998. *How Jews Became White Folks and What That Says about Race in America*. New Brunswick, NJ: Rutgers University Press.

Brodkin, Karen. 2005. "How Jews Became White Folks." In *White Privilege: Essential Readings on the Other Side of Racism*, 2nd ed., edited by Paula S. Rothenberg, 41–54. New York: Worth.

Bronson, J., and E.A. Carson. 2019. "Prisoners in 2017." *Bureau of Justice Statistics*. https://bjs.ojp.gov/content/pub/pdf/p17.pdf

Brooks, S. 2010. "Hypersexualization and the Dark Body: Race and Inequality among Black and Latina Women in the Exotic Dance Industry." *Sexuality Research and Social Policy* 7 (2): 70–80.

Brown, T., Angela M. O'Rand, and D. Adkins. 2012. "Race-Ethnicity and Health Trajectories: Tests of Three Hypotheses Across Multiple Groups and Health Outcomes." *Journal of Health and Social Behavior* 53 (3): 359–77.

Browne, Irene, and Joya Misra. 2003. "The Intersection of Gender and Race in the Labor Market." *Annual Review of Sociology* 29: 487–513.

Bullard, R. 2007. *Toxic Wastes and Race at Twenty—1987–2007: Grassroots Struggles to Dismantle Environmental Racism in the United States*. Report prepared for the United Church of Christ Justice and Witness Ministries.

Burchard, E. 2022. Research Overview. https://pharm.ucsf.edu/burchard/about

Bureau of Justice Statistics. 2016. Total Correctional Population. *Web:* May 28, 2017.

Bureau of Justice Statistics. 2017. Key Statistics: Incarceration Rate. https://www.bjs.gov/index.cfm?ty=kfdetail&iid=493.

Bureau of Justice Statistics. 2019. Prisoners in 2017. https://bjs.ojp.gov/content/pub/pdf/p17.pdf.

Bureau of Labor Statistics. 2015. https://www.bls.gov/.

Bureau of Labor Statistics. 2016. American Time Use Survey Summary. https://www. bls.gov/news.release/atus.nr0.htm.

Bureau of Labor Statistics. 2017. https://www.bls.gov/.

Bureau of Labor Statistics. 2021. American Time Use Survey Summary. https://www.bls.gov/news.release/atus.nr0.htm.

Bureau of Labor Statistics. 2022. Economic News Release: Union Members Summary. https://www.bls.gov/news.release/union2.nr0.htm.

Burgess, Melinda C. R., Karen E. Dill, S. Paul Stermer, Stephen R. Burgess, and Brian P. Brown. 2011. "Playing with Prejudice: The Prevalence and Consequences of Racial Stereotypes in Video Games." *Media Psychology* 14 (3): 37–41.

Byrne, Bryan Patrick. 2015. *A Surprising Number of Americans Don't Have a Toilet*. http://www.vocativ.com/253058/toilets-are-great.

Cahalan, Margaret, and Laura Perna. 2015. *Indicators of Higher Education Equity in the United States: 45 Year Trend Report*. Washington, DC: Pell Institute for the Study of Opportunity in Higher Education.

Calavita, K. 2000. "The Paradoxes of Race, Class, Identity, and "Passing": Enforcing the Chinese Exclusion Acts, 1882–1910." *Law and Social Inquiry* 251: 1–40.

Campos-Vazquez, Raymundo, and Eduardo Medina-Cortina. 2019. "Skin Color and Social Mobility: Evidence from Mexico." *Demography* 56 (1): 321–43.

Canaday, N., C. Reback, and K. Stowe. n.d. *The Southern Homestead Act: Race, Literacy, and Learning*. http://history.appstate.edu/sites/history.appstate.edu/files/Neil%20Canaday.pdf

Carmichael, Stokely, and Charles V. Hamilton. 1967. *Black Power: The Politics of Liberation in America*. New York: Vintage Books.

Carter, Prudence. 2003. "'Black' Cultural Capital, Status Positioning, and Schooling Conflicts for Low-Income African American Youth." *Social Problems* 50 (1): 136–55.

Cave, Alfred. 2003. "Abuse of Power: Andrew Jackson and the Indian Removal Act of 1830." *Historian* 65 (6): 1330–53. http://onlinelibrary.wiley.com/doi/10.1111/j.0018-23702003.00055.x/full.

Centers for Disease Control and Prevention. 2019. Health, United States, 2019. https://www.cdc.gov/nchs/data/hus/hus19-508.pdf

Centers for Disease Control and Prevention. 2016. Health, United States, 2015. *DHHS Publication No.* 2016-1232. https://www.cdc.gov/nchs/data/hus/hus15.pdf.

Centers for Disease Control and Prevention. 2011. Table 10. Low Birthweight Live Births among Mothers 20 Years of Age and Over, By Detailed Race, Hispanic Origin, and Education of Mother: United States, Selected Reporting Areas 2007 and 2008. http://www.cdc.gov/nchs/data/hus/2011/010.pdf.

Chammah, Maurice. 2016, September 15. Sandra Bland, One Year Later. https://www.the-marshallproject.org/2016/07/12/sandra-bland-one-year-later#.cJhX7yR9K

Charles, Camille Zubrinsky. 2003 "The Dynamics of Racial Residential Segregation." *Annual review of sociology* 29 (1): 167–207.

Charles, Christopher A. D. 2009. "Skin Bleachers' Representations of Skin Color in Jamaica." *Journal of Black Studies* 40 (2): 153–70.

Charles, Christopher A. D. 2011. "The Derogatory Representations of the Skin Bleaching Products Sold in Harlem." *Journal of Pan African Studies* 4 (4): 117–41.

Checker, Melissa. 2006. *Polluted Promises: Environmental Racism and the Search for Justice in a Southern Town*. New York: New York University Press.

Chermak, Steven M. 1994. "Body Count News: How Crime Is Presented in the News Media." *Justice Quarterly* 11 (4): 561–82.

Chicago Tribune. 2016, July 29. Officer Says Prosecutors Silenced Him in Sandra Bland Case. http://www.chicagotribune.com/news/nationworld/ct-officer-in-sandra-bland-case-20160729-story.html.

Choi, A., Herbert, K. Winslow, O., and Browne, A. 2019. Long Island Divided. *Newsday (Long Island)*, November 17, 2019. https://projects.newsday.com/long-island/real-estate-agents-investigation/.

Churchill, Ward. 2002. *Struggle for the Land: Native North American Resistance to Genocide, Ecocide, and Colonization*. New York: City Lights.

Cimbala, P. 1989. "The Freedmen's Bureau, the Freedmen, and Sherman's grant in Reconstruction Georgia, 1865–1867." *Journal of Southern History* 55 (4): 597–632.

Clark, Rodney, Norman B. Anderson, Vernessa R. Clark, and David R. Williams. 1999. "Racism as a Stressor for African Americans: A Biopsychosocial Model." *American Psychologist* 54 (10): 805–16.

Clear, Todd. R., and Natasha. A. Frost. 2015. *The Punishment Imperative: The Rise and Failure of Mass Incarceration in America*. New York: New York University Press.

Cohn, D., E. Patten, and M. Lopez. 2014. *Puerto Rican Population Declines on Island and Grows on U.S. Mainland*. Washington, DC: Pew Hispanic Center. http://www.pewhispanic.org/2014/08/11/puerto-rican-population-declines-on-island-growson-u-s-mainland/

Collins, Patricia Hill. 2004. *Black Sexual Politics*. New York: Routledge.

Comfort, Megan. 2007. "Punishment Beyond the Legal Offender." *Annual Review of Law and Social Sciences* 3: 271–96.

Connors, Kaela, et al. 2020. "Family Member Incarceration, Psychological Stress, and Subclinical Cardiovascular Disease in Mexican Women (2012–2016)." *American Journal of Public Health* 110 (S1): 77.

Cornell, Stephen, and Douglas Hartmann. 2007. *Ethnicity and Race: Making Identities in a Changing World*. Thousand Oaks, CA: Pine Forge Press.

Cosic, Damir. 2019. *College Premium and Its Impact on Racial and Gender Differentials in Earnings and Future Old-Age Income*. Urban Institute, March. https://www.pgpf.org/sites/default/files/US-2050-The-College-Premium-and-Its-Impact-on-Racial-and-Gender-Differentials-in-Earnings-and-Future-Retirement-Income.pdf.

Couloute, Lucius, and Daniel Kopf. 2018. *Report: Out of Prison and Out of Work: Unemployment among Formerly Incarcerated People*. Prison Policy Initiative, July. https://www.prisonpolicy.org/reports/outofwork.html.

Covington, Stephanie, and Barbara Bloom. 2003. "Gendered Justice: Women in the Criminal Justice System." In *Gendered Justice: Addressing Female Offenders*, edited by Barbara E. Bloom, 3–24. Durham, NC: Carolina Academic Press.

Crenshaw, Kimberlé. 1991. Mapping the Margins: Intersectionality, Identity Politics, and Violence Against Women of Color. *Stanford Law Review* 43 (6): 1241–99.

Dalmage, Heather. 2000. *Tripping on the Color Line: Black–White Multiracial Families in a Racially Divided World*. New Brunswick, NJ: Rutgers University Press. Dalton, Harlon. 2005.

Dalton, Harlon. 2005. "Failing to See." In *White Privilege: Essential Readings on the Other Side of Racism*, 2nd ed., edited by Paula S. Rothenberg, 15–18. New York: Worth.

Daniels, Jessie. 2008. "Race, Civil Rights, and Hate Speech in the Digital Era." In *Learning Race and Ethnicity: Youth and Digital Media*, edited by Anna Everett, 129–54. Cambridge, MA: MIT Press.

Darity, W. 2008. "Forty Acres and a Mule in the 21st Century." *Social Science Quarterly* 89 (3): 656–664.

Davids – TBA by author

Davis, Angela. 1998. "Masked Racism: Reflections On the Prison Industrial Complex." *Colorlines* 2. https://www.colorlines.com/articles/masked-racism-reflections-prison-industrial-complex.

Death Penalty Information Center. 2017, April. *Facts About the Death Penalty*. https://death pen-altyinfo.org/documents/FactSheet.pdf.

DeHart D., Shapiro C., and Clone S. 2018. "'The Pill Line Is Longer than the Chow Line': The Impact of Incarceration on Prisoners and Their Families." *Prison Journal* 98 (2): 188–212.

Democracy Now. 2016. *Dakota Access Pipeline*. https://www.democracynow.org/topics/dakota_access.

Desilver, D. 2015. "Businesses Owned by Women, Minorities Lag in Revenue Share." September 1. http://www.pewresearch.org/fact-tank/2015/09/01/businessesowned-by-women-minorities-lag-in-revenue-share/.

Diamond, Sara. 1996. "Right-Wing Politics and the Anti-Immigration Cause." *Social Justice* 23 (3): 154–69.

Dorman, Jacob. 2011. "Skin Bleach and Civilization: The Racial Formation of Blackness in 1920s Harlem." *Journal of Pan African Studies* 4 (4): 47–80.

Do Valle, Alice, Vanessa Huang, and Mari Spira. 2006. "The Prison Industrial Complex: A Delib-eration." *International Feminist Journal of Politics* 8 (1): 130–44.

Dozier, Raine. 2010. "Accumulating Disadvantage: The Growth in the Black–White Wage Gap among Women." *Journal of African American Studies* 14 (3): 279–301.

Du Bois, W. E. B., ed. 1904. *Some Notes on Negro Crime, Particularly in Georgia*. Atlanta: Atlanta University Press.

Dymski, Gary, Jesus Hernandez, and Lisa Mohanty. 2013. "Race, Gender, Power, and the US Sub-prime Mortgage and Foreclosure Crisis: A Meso Analysis." *Feminist Economics* 19 (3): 124–51.

EarthJustice. 2016. http://earthjustice.org/features/faq-standing-rock-litigation?gclid=CjwKEAiAjvrBBRDxm_nRusW3q1QSJAAzRI1tSFo9Zr0u2zCXMeM8RW4zPaLsCi8JrMViQMSL4o2NpBoCvXvw_wcB#.

Eckstein, Susan, and Lorena Barberia. 2002. "Grounding Immigrant Generations in History: Cuban Americans and Their Transnational Ties." *International Migration Review* 36 (3): 799–837.

eMarketer. 2013. "Digital Set to Surpass TV in Time Spent with US Media." *eMarketer*, August 1. http://www.emarketer.com/Article/Digital-Set-Surpass-TV-Time-Spent-with-US-Media/1010096#Ecc1XKrIcD8corwo.99.

Espinosa, Lorelle L., Jonathan M. Turk, Morgan Taylor, and Hollie M. Chessman. 2019. *Race and Ethnicity in Higher Education: A Status Report*. Washington, DC: American Council on Education.

Everett, Anna, and S. Craig Watkins. 2008. "The Power of Play: The Portrayal and Performance of Race in Video Games." In *Ecology of Games: Connecting Youth, Games, and Learning*, edited by Katie Salen, 141–66. Cambridge, MA: MIT Press.

Eze, Emmanuel Chukwudi, edited by 1997. *Race and the Enlightenment*. Malden, MA: Blackwell.

Farley, Reynolds, Sheldon Danziger, and Harry J. Holzer. 2000. *Detroit Divided*. New York: Russell Sage Foundation.

Feagin, Joe. 2001. *Racist America: Roots, Current Realities, and Future Reparations*. New York: Routledge.

Feagin, Joe, and S. Elias. 2013. "Rethinking Racial Formation Theory: A Systemic Racism Cri-tique." *Ethnic and Racial Studies* 36 (6): 931–60.

Feagin, Joe, and K. D. McKinney. 2003. *The Many Costs of Racism*. Lanham, MD: Rowman & Littlefield.

Ferguson, Ann Arnett. 2001. *Bad Boys: Public Schools in the Making of Black Masculinity*. Ann Arbor: University of Michigan Press.

Finkeldey, Jessica G., and Stephen Demuth. 2019. "Race/Ethnicity, Perceived Skin Color, and the Likelihood of Adult Arrest." *Race and Justice* 4: 567–591.

Foner, Nancy. 2008. "New York City: America's Classic Immigrant Gateway." In *Migrants to the Metropolis: The Rise of Immigrant Gateway Cities*, edited by M. Price and L. Benton-Short. Syracuse: Syracuse University Press, pp 51–67.

Fordham, Signithia, and John U. Ogbu. 1986. "Black Students' School Success: Coping with the 'Burden of Acting White.'" *Urban Review* 18 (3): 176–206.

Foster, Holly, and John Hagan. 2009. "The Mass Incarceration of Parents in America: Issues of Race/Ethnicity, Collateral Damage to Children, and Prisoner Reentry." *Annals of the American Academy of Political and Social Science* 623 (1): 179–94.

Fragomen, Austin T., and Steven Bell. 2007. *Immigration Fundamentals: A Guide to Law and Practice*. New York: Practicing Law Institute.

Frankenberg, R. 1997. *Displacing Whiteness: Essays in Social and Cultural Criticism*. Durham, NC: Duke University Press.

Frankenberg, R. 1993. *White Women, Race Matters: The Social Construction of Whiteness*. Minneapolis: University of Minnesota Press.

Franklin, John Hope. 1974. *From Slavery to Freedom*. New York: Alfred A. Knopf.

Free, M.D. 2017. "Wrongful Convictions: The African American Experience." In *Race, Ethnicity and Law* (Sociology of Crime, Law and Deviance, Vol. 22). Bingley, UK: Emerald Publishing Limited, pp. 7–25. https://doi.org/10.1108/S1521-613620170000022001

Friedman, S. R. 1969. "How Is Racism Maintained?" *Et Al.* (2): 18–21.

Frost, Peter. 2006. "Skin Color Preference in Sub-Saharan Africa." *Evo and Proud*, December 21. http://evoandproud.blogspot.com/2006/12/skin-color-preference-in-sub-saharan.html.

Fry, Richard, and Paul Taylor. 2013. *Hispanic High School Graduates Pass Whites in Rate of College Enrollment*. Washington, DC: Pew Research Center, Pew Hispanic Center. http://www.pewhispanic.org/files/2013/05/PHC_college_enrollment_2013-05.pdf.

Gabrielson, Ryan, Ryann Grochowski Jones, and Eric Sagara. 2014, December 24. "Deadly Force, in Black and White." *ProPublica*. https://www.propublica.org/article/deadly-force-in-black-and-white?utm_source=et&utm_medium=email&utm_campaign=dailynewsleter%2A%2A%23.

Gamoran, Adam. 2001. "American Schooling and Educational Inequality: A Forecast for the 21st Century." *Sociology of Education* 74: 135–53.

Garcia, Emma. "Schools Are Still Segregated, and Black Children Are Paying a Price." *Economic Policy Institute*, February 12, 2020. https://www.epi.org/publication/schools-are-still-segregated-and-black-children-are-paying-a-price/.

Garrison, V., and C. I. Weiss. 1979. "Dominican Family Networks and United States Immigration Policy: A Case Study." *International Migration Review* 13: 264–83.

Geller, Amanda, Irwin Garfinkel, Carey E. Cooper, and Ronald B. Mincy. 2009. "Parental Incarceration and Child Well-Being: Implications for Urban Families." *Social Science Quarterly* 90 (5): 1186–202.

Gelman, A., J. Fagan, and A. Kiss. 2007. "An Analysis of the New York City Police Department's 'Stop-And-Frisk' Policy in the Context of Claims of Racial Bias." *Journal of the American Statistical Association* 102: 479.

Georgetown University Center on Education and the Workforce. 2019. "The Unequal Race for Good Jobs: How Whites Made Outsized Gains in Education and Good Jobs Compared to Blacks and Latinos." https://cew.georgetown.edu/cew-reports/raceandgoodjobs/

Ghosh-Dastidar, Bonnie, et al. 2014. "Distance to Store, Food Prices, and Obesity in Urban Food Deserts." *American Journal of Preventive Medicine* 47 (5): 587–95.

Gilmore, Ruth. 2007. *Golden Gulag: Prisons, Surplus, Crisis and Opposition in Globalizing California*. Berkeley: University of California Press.

Glenn, E.N., ed. 2009. *Shades of Difference: Why Skin Color Matters*. Stanford University Press.

Glennie, A., and L. Chappell. 2010. "Jamaica: From Diverse Beginning to Diaspora in the Developed World. Migration Information Source." http://www.migrationinformationorg/Profiles/display.cfm.

Godfrey, P. C. 2008. "The 'Other White': Mexican Americans and the Impotency of Whiteness in the Segregation and Desegregation of Texan Public Schools." *Equity and Excellence in Education* 41 (2): 247–61.

Golash-Boza, Tanya. 2011. *Yo Soy Negro: Blackness in Peru.* Gainesville: University Press of Florida.

Golash-Boza, Tanya. 2012a. *Due Process Denied: Detentions and Deportations in the United States.* New York: Routledge.

Golash-Boza, Tanya. 2015. *Deported: Immigrant Policing, Disposable Labor and Global Capitalism.* New York: New York University Press.

Golash-Boza, Tanya. 2012b. *Immigration Nation: Raids, Detentions, and Deportations in the United States.* Boulder, CO: Paradigm.

Golland, D. 2011. *Constructing Affirmative Action: The Struggle for Equal Employment Opportunity.* Lexington: University Press of Kentucky.

Gonzales, J. L., Jr. 1986. "Asian Indian Immigration Patterns: The Origins of the Sikh Community in California." *International Migration Review* 20: 40–54.

Gotham, K. 2000. "Urban Space, Restrictive Covenants and the Origins of Racial Residential Segregation in A US City, 1900–50." *International Journal of Urban and Regional Research* 24 (3): 616–33.

Gottschalk, Marie. 2016. *Caught: The Prison State and the Lockdown of American Politics.* Princeton, NJ: Princeton University Press.

Gould, Elise, Jessica Schieder, and Kathleen Geier. 2016. "What Is the Gender Pay Gap and Is It Real?: The Complete Guide to How Women Are Paid Less Than Men and Why It Can't Be Explained Away." *Economic Policy Institute. Web:* May 29, 2017.

Gould, Stephen. J. 1996. *The Mismeasure of Man.* New York: W. W. Norton.

Gray, Herman. 1995. *Watching Race: Television and the Struggle for "Blackness."* Minneapolis: University of Minnesota Press.

Greenman, Emily, and Yue Xie. 2008. "Double Jeopardy? The Interaction of Gender and Race on Earnings in the United States." *Social Forces* 86 (3): 1217–44.

Grosfoguel, Ramón, and Eric Mielants. 2006. "The Long-Durée Entanglement Between Islamophobia and Racism in the Modern/Colonial Capitalist/Patriarchal World-System: An Introduction." *Human Architecture: Journal of the Sociology of Self-Knowledge* 5 (1): 2. http://scholarworks.umb.edu/humanarchitecture/vol5/iss1/2.

Gutiérrez, Elena R. 2008 *"Fertile Matters." The Politics of Mexican-Origin Women's Reproduction.* Austin, TX: University of Texas Press Google Scholar.

Hamamoto, Darrell. 1994. *Monitored Peril: Asian Americans and the Politics of TV Representation.* Minneapolis: University of Minnesota Press.

Hamilton, Norma, and Norma S. Chinchilla. 1991. Central American Migration: A Framework for Analysis. *Latin American Research Review* 26: 75–110.

Han, JooHee. 2020 "Does Skin Tone Matter? Immigrant Mobility in the US Labor Market." *Demography* 57: 1–22.

Hannah-Jones, Nikole. 2016. "What Abigail Fisher's Affirmative Action Case Was Really About." https://www.propublica.org/article/a-colorblind-constitution-what-abigail-fishers-affirmative-action-case-is-r

Harper, Kathryn, and Becky L. Choma. 2019. "Internalised White Ideal, Skin Tone Surveillance, and Hair Surveillance Predict Skin and Hair Dissatisfaction and Skin Bleaching among African American and Indian Women." *Sex Roles* 80 (11–12): 735, 44–49.

Harper, Shaun R., and Sylvia Hurtado. 2007. "Nine Themes in Campus Racial Climates and Implications for Institutional Transformation." *New Directions for Student Services* 2007 (120): 7–24.

Harris, David A. 1999. *Driving While Black: Racial Profiling on Our Nation's Highways.* American Civil Liberties Union Special Report. Washington, DC: American Civil Liberties Union. https://www.aclu.org/racial-justice/driving-while-black-racialprofiling-our-nations-highways.

Harris-Perry, Melissa V. 2011. *Sister Citizen: Shame, Stereotypes, and Black Women in America.* New Haven, CT: Yale University Press.

Harvey, David. 2005. *A Brief History of Neoliberalism.* New York: Oxford University Press.

Hattery, Angela, and Earl Smith. 2006. The Prison Industrial Complex. *Sociation Today* 4 (2). http://www.ncsociology.org/sociationtoday/v42/prison. htm.

Hernandez, Kelly Lytle. 2010. *Migra: A History of the U.S. Border Patrol.* Berkeley: University of California Press.

Hernández, Ramona. 2004. "On the Age Against the Poor: Dominican Migration to the United States." *Journal of Immigrant and Refugee Services* 2 (1–2): 87–107.

Herring, Cedric, and Loren Henderson. 2016. "Wealth Inequality in Black and White: Cultural and Structural Sources of the Racial Wealth Gap." *Race and Social Problems* 8 (1): 4–17.

Herrnstein, Richard J., and Charles Murray. 1994. "Bell Curve: Intelligence and Class Structure in American Life." Simon and Schuster.

Hersch, Joni. 2008. "Skin Color, Immigrant Wages, and Discrimination." In *Racism in the 21st Century: An Empirical Analysis of Sin Color*, edited by Ronald E. Hall, 77–92. New York: Springer.

Hochschild, J., and V. Weaver. 2007. "The Skin Color Paradox and the American Racial Order." *Social Forces* 86 (2): 643–70.

Hoefer, M., N. F. Rytina, and C. Campbell. 2007. *Estimates of the Unauthorized Immigrant Population Residing in the United States:* January 2006. Department of Homeland Security, Office of Immigration Statistics.

Hollingsworth, David W., Ashley B. Cole, Victoria M. O'Keefe, Raymond P. Tucker, Chandra R. Story, and LaRicka R. Wingate. 2017. "Experiencing Racial Microaggressions Influences Suicide Ideation Through Perceived Burdensomeness in African Americans." *Journal of counseling psychology* 64 (1): 104. http://dx.doi.org/10.1037/cou0000177.

hooks, bell. 2000. *Feminist Theory: From Margin to Center.* Pluto Press.

Hondagneu-Sotelo, Pierrette. 1994. *Gendered Transitions: Mexican Experiences of Immigration.* Berkeley: University of California Press.

Hondagneu-Sotelo, Pierrette. 1995. "Women and Children First: New Directions in Anti-Immigrant Politics." *Socialist Review* 251: 169–90.

Hordge-Freeman, Elizabeth. 2015. *The Color of Love: Racial Features, Stigma, and Socialization in Black Brazilian Families.* Austin: University of Texas Press.

Horowitz, Carol R., Kathryn A. Colson, Paul L. Hebert, and Kristie Lancaster. 2004. "Barriers to Buying Healthy Foods for People with Diabetes: Evidence of Environmental Disparities." *American Journal of Public Health* 94 (9): 1549–54.

Horowitz, Juliana Menasce, Ruth Igielnik, and Rakesh Kochhar. 2020. "Most Americans Say There Is Too Much Economic Inequality in the U.S., But Fewer Than Half Call It a Top Priority." Pew Research Center. https://www.pewresearch.org/social-trends/2020/01/09/most-americans-say-there-is-too-much-economic-inequality-in-the-u-s-but-fewer-than-half-call-it-a-top-priority/.

Huelsman, Mark, Tamara Draut, Tatjana Meschede, Lars Dietrich, Thomas Shapiro, and Laura Sullivan. 2015. "Less Debt, More Equity: Lowering Student Debt While Closing the Black–White Wealth Gap." *Demos.* http://www.demos.org/publication/less-debt-more-equity-lowering-student-debt-while-closing-black-white-wealth-gap.

Hunt, Darnell. M. 2005. "Black Content, White Control." In *Channeling Blackness: Studies on Television and Race in America*, edited by D. M. Hunt, 267–302. New York: Oxford University Press.

Hunter, Margaret. 2005. *Race, Gender, and the Politics of Skin Tone*. New York: Routledge.

Hunter, Margaret. 2007. "The Persistent Problem Of Colorism: Skin Tone, Status, And Inequality." *Sociology Compass* 1 (1): 237–54.

Internationalcomparison.org. 2014. International Comparisons. http://www.internationalcomparison.org/intl_comp_files/sheet006.htm.

International Comparisons.org. 2017. International Comparisons. http://international comparisons.org/overview/

International Labour Organization. 2016. *Key Indicators of the Labour Market, 9th edition*. Geneva: International Labour Office. https://www.ilo.org/wcmsp5/groups/public/---dgreports/---stat/documents/publication/wcms_498929.pdf

Islam, Namira http://www.muslimarc.org/afternotfairandlovely/

Jackson, Daren W. 2017, January 14. "Why 'black-ish' Is the Show We Need Right Now." *WaterCoolerConvos*. Web: May 25, 2017. http://watercoolerconvos.com/2016/02/25/why-blackish-is-the-show-we-need-right-now.

Jackson, J. S., K. M. Knight, and J. A. Rafferty. 2010. "Race and Unhealthy Behaviors: Chronic Stress, the HPA Axis, and Physical and Mental Health Disparities over the Life Course." *American Journal of Public Health* 100 (5): 933–39.

Jacobson, Matthew. 1998. *Whiteness of a Different Color*. Cambridge, MA: Harvard University Press.

Jacobson, Robin Dale. *The New Nativism: Proposition 187 and the Debate over Immigration*. U of Minnesota Press, 2008.

Jefferson, Thomas. 2004[1787]. *Notes on the State of Virginia*. Digireads.com Publishing.

Jhally, Sut, and Justin Lewis. 1992. *Enlightened Racism: The Cosby Show, Audiences and the Myth of the American Dream*. Boulder, CO: Westview.

Johnson, Kevin. 2004. *The "Huddled Masses" Myth: Immigration and Civil Rights*. Philadelphia: Temple University Press.

Johnston, David Cay. 2015. *Divided: The Perils of Our Growing Inequality*. New York: The New Press.

Jones, David S. 2003. "Virgin Soils Revisited." *The William and Mary Quarterly* 60 (4): 703–42.

Joppke, Christian. 1998. "Why Liberal States Accept Unwanted Immigration." *World Politics* 50: 266–93.

Jordan, Winthrop. 1968. *White over Black*. Chapel Hill: University of North Carolina Press.

Kao, Grace, and J. S. Thompson. 2003. "Racial and Ethnic Stratification in Educational Achievement and Attainment." *Annual Review of Sociology* 29 (1): 417–42.

Kasperkevic, Jana. 2015, October 1. "Jesse Williams: 'Celebrity Culture? I Am Not Going to Participate in That.'" *The Guardian*. Guardian News and Media. https://www.theguardian.com/culture/2015/oct/01/jesse-williams-greys-anatomy-celebrity-culture-civil-rights?CMP=share_btn_tw.

Keith, Verna M. 2009. "A Colorstruck World: Skin Tone, Achievement, and Self-Esteem among African American Women." In *Shades of Difference: Why Skin Color Matters*, edited by E.N. Glenn. Stanford University Press.

Keith, Verna M., and Cedric Herring. 1991. "Skin Tone and Stratification in the Black Community." *American Journal of Sociology* 97 (3): 760–778.

Kelly, Gail P. 1986. "Coping with America: Refugees from Vietnam, Cambodia, and Laos in the 1970s and 1980s." *Annals of the American Academy of Political and Social Science* 487: 138–49.

Kelly, Sean. 2009. "The Black–White Gap in Mathematics Course Taking." *Sociology of Education* 82 (1): 47–69.

Kena, Grace, William Hussar, Joel McFarland, Cristobal de Brey, Lauren Musu-Gillette, Xiaolei Wang, Jijun Zhang, et al. 2016. "The Condition of Education 2016. NCES 2016-144." *National Center for Education Statistics*. https://nces.ed.gov/pubs2016/2016144.pdf

Kennedy, Merrit. 2016. *Lead-Laced Water in Flint: A Step-By-Step Look At the Makings of A Crisis.* http://www.npr.org/sections/thetwo-way/2016/04/20/465545378/lead-laced-water-in-flint-a-step-by-step-look-at-the-makings-of-a-crisis.

Khan, Aisha. 2009. "Caucasian, Coolie, Black, or White? Color and Race in the Indo-Caribbean Diaspora." In *Shades of Difference: Why Skin Color Matters*, edited by E.N. Glenn, 95–113. Palo Alto, CA: Stanford University Press.

Kijakazi, Kilolo, Rachel Marie Brooks Atkins Mark Paul, Anne E. Price, Darrick Hamilton, and William A. Darity Jr. 2016. "The Color of Wealth in the Nation's Capital." https://www.urban.org/sites/default/files/publication/85341/2000986-2-the-color-of-wealth-in-the-nations-capital_1.pdf.

Kim, Chang Hwan, and Arthur Sakamoto. 2010. "Have Asian American Men Achieved Labor Market Parity with White Men?" *American Sociological Review* 75 (6): 934–57.

Kim, Chang Hwan, and Arthur Sakamoto. 2014. "The Earnings of Less Educated Asian American Men: Educational Selectivity and the Model Minority Image." *Social Problems* 61 (2): 283–304.

King, C. Richard, and Charles Fruehling Springwood. 2001. *Beyond the Cheers: Race as Spectacle in College Sport.* Albany, NY: SUNY Press.

King, Marsha. 2008, February 3. "Tribes Confront Painful Legacy of Indian Boarding Schools." *Seattle Times.* http://courses.washington.edu/divrspol/classreadings/Tribespainfullegacy.pdf.

King, Ryan, Marc Mauer, and Malcolm C. Young. 2005. *Incarceration and Crime: A Complex Relationship.* Sentencing Project. http://www.sentencingproject.org/Admin/Documents/publications/inc_iandc_complex.pdf.

Kizer, Jessica M. 2017. "Arrested by Skin Color: Evidence from Siblings and a Nationally Representative Sample." *Socius* 3: 2378023117737922.

Kochanek, Kenneth D., Sherry L. Murphy, Jiaquan Xu, and Elizabeth Arias. 2019. "Deaths: Final Data For 2017." *National Vital Statistics Reports* 68(9): June 24. https://www.cdc.gov/nchs/data/nvsr68/nvsr68_09-508.pdf.

Kochhar, Rakesh and Richard Fry. 2014. *Wealth Inequality Has Widened along Racial, Ethnic Lines Since End of Great Recession.* Washington, DC: Pew Research Center. http://www.pewresearch.org/fact-tank/2014/12/12/racial-wealth-gaps-great-recession.

Kochhar, Rakesh, Richard Fry, and Paul Taylor. 2011. *Wealth Gaps Rise to Record Highs Between Whites, Blacks and Hispanics.* Washington, DC: Pew Research Center.

Kodras, J. E. 1997. "The Changing Map of American Poverty in An Era of Economic Restructuring and Political Realignment." *Economic Geography* 72: 67–93

Kopacz, Maria, and Bessie Lee Lawton. 2011a. "Rating the YouTube Indian: Viewer Ratings of Native American Portrayals on a Viral Video Site." *American Indian Quarterly* 35 (2): 241–57.

Kopacz, Maria, and Bessie Lee Lawton. 2011b. "The YouTube Indian: Portrayals of Native Americans on a Viral Video Site." *New Media and Society* 13 (2): 330–49.

Kovera, Margaret Bull. 2019. "Racial Disparities in the Criminal Justice System: Prevalence, Causes, and a Search for Solutions." *Journal of Social Issues* 75 (4): 1139–64.

Kpanake, L., M.T. Munoz Sastre, and E. Mullet. 2009. "Skin Bleaching among Togolese: A Preliminary Inventory of Motives." *Journal of Black Psychology* 36 (3): 350–68.

Krivo, L., and R. Kaufman. 2004. "Housing and Wealth Inequality: Racial-Ethnic Differences in Home Equity in the United States." *Demography* 41 (3): 585–605.

Krogstad, Jens Manuel. 2016. http://www.pewresearch.org/fact-tank/2016/07/28/5-facts-about-latinos-and-education.

Krysan, M., and R. Farley. 2002. "The Residential Preferences of Blacks: Do They Explain Persistent Segregation?" *Social Forces* 80 (3): 937–80.

Kuhn, Moritz, Moritz Schularick, and Ulrike Isabel Steins. 2020. "Income and Wealth Inequality in America, 1949–2016." *Journal of Political Economy.* https://www.journals.uchicago.edu/doi/10.1086/708815.

Ladipo, David. 2001. "America's Prison Industry." *New Left Review* 7 (x): 109.

Lambert, Bruce. 1997. "At 50, Levittown Contends with Its Legacy of Bias." *New York Times*, December 28. http://www.nytimes.com/197/12/28/nyregion/at-50-levittown-contends-with-its-legacy-of-bias.html.

Lamberth, J. 1994. *Revised Statistical Analysis of the Incidence of Police Stops and Arrests of Black Drivers: Travelers on the New Jersey Turnpike Between Exits or Interchanges 1 and 3 from the Years 1988 Through 1991.* http://www.lamberthconsulting.com/downloads/new_jersey_study_report.pdf.

Lamont, M., and A. Lareau. 1988. "Cultural Capital: Allusions, Gaps and Glissandos in Recent Theoretical Developments." *Sociological Theory* 6 (2): 153–68.

Lara, M., C. Gamboa, M. I. Kahramanian, L. S. Morales, and D. E. H. Bautista. 2005. "Acculturation and Latino Health in the United States: A Review of the Literature and Its Sociopolitical Context." *Annual Review of Public Health* 26: 367–97.

Lauderdale, D. S. 2006. "Birth Outcomes for Arabic-Named Women in California Before and After September 11." *Demography* 43 (1): 185–201.

LaVeist, Thomas A., and John M. Wallace. 2000. "Health Risk and Inequitable Distribution of Liquor Stores in African American Neighborhoods." *Social Science and Medicine* 51 (4): 613–17.

Lee, Erika. 2002. "The Chinese Exclusion Example: Race, Immigration, and American Gatekeeping, 1882–1924." *Journal of American Ethnic History* 21 (3): 36–62.

Lee, Jennifer, and Min Zhou. 2015. *The Asian American Achievement Paradox.* Russell Sage Foundation.

Lee, Trymaine 2019. "A vast wealth gap, driven by segregation, redlining, evictions and exclusion, separates black and white America." *New York Times.* https://www.nytimes.com/interactive/2019/08/14/magazine/racial-wealth-gap.html

Leonard, David. 2014. "Dilemmas and Contradictions: Black Female Athletes." In *Out of Bounds: Racism and the Black Athlete*, edited by Lori Latrice Martin, 209–230. Santa Barbara, CA: Praeger.

Levchak C. C. 2018. "Microaggressions, Macroaggressions, and Modern Racism." In *Microaggressions and Modern Racism.* Palgrave Macmillan, Cham. https://doi.org/10.1007/978-3-319-70332-9_2

Lewis, Amanda E. 2004. "What Group?: Studying Whites and Whiteness in the Era of Color-Blindness." *Sociological Theory* 22 (4): 623–46.

Lewis, K. M., N. Robkin, K. Gaska, and L. C. Njoki. 2011. Investigating Motivations for Women's Skin Bleaching in Tanzania. *Psychology of Women Quarterly* 35 (1): 29–37.

Lichter, D., D. Parisi, S. Grice, and M. Taquino. 2007. "National Estimates of Racial Segregation in Rural and Small-Town America." *Demography* 44 (3): 563–81.

Liebowitz, David D. 2018. "Ending to What End? The Impact of the Termination of Court-Desegregation Orders on Residential Segregation and School Dropout Rates." *Educational Evaluation and Policy Analysis* 40 (1): 103–28.

Lindsay, Matthew. 1998. "Reproducing A Fit Citizenry: Dependency, Eugenics, and the Law of Marriage in the United States, 1860–1920." *Law and Social Inquiry* 23 (3): 541–85.

Lippard, Cameron D. 2011. "Racist Nativism in the 21st Century." *Sociology Compass* 5 (7): 591–606.

Lipsitz, George. 2006. *The Possessive Investment in Whiteness: How White People Profit from Identity Politics*. Philadelphia: Temple University Press.

Littlefield, Daniel, and James Parins, eds. 2011. *Encyclopedia of American Indian Removal*. Santa Barbara, CA: Greenwood.

Liu, J. M., P. M. Ong, and C. Rosenstein. 1991. "Dual Chain Migration: Post-1965 Filipino Immigration to the United States." *International Migration Review* 25 (3): 487–513.

Logan, J. R. 2011. *Separate and Unequal: The Neighborhood Gap for Blacks, Hispanics and Asians in Metropolitan America*. Project US2010 Report. http://www.hispanicallyspeakingnews.com/uploads/documents/normal-docs/BrownhousingStudy.pdf.

Logan, J. R. 2013. "The Persistence of Segregation in the 21st Century Metropolis." *City and Community* 12 (2): 160–68.

Logan, J., and B. Stults. 2011. *The Persistence of Segregation in the Metropolis: New Findings From the 2010 Census*. Project US2010. http://www.s4.brown.edu/us2010/Data/Report/report2.pdf.

Long, Heather, and Andrew Van Dam. 2020. "The Racial Wealth Gap in 10 Charts." *The Washington Post*. June 4.

Lopez, Gustavo, Neil G. Ruiz, and Eileen Patten. 2017, September 8. *Key Facts About Asian Americans, A Diverse and Growing Population*. Pew Research Center. http://www.pewresearch.org/fact-tank/2017/09/08/key-facts-about-asian-americans.

Lopez, Mark Hugo and Susan Minushkin. 2008 *National Survey of Latinos: Hispanics See Their Situation in the U.S. Deteriorating; Oppose Key Immigration Enforcement Measures*. Washington, DC: Pew Hispanic Center.

Louie, Patricia, and Blair Wheaton. 2019. "The Black–White Paradox Revisited: Understanding the Role of Counterbalancing Mechanisms During Adolescence." *Journal of Health and Social Behavior* 60 (2): 169–87.

Lovasi, Gina, Malo A. Hutson, Monica Guerra, and Kathryn M. Neckerman. 2009. "Built Environments and Obesity in Disadvantaged Populations." *Epidemiologic Reviews* 31: 7–20.

Lundström, Catrin. 2014. *White Migrations: Gender, Whiteness and Privilege in Transnational Migration*. New York: Springer.

Lynch, Michael. 1999. "Beating a Dead Horse: Is There Any Basic Empirical Evidence for the Deterrent Effect of Imprisonment?" *Crime, Law and Social Change* 31: 347–362.

Malaria Atlas Project. 2013. https://map.ox.ac.uk/

Malpede, C. Z., L. E. Greene, S. L. Fitzpatrick, W. K. Jefferson, R. M. Shewchuk, M. L. Baskin, and J. D. Ard. 2007. "Racial Influences Associated with Weight-Related Beliefs in African American and Caucasian Women." *Ethnicity and Disease* 17 (1): 1.

Marr, Carolyn. n.d. *Assimilation Through Education: Indian Boarding Schools in the Pacific Northwest*. University of Washington Digital Collections. http://content.lib.washingtonedu/aipnw/marr.html.

Martinez-Cola, Marisela. 2019. "Visibly Invisible: Tribalcrit and Native American Segregated Schooling." *Sociology of Race and Ethnicity* 6 (4): 468–482. doi:10.1177/2332649219884087

Massey, Douglas, and Nancy Denton. 1993. *American Apartheid: Segregation and the Making of the Underclass*. Cambridge, MA: Harvard University Press.

Massey, D., J. Durand, and N. J. Malone. 2002. *Beyond Smoke and Mirrors: Mexican Immigration in an Era of Economic Integration*. New York: Russell Sage Foundation.

Master, Maureen. 2003. *Due Process for All: Redressing Inequities in the Criminal Provisions of the 1996 Immigration Laws*. United States Conference for Catholic Bishops. http://www.usccb.org/mrs/dueprocessforall.shtml.

Matlon, Jordanna. "Racial Capitalism and the Crisis of Black Masculinity." *American Sociological Review* 81 (5): 1014–38.

Mauer, Marc. 1999. *The Crisis of the Young African American Male and the Criminal Justice System*. Sentencing Project. http://www.sentencingproject.org/doc/publications/rd_crisisoftheyoung.pdf.

Mauer, Marc. 2007. "Racial Impact Statements as a Means of Reducing Unwarranted Sentencing Disparities." *Ohio State Journal of Criminal Law* 5 (19): 19–46. http://www.sentencingproject.org/doc/publications/rd_racialimpactstatements.pdf.

Mauer, Marc. 2009. *Testimony of Marc Mauer, Executive Director, the Sentencing Project*. Sentencing Project. http://www.sentencingproject.org/doc/dp_crack_testimony.pdf.

Mauer, Marc, and R. S. King. 2007. *Uneven Justice: State Rates of Incarceration by Race and Ethnicity*. Washington, DC: Sentencing Project.

McDougall, Andrew. 2013, June 3. *Skin Lightening Trend in Asia Boosts Global Market*. CosmeticsDesign-Asia.com. http://www.cosmeticsdesign-asia.com/Market-Trends/Skin-lightening-trend-in-Asia-boosts-global-market.

Mele, Christopher. 2016, November 29. "Veterans to Serve As 'Human Shields' for Dakota Pipeline Protesters." *New York Times*. http://www.nytimes.com/2016/11/29/us/veterans-to-serve-as-human-shields-for-pipeline-protesters.html.

Mellon, James, edited by 2002. *Bullwhip Days: The Slaves Remember: An Oral History*. New York: Grove.

Mendelberg, Tali. 1997. "Executing Hortons: Racial Crime in the 1988 Presidential Campaign." *Public Opinion Quarterly* 61: 134–57.

Menjívar, Cecilia. 2000. *Fragmented Ties: Salvadoran Immigrant Networks in America*. Berkeley: University of California Press.

Michigan Population Studies Center. n.d. *New Racial Segregation Measures for Large Metropolitan Areas: Analysis of the 1990–2010 Decennial Censuses. Michigan Population Studies Center—Institute for Social Research*. http://www.psc.isr.umich.edu/dis/census/segregation2010.html.

Miele, Frank, and Vincent Sarich. 2003. *Race: The Reality of Human Differences*. Boulder, CO: Westview Press.

Milkman, Ruth. 1997. *Farewell to the Factory: Auto Workers in the Late Twentieth Century*. Berkeley: University of California Press.

Min, P. G. 1990. "Problems of Korean Immigrant Entrepreneurs." *International Migration Review* 24: 436–55.

Mohai, Paul, and Robin Saha. 2015. "Which Came First, People or Pollution? Assessing the Disparate Siting and Post-Siting Demographic Change Hypotheses of Environmental Injustice." *Environmental Research Letters* 10 (11): 115008.

Monbiot, George. 2011, November 7. *The Self-Attribution Fallacy. George Monbio*. http://www.monbiot.com/2011/11/07/the-self-attribution-fallacy.

Monk Jr., Ellis P. 2014. "Skin Tone Stratification among Black Americans, 2001–2003." *Social Forces* 92 (4): 1313–37.

Monk-Turner, Elizabeth, Mary Heiserman, Crystle Johnson, Vanity Cotton, and Manny Jackson. 2010. "The Portrayal of Racial Minorities on Prime-Time Television: A Replication of the Mastro and Greenberg Study a Decade Later." *Studies in Popular Culture* 32 (2): 101–14.

Montagu, Ashley. 1997. *Man's Most Dangerous Myth: The Fallacy of Race*, 6th ed. Walnut Creek, CA: AltaMira.

Morawetz, Nancy. 2000. "Understanding the Impact of the 1996 Deportation Laws and the Limited Scope of Proposed Reforms." *Harvard Law Review* 113 (8): 1936–62.

Morgan, Edmund. 1975. *American Slavery, American Freedom: The Ordeal of Colonial Virginia*. New York: W. W. Norton.

Moss, K. 2003. *The Color of Class: Poor Whites and the Paradox of Privilege.* Philadelphia: University of Pennsylvania Press.

Moynihan, Daniel Patrick. 1965. *The Negro Family: The Case for National Action.* https://liberalarts.utexas.edu/coretexts/_files/resources/texts/1965%20Moynihan%20Report.pdf

Muller, Chandra, Catherine Riegle-Crumb, Kathryn S. Schiller, Lindsey Wilkinson, and Kenneth A. Frank. 2010. "Race and Academic Achievement in Racially Diverse High Schools: Opportunity and Stratification." *Teachers College record (1970)* 112 (4): 1038.

Murguia, Edward, and Edward Telles. 1996. "Phenotype and Schooling among Mexican Americans." *Sociology of Education* 69 (October): 276–89.

Murphy, Katy. 2013. "Affirmative Action Ban At UC, 15 Years Later." *San Jose Mercury News*, June 24. http://www.mercurynews.com/ci_23516740/affirmative-action-ban-at-uc-15-years-later.

Mustard, David B. 2001. "Racial, Ethnic, and Gender Disparities in Sentencing: Evidence From the US Federal Courts." *Journal of Law and Economics* 44 (1): 285–314.

Nadal, Kevin L., Yinglee Wong, Katie Griffin, Julie Sriken, Vivian Vargas, Michelle Wideman, and Ajayi Kolawole. 2011. "Microaggressions and the Multiracial Experience." *International Journal of Humanities and Social Science* 1 (7): 36–44. http://www.ijhssnet.com/journals/Vol._1_No._7_[Special_Issue_June_2011]/6.pdf.

Nathan, Debbie. 2016, April 21. "What Happened to Sandra Bland?" *The Nation.* https://www.thenation.com/article/what-happened-to-sandra-bland.

Negrón-Muntaner, Frances. 2014. *The Latino Media Gap.* Center for the Study of Ethnicity and Race at Columbia University. Retrieved from: http://www.columbia.edu/cu/cser/downloads/AdvancedExectutiveSummary.pdf.

New York City Bar. 2013. *Report On the NYPD's Stop and Frisk Policy.* http://www2.nycbar.org/pdf/report/uploads/20072495-StopFriskReport.pdf.

Ngai, Mae. 2004. *Impossible Subjects: Illegal Aliens and the Making of Modern America.* Princeton, NJ: Princeton University Press.

Ngai, Mae M. 2010. *The Lucky Ones: One Family and the Extraordinary Invention of Chinese America.* Princeton, NJ: Princeton University Press.

Ngo, B., and S. J. Lee. 2007. "Complicating the Image of Model Minority Success: A Review of Southeast Asian American Education." *Review of Educational Research* 77 (4): 415–53.

Noel, J. 2002. "Education Toward Cultural Shame: A Century of Native American Education." *Educational Foundations* 16 (1): 19–32.

Norton, Michael I., and Dan Ariely. 2011. "Building a Better America—One Wealth Quintile at a Time." *Perspectives on Psychological Science* 6 (1): 9–12.

Novak N. L., A. T. Geronimus, and A. M. Martinez-Cardoso. 2017. "Change in Birth Outcomes among Infants Born to Latina Mothers after a Major Immigration Raid." *International Journal of Epidemiology.* 46: 839–49.

Nowrasteh, Alex. 2017, January 25. *Little National Security Benefit to Trump's Executive Order on Immigration.* Cato Institute. https://www.cato.org/blog/little-national-security-benefit-trumps-executive-order-immigration.

Nwosu, Chiamaka, and Jeanne Batalova. 2014. *Immigrants from the Dominican Republic in the United States.* Migration Policy Institute.

OECD. 2020. *Income Inequality (Indicator).* https://doi.org/10.1787/459aa7f1-en.

Oliver, Melvin, and Thomas Shapiro. 2006. *Black Wealth/White Wealth: A New Perspective on Racial Inequality.* New York: Routledge.

Omi, Michael, and Howard Winant. 1994. *Racial Formation in the United States from the 1960s to the 1990s*, 2nd ed. New York: Routledge.

Ong, A. D., A. L. Burrow, T. E. Fuller-Rowell, N. M. Ja, and D. W. Sue. 2013. "Racial Microaggressions and Daily Well-Being among Asian Americans." *Journal of Counseling Psychology* 60 (2): 188.

Orfield, Gary. 2009. *Reviving the Goal of an Integrated Society: A 21st Century Challenge.* Los Angeles: Civil Rights Project/Proyecto Dereches Civile at UCLA. http://civilrightsproject.ucla

Orfield, Gary, Jongyeon Ee, Erica Frankenberg, and Genevieve Siegel-Hawley. 2016. "'Brown' At 62: School Segregation by Race, Poverty and State." *Civil Rights Project-Proyecto Derechos Civiles.* https://www.civilrightsproject.ucla.edu/research/k-12-education/integration-and-diversity/brown-at-62-school-segregation-by-race-poverty-and-state

Orfield, Gary, and Erica Frankenberg. 2014. "Increasingly Segregated and Unequal Schools as Courts Reverse Policy." *Educational Administration Quarterly* 50 (5): 718–34.

Orfield, Gary, and C. Lee. 2004. *Brown at 50: King's Dream or Plessy's Nightmare?* Cambridge, MA: Harvard University Civil Rights Project. http://performanceassessment.whatkidscando.org/featurestories/previous_years/color_of_learning/pdf/Brownat50HarvardCivilRghts.pdf.

Oza-Frank, R., R. Stephenson, and K. M. Venkat Narayan. 2011. "Diabetes Prevalence by Length of Residence among US Immigrants." *Journal of Immigrant Minority Health* 13 (1). http://dx.doi.org/10.1007/s10903-009-9283-2.

Pager, D. 2007. *Marked: Race, Crime, and Finding Work in an Era of Mass Incarceration.* Chicago: University of Chicago Press.

Pager, D., and H. Shepherd. 2008. "The Sociology of Discrimination: Racial Discrimination in Employment, Housing, Credit, and Consumer Markets." *Annual Review of Sociology* 34: 181–209.

Pager, D., B. Western, and B. Bonikowski. 2009. "Discrimination in A Low-Wage Labor Market: A Field Experiment." *American Sociological Review* 74 (5): 777–99.

Paradies, Yin, Jehonathan Ben, Nida Denson, Amanuel Elias, Naomi Priest, Alex Pieterse, Arpana Gupta, Margaret Kelaher, and Gilbert Gee. 2015. "Racism as a Determinant of Health: A Systematic Review and Meta-Analysis." *PLoS ONE* 10 (9): e0138511. http://.dx.doi:.org/10.1371/journal.pone.0138511.

Parameswaran, Radhika, and Kavitha Cardoza. 2009. "Melanin On the Margins: Advertising and the Cultural Politics of Fair/Light/White Beauty in India." *Journalism and Communication Monographs* 11 (3): 213–74.

Parenti, Christian. 1999. *Lockdown America: Police and Prisons in the Age of Crisis.* New York: Verso.

Parvini, Sarah. 2017. "A Hub for Iraqi Refugees, San Diego Is Making Way for New Faces—This Time from Syria." *Los Angeles Times,* February 18. https://www.latimes.com/local/california/la-me-syrian-refugees-el-cajon-20170213-story.html, accessed: May 29, 2017.

Paschall, K. W., Gershoff, E. T., and Kuhfeld, M. 2018. "A Two-Decade Examination of Historical Race/Ethnicity Disparities in Academic Achievement by Poverty Status." *Journal of Youth and Adolescence,* 47 (6), 1164–77. Doi: http://dx.doi.org/10.1007/s10964-017-0800-7.

Passel, Jeffrey S., and D'Vera Cohn. 2019. "Mexicans Decline to Less Than Half the U.S. Unauthorized Immigrant Population for the First Time." *Pew Research Center.* https://www.pewresearch.org/fact-tank/2019/06/12/us-unauthorized-immigrant-population-2017/.

Pellow, David Naguib. 2007. *Resisting Global Toxins: Transnational Movements for Environmental Justice.* Cambridge, MA: MIT Press.

Perez, Louis. 2003. *Cuba and the United States: Ties of Singular Intimacy,* 3rd ed. Athens: University of Georgia Press.

Pérez, Raúl, and Geoff Ward. 2019. "From Insult to Estrangement and Injury: The Violence of Racist Police Jokes." *American behavioral scientist* 63 (13): 1810–29.

Pettit, Becky, and S. Ewert. 2009. "Employment Gains and Wage Declines: The Erosion of Black Women's Relative Wages Since 1980." *Demography* 46 (3): 469–92.

Pettit, Becky, and Bryan L. Sykes. 2015. "Civil Rights Legislation and Legalized Exclusion: Mass Incarceration and the Masking of Inequality." *Sociological Forum* 30 (S1).

Pew Hispanic Center. 2006. *Cubans in the United States.* http://ewhispanic.org/files/factsheets/23.pdf.

Pew Research Center. 2014. *Wealth Inequality Has Widened along Racial, Ethnic Lines Since End of Great Recession.* http://www.pewresearch.org/fact-tank/2014/12/12/racial-wealth-gaps-great-recession/.

Piccorossi, Michael. 2012, June 18. *The Asian Americans. Pew Research Center's Social and Demographic Trends Project.* N.P. Web: May 29, 2017.

Pierre, Jemima. 2008. "'I Like Your Colour!': Skin Bleaching and Geographies of Race in Urban Ghana." *Feminist Review* 90 (1): 9–29.

Piketty, Thomas, Emmanuel Saez, and Gabriel Zucman. 2016. "Distributional National Accounts: Methods and Estimates for the United States." No. w22945. National Bureau of Economic Research.

Pomerantz, Dorothy. 2011. "The Highest-Paid Men in Entertainment." *Forbes*, September 12. http://www.forbes.com/sites/dorothypomerantz/2011/09/12/the-highest-paid-men-in-entertainment.

Portes, Alejandro, and Ramón Grosfoguel. 1994. "Caribbean Diasporas: Migration and Ethnic Communities." *Annals of the American Academy of Political and Social Science* 533 (1): 48–69.

Portes, Alejandro, and Jessica Yiu. 2013. "Entrepreneurship, Transnationalism, and Development." *Migration Studies* 1 (1): 75–95

powell, john. 2008. "Structural Racism: Building Upon the Insights of John Calmore." *North Carolina Law Review* 86: 791–816.

Priest, N., N. Slopen, S. Woolford, J.T. Philip, D.Singer, A.D. Kauffman, K.Mosely, M. Davis, Y.Ransome, and D. Williams. 2018. "Stereotyping Across Intersections of Race and Age: Racial Stereotyping among White Adults Working with Children." *PLoS ONE* 13 (9). https://doi.org/10.1371/journal.pone.0201696

Provine, Doris Marie, and Roxanne Lynn Doty. 2011. "The Criminalization of Immigrants as a Racial Project." *Journal of Contemporary Criminal Justice* 27 (3): 261–77.

Puumala, S. E., K. M. Burgess, A. B. Kharbanda, H. G. Zook, D. M. Castille, W. J. Pickner, and N. R. Payne. 2016. "The Role of Bias by Emergency Department Providers in Care for American Indian Children." *Medical Care* 54 (6): 562–69.

Quan, A. 2005. "Through the Looking Glass: U.S. Aid to El Salvador and the Politics of National Identity." *American Ethnologist* 32 (2): 276–93.

Quijano, A. 2000. "Coloniality of Power and Eurocentrism in Latin America." *International Sociology* 15 (2): 215–32.

Quillian, Lincoln, Devah Pager, Ole Hexel, and Arnfinn H. Midtbøen. 2017. "Meta-Analysis of Field Experiments Shows No Change in Racial Discrimination in Hiring over Time." *Proceedings of the National Academy of Sciences* 114, no. 41: 10870–75.

Rajgopal, S. S. 2010. "The Daughter of Fu Manchu": The Pedagogy of Deconstructing the Representation of Asian Women in Film and Fiction. *Meridians* 10 (2): 141–62.

Ratnasiri, A. W. G., Parry, S.S., Arief, V. N. et al. 2018. "Recent Trends, Risk Factors, and Disparities in Low Birth Weight in California, 2005–2014: A Retrospective Study." *Maternal Health, Neonatology and Perinatology* 4 (1): 1–13.

Reeves, Arin N. 2014. *Written in Black and White: Exploring Confirmation Bias in Racialized Perceptions of Writing Skills. Yellow Paper Series.* Chicago: Nextions LLC. http://www.nextions.com/wp-content/files_mf/13972237592014040114WritteninBlackandWhiteYPS.pdf.

Reidy, K.J., Hjorten, R., and Parekh, R.S. 2018. "Genetic Risk of APOL1 and Kidney Disease in Children and Young Adults of African Ancestry." *Current Opinion in Pediatrics* 30 (2): 252–259.

Reimers, D. M. 1981. "Post–World War II Immigration to the United States: America's Latest Newcomers." *Annals of the American Academy of Political and Social Science* 454 (1): 1–12.

Reisinger, D. 2011. *91 Percent of Kids Are Gamers*, Research Says. https://www.cnet.com/news/91-percent-of-kids-are-gamers-research-says.

Restall, M. 2000. "Black Conquistadors: Armed Africans in Early Spanish America." *Americas* 57 (2): 171–205.

Reverby, S.M. 2009. *Examining Tuskegee: The Infamous Syphilis Study and Its Legacy*. Chapel Hill: University of North Carolina Press.

Richie, B. 2005. "Queering Anti-Prison Work: African American Lesbians in the Juvenile Justice System." In *Global Lockdown: Race Gender and the Prison-Industrial Complex*, edited by Julia Sudbury, 73–85. New York: Routledge.

Riggs, M. 2014, March 27. *Florida Senate Takes a Modest Step Toward Drug Sentencing Reform*. FAMM. http://famm.org/florida-senate-takes-a-modest-step-toward-drug-sentencing-reform.

Roberts, Dorothy. 2012. *Fatal Invention: How Science, Politics, and Big Business Re-Create Race in the Twenty-First Century*. New York: New Press.

Robertson, Dwanna L. 2015. "Invisibility in the Color-Blind Era: Examining Legitimized Racism Against Indigenous Peoples." *American Indian Quarterly* 39 (2): 113–53.

Rodríguez, Clara. 1997. *Latin Looks: Images of Latinas and Latinos in the U.S. Media*. Boulder, CO: Westview.

Roediger, D. R. 1999. *The Wages of Whiteness: Race and the Making of the American Working Class*. New York: Verso.

Rondilla, Joanne L. 2009. "Filipinos and the Color Complex: Ideal Asian Beauty." In *Shades of Difference: Why Skin Color Matters*, edited by Evelyn Nakano Glenn, 63–80. Palo Alto, CA: Stanford University Press.

Rondilla, Joanne L., and Paul Spickard. 2007. *Is Lighter Better? Skin-Tone Discrimination among Asian Americans*. Lanham, MD: Rowman & Littlefield.

Roscigno, Vincent, and James Ainsworth-Darnell. 1999. "Race, Cultural Capital, and Educational Resources: Persistent Inequalities and Achievement Returns." *Sociology of Education* 72 (3): 158–78.

Rosenblum, Alexis, William Darity Jr., Angel L. Harris, and Tod G. Hamilton. 2016. "Looking Through the Shades: The Effect of Skin Color on Earnings by Region of Birth and Race for Immigrants to the United States." *Sociology of Race and Ethnicity* 2 (1): 87–105.

Rothstein, Richard. 2017. *The Color of Law: A Forgotten History of How Our Government Segregated America*. New York: W. W. Norton.

Rothwell, Jonathan. 2016, July 28. *Drug Offenders in American Prisons: The Critical Distinction between Stock and Flow*. Brookings Institution. https://www.brookings.edu/blog/social-mobility-memos/2015/11/25/drug-offenders-in-american-prisons-the-critical-distinction-between-stock-and-flow.

Rugh, J., and D. Massey. 2010. "Racial Segregation and the American Foreclosure Crisis." *American Sociological Review* 75 (5): 629–51.

Ruiz, V. 2001. "South By Southwest: Mexican Americans and Segregated Schooling." *OAH Magazine of History* 15 (2): 23–27.

Rural Community Assistance Partnership. n.d. *Still Living Without the Basics in the 21st Century: Analyzing the Availability of Water and Sanitation Services in the United States*. http://win-water.org/reports/RCAP_full_final.pdf.

Rytina, N. 2011. *Estimates of the Legal Permanent Resident Population in 2010*. Washington, DC: Office of Immigration Statistics, Policy Directorate, U.S. Department of Homeland Security.

Sagoe, Dominic, Ståle Pallesen, Ncoza C. Dlova, Margaret Lartey, Khaled Ezzedine, and Ophelia Dadzie. 2019. "The Global Prevalence and Correlates of Skin Bleaching: A Meta-Analysis and Meta-Regression Analysis." *International journal of dermatology* 58, no. 1: 24–44.

Salaita, Steven George. 2006. "Beyond Orientalism and Islamophobia: 9/11, Anti-Arab Racism, and the Mythos of National Pride." *CR: The New Centennial Review* 6 (2): 245–66.

Saleem, Muniba. 2008. *Effects of Stereotypic Video Game Portrayals on Implicit and Explicit Attitudes.* MS thesis, Iowa State University.

Sammon, Alexander. 2016, September 9. "A History of Native Americans Protesting the Dakota Access Pipeline." *Mother Jones.* http://www.motherjones.com/environment/2016/09/dakota-access-pipeline-protest-timeline-sioux-standing-rock-jill-stein/

Sanburn, Josh. 2017, May 27. "Flint Water Crisis: Where It Stands a Year Later." *Time.* https://time.com/4634937/flint-water-crisis-criminal-charges-bottled-water/, accessed May 29, 2017.

Sanchez, George. 1997. "Face the Nation: Race, Immigration, and the Rise of Nativism in Late Twentieth Century America." *International Migration Review* 31 (4): 1009–30.

Saraswati, Ayu. 2010. "*Cosmopolitan* Whiteness: The Effects and Affects of Skin-Whitening Advertisements in a Transnational Women's Magazine in Indonesia." *Meridians* 10 (2): 15–41.

Saraswati, Ayu. 2012. "'Malu': Coloring Shame and Shaming the Color of Beauty in Transnational Indonesia." *Feminist Studies* 38 (1): 113–40.

Sassen, Saskia. 1989. "America's 'Immigration Problem.'" *World Policy Journal* 6 (4): 811–832.

Sawyer, Wendy, and Peter Wagner. 2020, March 24. *Mass Incarceration: The Whole Pie 2020.* Prison Policy Initiative. https://www.prisonpolicy.org/reports/pie2020.html.

Schlosser, Eric. 1998, December. "The Prison-Industrial Complex." *Atlantic Monthly.* https://www.theatlantic.com/magazine/archive/1998/12/the-prison-industrial-complex/304669/

Sentencing Project, The. 2022. "Criminal Justice Facts." https://www.sentencingproject.org/criminal-justice-facts/

Shapiro, Thomas M. 2004. *The Hidden Cost of Being African American: How Wealth Perpetuates Inequality.* New York: Oxford University Press.

Shapiro, Thomas, Tatjana Meschede, and Sam Osoro. 2013. *The Roots of the Widening Racial Wealth Gap: Explaining the Black–White Economic Divide. Institute on Assets and Social Policy,* February. http://www.naacpldf.org/files/case_issue/Shapiroracialwealthgapbrief.pdf.

Shaw, Marcus. 2019. "The Reproduction of Social Disadvantage Through Educational Demobilization: A Critical Analysis of Parental Incarceration." *Critical Criminology: The Official Journal of the ASC Division on Critical Criminology and the ACIS Section on Critical Criminology* 27 (2): 275–90.

Shoenfeld, Sarah Jane, and Mara Cherkasky. 2017. "A Strictly White Residential Section": The Rise and Demise of Racially Restrictive Covenants in Bloomingdale." *Washington History* 29 (1): 24–41.

Siddle Walker, Vanessa. 2000. "Valued Segregated Schools for African American Children in the South, 1935–1969: A Review of Common Themes and Characteristics." *Review of Educational Research* 70: 253–85.

Simon, Jonathan. 2007. *Governing Through Crime: How the War on Crime Transformed American Democracy and Created a Culture of Fear.* New York: Oxford University Press.

Singh, Gopal K., and Stella M. Yu. 1996. "Adverse Pregnancy Outcomes: Differences Between U.S. and Foreign-Born Women in Major U.S. Racial and Ethnic Groups." *American Journal of Public Health* 86 (6): 837–43.

Skrentny, J. D. 1996. *The Ironies of Affirmative Action: Politics, Culture, and Justice in America.* Chicago: University of Chicago Press.

Slack T., Thiede B. C., and Jensen L. 2019. "Race, Residence, and Underemployment: Fifty Years in Comparative Perspective, 1968–2017." *Rural Sociology* (2019).

Smedley, Audrey. 2007. *Race in North America. Origin and Evolution of a Worldview,* 3rd ed. Boulder, CO: Westview.

Smith, Andrea. 2012. "Indigeneity, Settler Colonialism, White Supremacy." In *Racial Formation in the Twenty-First Century,* edited by D. M. HoSang, O. LaBennett, and L. Pulido, 66–90. Berkeley: University of California Press.

Smith, Stacy L., Marc Choueiti, and Katharine. Pieper. 2016. *Comprehensive Annenberg Report on Diversity in Entertainment.* University of Southern California. http:// annenberg.usc.edu/ pages/~/media/MDSCI/CARDReport%20FINAL%2022216.ashx.

Smith, Stacy L., Marc Choueiti, Ariana Case, Katherine Pieper, Hannah Clark, Karla Hernandez, Jacqueline Martinez, Benjamin Lopez, and Mauricio Mota. 2019. "Latinos in Film: Erasure on Screen and Behind the Camera across 1,200 Popular Movies." http://assets.uscannenberg. org/docs/aii-study-latinos-in-film-2019.pdf.

Snowden, Frank. 1983. *Before Color Prejudice: The Ancient View of Blacks.* Cambridge, MA: Harvard University Press.

Snowden, Frank. 1970. *Blacks in Antiquity.* Cambridge, MA: Harvard University Press.

Snyder, Thomas D., Cristobal De Brey, and Sally A. Dillow. 2019. "Digest of Education Statistics 2017, NCES 2018-070." *National Center for Education Statistics.*

Solorzano, D., M. Ceja, and T. Yosso. 2000. "Critical Race Theory, Racial Microaggressions, and Campus Racial Climate: The Experiences of African American College Students." *Journal of Negro Education* 69 (Winter/Spring): 60–73.

Span, C. 2002. "'I Must Learn Now or Not at All': Social and Cultural Capital in the Educational Initiatives of Formerly Enslaved African Americans in Mississippi, 1862–1869." *Journal of African American History* 87: 196–206.

Spiro, Jonathan. 2008. *Defending the Master Race: Conservation, Eugenics, and the Legacy of Madison Grant.* Burlington: University of Vermont Press.

Srauy S. 2019. "Professional Norms and Race in the North American Video Game Industry." *Games and Culture* 14 (5): 478–97.

Stamps, D. 2019. "Is it Really Representation? A Qualitative Analysis of Asian and Latino Characterizations in Broadcast Television." *American Communication Journal* 21 (1): 1–12.

Stannard, D. E. 1993. *American Holocaust: The Conquest of the New World.* New York: Oxford University Press.

Stanton-Salazar, R., and Sanford M. Dornbusch. 1995. "Social Capital and the Reproduction of Inequality: Information Networks among Mexican-Origin High School Students." *Sociology of Education* 68 (April): 116–35.

Stephens, Dionne P., and Paula Fernández. 2011. "The Role of Skin Color on Hispanic Women's Perceptions of Attractiveness." *Hispanic Journal of Behavioral Sciences* 34 (1): 77–94.

Stout, M. A. 2012. *Native American Boarding Schools.* Santa Barbara, CA: ABC-CLIO.

Stullich, S., I. Morgan, and O. Schak. 2016. *State and Local Expenditures on Corrections and Education. A Brief from the US Department of Education, Policy and Program Studies Service.* Washington, DC: Office of Planning, Evaluation and Policy Development, U.S. Department of Education.

Sue, Christina. 2009. "The Dynamics of Color: Mestizaje, Racism and Blackness in Veracruz, Mexico." In *Shades of Difference: Why Skin Color Matters,* edited by Evelyn Nakano Glenn, 114–28. Palo Alto, CA: Stanford University Press.

Sue, D. W., J. Bucceri, A. I. Lin, K. L. Nadal, and G. C. Torino. 2007. "Racial Microaggressions and the Asian American Experience." *Cultural Diversity and Ethnic Minority Psychology* 13 (1): 72–81.

Sugrue, Thomas. 2008. *The Unfinished History of Racial Segregation.* http://www.prrac.org/ projects/fair_housing_commission/chicago/sugrue.pdf.

Sugrue, Thomas J. 2014. *The Origins of the Urban Crisis: Race and Inequality in Postwar Detroit.* Princeton, NJ: Princeton University Press.

Szasz, Ferenc M. 1967. "The New York Slave Revolt of 1741: A Re-Examination." *New York History* 48 (3): 215–30.

Tahmahkera, D. 2008. "Custer's Last Sitcom: Decolonized Viewing of the Sitcom's 'Indian.'" *American Indian Quarterly* 32 (3): 324–51.

Takei, Carl, and Katie Egan. 2017, January 9. Trump and Sessions: Great for the Private Prison Industry, Terrible for Civil Rights. *American Civil Liberties Union (aclu.org)*. Web: May 28, 2017.

Tali, Kristal, Yinon Cohen, and Edo Navot. 2018. "Benefit Inequality among American Workers by Gender, Race, and Ethnicity, 1982–2015." *Sociological Science* 5 (20): 461–88.

Tatum, Beverly Daniel. 2003. *"Why Are All the Black Kids Sitting Together in the Cafeteria?" and Other Conversations about Race*. New York: Basic Books.

Taylor, Dorceta E. 2009. *The Environment and the People in American Cities, 1600s to 1900s: Disorder, Inequality, and Social Change*. Durham, NC: Duke University Press.

Telles, Edward. 2009. "The Social Consequences of Skin Color in Brazil." In *Shades of Difference: Why Skin Color Matters*, edited by Evelyn Nakano Glenn, 9–24. Stanford, CA: Stanford University Press.

Telles, Edward, and Liza Steele. 2012. *Pigmentocracy in the Americas: How Is Educational Attainment Related to Skin Color*. Americas Barometer Insight Series 73.

Thomas, Lynn M. 2009. "Skin Lighteners in South Africa: Transnational Entanglements and Technologies of the Self." In *Shades of Difference: Why Skin Color Matters*, edited by Evelyn Nakano Glenn, 188–210. Palo Alto, CA: Stanford University Press.

Thorpe, Roland, Jr., and Jessica A. Kelley-Moore. 2012. "Life-Course Theories of Race Disparities: A Comparison of the Cumulative Dis/Advantage Theory Perspective and the Weathering Hypothesis." In *Race, Ethnicity, and Health: A Public Health Reader*, edited by Thomas Laveist and Lydia Isaac, 355–74. San Francisco: John Wiley & Sons.

The Pew Charitable Trusts, 2010. *Collateral Costs: Incarceration's Effect on Economic Mobility*. Washington, DC: The Pew Charitable Trusts.

The Sentencing Project. 2013. http://sentencingproject.org/wp-content/uploads/2015/12/Race-and-Justice-Shadow-Report-ICCPR.pdf.

The Sentencing Project. 2016. http://sentencingproject.org/wp-content/uploads/2016/01/Trends-in-US-Corrections.pdf.

The Sentencing Project. 2021. https://www.sentencingproject.org/criminal-justice-facts/.

The State of Women-Owned Businesses Report. 2015. http://www.womenable.com/content/userfiles/Amex_OPEN_State_of_WOBs_2015_Executive_Report_finalsm.pdf

The Times of India. 2017. *Can Dev Patel Be the First Indian Actor to Win an Oscar?* http://timesofindia.indiatimes.com/india/can-dev-patel-be-the-first-indian-oscar-winner/articleshow/57351685.cms.

Todorov, T. 1984. *The Conquest of America: The Question of the Other*. Norman: University of Oklahoma Press.

Traub, Amy, Laura Sullivan, Tatjana Meschede, and Tom Shapiro. 2017, February 6. The Asset Value of Whiteness: Understanding the Racial Wealth Gap. *Demos*. http://www.demos.org/publication/asset-value-whiteness-understanding-racial-wealth-gap.

Trennert, Robert A. 1983. "From Carlisle to Phoenix: The Rise and Fall of the Indian Outing System, 1878–1930." *Pacific Historical Review* 52 (3): 267–91.

Tumlin, Karen, and Wendy Zimmerman. 2003. *Immigrants and TANF: A Look at Immigrant Welfare Recipients in Three Cities*. Occasional Paper No. 69. Urban Institute. http://www. urban. org/UploadedPDF/310874_OP69.pdf.

Twine, F. W. 1998. *Racism in a Racial Democracy: The Maintenance of White Supremacy in Brazil*. New Brunswick, NJ: Rutgers University Press.

Tyson, K. 2002. "Weighing In: Elementary-Age Students and the Debate on Attitudes Toward School among Black Students." *Social Forces* 80 (4): 1157–89.

Umberson D. 2017. "Black Deaths Matter: Race, Relationship Loss, and Effects on Survivors." *Journal of Health and Social Behavior* 58 (4): 405–20.

University of California Berkeley Labor Center. 2013. *Data Brief: Black Employment and Unemployment in November 2013.* http://laborcenter.berkeley.edu/blackworkers/monthly/bwreport_2013-12-06_64.pdf.

U.S. Department of Education, Office for Civil Rights. 2014. https://ocrdata.ed.gov/downloads/crdc-school-discipline-snapshot.pdf

U.S. Department of Homeland Security, Office of Immigration Statistics. 2010. https://www.dhs.gov/immigration-statistics.

U.S. Department of Homeland Security, Office of Immigration Statistics. 2016. *Yearbook of Immigration Statistics: 2015.*

U.S. Department of Labor. n.d. https://www.dol.gov/general/topic/statistics

Uzogara, Ekeoma E. 2019. "Gendered Racism Biases: Associations of Phenotypes with Discrimination and Internalized Oppression among Latinx American Women and Men." *Race and Social Problems* 11, 1: 80–92.

Vagianos, Alana. 2016, August 30. Remember Brock Turner? From 3 Months Ago? He'll Leave Jail on Friday. *Huffington Post.* http://www.huffingtonpost.com/entry/remember-brock-turner-from-3-months-ago-hell-leave-jail-on-friday_us_57c58c81e4b0cdfc5ac9256b.

Vaid, Jyotsna. 2009. "Fair Enough? Color and the Commodification of Self in Indian Matrimonials." In *Shades of Difference: Why Skin Color Matters*, edited by E.N. Glenn, 148–65. Palo Alto, CA: Stanford University Press.

Valdez, Zulema. 2008a. "Beyond Ethnic Entrepreneurship: An Embedded Market Approach to Group Affiliation in American Enterprise." *Race, Gender and Class* 15 (1): 156–69. http://escholarship.org/uc/item/8c8206b6.pdf.

Valdez, Zulema. 2008b. "The Effect of Social Capital on White, Korean, Mexican and Black Business Owners' Earnings in the U.S." *Journal of Ethnic and Migration Studies* 34 (6): 955–73.

Valdez, Zulema. 2011. *The New Entrepreneurs: How Race, Class and Gender Shape American Enterprise.* Palo Alto, CA: Stanford University Press.

Vickerman, Milton. 1999. *Crosscurrents: West Indian Immigrants and Race.* Oxford University Press.

Viruell-Fuentes, E. 2007. "Beyond Acculturation: Immigration, Discrimination, and Health Research among Mexicans in the United States." *Social Science and Medicine* 65: 1524–35.

Visser, M. Anne. "Shedding Light On Economic Opportunity: Skin Tone And Job Quality During the Great Recession." *Journal of Ethnic and Migration Studies* 43, no. 9 (2017): 1562–79.

Volscho, Thomas W. "Sterilization Racism and Pan-Ethnic Disparities of the Past Decade: The Continued Encroachment on Reproductive Rights." *Wicazo Sa Review* 25, no. 1 (2010): 17–31.

Wacquant, Loïc. 2009. *Punishing the Poor: The Neoliberal Government of Social Insecurity.* Durham, NC: Duke University Press.

Wade, Peter. 1997. *Race and Ethnicity in Latin America.* Chicago: Pluto.

Wagner, Peter, and Bernadette Rabuy. 2016, March 14. "Mass Incarceration: The Whole Pie 2016." Prison Policy Initiative. https://www.prisonpolicy.org/reports/pie2016.html.

Walmsley, Roy. 2017. *World Prison Population List*, 11th ed. International Centre for Prison Studies. http://prisonstudies.org/sites/default/files/resources/downloads/world_prison_population_list_11th_edition_0.pdf

Warren-Findlow, Jan. 2006. "Weathering: Stress and Heart Disease in African American Women Living in Chicago." *Qualitative Health Research* 16 (2): 221–37.

Washington, Harriet. 2006. *Medical Apartheid: The Dark History of Medical Experimentation on Black Americans from Colonial Times to the Present.* New York: Random House.

Watras, Joseph. "Progressive Education and Native American Schools, 1929–1950." *The Journal of Educational Foundations* 18, no. 3 (2004): 81.

Welch, Michael. 2002. *Detained: Immigration Laws and the Expanding INS Jail Complex*. Philadelphia: Temple University Press.

Western, Bruce. 2006. *Punishment and Inequality in America*. New York: Russell Sage Foundation.

Western, Bruce, and Becky Pettit. 2002. "Beyond Crime and Punishment: Prisons and Inequality." *Contexts* 1 (3): 37–43.

Western, Bruce, and Becky Pettit. 2005. "Black–White Wage Inequality, Employment Rates and Incarceration." *American Journal of Sociology* 111 (2): 553–78.

White, Frederick. 2012. "Ubiquitous American Indian Stereotypes in Television." In *American Indians and Popular Culture: Media, Sports, and Politics*, edited by Elizabeth DeLaney Hoffman, 1, 135–50. Santa Barbara, CA: ABC-CLIO.

White, Karletta M. 2015. "The Salience of Skin Tone: Effects On the Exercise of Police Enforcement Authority." *Ethnic and Racial Studies* 38 (6): 993–1010.

White, Michael J., Ann E. Biddlecom, and Shenyang Guo. 1993. "Immigration, Naturalization, and Residential Assimilation among Asian Americans in 1980." *Social Forces* 72 (1): 93–117.

Wildeman, Christopher. 2009. "Parental Imprisonment, the Prison Boom, and the Concentration of Childhood Disadvantage." *Demography* 46 (2): 265–80.

Wilder, Jeffri Anne. 2010. "Revisiting 'Color Names and Color Notions': A Contemporary Examination of the Language and Attitudes of Skin Color among Young Black Women." *Journal of Black Studies* 41 (1): 184–206.

Wilkes, Rima, and John Iceland. 2004. "Hypersegregation in the Twenty-First Century." *Demography* 41 (1): 23–36.

Wilkins, Amy C. 2004. "Puerto Rican Wannabes: Sexual Spectacle and the Marking of Race, Class, and Gender Boundaries." *Gender and Society* 18 (1): 103–21.

Wilkinson, Richard G., and Kate E. Pickett. 2009. "Income Inequality and Social Dysfunction." *Annual Review of Sociology* 35 (1): 493–511.

Williams, David R., and Chiquita Collins. 2001. "Racial Residential Segregation: A Fundamental Cause of Racial Disparities in Health." *Public Health Reports* 116 (5): 404–16.

Williams, David. R., and Chiquita Collins. 1995. "U.S. Socioeconomic and Racial Differences in Health: Patterns and Explanations." *Annual Review of Sociology* 21 (1): 349–86.

Williams, David R., and Selena A. Mohammed. 2013. "Racism and Health I: Pathways and Scientific Evidence." *American Behavioral Scientist* 57 (8): 10. 1177/0002764213487340. doi:10.1177/0002764213487340.

Wilson, Carter. 1996. *From Slavery to Advanced Capitalism*. Thousand Oaks, CA: Sage.

Wing, Jean Y. 2007. "Beyond Black and White: The Model Minority Myth and the Invisibility of Asian American Students." *Urban Review* 39 (4): 455–87.

Wingfield, Adia Harvey. 2008. *Doing Business with Beauty: Black Women, Hair Salons, and the Racial Enclave Economy*. Lanham, MD: Rowman & Littlefield.

Wingfield, Adia Harvey, and Joe R. Feagin. 2010. *Yes We Can? White Racial Framing and the 2008 Presidential Campaign*. New York: Routledge.

Wise, T. 2005. "Membership Has Its Privileges: Thoughts on Acknowledging and Challenging Whiteness." In *White Privilege: Essential Readings on the Other Side of Racism*, 2nd ed., edited by Paula S. Rothenberg, 119–123. New York: Worth.

Woldoff, Rachael A., and Heather M. Washington. 2008. "Arrested Contact: The Criminal Justice System, Race, and Father Engagement." *Prison Journal* 88 (2): 179–206.

Wollenberg, Charles. 1974. "*Mendez v. Westminster*: Race, Nationality, and Segregation in California Schools." *California Historical Quarterly* 53 (4): 317–32.

Wood, Forrest G. 1991. *The Arrogance of Faith: Christianity and Race in America from the Colonial Era to the Twentieth Century*. Boston: Northeastern University Press.

Wood, Phillip J. 2007. "Globalization and Prison Privatization: Why Are Most of the World's For-Profit Adult Prisons to Be Found in the American South?" *International Political Sociology* 1: 222–39.

World Prison Brief. 2022. "Highest to Lowest: Prison Population Total" https://www.prison-studies.org/highest-to-lowest/prison-population-total?field_region_taxonomy_tid=All. Accessed Feb 14, 2022.

Yeakey, Carol. 1979. "Ethnicity as a Dimension of Human Diversity." In *Human Diversity and Pedagogy*, 5.1–5.49. Princeton, NJ: Educational Testing Services.

Yosso, Tara, Laurence Parker, Daniel Solorzano, and Marvin Lynn. 2004. "From Jim Crow to Affirmative Action and Back Again: A Critical Race Discussion of Racialized Rationales and Access to Higher Education." *Review of Research in Education* 28 (1): 1–25.

Young, Julia G. 2017. "Making America 1920 again? Nativism and US immigration, past and present." *Journal on Migration and Human Security* 5(1): 217-235.

Yudell, Michael, Dorothy Roberts, Rob DeSalle, and Sarah A. Tishkoff. 2016. "Taking Race Out of Human Genetics." *Science* 351 (6273): 564–65.

Yuen, Nancy Wang. 2016. *Reel Inequality: Hollywood Actors and Racism*. New Brunswick, NJ: Rutgers University Press.

Zagorsky, Jay. 2006. "Native Americans' Wealth." In *Wealth Accumulation in Communities of Color in the United States*, edited by Jessica Gordon Nembhard and Ngina S. Chiteji, 133–54. Ann Arbor: University of Michigan Press.

Zinn, Howard. 2010. *A People's History of the United States*. New York: HarperCollins.

Credits

PHOTOS

PHOTO 1-1, p. 8: Time & Life Pictures/Getty Images

PHOTO 2-1, p. 38: © So-CoAddict/iStockphoto

PHOTO 3-1, p. 75: P20: 1208, Extension Bulletin Illustrations Photograph Collection, courtesy OSU Archives

PHOTO 4-1, p. 111: Screen capture from *black-ish*, Season 2, Episode 16

PHOTO 4-2, p. 113: AF archive/Alamy Stock Photo

PHOTO 4-3, p. 115: Courtesy of the Arabian Street Artists

PHOTO 4-4, p. 117: Gilles Mingasson/ABC via Getty Images

PHOTO 5-1, p. 139: Photographs and Prints Division, Schomburg Center for Research in Black Culture, The New York Public Library, Astor, Lenox, and Tilden Foundations

PHOTO 5-2, p. 142: Screen capture from Seoul Secret beauty ad

PHOTO 5-3, p. 144: Illustration by Srishti Gupta Roy, appearing in Bright Magazine, July 10, 2019 edition. Used with permission.

PHOTO 5-4, p. 149: Seyllou Diallo/AFP/Getty Images

PHOTO 5-5, p. 154: Kristina Robinson © 2014 BlackStar Creative. Photo by Noelle Théard

PHOTO 5-6, p. 158: buzzfuss/123RF

PHOTO 5-7, p. 166: By permission of Namira Islam

PHOTO 6-1, p. 174: Bettmann/Contributor/Getty

PHOTO 6-2, p. 183: AP Photo/Jacquelyn Martin

PHOTO 6-3, p. 199: Ariel Skelley/Getty Images

PHOTO 7-1, p. 229: Courtesy of Katrina Golash

PHOTO 7-2, p. 253: Meewezen Photography/Shutterstock

PHOTO 8-1, p. 255: Associated Press

PHOTO 9-1, p. 268: California Department of Corrections

PHOTO 9-2, p. 269: Frances Roberts/Alamy Stock Photo

PHOTO 9-3, p. 280: KENA BETANCUR/AFP/Getty Images

PHOTO 9-4, p. 289: Photo By Joe Amon/The Denver Post via Getty Images

PHOTO 10-1, p. 291: Collection of the University of Michigan Health System, Gift of Pfizer Inc. United States, J. Marion Sims: Gynecologic Surgeon. UMHS.30.

PHOTO 10-2, p. 313: Courtesy of the National Archives at Atlanta

PHOTO 10-3a, p. 313: Reproduced by permission of the American Anthropological Association from Anthropology News, Volume 46, Issue 6, page 43, September 2005. Not for sale or further reproduction.

PHOTO 10-3b, p. 313: © Corey Perrine/Augusta Chronicle/ZUMAPRESS.com

PHOTO 10-4, p. 315: Jim West/Alamy Stock Photo

FIGURES

FIGURE 2-1: "Median Net Worth of white, Hispanic, and black Households." Pew Research Center, Washington, D.C. (2014) . **FIGURE 3-1:** Source: Migration Policy Institute (2015). **FIGURE 3-2:** Source: U.S. Department of Homeland Security, Office of Immigration Statistics (2015). **FIGURE 3-3:** U.S. Department of Homeland Security, Office of Immigration Statistics (2018). **FIGURE 3-4:** Department of Homeland Security, Office of Immigration Statistics (2017). **FIGURE 3-5:** DHS OIS. **FIGURE 3-6:** Adapted from LA Times Graphics . **FIGURE 3-7:**Pew Research Center, Washington, D.C., June 12, 2019, https://www.pewresearch.org/fact-tank/2019/06/12/us-unauthorized-immigrant-population-2017/. **FIGURE 3-8:** DHS OIS (2016). **FIGURE 4-1:** Data from American Community Survey; Smith et al. 2016; Yuen 2016. **FIGURE 4-2:** Source: Monk-Turner (2010). **FIGURE 4-3 and 4-4:** "The Oscars diversity problem in charts", by John Burn-Murdoch, Chelsea Bruce-Lockhart and Liz Faunce, FT.com 07 February 2020. **FIGURE 5-1:** Source: Davids et al. (2016). **FIGURE 6-1:** Sources: PBS Frontline (2014) Stanford Center for Education Policy Analysis (2012). **FIGURE 6-2:** Snyder, T.D., de Brey, C., and Dillow, S.A. (2019). Digest of Education. Statistics 2018 (NCES 2020-009). National Center for Education Statistics, Institute of Education Sciences, U.S. Department of Education. **FIGURE 6-3:** NCES 2016. **FIGURE 6-4:** Snyder, T.D., de Brey, C., and Dillow, S.A. (2019). Digest of Education Statistics 2018 (NCES 2020-009). National Center for Education Statistics, Institute of Education Sciences, U.S. Department of Education. **FIGURE 6-5:** Source: Kena et al. (2016). **FIGURE 7-1:** International Comparison.org, 2017. http://www.internationalcomparison.org/intl_comp_files/sheet006.htm. **FIGURE 7-2:** Bureau of Labor Statistics, 2015. https://www.bls.gov/webapps/legacy/cpswktab3.htm. **FIGURE 7-3:** Bureau of Labor Statistics, 2015. https://www.bls.gov/webapps/legacy/cpswktab3.htm. **FIGURE 7-4:** Bureau of Labor Statistics, 2013. http://www.bls.gov/news.release/pdf/wkyeng.pdf. **FIGURE 7-5:** Source: Labor Department via FRED **FIGURE 7-6:** Source: Census Bureau **FIGURE 7-7:** Source: Pew Research Center (2017). **FIGURE 7-8:** Freeman 2011 and Bureau of Labor Statistics. **FIGURE 7-9:** Freeman (2011); U.S. Bureau of Labor Statistics (2013b). **FIGURE 7-10:** Source: BLS (2015). **FIGURE 7-11:** Desilver (2015). **FIGURE 8-1:** Norton, Michael I. and Dan Ariely 2011. "Building a Better America—One Wealth Quintile at a Time." Perspectives on Psychological Science 6: 9 DOI: 10.1177/1745691610393524. **FIGURE 8-2:** John R. Logan and Brian Stults, 2011. "The Persistence of Segregation in the Metropolis: New Findings from the 2010 Census." Census Brief prepared for Project US2010. http://www.s4.brown.edu/us2010. **FIGURE 8-3:** Data from Pew Research Center, 2014. **FIGURE 8-4:** Rakesh Kochhar, Richard Fry, and Paul Taylor. "Wealth Gaps Rise to Record Highs Between Blacks, Whites, Hispanics." Pew Research Center, Washington, DC (July 26, 2011). http://www.pewsocialtrends.org/2011/07/26/wealth-gaps-rise-to-record-highs-between-whites-blacks-hispanics/, accessed on January 17, 2014. **FIGURE 8-5:** Source: Kijakazi et al. 2016. **FIGURE 8-6:** Source: Shapiro, Meschede, and Osoro (2013). **FIGURE 8-7:** The Color of Wealth in the Nation's Capital Urban

Institute, 2016. **FIGURE 9-1:** Data from BJS 2016 **FIGURE 9-2:** Data from BJS 2016 **FIGURE 9-3:** World Prison Brief (2021). Data from Institute for Crime & Justice Policy Research, https:// www.prisonstudies.org/highest-to-lowest/prison_population_rate?field_region_taxonomy_ tid=All. **FIGURE 9-4:** Data from BJS 2016. **FIGURE 9-5:** Data from BJS 2016. **FIGURE 9-6:** Source: Bureau of Justice Statistics (2016). **FIGURE 9-7:** Source: Bureau of Justice Statistics (2016). **FIGURE 9-8:** Source: Bureau of Justice Statistics, Key Statistics, www.bjs.gov, 2017. **FIGURE 9-9:** Source: Rothwell (2016) **FIGURE 9-10:** Source: Stullich, Morgan, and Schak (2016). **FIGURE 10-1:** Data from MMWR 2017. **FIGURE 10-2:** CDC 2011, http://www.cdc. gov/nchs/data/hus/2011/010.pdf. **FIGURE 10-3:** Source: Bullard (2007).

Index

Note: Page numbers followed by *f* and *t* refer to figures and tables, respectively. Italic page numbers refer to images.